<u>Guess What I Saw Inside Your House</u>

"My 40 Years As A Home Repairman"

by

Rob Jaegge

With

Eric Abrams

Table of Contents

Introduction

Call me Ismael. Actually, don't because it's not my name and this isn't "Moby Dick." If you bought this book thinking it was, I don't know what to tell you because the cover really should've clued you in that it wasn't. Anyway, my name is Rob Jaegge and the title of this book is "Guess What I Saw Inside Your House." Maybe you picked up this volume right before boarding your flight and didn't read past the title so let me clarify, I have been inside your house. Okay, probably not your house but suffice it to say I've been in many. Not to rob you or as a Jehovah's Witness or even as a guest at your family barbecue. No, I was there to fix your refrigerator, freezer, stove or TV. That's what I do. I fix things. Yes, kids, there was a time when if something broke, you didn't just chuck it and get a new one. You fixed it and that's what I did for over forty years before my "retirement."

How many homes have I been in? Let's do the math; eight to ten service calls a day, five days a week, four weeks a month, eleven months per year (I got 29 vacation days) times forty years gives us roughly eighty-eighty thousand homes I've been in. So, yeah, I've certainly seen more than my fair share of shag carpeting and Formica.

A little about me. I grew up in a mid-sized community in Southern California and never left and why would I? My neighborhood and the surrounding areas are quiet, the scenery is beautiful and unlike most of Southern California, it's not too crowded. Plus, unlike most valleys, it's almost never too hot. Honestly, I can't think of a reason to leave.

When you think of a repairman or, as we prefer to be called, "appliance technicians," you'd probably guess that I always liked to fix things. Bullseye. Looking back, part of it was out of necessity. Both my parents died before I turned seventeen. No one in social services caught on about it for several years so my brothers, sister and I pretty much raised ourselves but that's another book. The point is if something broke, we didn't have the money to buy a new one, so we fixed it and I was pretty good at it.

Growing up, I really didn't enjoy reading. It's not that I had a learning disability or anything like that but for the most part reading just didn't interest me. What did and does is reading technical manuals and repair guides. To me, it's like solving a puzzle or problem. They just speak to me and no, I'm not Rain Man or the head nerd on "The Big Bang Theory." I'm just a regular guy who's really good at what's becoming, sadly, a lost art.

How'd I get into the repair business? Good question. After graduating high school, getting married in 1978 and starting college, I got a job with my wife's Uncle Jimmy. Uncle Jimmy worked at a TV service center in Chatsworth that needed a parts guy which was, as luck would have it, exactly what I was studying at the local j.c. In fact, I was in the last TV class before it all went digital.

I worked for Uncle Jimmy for about two years until one day I had to make a delivery to a television repair center in Thousand Oaks. That morning, three of their technicians had quit. After they talked to me a little bit they asked if I wanted a job? I explained that I was working for a member of my wife's family and they said they'd almost double what I was currently making (three dollars to five, it was 1979). Now, I loved Uncle Jimmy, but I had to feed my family which was about to get bigger.

I worked at this company for about eight months when one of the road technicians called in sick. Not being the kind of guy who liked being cooped up in a storeroom or office all day I volunteered to take over the guy's route. Basically, I covered a good chunk of Los Angeles County. On the way to Oxnard, I passed a branch of one of America's largest appliance repair companies and on a lark, pulled in and filled out an application.

Before I got home that day there was a message on my Record-A-Call, which was kind of a pre-answering machine, from the company to set up an interview which I did for that Saturday. I aced it, they offered me a job and I took it. When I got to the bowling alley to tell my wife, she wasn't exactly thrilled as this would be my third job in three years.

"What did you do that for? Why can't you stay in one place?" she said.

"Well," I replied, "three fifty more an hour plus great benefits."

I'm sure the fact that she was very pregnant had nothing to do with her coming around so fast. That was 1980 and I've been with them ever since. Until that "retirement" kicks in, which, by the time you're reading this, has already happened.

Now, here's a few things you might not guess about me based on my profession: I have three college degrees. I've taught at several colleges. My wife has a high-powered job in the medical profession. All my children are professionals including a doctor and lawyer. My son was a pretty good left-handed pitcher. He was in the Diamondback's system and got as high as AAA before getting hurt. Instead of gutting it out he decided he needed a fallback, so he went to culinary school and became a chef. Couldn't be prouder.

I say these things not to brag but to show that you can't judge a book by its' cover. It's one of the big lessons I learned along the way. Some of the most normal looking people were the biggest whack jobs or as my wife would prefer I'd say, "unique individuals." Some of the weirdest seeming people had the most common sense and were the most decent.

So, yeah, you can't judge a book by its' cover except for this one. It's exactly what it says it is; a peek inside suburbia from 1979 to today as witnessed by your friendly, neighborhood repairman. Now don't get me wrong, by no stretch did something interesting or unusual happen every day. There were certainly weeks and even months when the job was pretty boring. But I've been doing this over forty years, so you'd figure the law of averages would kick

8

in and something remarkable or way out of the ordinary, sooner or later would happen. Well, it did. I've been collecting these stories and anecdotes, one here, a few there and eventually they started piling up and one day I realized that I had a lot of them.

Now, I've been telling these stories to my friends and family for years and way more often than not someone will say, you should really put this stuff in a book. So, I did. A lot of weird stuff happens in the 'burbs. One last thing, the names of all the people have been changed except mine. I figure I probably won't sue myself and if I do, I have a lawyer in the family.

At any rate, I hope you enjoy reading this and that my (mis)adventures are as entertaining to you as they were to my family, friends and me.

Story 1 – Do Not, Under Any Circumstances, Get Rid Of That Television (1982)

One day in '84 I got a call to do a television repair. From the work order, there was nothing unusual except that it was on a weekend which meant I was making more money. To say it was one of the most unusual events of my life would be an understatement.

The neighborhood the job was in was in an older community. It was kept up to a point but there was nothing special that stood out. Then I pulled up to the house.

Believe it or not, the appearance of the house can actually give you a good idea of what to expect inside and maybe, what the client is going to be like. This one was average. The lawn was mowed and edged with good detail. The bushes and trees, old as they were, were looking well maintained and neat. The front entrance had four white columns that gave the appearance of holding up the front, but I was pretty sure they served no purpose other than to provide a sense of style. Yup, all pretty standard stuff.

What wasn't standard was all the cars that sat out front. Not so much the makes or models but the quantity. Two cars sat in the driveway, one car was parked on the sidewalk behind the two that were in the driveway, some were even parked on the lawn; they were just all over the place. Several cars were double-parked up and down the street. There were so many cars that parking for my service van was hard to find. The closest spot that I could find was three houses down the street and it happened to be right in front of a fire hydrant.

Luckily for me, back in those days, I always kept a thirty-gallon plastic trashcan with the bottom cut out inside my van for just this situation. All I had to do was place the can over the hydrant and for the little while that I'm inside the house, no one was the wiser. I parked, gathered my service tools and headed toward the house.

With the toolbox in one hand and the service order in my pocket, I walked toward the residence. Getting to the front door felt like going through a maze because of all the weaving I did to avoid the tightly parked cars. As I got closer, I noticed a large disturbance coming from inside the house. Something was going on. My first thought was that maybe it was a party, a family reunion, or something like that. But as I got closer it was what I didn't notice that was unusual. There was no music playing but there was a lot of talking going on inside. Honestly, I was there to do a job, so I really didn't care.

I knocked on the door loudly and waited a minute. The door was finally opened by a ten-year-old kid wearing a jacket and tie. The place was packed with people in suits and dresses with lots of conversations going on. No matter. The kid instantly knew what I was there for.

"Uncle Lenny, the TV guy's here!" he shouted.

Shortly thereafter, Uncle Lenny, a skinny, balding guy in his forties came up and introduced himself as the kid walked off.

"Hi, I'm Lenny. Thanks for coming out on a Saturday," he said as he shook my hand. "Let me take you to her."

We walked past several chatting people who were eating sandwiches, chips, taquitos, guacamole and drinking soda, coffee and adult beverages out of Styrofoam cups. It smelled terrific. Everyone seemed to be talking in the past tense except for Lenny.

"This set might be a little bit of a challenge for you…" he droned on explaining what was wrong with the picture in excruciating and unnecessary detail. You have to understand that over the years I've heard this countless times, and it's almost never true but he continued, "It was my father's so it's pretty old. He loved this set both watching and working on it and he always said that we should we never, never get rid of this TV."

Finally, we arrived at the set's location and I'll say this for Lenny, he didn't lie. The set, an old RCA combination cabinet, was a complete piece of junk. It was a vacuum tube chassis with no solid-state circuit boards anywhere. They hadn't made sets like this in years and mind you, this was the '80's. I didn't even know if I had the parts or if they still made the parts to fix this museum piece. For maybe the first time in my career I was about to be stumped. But I'm a professional and was already there, I figured I should at least look at it.

As Lenny was winding down his history lesson about all things old-television and his memories of his dad spending countless hours working on it, I pulled the set from the wall, pulling one corner and swiveled the other side so I could work in the rear of the television. I set up my reflection mirror in front of the unit. We do this so that we can turn the television on and see what the picture tube is doing without coming out from behind the unit.

Mind you, while this was happening, people of all ages were constantly coming in and out of the room and talking. Like I said before, the place was just packed. One sound that stood out was of a lady's voice in another room who was crying. Clearly, something was going on.

After carefully checking out the television I made my evaluation and determined that I needed only to clean a control and adjust the screen to fill the screen completely. This was a small adjustment. Because it was a no-brainer I found it impossible not to listen in on the conversations that were happening several feet from where I was working. It's human nature and yes, I was curious as to why this house was packed on a Saturday afternoon.

"Remember when abuelo took us fishing by the lake?" said a man in his mid-twenties.

"I don't think in all the times we were there we ever caught one, so we always ended up at...what was the name of that steakhouse?" his cousin asked.

"Gallagher's – Home of the 96-ounce porterhouse." both cousins shared a laugh. Another overheard snippet between two older women went like this:

"...If you had to guess, how many hours do you think Jimmy spend with that stupid television?"

"Too many to count. But he did work very hard and if that's how he wanted to relax..."

This was a wake. That's why the woman in the other room was crying. The patriarch of the family passed away a couple of days ago. I wouldn't have called a repair technician to come by just after a funeral, but they did, and I had a job to do.

Now even though the repair was simple, it was somewhat time consuming. Basically, the set needed a lot of adjusting. Earlier, Lenny told me that his dad would adjust the television himself, sometimes twice a week, and how overprotective he was of it.

His instructions were that under no circumstance was that television ever, ever to be replaced. I've heard of people treating classic cars like their children but never a TV set. So, after adjusting control after control, I retuned the complete chassis. While doing this, I noticed that there was a lot of service performed on it. It was easy to tell because one of the first things any good technician would do is to make a visual observation.

On the inside of the television cabinet was a very large paper container and an envelope. The paper container was wrapped with a string several times over and the brown paper envelope was leaning against the side of the cabinet. Both the envelope and the bundles had a very good layer of dust on top of them. Except I noticed that the envelope's dust trail had been disturbed recently. I also saw finger print markings in the dust. It was obvious that someone was in there within the last week or so.

I decided to investigate what was inside the envelopes because I wanted to see what had been done to the television in prior services. It's actually not that unusual for customers to keep copies of their service records taped inside their televisions. Maybe I could find some information that would help me with my repair and give me more time to eavesdrop.

Inside the envelope were not service repair orders. What I found was totally unexpected, but it was also a very great surprise. Money. Lots and lots of money! Ones, fives, tens, and twenties were in abundance, packed into that envelope. I didn't count it, but it was substantial.

Next was the string wrapped paper container. I wanted to see what was inside. Can you blame me? I carefully grabbed the container, cut the string off and opened the paper wrappings. More money! When all was said and done, I found six individually wrapped packages inside the paper container. There was a lot of money in here; more than in the envelope. Each individually wrapped package was about three inches thick and there were six of these little guys. Quickly doing the math in my head, there had to be over thirty grand in small bills. I've heard of people hiding money in mattresses but TV's? That's one for the books.

That's when I pulled it all together because what I overheard earlier hit me: the deceased worked two jobs and long hours for many years, and twice a week he played with the television claiming that it needed adjusting. Taking all of that into consideration, it became obvious that the father had been placing his hard-earned moolah inside the television for years. No one knew about this hidden treasure, otherwise it would have been found by now. So…what to do?

Here's one of those moments in life like you see in TV and movies, where the angel pops up on one shoulder telling you to do the right thing and the devil pops up on the other shoulder telling you to do the self-serving thing. I mean, here sat thousands of dollars in front of me and no one knew about it. I could slip the money inside my toolbox and buy that vacation home in Lake Tahoe I'd been dreaming about. Maybe even have enough left over for a power boat. Nobody would miss it because nobody knew about it. Should I keep the money or do the right thing? The television was as adjusted as well as it was going to be, it was time for me to make my decision.

As I was finishing putting the R.C.A. back together, Lenny walked in. He asked me how things were coming along? I told him that the television is running as well as it could considering its age; I had done everything I could. At last it was decision time. I cleared my throat, took a breath and said:

"First of all, I'm sorry for your loss. Just from what everyone was saying around me, I can tell your father was a good man."

"Thank you," said Lenny.

Then I continued,

"Now, I get this is a little unusual but is there any way I could speak to your mother? While fixing your father's television, I learned some things about him that I really think she would be interested in hearing."

After considering it for a moment, Lenny said, "Sure, why not? The wake is winding down anyway. Let me get her up here."

Lenny exited and from downstairs, I heard:

"Mama, could you come up here, please? The TV repairman found out something about dad that he wants to tell us," said Lenny.

As Jimmy's widow entered, followed by her family and friends, I thought about what to say. Honestly, I wasn't expecting a crowd. This was before I started teaching in colleges, so I wasn't used to speaking in front of large groups of people. Then again, it wasn't like I was going to be delivering bad news. I decided I was going to be subtle but to the point.

"Once again, thank you to everyone for coming. Before you leave, Rob, the TV guy, would like to say something to mother," said Lenny.

All eyes turned on me wondering what the hell was going on? A TV repairman speaking at a wake where he doesn't know anyone, let alone the deceased? I took a deep breath and said:

"Hi, everyone, I'm sorry for your loss. From being here a little while I've learned three things about Jimmy: he was a good man, he loved and was loved by his family and friends and he treasured this old TV. So much so that he wouldn't let anyone work on it or sell it. I think I know why…"

Now, I had their attention. Was it a rare, valuable set? No, it was a piece of junk. Is that where he kept his letters from the war? Not even close. I took out an envelope and placed it on the floor, then I removed one of the packages, broke it open, removed its contents and fanned the bills. The whole room was outright shocked. It was pin drop time. There were a lot of gasps. I'm not exaggerating when I say no one said anything for at least twenty seconds. It was like all the oxygen had been sucked out of the room.

I'm really glad that I had the presence of mind to remember to take in everybody's expressions as I panned the room. I'm not a mind reader but I swear a good chunk of them thought they were in for a payoff. I'm sure visions of new cars, vacations, jewelry bounced in their heads but not in all of them because I distinctly remember one nephew standing behind his grandma who was relieved that she would be financially okay. I later learned that that was a legitimate concern of the family.

I handed the money to Lenny who just stared at it. Let's face it, the man was stunned. When he regained his composure, he handed the bundle to his mother.

"Mom, look, pop did remember to take care of you."

I have never seen sadness turned to joy so quickly. The crying just ceased. Of course, she was still sad about her husband's passing but a whole bunch of worries were just alleviated. Then, it was like I could see the wheels turning in her head.

Mama practically screamed, "So, that's where he hid it!"

She explained that she'd been looking for the money for years - twenty to thirty of them. She thought the television was just a hobby for her husband. Something to tinker with like some people do with model trains, cars, tin soldiers, etc. She said that she and her husband were children of the depression and he never trusted banks. The TV was his piggy bank for over three decades. You know, now that I think about it, it's amazing how fast a crowd can turn around when money is found.

Now, for another moment of truth. The mother, son and whole family were ecstatic at my discovery. I could've walked out of there with the rest, partially done the right thing and everyone would've been happy. Tahoe, here I come. Sadly, I'm an honest person.

"So, in regard to the money," I said as everything in the room seemed to stop. "It has relatives."

With that, I took out the second bundle from the TV and slapped it down.

"Here's Uncle Sammy," I said as Lenny picked it up and handed it to his mother. From the back I heard a voice say, "Really? There's more?"

Yes, there was as I pulled out another bundle.

"Here's Cousin Brenda."

Bundle number two circulated around the room before making its way back to abuela or grandma. It was probably covered in drool. Time for bundle number three.

"Oh, here's Aunt Linda," I said as I dropped the bundle and it made a beautiful thud. Lenny picked it up and handed it to his mother. You know, now that I think about it, maybe I invented the mike drop.

As bundle number three started its circuit, the gasps and shock were still going strong. Yup, you guessed it, time for numero four.

"Looky here, why it's good old Uncle Hector."

By now, grandma's lap was getting pretty full, not that she was complaining, and I wasn't helping the situation because I reached inside the set and said,

"Thank you for coming, close friend of the family, Manny."

With that, bundle five made its way around the room. Time for the big finish. How many times in life do you get to be a showman because that was exactly what I was going to be. I reached inside for the last time.

"Last but not least, here's great and I do mean great, Uncle George."

Because it was the last bundle, there was going to be no trip around the room. I decided to give it directly to grandma. With great fanfare, I walked over to her, got on one knee and handed it to her. She kissed me on the cheek and her smile could've lit up the entire state and I felt good too because I had done the right thing. Jimmy, the patriarch, saved his money all those years working at the Post Office to provide for his family. This family was saved because of his actions, because of his generosity, because of his love for them.

Even after I had shown them what was at least thirty thousand dollars, a few family members looked inside the television to see if there was any more money still hiding. Like after pulling out six envelopes and the bundle, I hadn't thoroughly checked. Nope, the magic RCA was tapped out. I think it's fair to say that the tone of the house had changed pretty dramatically from when I entered until now. Thousands of found money will do that. What were once tears were now happy conversations and pure joy. I began to close up the television. It didn't take long. Now, for the big finish as I stood up and said

"And if I could say one last thing before I leave you," I started, "please buy a new TV. You can certainly afford it."

Everybody laughed as I walked out the front door. It was the closest I'd ever felt to being Sinatra. And I felt good. Really good. I had done the right thing. The money was not mine to keep; I hadn't earned it. It was theirs. I'd be lying if I said that I didn't expect to be slipped a few bucks for my honesty, but I wasn't. They stiffed me. All I got for my trouble was time and a half because it was a weekend and knowing I did the right thing. Oh well. Tahoe...

Story 2: Some People Just Should Not Own Appliances (2016)

It was a Thursday afternoon when my dispatcher called. She had another stop she wanted me to make. Apparently, a customer's dishwasher was spilling water on the floor and her garbage disposal was all backed up. She needed service as soon as possible. I turned on the sirens and hightailed it over there. What a minute, I'm not a cop so, instead I cranked up the Pink Floyd and hightailed it over there. What can I tell you, the first way sounded more impressive.

The address laid inside a newly built track home complex, complete with a security guard manning the front gate. I pulled up, turned down the Floyd, gave the guy my name and the name of the customer. After a quick phone call, I was waved through. Now the hard part, finding the place when more than half the complex was still being built and most didn't have numbers.

Fortunately, the customer's house did, and I pulled up and parked right in front of it. Like all the others in the tract, it was brand new. The outside landscape had not been planted and was just a pile of dirt. At least the driveway was paved. I exited the truck, walked up to the front door, which judging by the smell, was newly painted and rang the bell.

About a minute and a half later, a bohemian looking woman in her thirties, wearing ripped blue jeans and a paint stained tee-shirt, opened the door.

"Hi, sorry it took a while for me to answer but I was in the back feng shuing the patio. I'm Gabby."

I nodded like I understood or cared what she was talking about but ever the professional, I said, "Not a problem. I'm Rob. You're having a problem with your dishwasher and garbage disposal?"

"Unfortunately, yes," she said. "It's right over here."

We walked about twenty-five feet or so to the kitchen. I placed my toolbox on the floor and my work order on the counter next to the sink. In the sink, a reddish skin pulp like material and a green stringy fiber lined the bottom along with many small seeds. What happened?

On the far side of the room laid a trashcan which looked out of place in a newly modeled kitchen. There was a paper bag hanging outside the trash can lid and corn husks were all over the floor. It looked like someone threw the bag into the can in a hurry and missed.

"How's your day been going so far," she asked?

"Fine. I've already made two service calls and now I'm here," I responded. "What about yours," I asked more out of politeness. She took in a deep breath, never a good sign.

"Well, I woke up and meditated. After that, I went to my hot yoga class. There's a new yogi. Yogi Rashna. Totally changed my life. You must see her. After that, I met a girlfriend for lunch. Then I looked at paint and tile samples…"

Oh my God, clearly her parents knew what they were doing when they named her Gabby. I was praying that somewhere in her monologue she'd tell me why I was there and that it would happen before I was eligible for social security. Fortunately, she did.

"…And on the way home from the design center, I saw a farmer's market. My nutritionist told me that I needed to dramatically up my vegetable intake and that they have to be organic. My dream is to have three fully formed bowel movements per day…"

Not to judge but going number two three times a day is your dream? Not climbing Everest or starring in a play or even getting a promotion? Maybe to her, sitting on the can three times a day was like climbing Mt. Everest. I'm not even going to make a "because it's there" joke. Too easy. Anyway, she continued

"…So, when I passed the farmer's market, I took it as a sign and just had to stop. I bought so many vegetables, they almost had to close early," she said while chuckling.

Okay, so that's why the trashcan was over on the side of the kitchen. She was cleaning the vegetables that she had bought. But where were they?

The answer came soon enough when I walked over to the dishwasher and opened the door. Steam came pouring out because the dishwasher was in a drying cycle. The reason why the room smelled like soup was that all the vegetables were crammed inside and were being cooked.

I got out my flashlight and took a closer look inside. What a nightmare. The heat had caused the lettuce to melt onto the sides. There were red spots throughout because grapes had exploded. The now mushy turn-ups added an aroma that was anything but pungent. Partially cooked vegetables were dangling from the racks and there were slimy vegetable shards on the floor next to the drying element. There appeared to be tentacles attached to the sides. Good god, she didn't throw a squid in here, did she? Nope, it was a spaghetti squash or nature's perfect food because it comes in its own bowl but was now was a blown-up mess. I pulled out the top rack and then the bottom rack. The food was melted onto the racks and it was a mess. It was pretty obvious that earlier, the dishwasher was completely packed with veggies but why?

"Ma'am, why did you put vegetables inside the dishwasher," I asked?

Gabby told me she got the idea from a show on the Food Channel. Too bad she wasn't a regular viewer of the Common Sense Channel. I explained to her that most foods cannot handle long durations of heat. First, they cook, then they start to breakdown on a molecular level and melt. Also, by essentially boiling them, all the vitamins and minerals are stripped away.

Gabby's face gave nothing away. Finally, she spoke. It was a doozy.

"I guess I didn't realize that the dishwasher would cook the vegetables because I turned off the heating mode switch on the selector panel. Doesn't a dishwasher clean with cold water?"

No!

I was completely dumbfounded, and, for some reason, my mind flashed to former baseball manager Dick Williams when describing why he didn't yell at his pitcher who bunted with the bases loaded and only one out. The opposing pitcher picked up the ball, fired it to home and the catcher threw the ball to first, killing the inning and the rally. Williams said yelling at his pitcher would've been like asking a guy who was wearing a turd on his head, why he was wearing a turd on his head? What rational answer could he give? Instead, I launched into a little dishwasher 101 but for five-year-old's. Maybe I was giving her too much credit.

"Ma'am, that's not how dishwashers work."

"They don't," she said back?

"No. The plumbing in any dishwasher is hooked into the hot water side. Hot water always enters the dishwasher at around one hundred and seventy-five degrees Fahrenheit but what caused this disaster most likely was the drying mode."

"How?"

"Well, the pump had forced the produce into the drainage system, then down into the house drain. Since the dishwasher's drain hose was stopped up, the water was exiting through the top aerator. That's why you have water seeping out. And because all the plumbing lines in the kitchen are connected, this mess got into your garbage disposal causing it to back up."

"Ohhh," she said but I'd bet everything I had that she still had no idea what I was talking about. What she said next confirmed it.

"So, you're going to clean this up and fix it, right?"

"Ma'am, it's not my responsibility to clean up this mess, it's yours. You can hire someone to do it, but it isn't going to be me," I said politely but firmly. In her mind, she still was undeterred.

"Okay, I understand. But the company's going to give me a replacement, right? It's still under warranty."

I took a breath.

"I'm sorry but there is no way your warranty or any warranty ever written would cover this."

"Why not?"

"Because a warranty only covers an appliance that fails in doing what it's supposed to do. I dare say that no one has ever tried to wash vegetables in a dishwasher. They're not designed for that. Now, if it failed during a normal operation, then you'd have an argument," I said way more reasonable than this situation called for. What she said next took me completely off-guard.

"But it's normal for me."

I laughed. I didn't mean to but there was no way I could stifle it. How could anyone not in this circumstance? Clearly, this woman wasn't all there or to put it in her terms; she was a cup of leafy greens short of a green smoothie.

"Ma'am, that may be, but it doesn't change anything. What I suggest you do is clean out the dishwasher as thoroughly as possible, then call a plumber. If you're lucky, only the dishwasher is destroyed and not most of your plumbing. It would take a miracle for you to not need a new dishwasher. I'm sorry."

She just stood there speechless. You would've thought I'd killed her. I put my flashlight back inside my toolbox and picked up my work order. Just before leaving, I turned around and said

"Next time, wash your veggies in the sink and let them dry naturally. Namaste."

To quote that great philosopher Forest Gump, "Stupid is as stupid does."

Then I left.

Story 3: The '70's Man (1992)

Ah, the seventies. The decade that gave us disco, leisure suits, "Three's Company" and jogging among other things. For some people that decade remains a magical memory. For at least one family, they're still living it this very day.

The house was pretty run down. The yard had not been attended to for a long time and I mean a long time. In the driveway there was a car that looked like it had been stripped for parts and, of course, a Volkswagen bus with yellow peace signs and fluorescent flower decals all over it. It sort of looked like the bus from "The Partridge Family" if Mrs. Partridge got stoned midway through decorating and gave up. Something was hanging from the rear-view mirror. I looked and saw flowers tied in a bow and the obligatory dream catcher that was probably purchased or bartered for at a Dead show.

Somewhere behind all the overgrown plants, lurked a front door. My mission: find it. I crawled through the plants and made pretend I was in a Vietnam war movie. Somehow, I found it. It was painted lime green with a big smiley face on it. I knocked on the door and attempted to stand up, but I had trouble. Plants had grown around the door's entrance, blocking it partially. Off to the side were, I think, a chair and a table. Not too sure, plants overtook the porch some time ago. Put it this way, if it was man versus nature, man got his butt handed to him.

I knocked a bunch of times. After the fourth time or so, I think I heard someone say, "Be with you in a minute, man." About three minutes later, the door finally opened. Standing in front of me, to my eye's disbelief, I found me a hippy!

The dude stood about six feet, rail skinny with long dark brown hair, head band, a scraggly beard and small rose-colored glasses. He had on baggy pants, which I don't think have ever been washed and a tie-died shirt. I believe anthropologists would call him "'70's Man." Then he spoke. He sounded exactly like Tommy Chong.

"Heyyy, man! Great to see you. I've been waiting for you to arrive. Would you do me the honor of entering my organic home, man?"

Then he went in for the hug. Since there was a distinct possibility that the guy was crawling with body lice, I stuck out my hand instead.

"That's why I'm here," I said. "I'm Rob."

"I'm Freedom."

I immediately checked my work order. Trust me, the name "Freedom" would've stuck in my brain.

"According to this, the man who set the appointment is Eugene Lipski."

"Oh yeah. That's my bourgeois name. If you don't mind, I like to go by "Freedom," man."

"Fine by me. Hey, isn't that just another word for nothing left to lose," I said quoting the Janis Joplin lyric. He just stood there.

"Whadaya mean, man," he said?

"You know, from the song? "Me and Bobby McGee?""

"No idea what you're talking about, man."

Thinking back, it kind of made sense that he didn't know. That song was from the sixties and Freedom was clearly a seventies dude. We entered his organic home. As we walked through the living room, I couldn't help but notice that everything was decade appropriate. The furniture was mostly wicker. There was lots of macramé art hanging on the walls with a smattering of god's eyes. There were no doors either. In their place were hanging beads. All the photos looked like they were from 1978 at the latest. Off in the corner were a lava lamp and a five-foot tall bong. I guess it was their version of an entertainment center.

Freedom began explaining what the problem was with his appliance. Of course, every sentence had a "man," "dude" or "far out" at the end of it. I did my best not to crack up. Trust me, it was hard to keep a straight face. I did not want to know what he was up to. As far as I was concerned, it was none of my business, man.

The more we talked, the more he seemed to warm up to me and for good reason, you see, I too was a seventies man with a pony tail down to my butt and a full-on scraggly beard. I may have even gone to a Foghat concert. And while I had left that decade far back in the rear-view mirror of my old Pinto, Freedom had not but he was touched that I could speak his seventies man lingo. In fact, at one point, we had an entire conversation where all any of us said to each other was the word "dude" and we understood each other perfectly.

You see, "dude" can pretty much mean anything. People are impressed that the words "shalom" and "aloha" have multiple meanings but, trust me, they have nothing on "dude." It can mean "hi," "no way," "awesome," "you're kidding me," etc. The list is pretty much endless. It's all about the inflection. For me, it was fun speaking in seventies again. I imagine it's like someone from the old country who hadn't had a chance to speak their native tongue in years.

We walked around the corner and entered the kitchen. It was dark as we entered in. Freedom turned on the light which barely did anything. The kitchen walls were painted a light shade of purple and stamped on the purple paint was a silver paint imprinted with a sponge. What put the whole room over the edge was what is stuck on the walls, chewed gum.

Freedom explained to me that it had all started innocently enough. One day, he was chewing gum when the phone rang. He didn't like to talk when he was chewing gum, so he took it out of his mouth and stuck it on the wall for later. I asked him why he didn't just throw it out? You would've thought that I had just punched his mother in the face by the look on his. Then he patiently explained that the gum had plenty of flavor left in it and that it would've been wasteful and disrespectful to Mother Earth to throw it out. He then pointed to the very same piece that was still on the wall as if it deserved landmark status or something.

Here's the thing, the entire wall. Scratch that. The entire room, except for one wall, was covered, wall to door with gum. The wall that wasn't covered in gum, was covered with the discarded aluminum foil from the gum which, again made perfect sense because, back in the seventies, the aluminum foil had a sticky adhesive on it. Perfect for sticking on walls. Far out!

"This is all from you," I asked, more than a little incredulously?

"No man, my old lady and daughter joined in, man."

Two "man"'s in one sentence. Kind of impressive. I swear, Freedom just about teared up. As for the walls, it was remarkable and disgusting at the same time. A tough feat to pull off.

I started to repair the appliance when a woman entered the room and stuck the newest piece of gum on the wall. She had long blonde hair and was wearing a flower print dress. Of course, she was dressed decade appropriate, that decade being the seventies. Freedom saw her wander in.

"Moon Honey, I want you to meet the repair dude, Rob. Rob, Moon Honey. Moon Honey, Rob."

I put out my hand and instead of shaking it, I think she read my palm.

"Rob," she said. "What an unusual name."

Now I really had to struggle to keep it together. The best I could come up with was, "not where I come from," meaning the planet Earth. She just shrugged. Then she started conversing. I'll say this for her, she didn't end each sentence with "man."

"So, what do you think of our gum wall," she asked?

"I can honestly say that I've never seen anything quite like it," I said truthfully.

She continued, undaunted.

"What a lot of people don't get is that all the gum creates a cosmic warmth for the kitchen and the kitchen is what powers the family. Think about it."

I didn't. Freedom, again, could not have been prouder or more impressed.

"I told you my old lady was deep, man."

No, he hadn't. Now, here's the slightly strange part. She did have a point. The kitchen was warmer than the other rooms and I didn't see a space heater anywhere. Then it hit me. The gum and foil were acting as insulation. All rooms being equal, the kitchen is the warmest because of the oven. Whenever she baked her homemade bread or funny brownies, the heat would remain trapped in the kitchen. It was almost smart. I said "almost."

I finished up the repair when a mouse darted through the kitchen. Surprisingly, they didn't freak out. I volunteered my help.

"Looks like you have an infestation problem. If you'd like, I'd be glad to give you the number of an honest exterminator."

Moon Honey was not happy and said so.

"You mean to murder one of God's little creatures? What right do I or any of us have to do that? They shouldn't call them "exterminators," they should call them "murdernators.""

Luckily, Freedom jumped right in to save me.

"Moon Honey, he doesn't know any better, babe. Out there, murder is a way of life."

From then on, Moon Honey was my bestest buddy.

"Freedom's right and I am so sorry. I shouldn't impose my things on you. Not cool."

"Don't worry about it. I'm not uptight or anything, man," I said by way of forgiveness.

"Bitchin'," she said back, and it was.

They really were kind of adorable together, Freedom and Moon Honey, standing side by side as I filled out the repair bill. It was obvious that the drugs from the 1970's really had messed them up, or had they? I mean, yes, they weren't quite all there but they were happy.

I handed the bill to Freedom. He placed my clipboard on the table and sat down. Moon Honey excused herself and left the room. He stood up, turned around and opened the kitchen cabinet door and pulled out a coffee can. He opened it and pulled out a wad of cash. I watched him with curiosity, how much money was he going to pull out?

"Is this enough, dude," asked Freedom?

I walked over to the counter. There was a lot of money on there. The bill came to a little over one hundred dollars. It would've been so easy to rob these gentle hippies blind but, once again, I'm an honest man so, I only took out what was needed to cover the bill. This was the right thing to do. I was surprised they didn't try and pay with magic beans.

"Thanks, man! I knew you were honest!"

He was testing me, and I passed. Groovy! Freedom wasn't done with me yet, though. He walked around the corner and opened another cabinet and pulled out a large plastic baggie full of a green, leafy-like substance. I don't want to cast aspersions, but I think it might've been marijuana.

"Hey man, have some Maui Wowie. Don't worry, man. It's completely pure. We grew it out in the back, in the bus."

The bag he was holding easily weighed over five pounds. The street value could have been in the thousands. Freedom and Moon Honey were pot farmers as well as gum collectors.

"I can't, man. It makes me paranoid," and I didn't want to go to prison which really would've made me paranoid. Freedom was disappointed but recovered quickly.

"Hey man, I understand. No matter what, we'll always be brothers, man."

Amen, Freedom. Amen. It was past time for me to leave.

"Catch you on the flip-side," I said in seventies speak for "goodbye."

"Not if I catch you first, man," said the man who I had come to know as "Freedom."

Now, I can't say I didn't enjoy my brief sojourn into the seventies, but it was sure nice to get back to the twentieth century.

Freedom and Moon Honey did stick with me though. In fact, I found myself ending some of my sentences with "man," "dude" and on one occasion, "dig." Trust me, my fellow techs cured me of that real fast. And one evening, the phone rang while I was chewing gum. I found myself taking it out and almost sticking it on the wall. I said "almost."

Story 4: Cold Feet (Late '90's)

It was September and it was crazy hot. To be honest, I was getting a little fed up with it. I mean you expect it to be hot in July and August, but it was mid-September and according to the news, we were looking at a high anywhere from 95 to 110 depending on where in the county you were.

On the work order, the complaint read, "losing food, frost and a smell." It was a long drive out to the house, about an hour or so. Not that I was complaining, mind you. The longer the travel time means the longer I could spend in the cool confines of the air-conditioned truck. I pulled up to the house which looked pretty normal. As I walked up to the door, trying not to completely sweat through my shirt, I noticed there were several pairs of shoes at the entry step.

I knocked on the screen door which was broken on one of its hinges. A few minutes went by, then the front door opened. An elderly lady opened the door.

"Are you the man from the appliance center?" she asked.

"I am. I'm Rob."

"I'm Elenore. Please come in," she said.

As I set foot inside, I couldn't help but notice that the house was old both inside and out. The entire place could've used a fresh coat of paint and that would've been just for starters. The current color was faded French Country yellow and very eighties. The furniture was old and covered in plastic. Ideal on a day when it was fast approaching triple digits and it wasn't even noon.

Another thing I noticed was a trail of wet footprints seemingly from the refrigerator to the front door which was a little odd. Was she just coming out of the shower? Probably not because there were no wet footprints on the wooden stairs. Also, upon closer inspection, they weren't footprints. They were shoeprints.

We walked slowly through the living room which was to the left of the front door and to the kitchen which was pretty large. The refrigerator was located right in front of the wall cabinets and had a sleeping bag and a pillow in front of it. I had no idea what that would be doing there. I mean, if she had guests staying over, why would they be in the kitchen? The kitchen wall was at least twenty feet across. The cabinets, the counter top and the flooring all looked like they were original to the house, so we were talking about thirty years.

As we walked closer, I noticed that there was a medium sized cooking pan located just right of the fridge that had water in it. Maybe it was for a dog.

Elenore told me that the temperature on the refrigerator side was not cold enough. She also explained that the freezer had frost inside. I opened the refrigerator door and was almost knocked unconscious by the odor. For some reason, the insides smelled like an old, sweaty gym bag. What was causing it? I then looked to my left and saw clear plastic wrap taped to the wall that separates the freezer and refrigerator. It ran the full length of the unit, top to bottom. I closed the refrigerator door and opened the freezer. To my surprise, there was plastic taped inside the freezer top to bottom in such a way that the freezer door would close and seal the best it could. Looking down at the bottom there was two cut outs, oval in shape, two or three inches apart. What were they there for? Had rats somehow gotten inside? That could explain the smell.

Inside the freezer, the ice maker was making ice and the bin was full. Frost was hanging from the ceiling. One shelf down, frozen food was tightly packed in and below that contained the answer to my question. Each descending shelf had work boots with socks stuffed inside. I counted five pair on two shelfs. Two shelves with stinky boots inside. Why? Was this tonight's dinner? If nothing else, at least I could say I knew where the smell was coming from.

About a half hour had passed since I entered the abode and the kitchen was hot just like the rapidly rising temperature outside. I was sweating through my undershirt as old Elenore was explaining the problems. I asked her if she could turn on the a.c. so we could both cool off. She replied that the house contained no air conditioning. Then I asked her why she kept boots inside the freezer. She smiled and began her lecture and whether I liked it or not, I was her audience.

"Rob, a while ago I read in a magazine…"

Moron's Monthly, I thought to myself. She continued,

"…that the feet are the air conditioners for the body…"

This wasn't true. If anything, it's a person's head that regulates body temperature. Still, she went on.

"…Logically speaking, of course, if you can keep your feet cold, your whole body will be cool. Now, how do we do that?"

I really think she was expecting me to raise my hand or something. Instead, I pretended like it was rhetorical and said nothing. This threw her off, just a little.

"…By making sure that what we put our feet in is cold which is why you saw the boots in the freezer…"

Duh, of course. Makes perfect sense.

"The reason why there are so many boots is that I like to rotate them so when the pair I'm wearing starts to lose its coolness, I have several other pairs of boots to use throughout the day."

Okay, so that was one mystery solved. Now for the remaining one.

"Interesting," I said. "Can you tell me about the two oval holes at the bottom of the freezer?"

She could not have been happier to have someone to explain this to. As the temperature was rising, my patience was lowering.

"But around the house, I do something a little different. You see, several times a day I walk over to the pan that has water in it…"

So, it wasn't for a dog. She droned on.

"I step in the pan, making sure to thoroughly wet my feet and shoes and socks completely…"

That explained the we foot prints. Now for her crowning achievement of idiocy.

"Then I walk over to the freezer, open the door, lie down and put my feet in the holes until the water on my feet is nice and frozen…."

"Really?" I said. "And the sleeping bag?"

"I was just getting to that. Sometimes it can take a while for my feet to freeze and I like to be comfortable. Sometimes, I can get quite sleepy," she said, laughing.

"Sure, frostbite can do that to you," I wanted to say but didn't.

"I do this several times a day and have never felt a need for air conditioning."

I couldn't help but laugh which Elenore did not find the least bit amusing. I asked her why I was there.

"You're being very rude. The people at customer service where I bought the refrigerator told me that they would replace the unit if you could not fix it."

I laughed again.

"Ma'am, let's go down the checklist: first, you want to get rid of the smell? Stop putting sweaty wet work boots and socks in the freezer. Second, you want to get rid of the frost? That's easy. Stop leaving the freezer door open and get rid of the dang plastic."

Now it was my time to lecture in a stiff voice.

"Frost builds up in a freezer when warm, humid air from the outside combines with the cold, dry air from the inside. This causes a thermal reaction which results in the frost you're complaining about," I said in my best professorial voice.

"Same goes for "losing food." By keeping your refrigerator door open, of course food will spoil. All you have to do is use the unit the way it was intended, and you won't have any problems," I continued.

"I want a new refrigerator," she insisted.

With that I completely lost my composure and busted out laughing. After a minute or two I regained it and said:

"I'm not going to recommend that we replace a $600 refrigerator because you want to put work boots and your feet inside it."

"Well, I never. I'm going to call your supervisor," she harrumphed.

"Please do and if you wouldn't mind, tell Gene that I'm going to be a little late for his barbecue on Sunday."

With that, I picked up my toolbox and left the house. Good thought freezing your feet in your refrigerator on a hot day. Based on her behavior, I'm guessing she stuck her head in there way more than once.

Story 5: The Go Back (2002)

A "Go Back" or a "Return Visit" or "Do Over" are pretty self-explanatory but in case they're not, it means going back to a residence for a second time for the same issue. All our repairs have a limited guarantee, usually sixty days. Now, for the customer, it's often free but for the company it's a loss of revenue and time. We get paid, they don't. Still, most of the time these calls are pains in the butt for various reasons including that the customer didn't follow directions, or the first repairman screwed up and now I had to clean up their mess. Something that's not very appealing to me.

As repairmen our mind set is pretty straight forward: get the job done and move onto the next one. Except for the strange calls. This is one of them.

This was one of those Go Back's where I did the initial repair. It was at an apartment complex which is never fun. Parking can be a bitch and sometimes a lot of walking's involved carrying a twenty-five-pound tool box. Don't even get me started about when elevators don't work. You try walking up seven stories lugging a heavy Craftsman tool box.

After I parked the truck about two blocks away from the complex and walked up, I began to recognize the place. It was the stoner's building. It was near a liberal arts college so that made sense. The main stoners were four guys who lived together and were loaded pretty much twenty-four seven. At least they were harmless. I knocked on the door and after about five minutes, the door opened revealing a guy in his early twenties with a scraggly beard and red eyes who was wearing a Baja hoodie, one of those sweatshirts with material like a burlap sack that had strips going down vertically. The Dave Matthews Band played in the background. He greeted me warmly.

"Thanks for coming, man! Good morning..."

It was two in the afternoon. He introduced himself as Ryan and invited me in. Inside were three other geniuses, equally loaded but not nearly as ambitious as Ryan because they hardly moved at all. At least Ryan opened the door. Hey, baby steps.

"So, what seems to be the problem," I asked?

"Problem?" he repeated back to me, somewhat confused before righting himself. "Oh, yeah, it's the freezer!" he said as if he just discovered the theory of relativity.

I immediately threw the ball back in his court by saying, "What about the freezer?"

He walked over to the appliance and I followed. Ryan opened the freezer door.

"So, like, inside the freezer, there's a whole bunch of sticky stuff. I talked to my dad and he said that we should get a new one for free because…" He couldn't complete his thought.

"Let me take a look at it,' I said, saving us both some time.

Yes, there was indeed a amber sticky substance on the freezer walls. It was beer. Either Ryan or one of the other members of the Algonquin Round Table he lived with, put a six-pack in the freezer and it promptly exploded leaving the amber sticky marks all over the freezer walls. I was pretty sure that Ryan had omitted this little detail when he talked to his father. It was up to me to break the news to him.

"Ryan," I said. "I can't replace the refrigerator because it was damaged by your actions."

No response. I felt like I was talking to a monkey, so I tried again.

"The problem was caused because you put beer in the freezer and it blew up. That's your fault."

"It is?"

I nodded affirmatively. It was around this time that I confirmed for myself that I wasn't a big Dave Matthews fan.

"Uh-oh," he said. "I'd better call my dad."

Ryan dialed up his old man and I just heard his end of the conversation. In an instant, he transformed from stoner to dutiful son. It was almost impressive.

"Daddy, hi!…Classes are going well. I'm really enjoying the academic environment. You were right to send me here…Yes, the repairman's here. He says he won't replace the refrigerator…"

I heard screaming loud and clear from the other end. Just then, Ryan turned to me and said, "Dude, he wants to talk to you." He handed me the phone. Great. This was just what I needed.

"Hello?…Yes, I'm with the appliance company," I managed to get out. He immediately started yelling at me.

"Don't try and pull this bait and switch crap with me! I'm not like the suckers you and your ilk rip off on a daily basis. I'm a district attorney. You will replace that refrigerator for free as specified in the warranty!"

What a dick! Still, I took a deep breath and tried to reason with him.

"Sir, the reason why the unit does not work is because your son, the fruit of your loins, put a six pack of beer in the freezer and it exploded. That's not our fault."

Hey, you can't say I didn't try and reason with him. He wasn't having any of my highfalutin logic.

"I don't care!" he practically spat back at me. "You guys owe me one refrigerator of equal or lessor value. I got it under sixty g.d. days ago!..."

For some strange reason, I didn't lose my cool. Maybe it was the smell of the patchouli oil or the thirty-five-minute Dave Matthews Band cover of Little Feat's "Dixie Chicken" that distracted me. Nah.

What caught my eye was that while Ryan's dad was hollering at me, I saw his son had picked up a small bowl and plastic kitchen ladle. The kind you use to put soup into bowls except that Ryan wasn't getting ready to work in a soup kitchen. Instead, he was scraping the frozen beer remnants of the walls of the freezer. He did manage to get most of it off. Was he just cleaning it up knowing that he wouldn't be getting a new one? My conversation with Stoner, Senior was mercifully coming to an end.

"Look, even if I wanted to, I couldn't," I said. "It's against company policy to replace a working appliance, even if it's under warranty, if the reason it's broken is because of misuse. This incident, I'm afraid, fits squarely into that category."

Click.

The son of a b hung up on me.

I returned the phone to the counter when I saw that Ryan had his bowl of beer shavings underneath the water dispenser of the refrigerator. He added just a short blast of water. I was watching very closely and was most curious to see what he was going to do.

Ryan started mixing the beer and the water together. I'll give him this, he was very meticulous about the process. I couldn't help but think that if he put this kind of effort into his studies as he did into mixing beer and water, he might be a doctor by now.

After a few minutes, he placed the spoon on the counter top and with two hands began to drink the beer solution. He raised the bowl way over his head making sure to get in the last drop. I was waiting to see if he was going to lick the bowl like a dog. He did not. I charged dad $160.00 for the visit and time being forced to deal with his and his son's stupidity. Well that was the first visit.

Now for the "Go Back."

This time I didn't have to park on the street, I was able to go to the visitor's section of the complex. Still, I had to walk a long way to the apartment. As I approached the front door, nothing had changed from the outside. Beer cans and trash were still strewn all over the walkway. I knocked on the door and waited. The door opened, and someone was standing there but I couldn't see who. It was the combination of the screen door and the sun shining in my eyes that prevented me from seeing who it was. But, sight is only one of our senses. The second he opened his mouth

"Dude!"

I immediately knew it was my old buddy, Ryan. You would've thought we had grown up together or something. The blessed reunion continued.

"Hey man, you're back! Awesome," he said as he invited me in and I returned the greeting.

"Hey man. Looks like the party's still going on!"

We both smiled at each other and walked over to the refrigerator while Phish played in the background. At least it wasn't Dave Matthews. I placed my work order on the sink and my toolbox on the floor.

"So, what's up with the fridge?" I asked.

Ryan looked at me quizzically and said, "Nothing Man, I just wanted to ask you a question." I looked at him and said, "What?," surprising myself.

"Yeah man, I called dad and made up a bogus story to call you back, I just wanted to ask you this one question."

"OK, you got me back here, so what's your big question?" I asked.

Ryan looked at me with those sweet, innocent, red eyes and said "Man, do you remember when you were here last? I had the best light beer I've ever had, and I don't know how I made it. Do you? It's been driving me nuts!"

That was the big question?! I started to laugh and said, "Man you must have had a real good party that day if you couldn't remember what you did."

He kept staring at me with wonder. I almost felt like reminding him to breathe.

"OK, I'll tell you how you made the beer."

Ryan's eyes opened wide. He was excited over the prospects of relearning how to make more light freezer beer.

"You put a six pack of Lowenbrau into the freezer and it blew up," I explained.

Based on his reaction, you would've thought that I had just distilled the secrets of the universe to him.

"Now I remember! Then I scraped the beer off with the ladle and added water! You are so cool, man!"

He went in for a hug, but I took a step back. If his feelings were hurt, it passed in a nanosecond. Ryan started bobbing his head and snickering like he was in a MTV cartoon.

I reached over to the sink and picked up my paperwork that needed to be filled out. But what to charge? I hadn't actually done anything, but I still had to drive there. I asked Ryan who was going to pay the bill? If it was him, maybe I'd give him a break. Believe it or not, the guy was growing on me. Thank God, he wasn't my son.

"Dude, my dad's paying."

The same dad who hung up on me. Mr. District Attorney? Well guess what, no break for him. I wrote the bill out for $100.00 dollars and Ryan handed me his dad's credit card.

Ryan signed it and we both walked to the front door. He looked at me with these eyes of doubt and asked, "Dude, I forgot to ask you something. Could you talk to my dad and tell him what you did?"

I looked at him and said, "Man, there is no way I'm calling your dad. If he finds out what you did he will cut off your money! Make up something, I have to go. Later dude!"

I started to exit the slum that was once an apartment and out of the corner of my eye, saw Ryan put a six-pack of Lowenbrau into the freezer to recreate his experiment in stupidity. Unbelievable.

I left the place and because this was before cell phones, I quickly located a pay phone. Who did I call? Ryan's dad!

After a few minutes of dealing with his secretary, I finally got through to the man himself. I identified myself and after a few moments of pleasant chit-chat about our families and golf games…of course we didn't. The guy was a dick, remember?

"I'm an extremely busy man. What is the reason for this call," he asked, pompously.

"It's about your son, sir."

"What about him?"

"Well, he's a drunk and a drug abuser. Plus, his apartment is probably a health hazard. You really should do something."

Now, I had his attention. His tone changed, almost bordering on concern or how his son's screw-ups might affect his next election.

"What should I do," he asked?

"Make a surprise visit."

"Why?"

I thought D.A.'s were smart.

"To see how he really lives. If he knows you're coming, he might get off his ass and clean up the place."

His tone went right back to the way it was before.

"I don't have time to fly across the country for this nonsense."

"Fine. If you don't come here in a week, I'm calling the sheriff's department and have them shut the place down." Then I hung up on him. It felt good.

A week went by with no visit from pops, so I called up the sheriff's department who instantly condemned the place and arrested Ryan and his buddy for possession. Believe it or not, I did do this for Ryan's own good. The way he was living had no good ending and the apartment was so squalid, it was unsafe.

So, whatever happened to young Ryan? Well, I'm proud to say that this little incident was a real wakeup call for him. After making bail and getting probation, he entered rehab and turned his life around. He began taking college seriously, graduated with a 3.8 and went onto a very prestigious grad school. After that, through dint of hard work, he went on to become the head of a major Fortune 500 corporation and is very involved with numerous charities. Yeah, right.

Last I heard, he got expelled from college and sells sunglasses to tourists on Venice Beach. But at least he knows how to make really good light beer in the freezer. Unless he forgot again.

Story 6: The Cat's Pajamas (1990)

Question; how does mold grow in a freezer when it is freezing inside? This is a question that I cannot answer but this one bizarre couple could.

For the most part, I was having a pretty boring week. Lots of ice makers, dishwasher pumps, racks, washer timers, plugged dryer vents, etc. All normal stuff. Then it happened. My dispatcher sent me a special code on my beeper. Code 500. Code 500 means special attention is needed on a repair and I was to call the office as soon as possible. In short, drop whatever it was I was doing and call the office and talk to the supervisor on duty.

Of course, I received the code just as I sat down for lunch. My lunch period is my time. It's the only time I get to collect my thoughts. Trust me, with all the crazy things going on in my day, I need my time. So, I was going to wait my full 30 minutes and eat my lunch like a human-being. I wasn't too worried. For all they knew, I was waist deep in a repair and didn't see the code. Also, right outside where I was eating, there was a pay phone I could use. This was before cell-phones.

My beeper went off three more times as I was eating lunch. Okay, this problem must be pretty significant if they needed to find me that urgently. I had swallowed the last bite of my burger when my beeper went off for a fifth time. What the hell was going on? I could only imagine.

I exited the restaurant and walked over to the pay phone and realized that it was brand spanking new. The phone company had just replaced it because it was clean, the numbers were all legible and didn't stick. And the biggest give-a-way that this phone booth was new; a homeless person hadn't defecated in it yet. It was entirely possible that I was the first one to use it. Yup, things were definitely coming up Rob.

The routing office had an 800 number that we were supposed to call when beeped. This made it easy for me and my fellow techs because we didn't have to walk around with a bunch of quarters in our pockets.

I dialed and on the third ring, one of the ladies in the dispatcher's office picked up. It was Jill, someone who I had worked with for several years and whom I could trust.

"Hey Jill, it's Rob. I'm responding to the code. My beeper went off five times in thirty minutes. What's up?"

"Hey Rob, I'm not sure. Let me put you on hold and find out," she said.

"Sure thing."

I was on hold for about a minute when she came back on the line.

"Rob, I checked, and I have no idea why you were beeped."

"False alarm, I guess," I said.

"Must be," she said.

"Okay, I'm sure I'll talk to you later…"

Just as I was about to hang up, my beeper went off again. Something was happening.

"Ah, Jill. It went off again. Would you mind rechecking?"

Jill put me on hold again. At least five minutes had passed. Around minute three, a man walked by who wanted to use the phone. I told him that I'd probably be a few minutes. He did not respond to this news in the spirit in which it was intended, instead spewing a trail of profanities as he walked off. Jeez, buddy, it's not that big a deal.

Jill came back on. Apparently, it was Ralph, a supervisor who I didn't get along with who had been beeping me non-stop. Simply put, Ralph had his head up his ass on a regular basis. Knowing this, Jill transferred me to Jose, a supervisor who I did get along with.

Jose explained to me that there was a technician at a home right now that thinks he's in danger from the customer and is requesting immediate help. In situations like this, when there are special or dangerous conditions, we have special phrases or keywords that will start a process without alerting the customer. We call them codes. For example, if someone is in danger when speaking to the office, he'd request a part that doesn't exist, which notifies the person on the other end that there's a problem.

Jose advised me that the call was a Code 3, which means that the customer is getting violent and the tech should leave but can't. Unlawful restraint would be the legal definition.

The address Jose gave me was very close to the location where I was calling from. At that time, we did not have computers or g.p.s. to get around. As anyone who lived in Southern California prior to around 2005 knows, if you needed directions, you relied on the good, old Thomas Guide, a book of maps that everyone had in their cars.

After locating where I needed to go, I could only wonder what I was getting into. I had to believe that if it was really bad, the office or the tech himself would've called the police. The important thing was that one of my fellow technicians was in trouble and I was the closest person who could help.

The drive was ten minutes down the road. I had to stop the truck and double check the Thomas guide to see if I had the right street because someone, probably teenagers, removed the sign from the pole. As I was rechecking the location in the guide, an older man walked by wearing a tuxedo with tails, holding an ivory tipped cane. On closer inspection, it wasn't a modern tuxedo because over his socks, he was wearing spats. Plus, he was wearing a monocle. Great, I had just hallucinated Mr. Monopoly. This man was really out of place in this neighborhood or any neighborhood.

After a moment or two to get my bearings, I realized that I was on the right street and the address was several houses down at the end. The man in the tuxedo continued to walk at a casual but bouncy stride as I drove by him. There was another one of the company trucks parked on the corner. I think the technician was taking a nap. I did not want to know, so I drove on. I was on the right street.

I found the house. As I exited the truck, I thought it best to grab a small part so when I knocked on the customer's door, I would give a false appearance that I was bringing a part to the other technician. I grabbed a leftover part from an earlier job and just as I did, Mr. Monopoly passed. He was going to the same house I was. Why was this man in a tuxedo, top hat and cane? A costume party? Dementia? Honestly, I really didn't care. These days, why be normal? I heard that someplace and it kind of stuck with me. Top hat and tuxedo wouldn't even crack the top twenty weirdest things I've encountered on this job.

As I walked up to the door, the walkway was not really normal. Someone used cracked old glass to form a walking path and even framed the pieces of glass to make lights light up. The front door's standing area also had the same glass cemented to the ground. The front door was just freshly painted. I could smell the paint, it hadn't dried yet. The doorbell switch was not attached, just two wires were dangling out. You think that was going to stop me? I grabbed the two wires and touched them together. The doorbell rang. It played a tune that I didn't recognize except that it sounded old.

I could hear footsteps. They were small steps, short in duration. It was a hard type heel shoe, almost like tap dancing. The door opened slowly and squeaked as it did. It wasn't the paint that caused it. Once opened, it revealed a lady in her seventies or eighties dressed in a 1920's flapper dress. She had a champagne glass in one hand and a cigarette in a long holder in the other. She was wearing a cloche hat. You've seen them in old pictures. They're kind of bell shaped and made of felt. There was also a horrible and stagnant smell of cigarettes escaping from the house and into my face.

"Hello, I'm Rob. The other technician sent for me. Can you take me to him," I said as non-threatenly as possible? Yes, she was old but quite possibly mentally unbalanced.

"Oh, you must mean that other chap who was here earlier. He left. What a bluenose. Not fun at all. At. All," the geriatric Daisy Buchanan replied.

I was confused for a moment until I realized that she was speaking to me as if she was still in the 1920's. I later found out that "bluenose" meant someone who doesn't like to have fun. Trust me, I looked up a lot of things when I got home from this job.

"So, he's not here anymore," I asked wanting to be as sure as possible?

"Yes, he bloused about a half-tick ago. Now, are you coming in or not?"

I must admit that curiosity got the best of me. I wanted to see what was going on inside there. I just hoped I didn't end up like the proverbial cat.

I entered the house and closed the door behind me. As I grabbed the door knob, I noticed a sticky greasy film on the knob itself. What was this substance? I could not tell what it was at that moment. The house interior was not lit up well enough for me to tell but the smell from my hand told me it was nicotine from her smoking.

The lady began to escort me into the living room entrance and I followed. The smoke was so thick that as we walked through the hallway a swirling vacuum of smoke twirled just behind us. I don't think she ever opened the windows in the house. As we slowly walked, her hips swung side to side as they did in the roaring 1920's. Disturbing to say the least. Honestly, I was just waiting for her to through-out her back as she knocked the shoe heels on the floor.

As we walked toward the laundry room I observed the furniture. It was old, I mean 1930-1940's. It was in great shape though and for some reason, not covered up. I could also see a stain of smoke across the top of the chair backs and seat marks where people had sat. Between the chairs were champagne bottles and four glasses. The stain marks might be from the sun light reflecting off glass and onto the upholstery although I couldn't say for sure.

A few steps into our walk and to my right, was Mr. Monopoly standing there still in full dress, with his hat in hand pressed to his chest and walking cane perched and prompted forward. He spoke as I walked by, "greetings and welcome, young man!".

"And hello and greetings to you, good sir," I said in my best approximation of 1920's speak.

This was a little creepy. I had a 1920's flapper in front of me and the tuxedoed man following me. The clanking sounds of all the shoe heels was also a little alarming. Two heel sounds from her and three from the tuxedo man, one being his cane. I still didn't know why I was being escorted. To skin me alive?

On the walls were pictures of old actors and actresses. All of the photos were in black and white and yellowed because of the time that has past. I didn't recognize any of them and I don't think my grandmother would have either. Probably because their heyday was before talkies.

As we walked through the parlor, I heard music playing. "…Yes, we have no bananas…" was the only lyric I could make out.

As a music buff, I could not relate to that time period at all. It just seemed like a lot of nonsense words. We were almost to our destination when the music skipped a track. The lady was playing a 33 or 18 on an old diamond tip photograph. I could only think that the diamond needle would tear the old plastic records groves to a point where no legible music would come out. Not that that would've been a bad thing.

We finally got to the kitchen and it too was from the 1920's. The sink was made of solid steel with four standing legs and a wrapped drain pipe as plumbing. The stove, white in color, had two doors and a chrome cooking area. It was perfectly polished as if it was never used.

The lady and I entered the laundry area and Mr. Monopoly stayed in the kitchen. The refrigerator was not really in front of us but just off to the right. I was shocked that it wasn't an ice-box. I also noticed that there was a pair of pliers clamped on the washer timer knob. They broke the knob and due to the age of the washer, no parts were available to fix it.

The laundry room was of newer construction and didn't match the rest of the home in the least. Best guess is that it was a storage room that was converted or redone. There was also a window with a sliding lever off to the left. I could not help seeing it, being the only light in the room, it kind of stuck out.

Standing in front of me was a brand new two-month-old refrigerator. Stainless steel in color with three doors. The two top doors were French doors meaning they were side by side and opened outward. One door had an icemaker and on the bottom was a forward sliding door that comprised the freezer section. Needless to say, it didn't match anything in the whole house. Naturally, I gravitated towards it because it was as out of place as I was.

The lady stopped in front of the refrigerator, just off the right side. I placed my toolbox on the floor with the paperwork on top of it. Then I walked to the left. The lady started to describe what the problem was again.

"Young man, there is a ghastly green mold inside the freezer and it's all over the place. On top of that, there is a slick amber film that's covering everything. It's bananas," she explained.

"Uh-huh," was what I managed to get out. She stood there in her pose, left hand on her hip and her right holding her cigarette poised in the air. Her head angled upward to the right as she took a drag. She explained further,

"Whatever it is, it's making me pull a Daniel Boone."

"A Daniel Boone," I asked?

"Yes, a Daniel Boone," she said as if that made sense. Then she mimed throwing up and I understood.

"I don't know what it is, but you need to figure this out or give me a new refrigerator," she said. She shifted her head to her right and walked out of the room. Noisy heels clacking on the floor with each step.

Back to the problem at hand. Something was going on here. I opened the refrigerator doors and found sixteen bottles of champagne inside but no bathtub gin. Anyway, that was a lot of champagne for two people. Maybe she had a party, maybe she was a drunk.

I closed the doors to the refrigerator and tried to open the freezer door. It wouldn't budge. I needed to take a different approach to open it. First things first, I need to see what I was doing. I'm funny that way. The light switch was located just outside the entrance. So, I wrapped my stinky hand and flipped the switch. It barely made a difference. The light was as dim as Daisy and Mr. Monopoly.

Next step, open the window enough so that light could come in and I really needed to vent this room, so I could breathe. I closed the door that divided the kitchen and the attached room I was in. Finally, decent air and light.

Next to the washer was a running sink with old towels draped alongside it. One old trick is to heat up the seal with warm water. As I placed the towels on the floor, I heard the sound of glasses clanking together. It sounded like my 1920's time warped customers were drinking. Didn't they know that prohibition was still the law of the land?

I poured the warm water onto the freezer door seal. It took about three attempts but finally the door seal broke free to a point where I could almost see inside. It took a little effort, but I finally got the door open completely.

The flapper was correct, there was something green inside and an amber food sticky film throughout the freezer compartment. As mysteries go, it was pretty easy to solve: the green material was from a champagne bottle that exploded. The green material being the shards of glass from the bottle and the sticky material being the champagne that sprayed all over the place.

The glass was all over. Small pieces and large from the neck with the main body still intact and laying on one of the wire shelfs. Good thing, there was no food inside or it would've been ruined. The damage seemed to be limited to the freezer.

I grabbed the tools from my toolbox that I'd need to remove the freezer door from its mounts and as I stood up I could hear the flapper in conversation with Mr. Monopoly. They were laughing about something. Perhaps about the Kaiser. Yes, they were drunk.

I grabbed the doors and moved the refrigerator a little to the left and proceeded to unplug the power source. I removed the freezer door and used the warm water and a pair of pliers to remove the glass bottle piece by piece and then used some old rags that were laying around to clean the champagne from the side walls. What a sticky mess. It wasn't the bee's knees.

This process took a while. Champagne does not dissolve very fast. I also needed to be careful not to cut myself from any leftover glass shards. Eventually, I finished cleaning the compartment and proceeded to reinstall the freezer door. Thankfully, it's a lot easier replacing the door than removing it.

As I normally do, I always cleaned up my work area. So, I placed the dirty rags into the wash sink and left the broken champagne bottle in the old wash bucket. I also placed the bucket in the wash sink. There was not a trash can around and I wanted the 1920's lady to see what I found.

My paperwork was inside the toolbox. So now it was time to figure out her bill. The warranty on her refrigerator does not cover exploding champagne bottles and I needed to reset her pompous attitude. I also wondered if she knew that women had won the right to vote. Perhaps it would be best if she hadn't.

I finished writing up the bill, so I opened the door and before calling out to her, I thought it might be best to take a look around first. From the door opening I could see through the kitchen and just a few feet into the living room. Then I called out.

"Hello-Hello, I'm all done here."

"I'll be right there, I just need to finish this last sip," she said back. I wouldn't want to get in the way of somebody's eighth glass of champagne, so I waited. Seconds later I heard the unmistakable popping sound of a bottle of champagne being opened. That was pretty damn nervy, I thought.

I called out for her again. "Ma'am, are you coming to see what I found?"

"Fine, I'm coming," she said. "Why must everyone be in such a rush these days?"

Hey, they didn't call it "The Roaring Twenties" for nothing, right? I could now hear her ankling towards me.

As she turned the corner to enter the kitchen I noticed that her make-up was smeared and her dress was not buttoned up correctly. Looks like the geriatric Tom and Daisy Buchanan had been making out in the other room with me in the house. Well good for them, I guess.

Daisy stopped walking to fix herself up, not realizing that I could see her. I backed up a little to make it look like was just coming into view. She now saw me and greeted me with a kid voice.

"Ok, young man, what did you find?"

As I stood in the door way, it was even more apparent than before that she was not all together mentally or physically. Trying to stay professional, I turned to the wash sink and picked up the old wash bucket. The one I put the broken champagne bottle in along with all the other broken glass from the freezer.

Her eyes opened wide and started a rant.

"No! No! No! Oh god, no! What did you do? Albert, come see what happened to one of our babies and the room! Hurry, just hurry!"

At least I now knew Mr. Monopoly's name, Albert. Drunk Albert.

As Albert ambled in, there was the sound of crashing glass and wood. He yelled out,

"I'm coming, darling dearest! I'll be there in a half-shake."

The flapper placed both of her hands over her face and turned away from me as she dropped her glass and cigarette into the sink. She slowly started walking straight into Albert's arms and they both started crying. They probably hadn't been that distraught since Calvin Coolidge won a full term.

"What is it, my dearest," pondered Albert?

"Albert, one of our baby's is dead," she said as her sobbing continued.

Albert did nothing but cry with her and he did not speak an intelligible word. With the amount of alcohol that was sloshing in his innards, it was a miracle he could stand upright.

I did not know what to do at this point. The refrigerator was working fine and had no real problem to begin with. The crying flapper just flew off to never-never champagne land and I was at a crossroad. Stick around and wait for them to come back to earth or leave so I can breathe clean air again? Guess what I choose.

I decided to mosey on out of there. Let them deal with their own issues, right? It didn't quite turn out that way, however because as I started to leave, Albert reached out and grabbed my arm and said with a drunken slurry voice,

"I will hunt you down and kill you."

This is what he probably said to the other tech which necessitated me being there in the first place. I forced him to let go as I grabbed his arm with my hand. As drunk as he was I don't think that the bruise I left on his arm would register for days.

Albert let go of me and embraced his soused lady again. Consoling her as she cried he said, "There, there, Dorothy. We shall get through this. By god, I swear it!"

I left them in that position inside the kitchen. The black and white scene was right out of an old timey movie. What Albert and Dorothy didn't realize is that when she dropped her glass into the wash sink, she also dropped her credit card. I wrote down the number when they were embracing and left a copy of the bill on the kitchen table top. I left them and the 1920's behind as I sought clean air.

I didn't feel too badly for them though. Surely, the news of Lindbergh landing in Paris would cheer them up…and give them another excuse to get drunk.

Story 7: The Refrigerator From Hell (2018)

How far can a person take their religion? If you watch or listen to regular TV, cable, or dish you will find a small assortment of religious stations, each praising the Lord in their own, shall we way, "unique" way. But what if it goes a little too far? Or really far?

It was a wonder sunny day, with the temps in the mid 80's... no it wasn't. It was raining like a bastard with wind blowing from all directions and just an ugly cold day. Not the day you would ever want to be out in.

Around two o'clock, I had just left the local fast food place that I visit regularly. I say that with confidence due to the fact that they know me by name and on occasion know what I'm about to order. I could not be prouder. Now, it was time to go to the job.

The house was located in a housing track that was built somewhere in the 1960's and a few of the houses looked like they had never been upgraded. As I pulled up the address on the work order, there were a few cars parked in front of the house, mostly American. I had to park the truck two houses down from the address...in the pouring rain.

The home had had some work done to it recently. The driveway had fresh concrete, the planters and the yard had newly planted plants. There was a walkway leading up to the front door. The house itself had modular tile encompassing the entire front. Whoever the contractor was had done a great job. The front door was made of solid wood, not pressed. The entry had an overhang of several feet that I couldn't wait to get to because, again, it was pouring. Wrath of God type of rain.

I hurried to the front door. One thing I really hate is getting my feet wet. Socks take forever to dry when you're wearing them, and you're reminded of that fact every time you take a step and squish. Because it had been raining for several hours, the street curbs were overflowing. The water was rising to sidewalk level.

I ran to the back door of my truck, opened it and grabbed my toolbox. It was a good two hundred feet to the house. I ran faster than I ever had in my life across the street and up to the front door. Once there, I turned to the right and up the steps. The plants in the planter were all overflowing with water and there was a better than average chance that they'd uproot and float away. Time would tell.

I knocked on the door and when it opened, standing in front of me were two nuns. That was a new one on me. One of the nuns invited me into the house. Why were there nuns here? Was it a nun convention or was the economy so bad that the church had them selling Amway? We made small talk about the weather as I entered. I was asked to take my boots off and I complied. My socks were soaked, and I left squish prints with every step I took.

On the walls were paintings and photos of the Pope, the Last Supper, Billy Graham, Jimmy Swaggert and every other televangelist you could think of. There were plenty of statues of religious icons, saints, disciples, you name it and at least a half a dozen crucifixes. What really tied the room together was a huge, black velvet painting of Jesus Christ hovering over the continental United States. I just hoped that the good god-fearing people of Alaska and Hawaii aren't reading this and feeling left out. There were also plenty of rosary beads on virtually every flat surface. It looked like the Vatican had a going out of business sale and this woman had purchased all the inventory.

After taking it all in, in all its splendor, I was pointed to the kitchen and to get there, I had to walk through a study room area. Inside were five young people sitting with two priests. Each of them had a bible in their hands. I assumed that they were a study group meeting at the house. I could not have been more wrong.

I continued to walk into the kitchen, the lady of the house was there wearing a sundress with shoulder length hair looking nice and sane. Also, there was Father Joe. Father Joe was and is the priest at the church I attend. Why was he there? Had someone died recently? The Father greeted me warmly.

"Rob, what a wonderful coincidence that they sent you here. Good to see you. How's the family?"

"Small world," I said. "And everyone's doing fine. Thank you for asking."

"I bet you're wondering why we're here," Father Joe came back with.

"You could say I'm a little bit curious."

"I'll let Bernice explain."

With that, Father Joe pointed to Bernice, the woman in the sundress. As I placed my tools on the floor, Bernice cleared her throat and spoke.

"Every night, around midnight, the witching hour, there's a terrible, ghastly noise from downstairs. I was so scared but after a week of hearing this awfulness, with God's help, I was able to summon up the courage to come downstairs."

She was starting to shake a little bit. Father Joe put his hand on her shoulder and nodded, giving her the strength to continue.

"And when I came downstairs to the kitchen, in this very room. I saw it."

"Saw what," I asked?

"The work of Satan himself."

Yeah, the decorating scheme was a little bit tacky, but I don't think it was fair to the decorator to call it "the work of Satan himself." But, that wasn't what she was referring to.

"I saw the refrigerator travel across the floor, as if possessed. It's possessed by evil spirits or the devil or both. I was so scared. And the refrigerator doors clanged and vibrated fiercely like something horrible was trying to burst out. Sometimes, when I came downstairs, the doors would be open when I knew, for a fact, that I had closed them the night before!"

Beatrice started sobbing. I scrunched my feet as hard as I could to keep from laughing. I turned to Father Joe and said

"And you and the sisters are here for spiritual support," I asked hopefully?

"No, Robert. We're here to perform an exorcism on the entire house but mainly on the refrigerator."

Oh-kay.

I asked her if she could describe the noises a little better. Loudness, octave level and duration, that kind of thing. She just looked at me like I was crazy. Yeah, I was the one who was loco. Obviously, she had no idea what I was asking her to do. Father Joe tried to help by rephrasing the questions but had no better results than I did. Beatrice didn't say a word.

From the other room, I heard the five or, so people start to sing a hymn from the bible. Father Joe pulled out his bible and began to recite a verse. One that I did not recognize. What were they doing?

Bernice exited the kitchen and walked to the study group people where she was consoled. At the same time, the two nuns entered the room from the other side entrance.
All nine of them were now in the same room singing a hymn.

Father Joe was still in the kitchen reciting a verse, and he turned a page, turned to his left and entered the room where everyone congregated. I was now all alone...with the refrigerator from hell. Time to get to work.

The refrigerator, that I nicknamed "Regan," after the little girl from "The Exorcist," was an older Norge, built in 1984 and it was still running. Maybe it was possessed.

I opened the door and turned off the thermostat. This stopped the power to the rest of the motors. The compressor stopped functioning and as it slowed down to a complete stop, it shook with an off-balance motion moving the refrigerator a few inches forward. Good thing there was a priest in the other room in case things got, you know, weird.

I waited a few minutes and turned the thermostat back on. The system restarted with no problems. Then I let a few more minutes pass and turned off the thermostat again and the shaking continued. Suddenly, the singing stopped and the whole crew of holy people entered the kitchen. It was a little tight in the small room for all ten of us. This was not my normal working environment.

Father Joe continued with his reading. I had no idea what he was saying because it was in Latin. The phrase "Dominus Refrigeratius" might have been uttered but was probably just in my head. The chanting continued with all ten of us in the kitchen.

Back to reality or at least, my version of it. The motor mounts inside the compressor had broken away and the only way to fix the problem was to replace the compressor. Easy to say for me but three hours of work and lots of trouble to actually do the job. Being in the middle of the Vatican's kitchen probably wasn't going to help matters either.

Father Joe grasped his rosary beads and continued the sermon and started speaking Latin which, I thought was a little rude because I had no idea what he was saying. That little part of me thought it best to keep my mouth shut, at least until Sunday when I would see Father Joe again and bring in my microwave to get blessed. Just a little preventative measure because the last thing I'd ever want is for my microwave to get possessed. Not only because the evil could affect my family and me, but it could also it screw-up the popcorn setting.

With all eleven of us in the kitchen, not including Satan, I needed to do something to get a little space for myself and move these people someplace else. They were interfering with my job and annoying me too. So, I raised my hands and with a slow motion, pointed to the other room. I did it with a flourish too and after a few times, they started walking out.

The Nuns led the way and the junior priest followed trailed by the study group. Bernice was the last to leave, with her arms raised high in the air, saying "Praise the Lord". Father Joe was the only one who did not leave. Maybe he felt it was his responsibility to stay with the evil appliance.

At this time, I walked over to the wall phone and called my office and asked for the parts department. When one of the parts persons answered, I gave them the model number and a description of the part I needed. After being on hold for about two minutes, the parts person came back on the line and uttered the best three letters I could have heard in this instance, N.L.A. N.L.A. means parts "no longer available." Hallelujah! There was no way I could complete the repair and would get to leave.

Father Joe turned the page in his Bible and before he restarted reading from the next page, I placed my hand on top of the good book so that Father Joe could not continue. That was going to cost me a couple of dozen Hail Mary's down the line. I turned to this man of God and said,

"Father, with all due respect, the refrigerator is not possessed. It has a bad compressor which causes the unit to shake. Because this appliance is so old, they no longer produce replacement parts."

I suggested that Bernice had three options; get a new refrigerator, visit local salvage yards to see if they had the old part or learn to co-exist with Satan in the lettuce crisper.

Father Joe was still a little shocked that I stopped his sermon in mid-stream. Bernice was in the next room. She now had her hands in front of her face, crying out the phrase "praise the Lord" over and over until she landed on the couch. Was I the only one who wasn't nuts here?

One of the priests and one of the nuns came to her assistance. One of them asked her if she was all right. Bernice blurted out, "I was hit by something and now I can see spirits!"

She claimed she could see evil demons and it was now her mission to destroy them the best she could. Hey, we all need a calling, right?

One of the priests stepped back to give Bernice a clean visual of the kitchen which Father Joe and I were still standing in. She jumped to her feet and rushed in. It was obvious that her new mission was to rid the area of demons.

Father Joe and myself turned to look at her and see what she was going to do. Then Bernice grabbed the Bible from Father Joe, closed the book and started with her own anti-evil spirit chant. Then she stopped. Looked at both of us and stepped back in shock.

"Father Joe, there is an evil spirit right next to you and next to the repairman, I can see him clearly."

Father Joe's face just dropped. What was she going to do?

Father Joe and I faced each other with confusing looks. There was an evil spirit between us? The only evil thing between us was the bill I was going to give them. At that moment, a flash on light came into the living room and bounced off Bernice's glasses.

"It's here and it's horrible! Don't you see?!"

The nuns all came rushing over as did the junior priests. I decided to take the lead. I figured that the time I spent in mass and church in general must have taught me something about spiritual matters.

"Father, I believe I'm the one most qualified to help this poor soul," I said.

I went up to Bernice and removed her glasses from her face and made her keep her eyes shut.

"Bernice, I see something. Don't move or open your eyes!"

"I won't. I won't!" she said back.

Was I going to chant a special verse from the good book or recite an anti-demon chant from the 1400's. Nah, too much of a hassle. I grabbed a dish towel from the sink, wiped the smudge from her glasses, put them back on her face.

"You may now open your eyes," I commanded.

She did and was amazed by the miracle I had performed.

"Yes, the spirit is gone! Show me what you did so that I too can fight evil."

I looked at Father Joe and said, "she is your problem now and I wish you the best! See you Sunday and I don't want to hear anything about this whatsoever."

Pretty ballsy of me to order around a priest. I'd have to be extra good for the next couple of days to make-up for that borderline blasphemy I had just committed on this anything but routine service call.

Right after I had performed this "miracle," Bernice dropped to her knees in front of one of the many crucifixes and started speaking in tongues. Father Joe and I looked at each other and for once were in total agreement; Bernice was nuts.

I picked up my tools and walked to the front door and said goodbye to the entire group.
I think the Lord was listening to what I had to say because the rain stopped just enough so I could walk at a comfortable pace back to my truck and not get wet. Once I got inside, it started pouring again.

On the drive home, I thought about revising my business card. Currently it read, "Senior Service Technician." I thought about adding the phrase, "And Satan Vanquisher." Yup, maybe I had missed my calling.

Story 8: Check These Out? (1995)

I think the title of this story does not do the experience justice.

The house I pulled up to was nothing special. Completely average in all respects. I knocked on the door and was greeted by Bill, a middle-aged man who was losing the battle to keep his hair. Plus, he was tall and had the makings of a first-class beer belly, so the toupee wasn't exactly helping matters.

The other thing that stood out about him was that he was wearing flip-flops. Mind you, it was winter and easily below fifty degrees outside. Nevertheless, he beckoned me inside and I followed. The flooring was worn but kept up and the furniture was old and dark in color. Bill, then, escorted me to the kitchen area where the job was.

The kitchen had new appliances all with stainless steel fronts and the area I was to work in was nice and comfortable. Bill explained to me what was wrong with the dishwasher and how it was broken. This I greatly appreciated because this kind of honesty from a customer does not come along very often.

I started repairing the dishwasher as I normally do. I told Billy what part had failed and that I was going out to the truck to get a replacement. As I started to move toward the doorway, his hand reached out and grabbed my arm stopping me in my tracks. He looked at me with an innocent expression, paused for a few seconds with his face tilted slightly.

"Can I ask you a question that does not have anything to do with the dishwasher?" he asked.

"Why don't you ask after the repair?" I replied, which seemed to satisfy him.

I left, got the part, re-entered the house and started fixing the unit. Bill was sitting at the kitchen table looking at the newspaper waiting for me to finish with the dishwasher. Something was on this man's mind and I had no idea what. Honestly, I kind of took my time. This is a technique we call "stringing out the repair." Finally, I finished and still had no idea what was coming.

I stood up and took him through the work I did and demonstrated that the dishwasher was done and was now working fine. He rose up from his chair and stepped into my direction and seemed happy with the job I did. I then turned around to grab my clipboard, which had the repair order.

As I was making notation on the order, Bill commented on my professionalism and he asked again if he could ask me a question now that the work was complete?

"That's fine," I said.

"It has nothing to do with the dishwasher or any appliances at all," Bill explained.

"Okay. Shoot."

Over the years, I've had many customers ask my opinion on completely unrelated matters like house repairs, car repairs, even family problems. Someone once even asked if she should go through with her upcoming wedding. Even with all that experience, I still couldn't have prepared for what came next.

"So," Bill started a little uneasily, "My wife, Ginger had some work done and we'd like your completely unbiased opinion."

"Haven't you asked your friends?"

"Yeah," said Bill, "but they just told me what I wanted to hear."

"What about your family?"

"Nah, it just wouldn't feel right to ask them. But I can tell you're a straight shooter. It won't take long, and you'd really be doing me a solid."

"Okay. Work on what?"

"Ginger," he called off. "Come on out. He'll do it!"

In the rear of the house, down the hallway came the missus. She walked at a normal pace and had on a pair of Daisy Duke shorts and a blue, button down shirt. Ginger entered the kitchen to my left. She was a very attractive, petite redhead. She and her husband were facing me.

"So," I asked, "Can you define your question better? What, exactly, am I looking at?"

With that, Ginger unbuttoned her shirt and took it off completely. No bra. She was topless. Bill was right, it would've been inappropriate to ask his family. Now, in the past, I have been trained to handle many situations, believe it or not, including this one so, I took a moment, looked straight at them, I mean her, and said,

"They look absolutely great. Whatever procedure you had done, it was completely successful."

And I wasn't lying. She did look absolutely great. Every straight man's wet dream. Ginger could model in a magazine fold out spread. Seriously, centerfold material.

She started to blush a little and her husband smirked. Honestly, I didn't blame him. Bill asked me what it was I liked about her new breasts. There were so many things I could've said and many of them would've been obscene, but I decided to be a professional.

"Let's see, to start with, both breasts are perfectly symmetrical. They're the perfect size. Not too big. They look natural. Truly a great job."

Just to be clear, she was, maybe, two feet away from me. Did I wake up in a porno? I pinched myself. Nope. But here's the thing, after the initial elation at seeing these surgically enhanced beauties, I started feeling uncomfortable. I don't care how much training you have, you can never prepare for something this intense. Think about it, how could you? The company's going to hire a woman to stand naked in front of trainees? I'm sure the stockholders would love hearing about that. Then again, once word got out I'm sure the number of applicants would skyrocket. Anyway, what were seconds, began to feel like hours.

Awkward tension filled the room. It was at this point, that Bill crossed the line. He reached out and grabbed my right arm and tried to place it on his wife's left breast. To all of you who think I was nuts not to feel this gorgeous lady up, I have three responses. The first is how easily this could've been turned around. What was to stop them from saying that I was the one who initiated contact? It would've been their word against mind and I was outnumbered three to one, I mean two to one. The last thing I needed was that legal headache. Second reason is that nobody touches me, let alone grabs me, without my permission. Third and most importantly, I was and am a happily married man.

So, I jerked my hand back and asked Bill not to touch me again. The whole situation went from an incredible, gorgeous, sexy, topless lady and became an ugly one in nanoseconds. Bill was stunned and looked offended.

Leaving quickly was the only thing smart course of action and I took it. I left the house and walked down the driveway while both of them were standing in the front doorway waving at me wishing me a safe drive and yes, Ginger hadn't bothered to put her shirt back on. Possibly too much "experimenting" in their younger days, I'd guess.

To sum up, it was an average neighborhood but with an amazing view.

Story 9: Harmless Practical Jokes (1982)

Being a service tech or repairman can be a trying job at best. Good times or even good jobs do not happen very often. Think about it, you're constantly on the road, since you're in someone else's home, you never really feel comfortable and as described earlier and after, the customers can be, let's just say, eccentric. As a result of all these circumstances, morale can sink, and nerves stretched to the breaking point. Although we may not always seem it, techs are human beings and human beings can have bad days.

One of the duties of a manager is to keep the momentum going from month to month. On Thursdays of each week the crew met at our satellite office to discuss any new policy changes or contest results of said changes.

One Thursday, our supervisor brought up a problem about morale. He said he agreed that having a working unit so far away from home base could be stressful. He also stated that he heard harsh comments were being made about other techs which is pretty much the worst thing for morale. So, yes, the supervisor knew he had a problem on his hands and tried his best to fix it. What he did was give a speech. Unfortunately, his speech was to morale what the Hindenburg was to blimps.

What could this man have possibly said that was so bad? Well, it wasn't so much what he said but how he said it. First, he addressed the problem in an upbeat manner. So far, so good. Basically, he said that we should try and have some fun. I'm liking it fine. Then he made his crucial mistake in not expecting us to take him literally. You've got to understand that most techs are pretty literal people. We have to be. To fix a major appliance you can't guesstimate what to do. You have to be exact or we'd be out of a job. So, what did he say? Even though it was over twenty years ago, I remember it exactly:

"Harmless practical jokes are great for the morale of the unit."

If he tried, he couldn't have thought of something more wrong to tell a room full of techs. Nearly all of us, including myself, are practical jokers. If that's not bad enough, we're pretty smart guys who are well versed in electronics and know our way around power tools. The man gave us blank check and I was going to be the one who exploited it. You can't open the door to mischief and not expect us to walk through. Heck, most of us were what you might call practical joke enthusiasts. In fact, I may even have a little brown book somewhere containing every practical joke I've ever played and ideas for new ones.

Granted, most of the jokes we do are pretty simple like placing grease or a sticky substance under the door handle of a service van or replacing training VCR tapes with movie tapes left by customers. I'm not saying they were always pornographic but sometimes…

Sometimes the jokes even serve an actual purpose like giving one of my co-workers his comeuppance. One time, a tech, let's call him Billy, swore that he could sell more laundry detergent himself in one month than the entire crew combined. You could wash the clothes for the entire state of Rhode Island for a year with that much suds. I mean, the numbers are insane: one tech versus twenty-four. So, I decided to take him up on his verbal boast. That night after our shifts ended, we opened his work truck and loaded four pallets of soap into his truck. The truck was not able to handle the weight. It sunk down onto the overload supports and flattened the tires. It's really a minor miracle that its axles didn't snap.

The next morning, around seven-thirty, several techs gathered around this truck waiting for Billy to show up. When he did, someone asked, "Do you still think you can sell more laundry detergent in one month than the rest of us combined?"

"Yup," said Billy.

"We took the liberty of helping you out," I said.

Still having no idea what we were getting at, Billy opened his truck and saw all the suds that were crammed in there. All of us broke out in laughter and nobody asked who was responsible. His expression was priceless.

"Ha, ha," said Billy. "Now how am I supposed to get all this out of my truck?"

"The answer seems pretty obvious to me," another tech said. "Sell it."

I didn't think it was possible for there to be more laughs than when Billy first opened his truck but there were. The look on Billy's face was again, priceless.

Other pranks techs play on techs involve each other's trucks like pulling up and seeing someone's vacant vehicle. Sometimes, when this happened, I placed an ice cube on the driver's seat. By the time the driver returns and sits on his seat, the ice cube will have melted and be easily absorbed onto the seat of his pants. By the time the tech realized what happened it was too late. He had a nice stain on his sitting place.

Another joke is turning the heater on during the summer time. Shockingly, in ninety plus degree Southern California summer weather, it takes no time at all for the truck to get hotter than a sauna. This is an especially good prank to play on rookies because a service truck's cabin is laid out differently, so it often takes a long time for the poor sap to find the heater and turn it off. Once I heard hours had gone by before the guy wised up. He did lose some weight that day though. But back to the supervisor. The man who so generously gave us that lovely challenge.

Now, a great practical joke should be personal. It should be relevant to that particular individual. Luckily, I remembered one day when the supervisor was in his office doing whatever the hell supervisors do. Because it was around lunchtime, a lot of people go in and out of the building eating lunch, running errand, etc. The supervisor came in carrying a number of items including a bag of popcorn. It was a small, single serve one. He stepped out of his office to attend to something and when he came back, almost all of the popcorn was taken from the bag.

The second the supervisor found out that some of his precious popcorn had gone missing, the man threw a gigantic hissy fit. You'd think someone had stolen the Hope Diamond instead of a bunch of popped kernels. The guy went nuts. He slammed the office door, kicked his chair and threw papers everywhere. I'm shocked he didn't have a coronary. Later that afternoon, he calmed down and apologized for his actions.

Yes, that little incident would be the inspiration for my greatest prank ever. After work, I stopped by the supermarket and bought ten pounds of popcorn kernels. Do you know how long it takes to pop ten pounds of popcorn? Trust me, hours went by.

That next morning, I went into work really early, way before anyone else. You see, a few days earlier I spied a small hole in the roof of the office, around two square feet. The perfect size to pour the six oversized bags of popcorn into and all over the supervisor's office. This process took around ten minutes to accomplish. If I may, let me paint you a picture:

The office was filled four feet high with popcorn. It not only covered his office but the desk and the two chairs in front of it. To top it off, I made sure to have a bag of popcorn, the exact size and brand that had gone missing, and dropped it on top of the pile. It was like the cherry on the sundae. The prank was almost perfect. It just needed that one last touch to lend some elegance. What I needed was a note to place on the office door for the supervisor to see before opening it.

It read, "I'm sorry for taking the popcorn so here's another bag to replace it, plus a little interest."

Shortly thereafter, the techs started coming in and making their morning calls confirming their appointment for the day. They saw the popcorn in the office and did nothing. I'd love to say it was because of solidarity but it was mostly because no one wanted to get yelled at.

Finally, around eight-thirty that morning, the supervisor showed up. He had a big smile on his face and seemed to have a better attitude that day. As he entered the building a few of the techs, including myself, were leaving the building to start their road routes. Of course, we had to re-enter the building to see what was about to unfold while staying far enough behind not to be seen.

Coffee in his left hand and his briefcase in the other hand, the supervisor spied the note, read it and smiled. Behind him, all the techs gathered behind him, waiting to see what was about to happen. He placed the key into the lock and turned the door handle. The door opened outward and with a crunching sound, four feet of popcorn poured out of his office! The laughter from the techs was the highlight of the whole week!

Who cleaned the mess up, well, I never knew and to this day, unless he's reading this, he still has no idea it was me or maybe not. My mind has been known to fade at times.

Story 10: Keys (2010)

For most of my career I have had the opportunity to train new employees. Honestly, I did not keep count how many, but that did not matter. Part of the training process was letting the new guy drive the truck. Why? Probably to see if he could drive the truck. Here's the story of two trainees that could not. I swear that all this actually happened just as I'm about to describe it.

One day, I was assigned a new trainee, Dave, who was driving the truck. We pulled up, across the street from the job site and parked close to a stop sign. Everything was going according to plan. We were making good time on the day and the upcoming repair was simple. Even Dave managed to not annoy me too much and even if he did, it would only be a short-term problem because his apprenticeship with me was almost over. What's that old saying, we make plans and God laughs? Well, Dave walked to the rear of the truck, reached into his pocket, pulled out the keys and <u>promptly dropped them down a storm drain grill</u>. Someone somewhere was laughing but it wasn't me.

Cut to twenty or so years later.

I had just finished training four new guys and all four were out on their own. It was not unusual for the trainees to call me throughout the day to ask questions. Really, I did not mind. Believe me, if they were unsure of something, I'd much rather they call then to try and fix it on their own and make it into a much bigger problem. One day I received a call from one of the newbies. I answered it only to be greeted by hysterical screaming on the other end. I could not tell what he was saying so I screamed back.

"Calm down and talk slower! Take a deep breath!"

There was a pause for a few seconds and then Steve started to explain what happened. You guessed it, he had dropped the keys down a storm drain just like the other trainee did twenty years prior.

After I stopped laughing, I asked him if he could see the keys? He said no. I asked him to explain in as much detail as possible, what kind of sound did they make as they went down the drain? Steve replied that the keys made several clanking sounds before they stopped. Great, it was pretty obvious that they had fallen down into the main storm drain. What to do?

I told Steve that he needed to go down there and retrieve them. I hung up the phone, figuring that he could handle this small task. Several minutes had gone by and the phone rang again. It was Steverino. Was he screaming? Nope. He was crying. Again, I told him to calm down. He said that he had two problems. One, he could not see the keys from the storm drain and two, he could not fit his arm through the grill to see any better.

I was lost for words. Honestly, I was laughing after I hung up. Composing myself, I answered his question.

"Do you see a manhole cover somewhere in the street?"

"Yes," he answered.

"Okay, Steve, what you need to so is lift the manhole cover, go down the hole and find the keys," I said back. He hung up.

Several more minutes went by and my phone rang again. I'm sure you'll be shocked to discover that it was Steve.

"OK, what happened?" I asked.

"Umm, actually, I'm stuck," said the really anxious trainee.

"Stuck where?"

"Stuck in the manhole. The ladder's preventing me from going down."

It was for times like this that the 'mute" button was created because, by now, I was laughing so hard, if he heard me, it would've only made things worse. Damn, it was pretty funny though. After a few seconds, I somehow managed to calm myself down and unmuted the phone. I explained that I was only a few miles away and that I would be right over. This seemed to calm him down a little. I hung up, called my boss and explained what had happened. He cracked up too.

I hopped in my truck and after a few minutes, made a right turn on the street where Steve was. Already, there were three people hovering around the manhole cover. I slowly pulled up and parked alongside the other truck. I got out, wondering why these three people, two women and a man, were out there. The man turned to me with a stupid smile on his face. He asked me if I was here to help out the guy who was stuck? Yup.

I walked over to the manhole and stopped right at the edge. I looked into the hole and yelled "Steve!" Nobody answered. I called again. Nothing. The bystanders were now looking at me with concern. Honestly, I did not know what to do. So, I walked back to the truck and grabbed the phone and dialed his number. Thankfully, he answered.

"Steve, what's going on?"

"Rob, thanks for calling. I think I'm okay. I'm using my phone as a flashlight."

"Why didn't you just bring down a flashlight?" I asked.

"I couldn't fit down the manhole with the regular flashlight, so I left it."

I couldn't help but shake my head. Right around then, the boss pulled up. He saw me talking on the phone and walked over and knelt beside me. From my phone we could hear the sounds of splashing shoes and a verbal echo coming from the phone.

Now there were five of us standing around the manhole cover listing to my phone. I asked Steve if he knew where he was going? He said he had no idea but was still looking. Suddenly, in the background, a fire truck turned the corner with the lights on and was heading our way.

Steve was still speaking over the phone. Mostly random stuff. He still had no idea that he had an audience listening in or I'm pretty sure he would've mentioned his hemorrhoids. The firemen were now huddled round the manhole, listening with interest. The captain looked at me wanting to know what happened. Steve was still talking as I explained, as best I could, to the captain about how he was having trouble locating where he was and couldn't find a way to come back up. The captain, clearly, was concerned.

By now, a short time had passed. Many of the neighbors in the area gathered around the manhole. I had my focus on the phone, listening to what Steve had to say. He had been walking around the drain system for about thirty minutes or so. Seemingly, from out of nowhere, from the phone, I heard "I found the keys!!!" The gathered crowd cheered with delight. It was so loud that I had to mute the phone again. After it had died down somewhat and I could have a normal conversation again, I unpressed mute.

"That's great! Can you find your way back to the manhole?"

"I don't know, Rob," he replied, then continued, "Hey, what's that sound? Are there other people around?"

I looked around at the surrounding gawkers, neighbors, firemen and our boss which now numbered around forty or so people and didn't know what to tell him. Should I tell the truth, or should I lie? I hedged and said that I had a little help. As soon as those words left my mouth, a police car pulled up followed by a local news crew. Just Steve's luck that today turned out to be a slow news day. Before I knew it, they were up and running and recording everything we were doing. In my mind, I revised the count to fifty people who had gathered.

Of course, Steve had no idea about any of this circus that had developed because he dropped the truck keys down the sewer. I could hear him walking but I wasn't sure what direction he was heading. He started talking again and I had to ask the crowd to quiet down so I could hear him. More like a yell, really.

"Rob, the light from my phones started to get a little dim," he said.

"Can you see any light," I asked?

"No."

Now, I was starting to get worried. The fire captain stood up and gave some commands to get the necessary equipment off their truck. The two police officers started to make their way closer to where I was, and the news crew started filming from their vantage point. Steve was still walking, I could hear his feet splashing in the water. All of a sudden there was a big splash and a thud. He had fallen in.

I yelled into the phone. "Are you all right?!"

The crowd grew quiet. I yelled out a second time. He responded by saying,

"I'm all right, I tripped over something. Give me a second, the battery's getting low"

I told him to try and save the power in the phone. He did not respond right away. His silence was broken by this revelation

"Rob, I just tripped over a dead body!"

Holy crap! The situation took a strange turn from a big laugh to a huge problem. The police officers and the fire captain now took charge. I moved out of the way but not too far because Steve was still my responsibility and one of the officers asked me to stay close. My boss and the rest of the crowd were asked to step back and stand on the curb. Even the television news crew backtracked a little but still close enough to see.

Three of the firemen had returned from their truck, each carrying their gear. They placed a tripod over the hole and snaked a rope through the top, down the hole. Some of the other firemen attached the other end of the rope to a wench on the firetruck. Essentially, they were setting up a rope / pulley system to pull Steve out.

Apparently, this was only phase one of the plan because phase two involved some of the other fireman going down a different manhole further down the street carrying a board with straps on it and some other equipment that I couldn't quite make out. Some time had passed and the crowd standing on the sidewalk had become totally silent. Steve was getting a little antsy too. Not that I blame him. I wouldn't want to be stuck in total darkness with a dead body either. The news crew continued walking closer and closer with the camera guy leading the way. They sensed a big scoop now because what was once a human-interest story could now, potentially, be a murder or accident. The silence was broken by the man we were all waiting for.

"Hey! Can you still hear me," yelled Steve? I assured him that we could. He continued, "It's not a dead body, just a pile of leaves!"

This was the best news I had heard in a while. I told Steve that there are fireman looking for him inside the drain system and not to be scared when they approach. One of the firemen, who didn't go down the manhole, asked Steve to yell so that his compatriots could better find him. Steve started yelling like a crazy person, which I would've done if it was me down there.

The news crew didn't hear what the fire captain requested and immediately thought that something bad had happened in the down below. The reporter started talking into his microphone. What we didn't know at the time was that the reporter had gone live and was in full-on local news reporter who wanted to get hired by the network mode.

"Good afternoon, everyone. This is Gordon Keeley and I'm at a busy intersection where a repairman is helplessly trapped in the city's sewers. Earlier, he thought he had stumbled upon a dead body, but it turned out to be a pile of leaves. One of the few lucky breaks to befall this helpless repairer of appliances…"

This guy was good. You would've thought World War III was about to break out. Before I could be too impressed by the blow-dried correspondent, I heard Steve yelling over the phone.

"I see a light. It's moving. I see someone. Is it you?"

"No," I said, "It's a fireman coming to find you. By the way, you might want to watch what you say because we're on TV--"

"Thank God, my 'roids are really acting up like a bastard. Must be the stress" he said back. I'm guessing he didn't hear the part about going out live on television.

The crowd heard the first part and not the second and began cheering. The camera man ran around to film the response. Both the officer and the fire captain shook hands with delighted smiles.

"Great news from the manhole as local fireman are confident they located the trapped repairman and are awaiting his near return" said the reporter.

The fireman started to come out of the manhole one at a time. Now the news crew was right on top of us. The first fireman yelled down into the manhole, "We are almost ready to pull you out."

The other fireman tied the rope around Steve's waist, so he could be extracted. "Wait, there's a problem," said one of the firemen. I was pretty sure what it was. Steve was really fat like easily forty pounds overweight. He just might not fit out of that hole. From the manhole, I heard, "does anyone have any Vaseline?" Not surprisingly, one of the news guys did and handed it to a fireman and down the hole it went.

A few moments passed and then we heard that Steve was on the board and ready to be extracted. The wench was activated and started doing its job slowly. Just to be safe, a bunch of firemen had their hands on the cable with the captain directing all the while.

The first thing we saw out of the hole wasn't Steve's head, it was his arms. He was so fat that the only way out was for him to raise his hands up and it was still a tight fit. I'm guessing that's why they needed the Vaseline.

My boss walked over to me, we both looked at each other and knew exactly what was going to happen and we weren't in the least bit disappointed because the second Steve's head appeared, the news crew got their live shot. The reporter didn't miss a beat.

"It's a miracle as the firemen and police have heroically saved a young man from the clutches of the sewer. A young man who has one child and is expecting another in eight months..."

Wow, that was some pretty in-depth reporting there. And as Steve was finally pulled out to safety, one thought kept bombarding me; maybe, in the future, we should keep two sets of keys.

Story 11: Deep Hearted Family (2005)

How far would you go to take care of you family and what kind of sacrifices would you make? Here is a story that caught me completely off guard in the best possible way.

It was a Friday and it seemed like the day and week would never end. Believe me, the weekend couldn't get here fast enough. Fortunately, I had only a few stops to make. It should've been simple and quick but, of course, it wasn't. Service stop one was just a stopped-up drain in a washer, which I knocked off in twenty-five minutes. Stops two and three were a colossal waste of time. Some things you just can't stick down a garbage disposal and expect it to work like rice and bones and while it was fun to leave and say, "not my problem," I still had to drive there.

The day was half-way over and it was time for lunch, namely fast food again. This seems to be the life of a service tech. Lots of diners, food trucks but mostly fast food hang outs. Although, I do enjoy the challenge, of trying to get quality food at a decent sized portion for five bucks.

After thirty minutes, lunch was over and my next stop, at least on paper, seemed to be nothing out of the ordinary. "Food freezing in the Refrigerator" said the complaint written on the order. What caught my eye was the address. The street name was one that I had never seen been down before. Also, I didn't recognize this area of town. So, I grabbed my trusty Thomas Guide book and proceeded to find the location. It was a gated community in Bel Air, which was way outside my normal route. No wonder I didn't recognize it. It's also one of the richest neighborhoods in America.

My first thought was "wonderful, a bunch of high class snooty's who were going to stick their lifestyle and money in my face." This was going to be an interesting service call, I can just see it coming. Why were they calling on a repair person anyway? Usually, rich people just throw away an appliance that isn't working and buy a new one. Okay, so, maybe my attitude going in wasn't great, but I knew the traffic was going to be horrendous and it was. It took me sixty minutes to travel about ten miles.

Thankfully, it was a nice day in the mid-seventies. I rolled down the driver's window and cruised along at a snail's pace. I had a chance to look around at the neighborhood. Lots of buildings, side streets and cars. Dirt lots. A little run down in places. People of all walks of life were walking and or standing in places. This was not a great part of town.

The light at the intersection turned red. I was first in line and waiting for it turn green, so I could drive another five feet before stopping. Something hit me at that intersection. It was night and day. The street in my rear-view mirror was like something almost out of a war-zone, but looking out the windshield, the other side of the street, was almost perfect.

The trees were all well-groomed. The park benches were freshly painted and the people sitting on them looked like something out of a Gap ad instead of someone you'd see on those Old West "Wanted Dead Or Alive" posters. The flowers and trash cans were equally clean in a good way. The light posts looked like they had never been touched. The sidewalks were all new. It was like, what I imagine, going to a movie studio is like. On one side, you have the Wild West Street and ten feet away, you have New York City Street. It really was that jarring a difference. The reason for it all popped out at me as I inched past the "Welcome to Bel Air" sign.

It was simple, money on one side of the street and no money on the other. What a night and day experience. Yes, things were nice around here but maybe a little too nice. As I continued my descent to the address, I noticed a few people walking with well-groomed dogs at their side, watching or staring at my truck as I drove by. Was this something right out of an old movie or didn't these people have jobs? It was two in the afternoon.

About a short mile down the road I found the street I needed to make a left turn on. I had to slow down the truck a little more than normal because the road was made up of concrete pressed into cobblestone and it was wet. Normal asphalt wasn't good enough for these people, though it would've been just fine by me as my tires started to slide on the wet tile. As I completed the turn, I noticed two long rows of rose bushes on the left and right. At the end was a guard house. These people lived in a gated community.

As I slowly pulled up to the guard house, I saw two guards inside eating pizza. One of the guards leaned his chair back and with an attitude wanted to know why I was here. Honestly, I think he was more upset that I disturbed his gorging.

"I'm here to see the Symington's at 1455 Stradella Ave," I said.

The guard reached out and started typing something on a computer terminal. I think he was looking for the homeowner's authorization to enter.

"OK, you're cleared," he said, in between bites. I responded, "Super, hey, what was the light change on your screen?"

"I just took you truck's picture. Your photo and the registration just came through."

Honestly, I thought that was kind of cool, but I decided to pull away before he pulled up my G.P.A. or tax forms. Some hassles just aren't necessary.

My destination was just a short ways around the corner. This neighborhood was even more beautiful on the inside. I mean, there was nothing out of place. Maybe this is where they filmed the "Stepford Wives." Maybe I was actually in the movie. Nah.

I saw the house. Out front and standing on the street was a man in proper suit and tie waving at me. Usually, I don't get a welcoming committee.

Maybe I was moving up in the world. I pulled up slowly and said hello. He responded with

"Hello, my name is Rodney. Yes sir, you are at the right place. Please pull your truck up and park over on the side of the driveway."

I did as he asked and exited my truck. Rodney came up and re-greeted me and I shook his hand. Honestly, a pretty firm shake for a rich guy.

"Hi, I'm Rob. I'm here to fix the refrigerator. Let me grab my toolbox."

"Sure. I'm certainly not here to tell you how to do your job," said Rodney.

We walked to the side entrance of the yard. The gate was motion sensitive so, as we got closer it opened all by itself. Hey that was something I had never seen before.
Both of us went through the gate and turned left heading to the living quarters just adjacent to the garage doors but within fifty feet from a gorgeous swim up pool. I did not want to stare too hard but it's hard not to notice these things.

Rodney and I stopped at the entrance to the house where a small box was next to the door. He opened it up and pulled out blue shoe coverings.

"Excuse me," said Rodney. "Would you mind putting on these shoe protectors? The interiors were recently redone and we're trying to keep it as pristine as possible."

"You mean, you don't want my dirty shoes in your house," I said back. Rodney didn't know if I was serious or not so, I cracked a smile and said, "Sure, no problem."

As I put them on, and they were easy to put on, Rodney sighed and after I was finished, we entered the house and yes, I was out of place. These people had money and had no qualms about showing it off.

Rodney and I walked to the right and down a short hallway. The carpet was perfectly maintained except for wheelchair tire marks. The walls and trim showed no flaws anywhere. On the walls were several rare paintings from the previous century. No "Dogs Playing Poker" hung on the walls here. Gold statues and old antique serving trays were also prominently displayed. It felt like I was in a museum and not the fun kind where they have airplanes and astronaut ice-cream. Life was good around here and it showed, I guess.

We then entered the kitchen. It was huge. At least nine hundred square feet with two islands in the middle standing twelve feet in length. There were fifteen to twenty pots and pans, all cooper, hanging from the ceiling. The cabinets were all white with engraved glass on each door with gold knobs. If I didn't have good old Rodney to act as Sherpa, I might have easily gotten lost in here. Off to the right was the refrigerator I came to see. I placed my tools and paperwork down. Rodney looked at me and said he would be right back. He was going to go and get someone.

I started looking at the refrigerator to see what the problem was. There was a clicking sound coming from the inside and that normally means that the air damper was not closing like it's supposed to.

Rodney was gone for more than a few minutes. This gave me some time to check things out inside the refrigerator. How often did I get the opportunity to see what rich people ate anyway? I cracked open the doors and to my disappointment, it was mostly normal, everyday food including some store and not name brands. There were some chilled bottles of booze but nothing really out of the ordinary. I did see four mid-sized salt-water fish carefully wrapped in plastic bags.

Each of the plastic bags weighed about four pounds with the heads still on but the insides removed and then sewed back together. My first thoughts were, they were fish surgeons or, more likely, they recently went to Chinatown and bought some fish. I was kind of proud of myself for figuring this out until I later realized that I was wrong.

Rodney entered with an extremely well-dressed lady. He greeted me and apologized for taking so long. I wasn't dying to set back out into rush hour traffic so, it wasn't a big deal and I told him so. Then the woman, who never introduced herself, spoke

"Young man, have you found out what's causing all the trouble?"

"Ma'am, the air damper assembly had malfunctioned and that's what's causing the problems you've been experiencing with the unit," I said.

Then she gave me a discerning look that I wasn't quite sure how to read.

"Can I ask you a question," she inquired?

"Sure, what is it," I responded?

"Are all you service people as nice as you?"

I just looked into her eyes hoping not to upset her. What a weird question, I thought.

"Why do you ask," I responded?

"Oh, I just wanted to know."

What else was she going to ask? This honestly was a set up question. Experience told me that if I answered it, I would be opening up the door to many more questions which, was not my idea of fun so I decided to change the subject.

"Well," I said, "I have the part on my truck and I can take care of this right now."

I reached over to my paperwork and started writing up the estimate to replace the damper. As I was doing this, the lady looked down and reached into a pocket and pulled out a few hundred-dollar bills then turned to Rodney.

"Take care of this repairman" she commented before walking off. Rodney turned and looked at me and said, "Looks like you've been given the okay to fix it."

I exited the kitchen and turned down the short hall and into the antique gold room heading to the door. The truck was right there. It was a lot easier to navigate now that I knew where I was going. I thought I'd be in and out of there in a couple of minutes. I was wrong again.

As I walked back into the yard and headed to the front door, there was an elderly man in a wheelchair and a nurse caregiver that I could see through the window. I entered the house and greeted them as I headed to the kitchen. The caregiver was pushing the old man in the wheelchair down the hall then into the kitchen, exiting to another door that was leading to the backyard.

Rodney was exiting the kitchen as I entered, both from separated doors when a young man about twenty-five years of age appeared. He was well well-groomed and well-dressed wearing a suit and tie with not a hair out of place. This guy could've been on the cover of GQ or been named one of the top ten best looking best men in the world. Some lucky lady needs to catch this guy! He was like American royalty. Hell, I'm straight and even I was thinking about it.

I placed the part on the counter and began to open the toolbox. The young man went to the hall way next to the other room, leaving the kitchen. I took out the tools I'd need for the job and got to work. As I was installing the part, I placed one of my tools on the counter and made a quick glance out the kitchen window. There was a small table with an umbrella and phone on it. To the right, I saw the old man in the wheel chair. He was at the side of the pool and I could only see the front of the chair. He was alone. This situation really got my attention. What was going on? My heart stopped for a second or two or three. Common sense says that you do not leave a wheel chair person alone, especially by a pool. What are they doing?

I had to stop what I was doing and see what was going on. I put down the tool I had in my hand and started walking through the kitchen, so I could get to the backyard. Just as I came to the entrance of the backyard door, standing in front of me was Mr. GQ. We looked at each other and paused for a few seconds. He excused himself and said, "pardon me' as he passed. Shockingly, proper manners are not something I'm used to. Maybe there's something to be said for a Wasp upbringing.

What I couldn't see from the kitchen was the eight-foot fishing pole with an ocean reel leaning against the door. I decided to follow Mr. GQ who went back to the kitchen. He headed to the refrigerator. He opened the freezer door and pulled out one of fishes in a plastic bag. What was he going to do with that fish? Now, I was really intrigued.

Mr. GQ passed me again, heading through the kitchen and then back to the pool area. As he exited the house, he made a hand signal to someone. Who? The bag containing the fish was in his left-hand swaying back and forth. Yes, it seemed like they had things under control but damned if I still didn't want to know what was going on.

It wasn't like I could just drop what I was doing and go out there. I wasn't a guest, I was there to do a job, so I headed back to the worksite. I looked out one of the windows and to my right I saw the nurse / caregiver walking with a fishing pole in her hand.

I continued installing the part. I again turned to my right and looked out the window. I saw the caregiver and Mr. GQ working together to hook up the fishing line to the fish that was still in the bag and they handled it just perfectly. Obviously, they had done this many times before. When they were done, they handed the pole to grandpa who put the line in the pool and continued "fishing." This is what he did all day. He "fished" in his pool. Grandpa had a serene look on his face. He probably didn't know where he was or the context of what he was doing, but he was happy.

My job was now complete, and I began to clean up the site. I wiped down the area and left it cleaner than before I started. Honestly, the place was pretty spic and span to begin with, which made my efforts minimal.

I called out for Rodney and after a few moments, he came back in. I advised him that the job was done, and I also explained what the problem was and how critical the part I replaced in the refrigerator was. He nodded like he understood. He didn't.

Rodney then picked up the old part with one hand and transferred it to his other hand and back repeatedly like a basketball or, more accurately, like a nervous tick. I explained to him what the part was and how it worked. After I finished, he thanked me for the explanation and shook my hand.

"Mrs. Symington was right," he said. "You are unusually kind. Would it be all right if we could call you in the future should a problem arise?"

I didn't feel comfortable with the question. It's not like I enjoyed hanging out with a bunch of insanely rich people. One thing I did know about them was that if they felt like they owned you, they owned you and I didn't want to be their dancing repair-man monkey, so I punted and said

"If you should need a repair in the future, just call the main line and my supervisor can get ahold of me."

This way, should that the occasion arise, I could always decline without them knowing.

"Great," said Rodney. "May I have the bill?"

I looked at Rodney and told him that I have not started the paperwork yet. I needed a few minutes. Rodney pulled out the money from his pocket and advised me that Mrs. Symington said to give me this. Rodney placed the money on my work order. How much was there? At the time, I did not know.

"Are you sure this is what you want to do," I asked?

Rodney had no facial expression whatsoever. Kind of like Mr. Data on Star Trek or maybe a zombie. He just stepped back and reached out for the broken part again. Why was he so interested in that part? My better judgment left me, I just had to ask.

"Rodney, excuse me if I'm out of line here but I really want to know, why is the elderly man in the wheelchair holding a fishing pole and what's the deal with the frozen, gutted fish in the freezer?" Try saying that three times fast. Rodney answered with the barest hint of emotion.

"The gentlemen is Mr. Symington. Perhaps you've heard of him? Symington Wholesale?"

I honestly hadn't but, out of politeness, I nodded. Hot Rod continued:

"He is the owner of the house and the head of the family. Unfortunately, he has a medical condition very similar to Alzheimer's where he loses his memory from day to day. No matter what, he always remembers how much he used to enjoy fishing so, we take him fishing out in the backyard. And that is what we'll continue to do with him until the end."

I was taken aback by this. It was incredibly kind and thoughtful. I asked Rodney if it was his idea and he indicated that it was. Since he didn't clam up, I asked who looked after the old man throughout the day? It was the nurse / caregiver and Mr. GQ.

Just as he answered me, the nurse shrieked in the background. Not a shriek of terror but like she had done something that she wished she hadn't. I placed the money in my pocket, picked up my toolbox and Rodney and I began to leave.

We walked through the kitchen, towards the hall and then back through the antique room. As we entered the hallway we both heard two people making some funny noises. Yup, it was the nurse / caregiver and Mr. GQ who were walking by us with their hands in the air and heading to the kitchen sink. Clearly, they were going there to wash up. Best guess, someone touched the stinky fish. Wow, what a terrible thing to do.

Rodney, who was walking slightly in front of me, just stopped in his tracks. He turned his head to the left and stared right at them as they passed by. He turned to me and asked me if I wouldn't mind exiting the house by myself? I thought it best to do so, due to the fact that someone was going to get in trouble for washing their hands in the wrong sink or leaving dad alone by the pool.

Before leaving, I turned to Rodney, extended my hand, which he took, and said

"Rodney, I can honestly say that you're a good man and I admire you for the way you're looking after your elders."

The faintest of smiles crept over his face. I even detected the smallest of lumps in his throat. Something told me that my simple compliment really meant something to him. Maybe because he respected me or, more likely, in that house, he rarely got appreciation, let alone compliments. Dare I say, his voice even seemed to crack a little.

"Thank you," he said. "That's very kind of you to say."

I replied, "And it was even kinder of you to do."

And it was.

Story 12: Birthday Suit (1990)

It all started when the car broke down. I had it towed to the dealer to get it fixed. This was a big mistake. Slick, that's what I've decided to call the guy at the dealership, looked the car over and said he'd call me with an estimate. When he got around to calling me, I could not believe that he wanted $600.00 to do the brakes and rotors.

To those of you who may not know what something like that should cost, suffice it to say, that price is a total rip-off. Slick told me that that's what it would cost to do a quality repair. I told him not to have his guys touch my car. He said that any other garage or dealer in town would charge at least as much. Good thing I didn't plan on going to them, I said. I was going to do the repair myself. Slick laughed at me. Fine, I love proving idiots wrong.

On Friday I went to the auto supply store and bought all the parts necessary to fix the brakes including rotors, brake pads and some other stuff the guy at the counter told me I needed. The following day was when I'd get to work and fix the car all by myself. Lucky for me, that Saturday, my wife was having a girl's lunch at the house. The girls were to arrive around eleven o'clock or so. I did not have to attend the lunch. Oh, darn. The joy of having a bunch of women in the house talking about fashion and…whatever they talk about just excites me all over. I may even still have goosebumps.

As I began working on the car, the ladies started to arrive. I have to admit, I did not count how many of the wife's girlfriends came over. All I know is that I was getting greasier as I continued to work. It's a guy thing, I guess. Getting involved. Getting your hands dirty. Time just flew by. As I was finishing up on the brakes, I could hear that the ladies were in full swing. Lots of talking and laughing and for good measure, once in a while, a scream. Sounded like they were having fun. So was I. Fixing your car can be fun. Messy and greasy, yes, but fun to say the least.

I finished the brakes and checked whatever else I could check on the engine. I stepped back and started wiping my hands on my clothes trying to get off the grease. I moved the car into the street and drove it around the block to check everything, making sure I did things correctly and I did. I felt good. Not only was I experiencing the joy of self-sufficiency, but I had saved myself $400 in the process. I parked the car in the driveway and walked into the garage.

As I walked through the garage the back door opened and my wife approached and handed me the phone. Who was calling me on a Saturday? No one calls me on a Saturday. I asked who it was. She did not know so I picked up the phone and it was my old buddy, Slick. I rolled my eyes at the b.s. that I knew was soon to come. I was not disappointed. Slick told me that he would readjust the estimate down $75.00 if I brought the car into his shop right at that moment. Time for some fun.

"Really, you'd actually do that for me," I asked?

"We sure would," replied Slick.

"What have I done to warrant such generosity?"

"Believe me, my boss didn't want to, but I forced him into it because I'm concerned about your safety and you're such a good customer."

I had never been there before.

"My safety, huh? You really don't think I could do this repair on my own? I'm pretty handy," I said, trying to keep some self-control.

"We really don't recommend it. No offense, but a job like this is far too complicated for the weekend handyman. The systems in today's cars are a lot more complex than when you were working on cars in high school."

Condescend much?

"Yeah, you're right. They certainly are but here's the thing. I've already done the repair, the car's running great and the whole thing only cost me $200."

There were a few seconds of silence, but he would not be deterred.

"Why don't you bring it in and have our professional mechanics look it over, just to be safe? We'll only charge you $100. I'd feel a lot better."

By then, I was feeling too good to be truly mad and honestly, I kind of respected the guy for his tenacity. Guys who work at car dealerships never give up. That's why if there's a nuclear war, the only things that'll survive are cockroaches and them. I declined Slick's generous offer and hung up. As good as I was feeling, the real fun was about to start.

I opened the back door of the garage and started walking in from the garage door, through the living room which is right next to the kitchen. All the ladies were throughout the two rooms, talking and doing whatever it is they do. As I turned the corner, my wife yelled at me.

"Rob, do not enter the house wearing those greasy clothes!" she said with more than an overbearing attitude.

I looked at her and did not know why she would say that to me. Of course, I was greasy-dirty. I just finished working on the car. What would anyone expect? For me to smell like roses? In my defense, my shoes weren't that bad and yes, I did kind of understand why she'd have that reaction, but I did not appreciate the tone. So, I answered back, "OK, honey, I'll take off the greasy clothes."

Now, humor can take many shapes and I have learned, over the years, that some people do not appreciate mine. But, I was still in a good mood and like a good husband, I did exactly what I was told to do with, maybe, a little vindictiveness. I took off all my clothes in the garage. I was butt naked.

I opened the garage door and walked into the house. Nobody saw me standing there so, like all men above a certain age, I sucked in my stomach, made sure all my man parts were flopping in the afternoon breeze and flexed as hard as I could without straining anything too bad. I mean, I don't look bad for my age, but I think it's fair to say that no one's exactly clamoring to see me naked. Now, that I had gone through the checklist, it was show time. I swear I actually started to hum that song "The Stripper" without realizing I was doing it. It's that big, brassy song. You know it, trust me.

As I walked through the house, I made sure that I made a bunch of jerking motions as I turned the corner so that my now not private parts would swaggle a little bit more than normal all the while keeping my head straight ahead and noticing that the lady's voices were quieting down as I continued toward the kitchen. One of my wife's friends, a woman in her sixties, dropped her coffee mug, shattering it on the floor. Luckily, none of the shards hit me in my vulnerable position.

By the way, if you ever want to hear the sound of a bunch of hens going completely silent in an instant, try walking into the kitchen in your birthday suit. Now that I had their attention, it was time to truly milk the moment for the big finish. I moseyed over to the staircase and put my right leg on the first step to give everyone some nice side view of my dangle.

At this point I knew I was humming the song, so I cranked up the volume. After every step up, I accentuated it with a "da-da bump-bump." By the time I finally got to the top stair and had everyone's attention, I put my hands behind my head and swayed to the left. "Ba-dah." To the right. "Ba-dah." For the piece de la resistance, I flexed my butt cheeks in time to my humming. "Da-da-da-dum!" Then I said, over my shoulder, "Thanks everybody! You've been a great audience!" and exited to my bedroom.

Now, you might think that that would've been the end of the big lady's luncheon, but it wasn't. The event had a few more hours left in it although I do think it's fair to say that the rest of was a little more subdued to say the least. Believe it or not, I was now dreading the end. Not because I particularly enjoyed this type of thing because I knew that when it was over, my wife would kill me. I wasn't wrong.

"Rob, how could you do that?! Do you have any idea how embarrassed I was?! In front of my friends-," she said later.

Here's where I made my biggest mistake. I interrupted her.

'But honey," I said as sweetly as humanly possible, "you told me to remove the greasy clothes, so I did."

74

For some reason, she got even madder. "Don't you pull that crap on me! You know that's not what I meant…"

As the wife continued her rant I couldn't help but think, some people just don't appreciate the male form.

Story 13: Lost and Lonely (the '90's)

There are times that I really feel sorry or even pity for some people. This is a story about an elderly lady who had resorted to talking to her animals. Loneliness or forgetfulness, I guess.

A service call was scheduled for this customer's dishwasher. The housing tract it was located in looked like it was built in the early sixties or so. Well-kept lawns, hedges, flower pots and the occasional vegetable patch adorned the various yards. I pulled the truck up to the house on the service order. It was old but not rundown. It would need a new coat of paint in about three years, but the place didn't look too bad especially considering its age. As I walked up, I spotted an elderly lady who was standing outside watering the plants just adjacent to the front door. She waved to me. Looks like she could be a good customer. I walked up the walkway and she greeted me with all good intentions.

"Hello, young man. Thank you for coming so promptly," she said in a schoolmarmish voice.

"Not at all. I'm Rob."

"I'm Miss. Steglitz. Pleasure to meet you."

"It's a pleasure to meet you too. Your azaleas are looking lovely," I said.

"Thank you for noticing. The trick is to water them twice a day and to talk to them."

"You don't say?" That should've been my first hint on what was to come.

After that exchange, she walked me into the house. Did I say "house" because I meant greenhouse. There were plants everywhere. On the table, on the floor, hanging. Seriously, the place was just a few steps removed from that TV show, "Life After People." Maybe she was worried about running out of oxygen.

Aside from the vegetation, the place was decorated with furniture probably purchased about forty years ago but at least it wasn't covered in plastic like, so many elderly people's furniture is. I guess you have to keep stuff up in case you get a royal visit or something. The counters and pretty much every flat surface was completely cluttered with pill boxes, cat food, bills, the penny saver, etc. Let's just say that it wasn't the most hygienic home I've ever been to and leave it at that.

Inside the kitchen, the dishwasher I was to work on was off to the left of the entry way and a table with four chairs was to the right. Next to the rear sliding back door were two food and water dishes belonging to a couple of cats.

"Oh, I see you have cats," I said.

"Yes, Mr. Mularkey and Madam Whiskers. They give me so much joy."

"Terrific," I said not really meaning it.

Miss. Steglitz told me what was wrong with the dishwasher. Basically, the dishes weren't getting clean because the water pressure was wanting. Sounded to me like a problem with the pump blade and I was right. It wasn't a big deal and honestly, it would only take me about twenty minutes or so to swap it out.

I placed my toolbox on the throw rug next to the appliance, squatted down and got to work. Miss. Steglitz walked over to the table and sat down. Just around the corner were the two cats who walked over to the side chair and one of them, I think it was Madam Whiskers but don't quote me on that, jumped into one of the side chairs and the other cat, presumably Mr. Malarkey, jumped onto the tabletop. Madam came to rest to the right of her owner.

A copy of the local paper was on the kitchen table and if I had to guess, Miss. S had started reading it before I arrived.

"…"St. Matthew's Lutheran Church is having a bake sale this Sunday afternoon after services to benefit local families hit hard by the recent wild fires"…" she read aloud from the paper.

Okay, so this was a little weird. I don't think I've been read to since I was twelve and I wasn't too crazy about it then. Should I politely ask her to stop? No, I decided, that would be rude. After all, it was her house.

"…Congregants who wish to participate, please get in touch with Mrs. Johnston of the ladies' auxiliary and let her know what dish you'd like to prepare." She stopped for a moment. "Isn't that nice?" The cats nodded their heads.

Was that a rhetorical question or did she expect an answer? Just as I was about to say "yes," or "sure is" or something equally clever, she stopped me in my tracks by saying

"Yes, it is Madam Whiskers and Mr. Malarkey. Yes, it is"

I couldn't help but steal a glance at her and see that she was at the end of the table and that she had one cat to her right and the other cat sitting on a chair to her left. She was reading the paper to her cats! The lunatic, I mean "lady" picked up the newspaper and found the article she was looking for and continued to read out loud. This time it was sports. Something the cats could really sink their teeth into.

"Dakota Whitford hit two home-runs and helped Columbia High School edge out North Orange Prep four to one..." she droned on. "Head Coach, Fred Taylor, commented that Whitford has really come into his own during his senior year..."

As she was doing this, both cats had complete, intense focus on her. They nodded their heads and occasionally groomed themselves as cats are known to do, all the while, never leaving her side.

To this point the repair was going as normal as would be expected. Here's where the fun started. I stood up and tried to break into the newspaper reading.

"I'm almost done here," I said.

"Sshhh!!"

She was shushing me! More than that, she was giving me the evil eye. Unbelievable. In the moment, I was stunned, and she used my silence to continue reading to the freakin' cats.

I could not believe what she just did. Respectfully, I was told not to speak. The lady finished reading the article, looked right at me and asked me with a snide voice what I wanted. I told her that I wanted to go over with her what was wrong with her dishwasher, what I did to fix it and that I was going to be testing it soon.

"Fine," she said, more than a tad unpleasant.

As I turned my back to her the lady asked the cats if they wanted her to read the comics or the national news? Please let it be the comics section, I thought to myself. It's been so long since I've known what Nancy and Sluggo have been up to.

Ok, this lady is a little nuts. More than a little. And just my luck, she picked the national news. By the way, the cats had not moved from the spots they first sat. I continued repairing the appliance commenting to myself that while the dishwasher is in good order, Miss. Steglitz clearly wasn't.

She continued her civics class by reading aloud. "President Clinton met with President Boris Yeltsin in Vancouver today. First on the agenda, how much western investment in the former Soviet Union is prudent..."

I really wish she read the comics because this could not be more boring, I thought to myself.

It was now time to test the appliance. I shut the dishwasher door and turned it on. As the appliance began to run, she shushed me again with a glare accompanied by a raised hand with her index finger pointed directly at me. If I had continued to speak, she might've given me detention or worse, wrapped me on my knuckles with a ruler.

A millisecond went by, then she continued reading. By this time, I didn't know what to think. So, I just did my normal thing, checked out the appliance to see if it was working correctly. As we all know, dishwashers can be loud which couldn't have made crazy lady too happy so, to compensate for the increased volume, she raised her voice a few octaves.

I swear, Miss. Steglitz changed the sections of the paper at least three times while this was going on. I stood up and started cleaning up the small mess I made on the floor while leaving the dishwasher running completely unnecessarily. I turned to her and said, "I'm almost done here."

The lady, I guess had had enough of my interruptions. What was I thinking in trying to talk to her about something she called me about while she was reading to her cats? She turned her head toward me and said,

"Do not interrupt me again! My cats need to understand what is going on in the world" she said way too aggressively and went right back to reading.

"Her cats need to understand what is going on in the world?" I thought to myself. Were they planning on voting? This is bonkers. She continued reading,

"Today the U.N. voted to establish an international tribunal to prosecute violations of international law in Yugoslavia…."

In the moment, I didn't know what to think. Being put aside for a couple of cats doesn't exactly do wonders for your ego. This crap was stopping now. I finished cleaning up my mess and at the same time rewrote the repair bill a few dollars higher. Never upset the repairman is a great lesson for all. Around this time, the lady finished reading the society page column, so I walked over to the table and handed her the bill.

Without missing a beat, she reached down to her right for her purse, pulled out the credit card and thrusted it at me in a really aggressive manner. I wrote down the necessary numbers, had her sign the work order, ripped off her copy and placed it on the table right on top of her newspapers. I looked at her and knew I just had to say something. This is what came out.

"So, what school did you send the cats to?"

The lady looked at me with a puzzling look on her face. Another question, "How much does a semester cost?" The lady's eyes opened even wider.

"Why would you ask me such a bizarre question?" she asked.

79

"The reason I asked was because, as you must know from reading the paper and assorted books it that a dog's I.Q. is around sixteen at best and a cat's I.Q. is measured in the ten to eleven range."

The lady nodded her head in a positive faction. Where was I going with this, she must've thought?

"You know, a cat's I.Q. is hard to measure because most cats are either extremely intelligent and do not show it or completely instinctive."

She nodded affirmatively. I continued;

"One of my kids is going to school at a university and a year or two semesters runs around $17,000 dollars so I was wondering what it costs to put a cat through college?"

She was confused to say the least. To sum up, talking to your cats is all right, I guess. Some people talk to their plants but what is insulting is when you put cats over people. That's wrong! If you need a companion to talk to, I'd suggest a member of the human race. Heck, they'll even talk back to you.

So, just as Miss. Steglitz was about to attempt to answer my question, she turned to me, opened her jaw and yup, you guessed it, I shushed her.

Hey, if you're going to dish it out, you'd better be able to take it.

Story 14: Germs! (90's)

If I ever wondered what it would be like to work for Howard Hughes, this service call answered that question.

It was on a Tuesday when I got the call from one of my managers. She said she wanted to send me out on a "special call" and that it was a little "strange." One "special" and a "strange" didn't exactly sound promising. In the past, these two words lead to me doing a repair at a special "men's weekend" out in the middle of nowhere that involved a lot of howling. Pass. No, my manager, assure me, it's nothing like that.

"So, what's the deal with this call,' I asked?

"Well…" she said, "the last technician was asked to leave the house. Sorry but I have to take another call. Bye." She hung up. Looks like I was going on the "special call."

I arrived at a seemingly normal two-story house in a non-descript, residential housing track. Every house on the block had cars, plants, kid's bikes, etc. on their lawns. The house I was going to did not. Instead, it had eight-foot-high security gates surrounding the place, topped by barbwire. There was a main gate to the right of the driveway gate. I was starting to get madder at my manager. Where did she send me to? Was this a P.O.W. camp or the North Korean embassy?

The main gate was made of heavy bars with an arch at the top and all the bars were painted black at one point. I say, "at one point" because the color had badly faded to a dull black, mostly due to the elements and sun damage. Right next to the door was a newspaper that had been there awhile. Kirk Gibson had won Game One with a home run. Okay, so maybe it wasn't that old, but we were definitely talking months here. To put an exclamation point on this unwelcoming motif, the entire front of the residence was dotted with "Do Not Disturb," "Keep Out" and "Owner Has Gun" signs.

I pressed the doorbell and waited for a response. A speaker was just off to the side of the switch. Next to it was a small screen from which a lady's voice sprang out. It was old and raspy with more than a tinge of paranoia.

"Who are you? What do you want?" she barked out.

"I'm Rob. I'm here to fix your appliance," I said back.

"Hhhmmm…"

Did she think I was lying to her? After a moment or two, she buzzed me in and I opened the metal door, making sure I left it open just slightly. As I continued to walk towards the house, I noticed that there were no plants along the walkway, just brick and concrete. The lawn was a bright green. Almost too bright. I bent down to touch and when I got my hand back, there was green on it. She painted her lawn, or someone did. Okay, while that's a little bizarre, it's not exactly a crime. The whole front yard looked like a prison that was being spruced up for a last-minute inspection. Think I'm exaggerating? I had to pass through a total of four checkpoints with four different fences. Each one I was greeted by the shrew and eventually buzzed in. I had an easier time getting my first mortgage than getting to this front door. When I did, I knocked and waited for a response.

Off to my upper left was a small LED television screen that I didn't see turn on. A picture of a group of small animals came on, followed by the lady's voice. She wanted to ask more questions.

"Who are you?"

"I'm Rob."

"Who do you work for?"

"The appliance repair company."

"What did you come to fix?"

"Your air filtration system."

"How long have you been with the company?"

"Over forty years."

While a little overly thorough, these were essentially normal questions that I've been asked, although, not all at once, many times before. Next came the non-normal questions hard and fast.

"Are you married?"

"Yes."

"How many cars do you own?"

"Two."

Around this time, I stopped answering her questions, not that it stopped her. The interrogation continued. This time the questions became even more strange and personal. It was like she was reading from a script.

"How much money do you have saved? How many credit cards do you have? Are you circumcised? What's the square footage of your house? When did you lose your virginity? Who's the President? Where were you born? Do you have any lead fillings? If so, how many? Are you Jewish? "

I just stood there, somewhat agape. This is what she buzzed me through four gates to ask? At some point, I guess she realized that I had stopped answering because she stopped asking. There was a long pause and from the screen came a clicking sound. It sounded like a fingernail tapping on a table. What the heck was going on here? The image on the screen changed from animals to a person. The person who was conducting the inquisition. She was in her eighties, had long, stringy, unkempt gray hair and was wearing no makeup. She looked extremely weathered and perplexed.

"Why aren't you answering my questions?" she practically spat out.

What I wanted to say was, "because they're way out of line, what do they have to do with the job I was sent here to do and the second I get out of here, I'm going to super glue my manager's door with her inside. By the way, you're nuts."

I knew this would've only made the situation worse. From experience, I knew the best way to handle an agitated customer was to project a professional, calm and unaffected demeanor, which I did.

I gently put down my toolbox on the front porch, looked at the screen and as sweetly as possible said, "Ma'am, why are you asking me all these personal questions? They really have nothing to do with the reason why I'm here which is to fix your system."

She looked down at her piece of paper and didn't say anything, so I asked again, "Ma'am, this repair shouldn't take long. Why don't you let me in, I'll fix it and then I'll be out of your hair?"

There was no response. Just silence. I tried again.

"Ma'am, don't forget, you called us. Would you like me to help you or not?" Still nothing. She didn't answer.

After thirty seconds of silence, I bent down, picked up my toolbox and began to leave. Her voice crackled through the screen.

"Excuse me, sir. I'm sorry to put you through this. You cannot be too sure these days. I just wanted to find out if you were safe or not. I apologize for my questioning. Please enter the garage door to your left. Place your toolbox in the clear holding container then walk forward to the holding cell and remove your clothes. I will speak to you from there with further instructions."

My eyes opened. I was in shock. Holding cell? Remove my clothes? What the hell? I looked at the screen and asked, "My hearing isn't great. Would you mind repeating that again word for word?" She repeated her instructions. They didn't change.

"Please enter the door on your left. Place your toolbox in the compartment and enter the chamber where you need to take off your clothes and wait to be sprayed to sterilize you. There are clean clothes hanging on the wall for you."

The door was buzzed open, but I didn't enter the garage. Inside was a clear square chamber, like a shower stall, with several hoses attached to the walls and nothing else. The place was clean. Scary clean. Like you could operate in there. The hoses were all facing inward and it was a full-size spray tank large enough for a person to enter. A door handle protruded from one of the sides and a wooden step stool was inside.

A short puff of spray came out of the chamber. I guess it was her way of reassuring me that the chamber was safe. I backed up and looked up at the screen and said

"Ma'am, why do I need to be sprayed to enter your house? I assure you, I'm a hygienic person."

She answered back by saying, "I do not like germs so, I need you to be cleaned. Please enter the box so you can come in."

"Ma'am, I'm not going to do that," I answered.

She looked down at her paper again, reading something. Seconds passed. She looked up and said, "I'm sorry, sir, but I need you to fix my appliance. If you're not willing to comply with the protocol, you cannot leave my yard. How long you stay is up to you. I'll wait."

Oh my God, what was this lady thinking? She was going to keep me imprisoned in her front area until I complied? That's kidnapping or unlawful restraint which is a pretty serious crime. I tried to reason with her while being a little humorous.

"Ma'am, I take my clothes off for nobody. Trust me, I'm doing you a favor. You don't want to see me without a shirt off or worse."

My attempt at levity fell flat. Meanwhile, two minutes had passed. Then

"I have no interest in seeing you naked, sir. I just need to know that you're clean. Why are you being so damned difficult? Now, take off your clothes and step into the chamber for decontamination," she practically screamed.

With that, I picked up my toolbox and spoke into the intercom.

"Ma'am, I will be leaving now and do not call use back. We will not come back. Good day."

She screamed, "You cannot leave! I won't let you go! You will stay, and do as I command!"

Remember how earlier I left the gate just a little bit open? She didn't. This is what years of experience will do for you. I always leave gates open when entering a closed off area. Why? Just in case you need to make a quick exit from a dog or a complete nut job who likely hadn't left her house in years and probably stored her urine in clear, glass jars. So, yeah, all four gates were still open just a little bit.

She continued to scream, "You fool, don't you realize you're only making things worse for yourself? You're not going anywhere until I say so! I command you again!"

She commanded me again. Sounds serious. She must've had a camera mounted somewhere on the house facing the front yard with multiple angles because her voice continued coming through all the speaker boxes and LCD screens simultaneously. She continued

"It's locked! Don't make me angry! There's no way out!"

I opened all three gates which seemed to drive her further into madness. It's as if everything she ever thought was true was revealed to be false.

"No, you can't do that! That's not fair!" she bellowed.

And keep me here against my will isn't?

As I got to the main gate, it was locked. I guess the wind blew the newspaper I had used to prop it open away. Hagatha could not have been happier. She didn't need the speakers because her cackling was that loud.

"You shouldn't have defied me! Now things will only get worse for you! I tried to be merciful and now you will pay!..."

What she didn't know was that I always carried a small screwdriver. It's amazing what these things can do for instance, if you jam it into the backside of a security lock and turn it, nine times out of ten, you can get the latch to retract, which is exactly what I did. I showed her my trusty tool and opened the gate. Man, if you thought she was pissed before, that was like a 2.1 earthquake compared to the big one.

Keep in mind that I hadn't exited yet. I opened the gate as wide as it could go and left, then locked it. Then I jimmied it open and went back inside. After that, I got it open and left again. In and out. In and out. I did this no less than six times. I may have even skipped through the last time. Oh yes, I was having a grand time showing her just how easy it was to escape from her prison. Of course, she couldn't escape from herself but that wasn't my problem.

"Noooooooooo!! You can't leave, you bastard!" were some of the cleaner things she said. The rest does not bare repeating.

Somehow just exiting and leaving the gate wide open somehow didn't seem like enough. I needed to do something to truly piss her off, even more. So, I took out my screwdriver, held it to the metal posts of her gate and danced off, all the while clanging on each plank, just like a kid would do on a bike with a wooden stick to a fence. The dink, dink, dink sound the screwdriver made on the wall was beautiful.

After that, I got to my truck, placed my tools in the back and smiled as I faced the house. Shortly after I entered the cab, I called the police and then my manager with my findings. After my moment of triumph, I no longer wanted to punish my manager but let's just say I had easy shifts for the next six months. Still, I wonder how long it would take the crazy shut-in to get off her ass, close the gate and decontaminate herself before entering her house. Oh well, not my problem!

Story 15: Weight Lifting Family (Early 2000's)

Most of my service repairs are done Monday through Friday. Once or twice a year, I'd have to work on a Saturday. I had a co-worker who was off on vacation one week and I drew the short straw to cover his shift. Not that I minded all that much. Saturday was all overtime for me, the sweetest time of all.

The repair that was requested on the order form did not completely explain what needed to be done. All it said was that something was wrong with the refrigerator doors, which could be a number of things. I'd find out when I got there.

As I drove my work truck into the housing tract, it seemed pretty normal. This was just going to be a routine service call. Boy, was I wrong.

I walked up to the house and heard a sound coming from inside. It sounded like metal clanking together followed by grunts. The metal clanking sound repeated a few times as I got closer to the front door. I also heard someone being berated like, "do it you, loser," only the voice didn't say "loser." I cleaned it up. I rang the bell which was the opening notes of "Jingle Bells" which was an odd juxtaposition to someone being tortured inside.

After a few moments, the metal clanking sound stopped, and I could hear someone walking to the door. When it opened, I literally saw the biggest human being I've ever seen in my life. This guy was huge. Six foot five and easily three hundred pounds, all muscle. This guy was a body builder and yes, I did find it a little ironic that I was fixing the refrigerator of a man built like one. He had long, flowing blond hair. I stuck my hand out and introduced myself.

"Hello, I'm Rob. I'm here to repair your refrigerator."

He shook my hand and I somehow managed not to wince. The guy had a grip like a vise.

"Hey, I'm Blake. Come on in."

We entered into the foyer. Just off to my right was the living room. It would've been more accurate to call it the "lifting room." There was almost no furniture save for a large-screen TV that was showing ultimate fighting. Instead of couches, loveseats, coffee tables, etc. there were bench presses, curling benches, sit-up inclines, etc. It was like someone decided to open an L.A. Fitness in a private residence. It was packed with weights and weight lifting equipment. What I heard earlier was Blake finishing up his bench presses. I should also add that he looked vaguely familiar.

As we entered the kitchen, I noticed that it was very clean except for two food blenders and several plastic bottles full of what, I'm guessing, were body building supplements. There were also a bunch of smaller pill bottles like the kind you'd find at your local GNC. Whatever they were was none of my business.

"So, the work order was a little vague, but I understand you're having a problem with the door. Can you show me?"

"Sure, bro," he said. Hey, we were "bros." It sure beat being on his bad side. Blake opened the door and demonstrated what was wrong.

"Hear, that popping sound, bro? And it's not opening correctly. Any idea, bro?"

Actually, I did. I had seen this problem before. It involved lubrication and switching out the lower door hinges which had failed. It was a simple fix and it should only take a me a few minutes to knock it out, which I explained to my new bro, Blake. What I could not see from where I was standing was why the lower door hinges failed.

Blake sat down at the kitchen table. I re-opened the refrigerator door to verify where the popping sound was coming from. As I opened it fully, I noticed that the interior of the door was stocked with gallons of milk. There were at least eight gallons of milk and a few more plastic bottles. Inside the refrigerator itself were neatly stacked containers full of high protein foods, all clearly labeled like "chicken," "tofu, almonds," "sardines," etc. Trust me, you weren't going to find any pork rinds in this household. By the way, I just listed the foods that I had recognized. A bunch of the other containers had names that sounded more like chemicals.

I asked Blake to come over, so I could show him the problem and what I planned to do to fix it. He stood up and flexed the whole way over. Almost like it was a nervous tic or something. It was a little unnerving. I told him what I needed to do to fix the door and he grunted which I took to mean "go ahead." He really didn't know what I was talking about. I turned around and bent over, knelling in front on my toolbox. I opened the lid and found the wrench I needed to remove the upper hinge. As I reached for the wrench, the lady of the house came around the corner carrying a laundry basket. I stood up.

My initial thought was that she was a body builder too. She stood about six foot and must have weighed around one hundred and eighty pounds, all muscle. She was wearing a half-shirt which exposed her six-pack bare mid-riff. Hell, it was closer to a thirty pack. Contrary to my description, she was quite attractive. I tried not to stare but it's not every day that you're in an amazon's kitchen. I'd like to add that I've never felt more out of shape in my life. Honestly, I can bench press around one hundred and fifty pounds. But those two could easily lift that with one arm with me attached. Good thing I wasn't there for a lift off.

The lady put the laundry basket down on the counter and I noticed what was inside it. Lots of tights, unitards and masks. Then it hit me, there two were professional wrestlers! I had seen them on TV because my son was a big fan. I decided to keep the fact that I recognized them to myself because I felt it would've been unprofessional.

I began to remove the upper refrigerator door hinge. I stopped because I forgot to remove the milk and the other food from the door which, obviously, made the door a lot heavier than I wanted it to be. While moving the contents around, I noticed rectangular plastic containers that were labeled for the days of the week. I could sort of see what was inside and what I could make out were syringes, vials and needles. Looks like the former champ was a juicer. Again, not my business but disappointing nevertheless.

After removing all the gallons of milk, I continued to remove the upper door hinge. I had a little trouble removing one of the hinge screws. Someone crossed threaded it into the cabinet. Why do people do moronic things? Damned if I know.

Blake, who was still sitting at the kitchen table asked me if I needed some help. I told him, "No, I got it covered. Thanks." Good thing I didn't take him up on it because with his strength, he easily could've ripped the door off without even trying. Try filling out the paperwork on that one.

The bolt came out finally and I removed the refrigerator door. I carefully put it on the floor. The lower step up/down washers had worn off. Not surprising because of all that extra weight on the door. I told Blake and Mrs. Blake that I had the parts in the truck and I would be right back. As I left the room, they started talking. One sentence that did stand out was, "I hope he didn't see anything…"

They must've been talking about the steroids, like I was going to say anything. Apparently, one of the side-effects of juicing is acute paranoia. Besides, even if I was suicidal, which I'm not, and wanted to tell someone what I saw, who would that be? The cops? The promoter? Their clergyman? Safe bet that I was going to keep it to myself.

I went to the truck, got the door hinge parts, re-entered the house and walked back into the kitchen. I noticed that the milk had been moved around and some of the other food had been removed. What was in those plastic containers I removed?

Mrs. Blake, still in the kitchen, had a funny grin on her face, like she was hiding something. She was also flexing, just like her husband. What's that old saw about marriage; the longer you stay together, the more alike you become? Well, it appeared to be alive and well in this kitchen. I just hoped for her sake that she wasn't taking any of that stuff. Have you seen what 'roids do to women? They make them look like not women.

The old parts took no time to remove and swap out with the new ones. As I finished replacing the last washer, Blake approached me. I got a little nervous. Maybe he was going to threaten me if I said anything about what I saw inside his fridge. Great, now I was paranoid, and I've never touched the stuff. Anyway, I could not have been more wrong.

"So, bro, you like what you see here," he asked?

I really had no idea what he was talking about for a moment. Then he started flexing up a storm. His wife soon joined in. I still had no idea what he was getting at and it made me uncomfortable. I figured I should say something.

"Sure," I responded.

"You know, bro. I used to be like you. A little scrawny, no definition, weak…"

A little sales tip for any who may be reading this, it's a good idea not to insult people you're trying to get money out of. He continued.

"Then I started down a path that changed my life. You know what that path was made of," he asked?

'Illegal drugs," I said to myself?

I may not be the brightest bead on the rosary but I'm not idiot either. Apparently, his question was rhetorical because he answered before I could.

"Specialized training and custom nutritioning, bro. And if it could work for us, it can work for you too."

He and the missus started flexing again. I thought it best not to laugh. She chimed in.

"Sorry for not introducing myself earlier, I'm Raye."

We shook hands. She wasn't as strong as her husband, but I definitely felt it.

"What my husband, Blake, was alluding to, was that we're life coaches. We rebuild you from the inside and out," she said.

"Bro, our program is the way of the future. It'll change your life," he said. Clearly, they had made this pitch many times before. One thought that popped into my head, what if I like my life? Again, I kept it to myself. The pitch continued.

"What we do here is, we don't just train bodies. We rebuilt them. No one does what we do. Raye has an associate's degree in nutrition from Harpsburg Community College and I have over twenty years inside the squared circle," he said.

"That's professional wrestling," Raye said, trying to help out. Hey, if they brought it up, that's fine.

"I thought I recognized you," I said. The two of them beamed. I didn't say I liked him, just that I recognized him.

"Yup, I had me some battles inside that ring. Learned a lot and I can pass it on to you," he said.

I don't know if you've watched wrestling lately, but I didn't see the need to learn how to get hit by a chair. Honestly, it doesn't look like there's a lot to it. Blake kept talking and I kept pretending to listen.

"All the equipment you saw in the living room before, we use to help our clients achieve their dreams. To become better than they are, and I know we can do it for you. Ten sessions with us, will turn your life around," Blake said.

"And," chimed in Raye, "we are prepared to give you a twenty-percent discount, so the ten sessions will only be eight hundred dollars."

Eighty dollars a session? Yikes. back then, that was a lot of money to work out with a trainer. It still is, as far as I'm concerned when you can join the Y for about twenty bucks a month but who knows what degrees they have?

"You get a trainer, a nutritionist, a muscle guru and a friend," he said.

I wonder if the eighty bucks a session covered the drugs. Not wanting to offend them and get out alive, I told them that I'd think about it.

"Fine, bro, but don't wait too long. If you do, someone else is going to take your spot," said Blake. It was a chance I was willing to take. Also, I had a job to finish, so I turned back to the refrigerator.

The refrigerator door went back on the lower hinge with no problem and the upper hinge screw that had given me a little trouble coming out, went back in smoothly. The refrigerator door now opened and closed correctly. I knew that all that milk was going to be placed back into the door, so instead of using a grease to lube up the hinge, I thought it best to use a little Vaseline.

I was now sure of two things; that the door was going to work correctly and that I wasn't going to train with them. I started to replace the milk. At or about the fourth gallon, Blake asked me to stop. I told him that I needed to place a little weight in the door to see if it was going to work correctly which was true, but I also wanted to get a closer look at the steroids.

I was pretty sure that Blake knew what I was up to. I could just see it in his face. Raye stepped in and started putting the food back in herself, claiming that she needed to do some cleaning in the already clean refrigerator. Fine by me.

Then I turned to Blake and told him that the repair was covered under warranty. I also advised him that they might want to move some of the weight onto the shelving so the problem with the door would not reoccur.

I got up, presented them with their paperwork, shook their hands and headed to the front door. As I exited, we waved to each other and Blake told me again that he could only hold my space for a couple of days. I thanked him and told him I'd get back to him. Then I got into my truck and drove off.

Lastly, I told them that I had added some glue to the door gasket, so it would be best to leave the refrigerator door alone for at least an hour. No opening or closing. Let the parts settle, the glue dry and the lubrication set in. I ended my mini-lecture by saying, "If you have kids, be sure to pass it on—"

Raye jumped in and said, "Oh, we don't have kids." It was then that I said, quite possibly, the dumbest thing I've ever said. Completely without thinking, I blurted out

"Gee, I wonder why?"

They collectively sighed, and I quickly apologized but you really couldn't take back what I put out. Maybe what I said shocked them into getting off the juice. I highly doubt it but maybe. I got the hell out of there before Blake's sadness turned into full-on 'roid rage.

Better living through chemicals may appeal to some people but not to me. That night, when I got home, I cracked open a beer, grabbed a bag of chips and was a couch potato for the rest of the night. I felt like it was my own little protest against what I'd seen at Blake and Raye's house that afternoon. What can I tell you, at heart I guess I'm a rebel.

Story 16: One Big Rat (2010)

Have you ever seen a mouse? Have you ever seen a rat? What about a rat the size of a small dog? Well, I have.

I got a phone call for a service visit for a refrigerator that wasn't cooling correctly and the customer was irate to say the least. According to the order, the fridge was about eight months old. What could go wrong with a unit only eight months old? Sadly, for me, there was only one way to find out and that involved a home visit.

As soon as I got the address I knew it wasn't going to be a good day because the call was located in an area of track houses, probably built around 1960, that could best be described as "the hood." While pulling up, I couldn't help but notice all the debris that was scattered on the lawns. Stuff like flat tires, beer cans, a hubcap from a '68 Chevy, sagging lawn chairs, busted sprinklers, a bunch of Slip-N-Slides stapled together, etc.

All the homes were run down with foot and a half paint chips hanging off. Plus, the address numbers were all askew because the bottom nails were so corroded they couldn't hold anything anymore. I wanted to shout, "There's this wonderous new invention called aluminum siding! It's cheap and your house won't look like crap!"

I parked the truck and the lady was standing on the sidewalk waiting for me with both hands clinched in fists and placed on her hips. Her face had a mean look of disgust on it, kind of like Aunt Esther from "Sanford & Son." I got out of the truck and walked around the back to get my toolbox. As I opened the rear door, she began to speak, or should I say yell. Normally, I'd repeat what she said verbatim but not one clean sentence came out of her mouth. She couldn't go more than three words without cursing. This lady was pissed about everything and I was the one she was going to take it out on.

One of the basic rules of field work is for every obscene word spoken, the bill goes up by ten dollars and if there is no money involved, like a warranty job, let's just say that the unit may be left in the "off" position after I leave.

With my toolbox in hand and the lady cussing me out about everything, I walked slowly to the front door. Looking back, I should have broken off the repair after her first obscenity because common courtesy was something this lady did not have. Who knows what this lady's problem was but for the next hour or so, I was to bore the brunt of it.

And yet, I entered the house. Damn my professionalism. The décor inside was perverse to say the least. There were rattan chairs with big holes in the bottom, a black velvet painting of Dean Martin, cheesy, mismatched wood paneling, a broken lava lamp, a disco ball, old newspapers, filled up ashtrays. Nothing went together. At all.

The "lady" raised her right hand and pointed to the kitchen. The decorating didn't get any better in there. It was old and really run down. The cabinets and wall fixtures were as beaten up as the house and some of the cabinet doors were broken. The kitchen table had four seats; two plastic, one folding and one bean bag. The dishes in the sink must have been there for at least a few weeks or so. I swear you could see ants crawling on the plates. What a slob!

What shook me out of my stupor was the unique smell coming from the refrigerator. It was an odor I had smelled before. No doubt about it, it was a dead animal, undoubtedly in the refrigerator, probably in the rear. The most likely place was in the water tray under the unit. The question now was, how long since it had died? The centered rail of the unit was red hot. So hot your hand can burn if left on for more than a few seconds. Needless to say, that's not how it's supposed to feel.

Going back to the original complaint, her refrigerator was not cooling properly, and this was a little unusual. Usually, it means that a condenser fan motor in the back has stopped working and I didn't have to be Sherlock Holmes to figure out why. To sum up, we had a bad smell, a hot center rail, internal temperatures way too high and one pissed off lady. Yup, something was dead.

The lady was standing at my side as I pulled the refrigerator away from the wall. The kitchen floor hadn't been cleaned in a long time and it was worse under the unit. The wheels were sticking and slurping as I pulled on it. The lady saw what was under the refrigerator with no surprise and without skipping a beat, continued to verbally assault me. This repair could end up costing her thousands or the entire cost of her home.

As I was pulling the unit forward, I first saw it, the tail of the rat. It wasn't as long as I thought it would be. A second look told me that most of the tail was still inside the cabinet. I did catch a break though. For whatever reason, Aunt Esther decided to exit the kitchen and walked out of the house. I could see her in the backyard continuing her act. Maybe she wanted to see how it would play outdoors.

In my toolbox I always keep a towel large enough for me to sit on, just for this sort of situation. I sat down and removed the rear cover of the refrigerator. As I lowered the cover there was the rat. It was a big one, about the size of a small dog; weighing around four pounds. As I looked more closely, I noticed that the condenser fan blade had cut through the back of the rat's neck killing it in his tracks. I'm no coroner but my guess was that the rat had been there for about three days. I say this because the rat's body was not hard and dehydrated but a little squishy.

I could see that Aunt Esther had started walking back toward the kitchen door. She sidled up to it and stood in the doorway in her familiar pose, hands on hips with her neck projected outward, only a little meaner. I looked at her. There was five seconds of silence or enough time to take a breath of air. Then she continued with her verbal harassment. She wasn't breathing, she was reloading.

By now I was getting pissed off. I don't normally get upset with customers but cracks about my personal life and my family really crossed the line. Obviously, she didn't know me or my family. She was fishing but nowhere in my job description did it say I had to put up with this garbage. It was time to do something about it.

I looked at a pair of needle noise pliers in my toolbox and at the rat. I grabbed them and carefully pinched the rat's backside, lifting him off the floor. With a short flick of my wrist I aimed the body in her direction and Ricky Rat sailed through the air. It was like that scene in "The Natural" where Robert Redford hits that first homerun. Time stood still, and everything seemed to be in slow motion as Ricky Rat transformed into Super Rat because, man, that rodent corpse was flying! In my head, I swear, I heard that movie's theme song. Da-dum. Da dah-dah dum… By god, it was glorious.

As Rickey made his journey across the kitchen, doing a couple of 360's, the look on Aunt Esther's face was one of incomprehension and abject horror. Super Rat traveled about five to six feet before hitting and bouncing off her and landing on the dirty floor. The sound of dead rat's guts spreading over a short radius was to say the least, unique. A bloody squishy sound was heard. Kind of like a kerplunk. She screamed.

I looked at her with my best mean look and said, "If you kept your f**king rat out of the refrigerator it just might work correctly."

The look on her face was one of shock. She stopped screaming and stood up slowly in an up-right position. Her face was turning pale. I couldn't be sure if she was breathing or not, nor did I care. All of a sudden, she raised her hands to her shoulders and started to frantically scream in short hysterical outbursts. After about the fifth one, she fell over backwards. With any luck, she would stick to the floor which was like one giant glue trap.

I finished up the repair, so I could get the hell out of there, placing the rear cover back on the refrigerator and moving it back to the spot where it originally was. She was still screaming about how offended she was at what I had done. A terrible acting job to say the least. No Oscar in her future. Not even a Golden Globe.

I said to her, "This job is done, and you do not get an Oscar for your performance today. I've seen this act before. You have a mess to clean up. Good luck"

I grabbed my toolbox and exited the house. In the middle of the driveway I started laughing. It started somewhat quietly but quickly grew to a good belly laugh. It's fun watching how stupid people can be and what they will try to get out of paying for repairs.

A few moments later, I was in my cab of the truck and calling the dispatcher. My back was facing the driver's window when I heard a knock. It was crazy lady only this time something was different. Mainly because she appeared to be subdued and her hands were placed together like she was praying. The only thing missing was a halo above her head. She was up to something, but I didn't know what. I opened the window half way. In a calm voice, she slowly stated that she wanted to explain her previous conduct. She said she had a dual personality and the person in the house was not the real her.

I had no idea what to say or believe at that point. Was this her way of apologizing? No. She wanted me to come back into the house and clean up the rat. I kept a calm disposition, took a deep breath to steady myself and looked her right into her face and said

"Lady, you're so full of sh*t and it's funny. Now step back from the truck or I will drive over your feet."

I closed the window, turned up the radio loudly and shifted the truck's transmission into gear. As I pulled away, I looked at the side mirror and saw that Aunt Esther was cussing up a storm and started her tantrum again only this time in the middle of the street. I guess her first personality came back. Maybe they could team up and fight the rats together.

Story 17: Nothing Matches (2012)

Have you ever been inside a home where nothing matched, and I mean nothing? Well, I have.

It was windy day and the Santa Ana winds were easily blowing 20-30 mph, coming straight off the Lancaster desert. I don't mind the winds. Sometimes I even find them kind of soothing. As long as they don't blow my truck all over the road. That does tend to kind of harsh your mellow. The service call I was heading to was in a small town, somewhat out of the way, especially compared to the city life I was used to.

On the way over, I was treated to country windy roads, a few cliffs and views that would take your breath away. So much so, that I didn't even mind that it took me an hour and fifteen minutes to get there.

As I pulled up to the residence, there was pre- installed chain link fencing of non-uniform heights and different colors. It was odd, to say the least. Almost seizure inducing. The plants were somewhat overgrown, but I had seen worse. I parked the truck and obtained my toolbox from the rear.

The house was very old. Probably built in the 1940's or before. It could really use a fresh coat of paint as large hunks of it were peeling off. As I walked up to the chain link door, I noticed that there was a large amount of planting pots scattered throughout the small yard. Plastic pots, clay pots, and ceramic pots, all in different sizes with no uniformity at all. All were empty with several open bags of planting soil next to them. What the gardener of the house was waiting for, I did not know.

I tried to open the gate, but it was difficult. Nobody had been through this door in years. Somehow, I managed to wedge it open but as I turned around to close it, I think I may have broken the hinge because there was a snapping sound. From there, it was a short walk to the front door.

The front door was framed by planters on both sides and a rundown screen door. The roof line traveled to the rear and was elevated somewhat high up, just like the buildings you tended to see back east to make sure snow wouldn't pile up too high. Again, very out of place in this part of the country but I hadn't seen anything yet.

The steps leading up to the porch had some give as I walked on them. I noticed that three of the steps were replaced at one point in time because each replaced step was a different material. They needed to be painted too. Somebody's cheap handy work, no doubt.
As I knocked on the screen door I had a chance to check things out. On the patio were two benches. The one on my left, facing the house was had a metal frame with a red cushion and on my right, was a wood frame swinging bench with a blue cushion.

I didn't think the owner of the house heard me knocking, so I tried again, still with no response. I walked to the left of the patio and called out to the rear of the house.

"Hello, is anybody home?! I'm here to fix the stove," I shouted. Still no answer. Great, I had traveled all this way for a no-show.

I called the number on the work order from my cell-phone. This time I got a response. She said she'd be right there and I hung up. Why the confusion? She was in the rear of the house and could not hear me knocking. Finally, I could hear her walking. It still took her a good minute to get to the door. She opened it revealing a plump Mexican-American woman in her forties. She was very friendly.

"Greetings, senior. My apologies for the delay. I could not hear you. My name is Carmen," she said.

"No problem. I'm Rob. I'm here to help you with your stove," I said.

"Yes-Yes, please come in. I have been waiting for you."

We shook hands and entered the abode. It was hard to see due to the lack of light, but I was able to make out, just inside the door, vast amounts of collectibles ranging from small statues to china that was not anywhere close to a complete set. The furniture in the living room did not match either and believe me, I'm no interior decorator. The couch was Victorian and had a hand knitted cover draped over it. It was flanked by two chairs of different styles and colors. One was made of oak and the other of hand stained pine with metal straps binding the legs together. The coffee table looked like it was of good quality except that one of the legs was missing and the table was propped up with bricks and tape. Off to the side was a dress form mannequin draped with tan, hand woven knitted materials. On the couch was a large ball of packing twine with really big sewing needles. It looked like Carmen was making clothes out of it. If Martha Stewart saw this place, she would've crapped herself.

Just behind the furniture were three electrical cords bordering the outside of the room. Where were these electrical cords going to or where did they originate? Who knew? Maybe Carmen did but with this mess, I couldn't say for sure. On the wall were pictures of plants, trees and bushes. No photos of kids or family. Just landscaping. Kind of odd.

As we walked to the other side of the living room, we entered a short hallway where I noticed one of the same electrical cords on the floor that had masking tape to hold it down. The hall was only painted halfway, starting from the ceiling and ending in the middle of the wall. Whomever was doing the job, ran out of paint mid-way or just gave up. Well, that wasn't really my concern anyway. I was there to fix the stove.

We entered the kitchen which was pretty small. Maybe 12 feet by 15 feet. Just enough for one or maybe two people inside at the same time. We stopped at the kitchen sink and I placed my work order on the counter and my tool box on the floor.

"Carmen, what exactly is the problem with the stove," I asked?

"Well, Mr. Repairman—"

"Please, call me Rob."

"Well, Mr. Rob, the stove burners don't light up by themselves. They do light if I used another thing to light them," she said.

"Okay," I said. "I'm not exactly sure what the problem is so, let me have a look at it."

"Okay, good luck and when you find out what the problem is, just holler," she said before exiting. I assured her that I would.

In no time, I figured out what the problem was, so I got to work. No sparking from the burners but the gas was good. As a normal check, I turned on the oven just to see if the ignition coil would light up as well. This process does take a few minutes which gave me a perfect opportunity to look around.

On the counter were the dishes she just washed. None of the plates were the same. The forks and knives were all different too. The coffee cups, one from Disneyland, another was gold and the rest were chipped and scratched. I stepped over to the cookie jar. It was a smiling clown with a big crack in its head that was shoddily glued back together. The rest of the decanter set did not match either.

I then looked up at the cabinet doors. They were of different colors but the same materials. The counters had undergone several repairs because a bunch of the tiles stuck out more and were of a different color. The process was finished so I opened the oven door and tested the ignitor. It was not working. The display on the front console was completely dead so, it was definitely a power problem.

I opened my tool box and found my Voltmeter. I needed to see what was getting juice and what wasn't. On the kitchen floor was an old rug and overlaying the corners were four other rugs, none of which matched. They were covering up something but what?

Off to the side was the kitchen table. It was yellow and made of metal. There were two chairs, one of wood and the other pieced together with PVC piping on opposite ends. The sink had a big chip in the porcelain and it looked like someone tried to use epoxy to fill in the chip. It looked like crap. The only normal thing I had seen so far was the kitchen window located above the sink and, of course, it had a huge crack in it too. You know what the house reminded me of? Did you ever see that show about the Alaskan family living in the bush that never threw anything out? Bingo.

The corner of the rug was underneath the stove. I needed to move the stove a little, so I could see underneath. As I did, there was a loud bang from under the stove. Something just happened. Was it the load bag? I carefully moved the rug aside and noticed that those extension cords were traveling underneath the stove and somehow, one the legs mashed the cord to break it. The bang I heard was the cord shorting out.

Carmen bolted into the room, more out of concern for her stove than regard for my safety.

"I heard a bang. What happened?"

"Yes, I'm fine, thank you. But, have you heard that noise before?"

"I think last week, maybe," she replied. "I heard something like that last week when I closed the oven door," she said.

Just wonderful. Carmen was powering her oven with an electrical cord and it shorted under the rug. Serious major fire problem if I ever saw one. The whole place could've burned like a tinderbox but wait, it gets even better!

I looked at Carmen and asked, where does these electrical cords go? What are they plugged into? I thought my question was reasonable, but she just stood there. No answer and zero response.

With no answers forthcoming, I pulled the rug back enough to see for myself. Around the corner of the kitchen, the cords were taped to the molding with duct tape of every imaginable color. They traveled through the mismatched living room. As I walked through, Carmen stood there, not moving an inch.

The cords snaked under a small closet door. I needed to open it to check it out. I asked for permission, but she still did not move. I guess her batteries were low or something or she had crashed and needed to be rebooted.

I opened the closet door and found three rain coats, several sets of gloves that did not match and shoes of all colors. As I knelt down to check out the electrical cords, I noticed that they traveled upwards slightly. I needed to move the coats aside. Again, I called out to Carmen but got no answer. Maybe she was one of the robot hosts from "West World."

The electrical cords went through a hole in the wall that led outside the house. Now, it was getting interesting. Next to the closet was the bathroom. I took a short glance inside to find out if this was the cords destination. Shockingly, inside the bathroom, nothing matched. The base of the sink was blue, and the sink basin was white. The floor was comprised of three different types of tile and looked like they were laid down with Elmer's. Only one segment of the tile had grout and the rest had green mold under the white glue.

The soap dispenser was made of dark colored glass which was too dark for that room and, of course, the curtains were mismatched. There was no shower or bathtub. No room.

I can only guess that this lady has a decorating issue or something else was going on here. By now I knew that the cords final destination laid outside the home. I walked back to the kitchen to check on Carmen.

"Ma'am, are you okay?"

Finally, she came to and said, "I'm sorry."

"Ma'am, I'm checking to see why you are using electrical cords to power your oven and, by the look of things, your entire house."

For some reason she turned to her left and began to walk out to the enclosed patio area and wanted me to follow. As we entered the patio, I could see five large mounds of something that were covered by bedsheets. Carmen continued to walk to the other side of the room and exited.

On the patio, I saw two wagons and a small shopping cart. One was the kind a little kid would play with. It was a Radio Flyer or knockoff and could carry many pounds. The third was made of wire and had small wheels. What were they doing in this patio section? It made as much sense as anything else in the home.

We exited the patio and walked down a short driveway heading towards the front of the house. I could see the power cords dangling from the side wall and dropping under the gravel driveway, buried, and heading for the neighbor's house. The mystery was starting to come into focus. I was now getting a small glimpse of what was going on here. She had plugged two electrical cords into her neighbor's exterior wall socket and was using them to power her house. And I could see how she was able to get away with it because the adjoining yard were covered with weeds and various plant growths. Nobody could see what was happening.

We continued to walk in front of the house to re-enter the front door. What else had she done? Turns out Carmen was just getting started because she had also tapped into her neighbor's garden faucet and piped it to her own, so she could have water. The garden hose was also camouflaged with junk. Nobody could see what was going on unless you were looking for it. Give her this, Carmen was good.

By now, we were back in the kitchen. The electrical cord that was attached to the oven was burned beyond repair and it need to be replaced and I told her so. She just looked at me for a moment. Then she turned to her left and grabbed onto a small shopping cart. Then she just walked out the rear patio exit and into the back-yard area heading to the back fence. I followed her as far as the patio and she just kept walking. What the hell just happened here?

Around then I started looking around. The five mounds of something were right at my feet. What to do? Since the captain or the Carmen had abandoned ship I decided to lift each of the bedsheets to see what lurked underneath. What did I find? Large bags of rice, flour, salt, beans, oats, and more. More bags of flour had a U.S. Government symbol. Where were these things coming from? Probably the U.S. government. At least now I knew what the larger hand towing wagon was needed for. She was hording government food.

I had the opportunity to look around a little more and I found lots of canned food ranging from canned meats, veggies, fruit, etc. Also, all government issued.

It has been now about twenty minutes. Where did Carmen go? I went back into the kitchen and started to collect my tools. I needed to get out of there. What a way to get out of a repair bill. This was certainly new one. Don't like the estimate, fine, grab a shopping cart and walk the hell out.

Just as I started to go, I saw a small storage room off the side of the kitchen. Another room. Believe it or not, I'm not nosey but I was now emotionally invested. I peeked inside. No windows or light. Just crap and lots of it. It was overly packed with the strangest things. Broken hand tools, a building block of clear stone, a worn-out plastic plant, odds and ends from everything that could or would be found. Clearly, anything that she had found and could carry home went into this room. Broken or in good condition, it didn't matter. This pack rat room was packed to the gills.

I glanced at my watch and noticed that it had been forty-five minutes since Carmen walked out of the house. I keep asking myself, where did she go? Obviously, the oven was not going to be repaired today. I headed back through the living room, out the front door and toward my truck. I stopped on the sidewalk for a second to see if I could find her.

Placing my tools in the rear of the truck it finally came to me. If you look at the bigger picture, Carmen did not have a care in the world. She had a house, clothes, lots of food and all the city people providing her with their trash or throw-a-ways. That explained why nothing matched and why she did not need to lock up the doors of the house. Who would want to steal any of this crap from her?

As I drove off, I could only think what kind of life she was living. It was just her and she was perfectly happy doing whatever she wanted.

Her house was about ten houses from the main drag of the city. I turned the truck to the right and thought I would get some lunch at the local greasy spoon. About three blocks in and off to my right, there she was, Carmen! Just walking on the side walk with the shopping cart full of stuff she must have found someplace. I decided not to interrupt her bliss. In her own way, she was doing just fine.

In a weird way, I had come to respect her. Think about it, she didn't have to depend on anyone. Her needs were simple and provided for. She kept things simple and it appeared to be working for her. Adios, Carmen and don't eat too much government rice.

Story 18: The Sun Worshipers (1980's)

This story is about the time I got to see naked women and was paid handsomely for the privilege. To anyone who doubts that this is a great country, here's some irrefutable proof that is is.

It was a hot summer here in what we call the Southland. The temperatures were supposed to hit 110 around mid-day. That's hot for anyone. Even Satan would say that that's a bit much. There was a slight breeze coming up from over the west, but it was fighting a losing battle.

That morning, I arrived a little earlier than normal than the mandated start time of eight a.m. I entered the shop and the blast from the air conditioning unit was a welcomed treat. I walked over to the rack were the paper routed service orders were kept and found my orders for that day. I had eight. I just hoped that these houses had air conditioning.

I arrived at the third house around eleven. By now, the temp was easily 100 and climbing. The house appeared normal. Single story with a concrete driveway and side planters to the left. In the driveway sat a motor home covered with a tarp. I knocked on the door and stood there for a minute.

The door opened. The lady of the house stood inside the doorway. She was in her early forties, a brunette and was wearing a light blue house coat tied with a bow in the front.

"Hi, I'm Jill. Won't you come in," she asked?

"Hello, I'm Rob," I answered back.

She was quite attractive but what really stood out was the amazing, golden tan that covered her entire body. At least the parts that were visible to me. It was almost perfect. Maybe a little too dark but not insanely so. It was, flawlessly evened out and it appeared totally natural. Jill looked like the picture of health. I entered the residence and we walked into the dining area.

"So, what seems to be the problem with your television, ma'am?"

"Please, call me Jill. For the past week or so, the set has been freezing and we haven't been able to change the channel, even when we go up to the set and try and do it ourselves."

At this point, I really didn't know what the problem was, although, I had a rough idea.

"By the way," she said, "Do you a problem with sun worshipers?"

"Honestly Jill, I don't know what that is."

"How about if I show you," she asked?

At that point, Jill turned to her left and began to walk around the kitchen table. She stopped in front of a free-standing clothing rack and with her back towards me, she took off her housecoat and hung it on the rack. She was completely naked. Jill, then turned around and asked if I had a problem? I could not have had less of a problem and yes, she was tanned completely from head to toe.

"Good," she said, "Would you mind following me outside?"

I would've followed her to the ends of the Earth, but I settled for her backyard. A word about it. Clearly, this space was designed for two purposes; tanning and privacy. The entire area was ringed with Italian or Mediterranean Cypress trees. For those of you who aren't into horticulture, Italian Cypress trees have no branches and grow straight up with a potential height of one hundred and fifteen feet, although, these were closer to twenty. Since this was before drones, there was no way any neighborhood pervert could've found their way in to sneak a peek. Also, there were various tanning stations in the yard which were chez lounge chairs that were perfectly angled to get the perfect sun benefit at specific times. For instance, at 2:12, you would sit at tanning station one and for the next twenty minutes you would achieve "maximum rays," as they put it.

Jill lead me to the patio where the television was mounted on the wall about seven or eight feet in the air, enclosed in a handmade wooden box which was used to protect the tv from the elements. Jill reached for the remote. I didn't want to stare so I turned my gaze to the television. She demonstrated the problem and her earlier description was right on. The set would freeze on a channel for seconds at a time. Maybe the personalities on the screen were staring at her and forgot what they were supposed to do.

From inside the house, another voice rang out. It was a man's voice. It was Jill's son who was coming from the back bedroom and headed towards the kitchen. He was a teenager and fortunately, wearing clothes. Oh yeah, he was well tanned too.

"Jill, I need to get the set off the stand, so I can work on it. I'm going to go to my truck and get my ladder," I said.

What I didn't tell her was that I was going to splash cold water on myself. It was now 105. I knew this because of the thermometer in the backyard. So, I went to my truck and returned with the ladder. It was so hot out that even though I dumped cold water on my chest when I got to my truck, it was completely evaporated when I returned to the house. As I was bringing the ladder back, I noticed that the next-door neighbor was standing next to his mail box and was smiling at me. Clearly, he knew what I saw and was either jealous and/or got a kick out of my reaction.

"Enjoying the scenery," he asked?

"Yes, it's quite lovely," I said back.

"Best neighbors ever," he said before going back to his air-conditioned house.

Even though I never lived next to them, I'd still have to agree. I re-entered the house and went back outside to the porch. The son, whose name was Larry, helped me take down the set from its perch. I then went about the process of figuring out what the problem was. Apparently, I came up with something, but I'd be lying if I said I remembered what it was. Call me crazy but it was difficult to concentrate on the inner workings of a Trinitron when an attractive lady is completely naked in front of you without a care in the world. I wrote down my diagnosis and the parts I'd need, then Larry and me returned the set to the wooden box. At that point, I left.

A week or so went by and the temperature, mercifully, dipped. I went into work that morning and most of the techs had already entered the shop before me. I looked at the big board and saw that the sun worshiper's parts had come in and as the repairman who made the initial visit, I had the right of first refusal on the return. You think I'd turn it down? It was about to get even better.

Business as usual was going on with the various techs either on the phone talking to customers or gathered around the table. One guy was telling a story about a housewife that came onto him. A few technicians were sucked in by the content and gathered around the table and some of the bosses were too. I'd already heard it a few times and the amazing thing was that every time he told it, the story got bigger. In this version, the lady begged the tech to run away with her to Jamaica. In the original telling, she invited him to go bowling. I just rolled my eyes because I was sitting on pocket aces and couldn't wait to lay them down.

"Great story, Sam. How about I tell you what happened to me last week," I started and then I proceeded to tell them the entire sun worshipper story. About midway through, I heard this

"Oh, come on, Rob. That's total b.s.!" said Dougie.

If there's one character trait in myself I'm most proud of, it's my integrity. Lord knows, I absolutely have faults, just ask my wife, she'll list dozens without breaking a sweat. But I don't lie. Obviously, I couldn't let this stand.

"Excuse me," I said, "but are you calling me a liar?"

He knew he had gone too far and tried to back down.

"I'm not calling you a liar," he said back. "I'm just saying that there's no way things went down exactly like you said they did. You're exaggerating."

"Sounds to me like you're calling me a liar," I said right back. "Anyone else here think I'm making this up?"

More than a few of the techs shrugged indicating that they didn't one hundred percent believe me. Good, my plan was working to perfection. The bait was put out, now time to reel in the suckers.

"I have to go back there today on a return and will cover any bet that what I said was a hundred percent true. Hell, I'll even give you four to one odds."

I knew that I had their complete attention now. The entire crew of twenty to thirty techs, two support people, two parts personal employees and three bosses were already mentally spending my money. I knew I had them. The guys were getting their wallets out. Some even ran to a nearby ATM. With this much money involved, we needed to be organized. That's where Lucy came in.

Lucy was a sweet but no nonsense older lady who had worked in a support capacity with the company for years. Everybody trusted her and with good reason. Put it this way, if you gave her money to hold, by the time you came back to get it, not only would the principle be there but she would've added three percent interest. So, yeah, nothing bad could be said about her.

I turned around and asked for her assistance. She got up from her chair and walked over to me. I looked at her and asked her if she was listening? A little embarrassed because of the content, she admitted that she had. I asked her to hold the money and keep track of all the bets by who and how much. She agreed. The money went flying in her direction and she took special care to get the information down accurately. Even the bosses got in on it which was technically against company policy but who doesn't like, what was sure to be, free money?

When all the bets were written down and all the cash was collected, it was placed into a brown folder. Lucy sealed it and placed it in her desk. Now, we needed someone to go with me for two reasons: to help me bring down the television set from the perch and to verify my story. This created a little bit of a debate. Money tends to do that.

We needed someone who had no allegiance to anyone in the shop and someone honest. You might think these two traits naturally go together but not necessarily. After a short debate, the techs looked around and unanimously picked one of the parts support persons, Ira. Ira was perfect. He was from the mid-west and had only been with the company for six weeks, so he had no loyalty to anyone there and was a bit on the naïve side. Even more perfect, he hadn't been privy to the conversation. We called him over.

Dougie, the guy who called b.s. on me, started to talk to Ira. He was a little intense so that and the fact that Ira wasn't used to be singled out, made him a bit hesitant.

"Ira, I need your help on a call. We're leaving in a few minutes. Get ready," I said to him.

Before we left, Dougie spoke to Ira and issued the following instructions: we want you to look for something out of the ordinary and be prepared to tell us exactly what you saw when you get back. He agreed, and we were off but just before exiting, I turned to the crowd and said, "Easy money." All the techs and bosses let out a profound laugh. One that could have been heard for miles. I then told everyone that we'd be back around ten-o'clock, pulled the service order, picked up the parts and left.

About twenty minutes later, we pulled up to the sun worshiper's house. I parked the truck right in front and exited with my partner for the day. While in the driveway, I turned to him and said, "I'm only going to say one thing to you, look only at their eyes, nowhere else. You're going to want to look elsewhere, but don't. Put it this way, look without looking. Understand?" Ira nodded "yes," still not knowing what he was getting himself into.

We continued walking until we reached the front door and knocked. Jill answered and again she was dressed in a house coat. She was very welcoming and as we stepped inside, she turned to me and asked, "Your helper, is he ok?" I replied that he was.

With that, Jill turned around and removed her house coat, placing it on the rack. Ira now had a complete view of a beautifully tanned naked lady and I had just won a lot of money. However, Ira almost lost it, hyperventilating a little. I patted him on the back and gently but firmly reminded him of our earlier talk and how he had given me his word. With that, Ira nodded, and his breathing returned back to normal.

Jill walked us towards the backyard and the TV and I followed. A few steps in, I turned around and noticed that Ira hadn't moved so I had to give him a little shove to get him to snap out of his trance. We preceded to go outside.

Once in the backyard, we went to the TV. What I didn't notice was that there was someone else in the backyard with us. It was Jill's mother who was easily eighty and also naked. I don't want to be cruel but yuck. No one wanted to see this. She looked like a combination of a dog's well used leather chew toy and a worn-out catcher's mitt with eyes. To this day, whenever I think of my grandmother, I still get slightly repulsed. Of course, Jill introduce us and we both had to shake her hand. Frankly, I'm surprised we didn't go blind. Yes, she was tanned.

I placed my tools down on the table that was just under the television. I looked at Ira and said, "Now do you see why I needed your help?" Ira responded by saying "yup." We set up the two-person ladder so that Ira and me could climb up and bring the set down. Don't forget, this was before flat screens and this television easily weighed over one hundred pounds. Ira and I climbed up the ladder, removed the set from its case and brought it down so we could work on it.

I opened my toolbox, got out a Philip's Head screwdriver and removed the back of the set and went about fixing the problem. Just as I was getting started, I heard a female's voice. It was one of Jill's daughters. Jill told her daughter, Kitty, that there were guests in the backyard. Kitty didn't say anything back, she just walked through the rear door and right outside.

Kitty was in her early twenties, blond, perfectly tanned, gorgeous and completely naked except for bikini bottoms. She looked like she stepped right out of a center-fold. Without missing a beat, she said hello to both of us. I thought Ira's eyes were going to pop out of his head. I quickly regained my composure and continued with the repair. I couldn't say the say same for Ira who, despite my earlier warning, was staring at Kitty. Who could blame him? She was sexy as hell and about the same age of him. Ira was definitely heterosexual. I cleared my throat and he got the hint and stopped staring at least for a while.

I had installed the new parts into the set and tested it. It worked fine so I put the backing plate back. Ira had started staring at the daughter again. This had the potential to get ugly, so I whispered to him to snap out of it and if he couldn't, look at grandma who looked like an old catcher's mitt.

By now, I had the back of the set on and it was time to place it back on the stand. After that, all that remained was the paperwork. As I was cleaning up my tools, the front door of the house opened. It was the rest of the sun worshipper family coming home. Al, who I later found out was Jill's husband, called out

"Jill, you home?!

"In back, hon. And we have guests. Kids, take off your tennis clothes and place them in the laundry room," she said back.

What I was expecting was children which would've been really uncomfortable for obvious reasons. Instead, we heard back voices belonging to young adults. Wonderful, I thought.

I turned to Ira and said, "let's get this television up there so we can finish up and leave." We lifted the television up to about waist height and turned around, facing the mount with our backs to Jill and her mother. We began to lift upwards to place the television on the top of the ladder.

Now just a side note about gravity. Objects come down a lot easier than they go back up. Ira had zero upper body strength. He could not lift above his chest. Kids today. Now we had a real problem. We placed the television back on the table. I instructed him to get underneath and place his hands shoulder height. By him lifting with his legs, we were able to get the television almost to the top of the ladder.

To the rescue came Al. He walked up to us and said, "Let me help you out." Did I mention that he was also completely naked? Well, he was so, here were three of us lifting. Two of us with clothes, one without.

The television was now on the stand and I began to re-hook up the cable. Because Ira's back was turned, it wasn't until this moment that he noticed that Al was sans clothes. He was shocked, to say the least. Finally, we got it up and working. The job was done.

I cleaned up the small mess I made and all of us walked into the kitchen where we finished the paperwork and I talked them through the repair and the new parts I installed. It was all very businesslike except for the nudity, of course. As I was winding down the explanation the two young adults who had been playing tennis entered. I'm happy to say that they were female, stunning, tan, completely hairless and most importantly, of legal age. Now the entire family was in front of me and wearing their birthday suits.

Do you know how hard it was facing the entire naked family, no pun intended? All I could think of at that moment was not getting caught sneaking a peak by Al. There were four gorgeous naked women not five feet away. I am a man, you know. Whenever I was about to lose myself, I glanced at grandma and my problem stood down. Ira was still spellbound.

I handed the paperwork to Al who handed it to Jill who signed it and returned it to me. I tore off the bottom sheet and handed it to her. As Jill and Al shook my hand, one of the daughters was walking by and Ira was gawking at her. Unfortunately, Al noticed and was none too pleased.

"What exactly do you think you're looking at, young man," he said in a deep, scary voice to Ira who just stammered. Ira was so intimidated that he almost went into cardiac arrest. This could've gotten real ugly, real fast so I decided to step in. I said

"Ira, it's time to go so that these nice people can get on with their day. Wouldn't you agree?"

He half nodded and gulp which I took to take that, yes, he agreed with me. I turned and grabbed Ira and started to escort him to the front door. We walked briskly because I didn't want to inflame the situation any further. We needed to get the hell out of there now!

I pushed Ira outside and he headed straight to the truck. Just as I was about to follow him, Al asked for a word with me. I walked back inside and told Ira to keep going. I looked at Jill and Al directly in their eyes, which I think they appreciated. Al turned to me and said,

"I'm sorry about going off on your partner. It's not like we don't get that reaction from time to time."

I responded by saying, "He should have not stared, no exception." But really, come on. They were naked! Jill and Al both smiled and closed the door. I left and headed to my truck

Ira was in the passenger seat and just as I opened the door and headed into the cabin he blurted out, "I'm so sorry! I couldn't help myself."

"I think it's best that from now on we leave you back at the shop where it's a little more safe," I said back.

Ira didn't put up an argument. I continued, "Also, do me a favor? Clean yourself up. You've have spit all over your shirt." As Ira tried to clean himself up as best as he could, I drove us back. Finally, the payoff.

We got back to headquarters around 9:45. Remembering that I said we would be back about 10:00? The parking lot was packed. Everybody was dying to know whether I was full of crap or not. I couldn't wait. The both of us got out of the truck and headed inside where I was greeted by Dougie, the guy who kicked this whole thing off.

"Look who's here, Mr. Integrity, or as I like to call him, the guy who's going to make my car payment this month," he said. Keep digging, Dougie. Keep digging.

I walked through the main area and headed to the back where at least twenty techs where sitting. They were soon joined by three bosses. They were all waiting for me to say something or break down and admit I was wrong. I just walked over to the counter where the phone bank was. I placed the work order on the table and turned around. The entire group stared at me. I just stood there. I was in no rush. Again, I knew I was sitting on a winning hand and decided to milk it a little bit.

Ira entered shortly thereafter looking a little paler than the last time anyone had seen him. It was the moment of truth. Gene, one of the bosses, whistled to shut everyone up. Then he turned to Ira.

"What happened at the call? Were the customers naked or did Rob make the whole thing up?"

You could've heard a pin drop. Finally, Ira took a deep breath and said, "Yes, they were naked. The whole family including the grandma. I think I may need therapy." There are some things you just can't unsee.

Everybody winced. Trust me, whatever they envisioned was nowhere near as bad as the real thing. The silence was broken by another wise guy who didn't believe me.

"They're in this together, he told you what to say!" the joker said.

I looked directly at this idiot and said, "I can honestly say that the only thing I said to Ira was to look at the customer in the eye." Then I turned to Ira and said, "We almost had a problem too, didn't we?"

Maybe it was wrong to embarrass him, especially when it was unnecessary. I just wanted to prove to the guys that I wasn't making it up and I thought the added detail of Ira pretty much wetting himself would help.

He practically sputtered out, "I didn't know what to expect! I'm not a service tech. I work in the shop. I was just there to help fix a TV. I didn't know I was going to be looking at a whole family of nudists!"

This clinched it. Ira was clearly telling the truth. No one could've acted this out and convinced this crew. I told Ira to take it easy and that he wouldn't have to go out again if he didn't want to. I then offered to buy him lunch. With my soon to be windfall, I could afford to be generous.

Even though I was proven right, the guys still wanted all the details and then some that I could supply. It was like a police interrogation. They wanted to know what the women looked like. Were they hot? Did they come on to me? It was endless. I didn't blame there. If I was them, I'd probably ask too. By now, the phones were ringing. People out in the field wanted to know what happened. I got a kick out of hearing their versions being relayed back

Now, the payoff. Lucy entered carrying the envelope that contained who bet what and how much, plus the cash. She actually read it out loud. I don't know why she did this since the money was already collected but I sure did appreciate it. After she was done, she walked over and handed me the envelope. It was more than a thousand dollars.

Lucy, felt like twisting the knife in their backs even more which I absolutely loved. She said that from now on when Rob says something, they should believe it. The other techs came back at her and me with weak comebacks. They had nothing. I was proven right and had the moolah to prove it. From that day on, a new phrase in the shop was born, Lucy's word is law.

One of the techs asked if I would copy the address and pin it on the board. The look that came from Lucy's face was not a good one.

It was a special moment, one that will last in my mind forever. It was not the money. Just the truth. Okay, maybe it was a little bit the money.

That afternoon, Ira and me had steak at the Pacific Dining Car. Even though I've had superior cuts of meat in the past, that steak was the best I ever had. Easy money sure does go down easy.

Story 19: They're Always Hungry (Late '80's)

Here's a story I tell my customers on an almost daily basis. But before I do, ask yourself this question; how far would your kids go to get food?

I was called out on a job to repair a refrigerator. According to the work order, the fridge had a cooling issue. Pretty straight forward, or so I thought. As I drove up to the house I noticed toys all over the front yard, driveway and porch. We're talking action figures, bikes, footballs, bats, toy guns, cleats, balls, etc. It was like one big playground. Being the smart guy, I am, I was able to deduce that this customer had kids. Lots of kids and what I later found out, uncontrollable kids.

I rang the bell and the lady of the house answered the door. If I had to guess, I'd say she was probably in her late thirties, but she looked at least ten years older and tired. This woman needed a nap like nobody's business. She wasn't wearing any make-up, probably hadn't washed her hair in days and I'm pretty sure she had peanut butter on her neck but as I was about to find out, that was the least of her problems. Honestly, it looked like she was suffering from PTSD.

"Hi, thanks for coming. I'm Stephanie."

"I'm Rob, what's the problem with the refrigerator?"

I swear, I thought she was going to pass out on me as she lead me into the house. Now, I don't know if it was her decorating theme but everywhere the eye could see were kids' clothes, sports equipment, backpacks, video game headsets, controllers, juice boxes, etc. Seriously, it was like a Toys R Us and an OshKosh store had blown up and nobody bothered to clean it up.

Now, having kids myself, I know they can be messy and it wasn't like I expected customers to make their places of residence model home perfect for me but at some point, hygiene has to enter the equation.

I mean, why would there be shirts and pants on the kitchen floor? It's understandable in somebody's bedroom or even their bathroom but the kitchen? Somehow societal norms had broken down big time. Yup, his place was way more than "lived in."

As I walked into the kitchen area, the place stunk so bad it was beyond overwhelming. Plus, the amount of dirt and filth could not be measured by any rational thought. Put it this way, the floor was so sticky I was afraid to put my toolbox on the floor because I thought I'd never be able to pry it off. How families could live like this is beyond me.

I looked at the refrigerator and what I saw was indescribable. Now, it's always best to have the customer explain what the problem is just so that there's no misunderstandings later on down the line.

"Ma'am—"

"Stephanie."

"Stephanie, what exactly is the problem with the refrigerator?" I asked.

"There seems to be a cooling problem."

"Could you please be more specific?"

"Well, maybe not a cooling problem, per se, but the food isn't staying cold inside the fridge long enough."

My head was starting to swim. "The food isn't staying cold inside the fridge long enough?" What did that even mean? She continued:

"I have four young children, all boys, ranging in age from seven to fifteen. Every Saturday we all go to the Costco Warehouse to do our grocery shopping…"

Now I was the one fighting to stay interested, but she went on:

"And we end up spending $300 plus per visit. That's a lot of money…"

I nodded still wondering what any of this had to do with me.

"But all the food is gone by the following Tuesday. How is that possible? How can all that food be gone so quickly?"

Now let's think about this; young boys do eat. They eat a lot and all day and night long. They're boys and some of them, clearly, are going through puberty. Eating is the closest thing they have to having a job.

"Ma'am—"

"Stephanie."

"Stephanie, I'm not really sure why I'm here…"

At this point, it wouldn't have surprised me if she said something along the lines of "Why are you here? Why am I here? Why is any of here? Wasn't it Nietzsche who once said…" Actually, that would've made a lot more sense than what happened next.

"Let me show you," she said.

She took me to the appliance and showed me the problem. The door handles were cut by a saw in two places. The cuts were horizontal to the ground, waist high and the door on the left side was damaged. I looked at the lady, sorry, Stephanie and asked her what happened.

"O.K., I put a bike chain around the door handles and locked it so that the refrigerator doors couldn't be opened. But Tyler, he's my oldest, went to the garage and picked up his father's power saw and cut the door handles off. He's always been good with his hands. Takes after his father..." "Yeah, he's a real craftsman," I thought to myself.

I looked closer at the refrigerator and saw that crazy lady was telling the truth. If anything, the saw cuts were a lot worse than they seemed because they appeared to get deeper on each pass. Not only were the door handles destroyed, the ice and water dispenser and the left side of the freezer door were so damaged that they could not be repaired. Here's where it got even weirder. Stephanie looked at me and said,

"I'm just so glad I'm covered through my house warranty."

I didn't know if I should bust out laughing or ask her if she was delusional. On what planet would a service warranty cover a teenage lunatic carving up an appliance like it was a character in a "Texas Chainsaw Massacre" movie? Suffice it to say, we weren't talking about normal wear and tear here. The nerve of some people. But, looking around the house I can understand to a point why she made that comment. Hell, if I lived there I'd say something crazy to get a new appliance too.

I had to cover myself somehow, so I took a professional approach to this comedy act. I called my office and had them look up all the parts I needed and the prices. The handles priced out to be $92.00 each. The front panel was around $60.00, and the freezer door priced out to be $1020.00. The total parts with tax came to over $1300.00. Then the labor to install the parts would have come to another $600.00. The total repair came to $1,900-2,000. I'm not really a math person but doing this addition sure was fun.

Stephanie looked over my shoulder and saw the prices that I was quoted and was likely doing her own calculations although with her, she could've been thinking about her past lives. Now, I had to spring the bad news to her. Finally, some fun.

"Stephanie, I'm afraid I have some bad news. Since your children damaged the unit with a power saw, the warranty is void..."

"I don't understand," she said.

"The warranty is no good. If you want me to do the repair, I can—"

"Great!" she said as she smiled.

"But it'll run you around $2,000."

Suddenly, things weren't so great anymore and her smile disappeared completely. I'd be lying if I said I knew what she was thinking because she did not move. Not a muscle. Frozen to the floor. I was waiting for some kind of reaction. Anything, even yelling would have been something. On the plus side, I could see that she was breathing. Maybe she was finally getting the sleep she so desperately needed.

So, what to do? I left the house. She was still standing motionless as I exited. Thank God, my feet didn't stick to the floor. That would be bad.

Story 20: How Not To Fix Your Car (2007)

Have you ever had the chance to lend your opinion on a subject you know well and the person you are trying to help declines your advice? Well, on this occasion, I tried to help and what happened was right out a movie.

Occasionally, I take an automotive class on Saturdays. The local college offers several throughout the week but only a few on the weekends. One Saturday mid-morning, as I was on my way to the project car I was assigned, I saw four guys, in their twenties, looking into a S10 Chevy truck. While I was trying to mind my own business, it was hard not to overhear their conversation. It was mostly about girls they were working on, what great athletes they were in high-school, etc. Their conversation was littered with a lot of "bro"s and "dude"s. Put it this way, the b.s. was flying out hard and thick.

I started working on my car. The project I was given wasn't too difficult, so I was alone. But still, I could not help from laughing on the inside at the four guys. Why was I laughing? Because it was blatantly obvious that they had no idea what they were doing. Hey, that's fine. This was a class and the whole idea is to learn something, but these guys were so cocky in their ignorance that it was beyond ridiculous. After about twenty minutes or so, I just couldn't take it anymore, so I walked over to them and asked what they were trying to do? All four of them stopped talking, looked at me with blank expressions and wanted to know why I was intruding on their truck?

"Thanks, we appreciate it but it's under control, bro. If we need help, we'll be sure to ask for it," said Guy #1.

"Okay. No problem," I said back. Yes, I just got brushed off but at least they were polite about it. I walked back to my project car and continued working. I began removing the old serpentine belt. Basically, a serpentine belt drives other devices on an engine like the alternator, water pump and air conditioner.

Just as I was about to remove the old belt, one of the guys walked over to me and asked if I could show them how to set the rack under their car so they could lift it up? What the heck, they were polite, and I was on pace to finish ahead of schedule so I put down my tools and walked them through what they needed to do. With their truck now in the air, I went back to complete my project.

As I was trying to install the new belt, which was an exact replacement, I was having trouble threading it in. This belt had an attitude. There's a reason why they call them "serpentines," it's because they are more than capable of sliding all over the place. Trust me, on this, it comes from years of experience.

By now, my neighbors were under the truck, looking up and talking. What they were saying did not make sense. I continued installing the new belt even though that bastard was fighting me every step of the way. Eventually, I finished up and saw that the four guys started taking the transmission fluid out of the lower transmission pan. It was a mess, to say the least. Transmission fluid, which is red, spilled all over the floor and covered their clothes. It was like the prom scene in the original "Carrie" except these guys had longer hair. I readied my project for start-up testing.

Another one of my classmates, Al, not one of the truck guys, walked over and asked how I was doing? We talked for a while, mostly about the cars we were working on and he sympathized with me about my battle with the belt. Threading those bastards is easy in theory but not always in practice. That's why your local rip-off artists, I mean mechanics, charge so much to replace them. After a few moments, Al looked over at the circus that was the truck guys and asked what the hell was going on over there? My response: "They're rookies."

We continued watching the four stooges as they lowered their truck to the ground. What these geniuses forgot to do was pick up the tools they dropped on the ground including several hand wrenches, rags, and who knows what else and that were now all covered in red transmission fluid.

Al and I stood at my car for at least ten minutes watching this comedy that was unfolding right before our very eyes. All four of the guys were talking about how much transmission fluid they needed to put back into the truck. One of them looked at me and asked if I could answer a question? I'm a nice guy and I wanted to get a closer look at the insanity, so I said "sure."

Their question was, "How much transmission fluid do you need to replace back into the truck?" According to the paper work they obtained, the total fluid capacity of the truck was twelve quarts. I told them that since they could only estimate how much fluid drained from the truck, they needed to add at least four quarts and then start it up, let it run for a few minutes and then check the dip stick to see the level. After that, add one quart at a time as needed until the transmission was full. One of the bros said I was wrong and I didn't know what I was talking about. Clearly, my help was not needed any more.

I walked back, standing in front of a workbench just in front of my car. Al was still there and looked at me with a big smirk. We both were watching the rookies.

Against my advice, the rookies added all twelve quarts to the S10 truck. One of them said it was time to start the engine and test the fluid level. Now, when you add transmission fluid to a car or truck, you need to pull out the transmission dip stick and add the replacement fluid through the tube on which the dip stick is mounted. What these geniuses forgot to do was reinstall the dip stick which was laying on the work bench, right in front of their truck.

Al and me yelled "Wait!" at the exact same time, which was darn nice of us, if I do say so myself. Was this courtesy appreciated? Nope. One of the rookies turned around and waved his hand dismissively.

"We got it, bro," he said.

The instructor heard our yelling and looked over in our direction with concern. Because Al and me knew what was about to happen, we walked over to the rear of my car and ducked down behind the side windshield. One of the rookies was inside the truck, the other three were standing in front of it. He started the engine.

A quick note: inside the transmission is a pump. The pump pumps fluids throughout the transmission to the various lines. While this is happening, the pump produces a great amount of pressure. Exactly how much depends on the make and manufacturer. What the rookies didn't realize is that the uncapped fluid needed to go someplace especially when the transmission was over filled.

The truck was started and mere seconds later, a red stream of transmission fluid shot out of the dip tube, into the air on an upward trajectory right onto the building's windows. It was like a scene in a movie when someone strikes oil. Make that a gusher. It continued as long as the engine was running, which it still was.

The three rookies standing in front of the truck turned as the fluid shot right by them. The red liquid hit the window and splattered in an oval type pattern. When all was said and done, the fluid sprayed an area about fifty plus feet in both directions, thirty to forty feet upward and covering the car on the other side of the truck, all the benches and just about everything in its spray path. Most of our car was doused. If you didn't know any better and just walked in, you'd swear you were entering a slaughter house or murder scene.

Finally, the truck's engine stopped, and the four rookies just stood there, slack jawed, covered in sticky, red, transmission fluid. Those "Bon Jovi" t-shirts and torn jeans were completely ruined. A dead silence came over the shop.

The instructor walked over behind the truck, just outside the spray pattern. Most of the students inside the shop started to walk in the direction of the accident, not that I blamed them. How often did you get to see someone screw up so big time?

All four rookies were standing in front of the instructor, awaiting their punishment. Was he going to scream or slap them like Patton? I had to see this, so I got up closer. I really wanted to start laughing even though I knew it may have been somewhat tacky. But, sometimes you just can't control myself, so I started cracking up, followed by Al and the rest of the class. I'm only human.

Several minutes went by and the laughing finally stopped. All throughout this, the instructor didn't move a muscle. He just stared directly into their eyes like the drill sergeant in "Full Metal Jacket." His slow burn was something to see. Smoke may, very well, have come out of his ears.

After, what seemed like an eternity, but was probably a minute, the instructor turned on his heels and walked slowly across the shop and into the bathroom. From inside the bathroom, even though it was muffled, I heard some of the foulest cursing ever known to man. I don't know if some of the acts he described were even physically possible, even for Olympic gymnasts. After his rant subsided, I heard what sounded like someone punching the metal stalls. Finally, there was the sound of a door opening and a funny squeaking noise. It was a wash bucket on wheels.

Emerging from the bathroom, came the instructor. He was pushing a wash bucket with a long handle mop and under the other arm were a bunch of rags. He wheeled slowly over to the rookies. So slow, it looked he was truly savoring the moment. He did not say a word as he continued to approach them.

The whole class was watching, waiting to see what he was going to do. I was hoping yelling would be involved but I was wrong. I guess he had gotten it out of his system in the bathroom. The instructor raised his arm and dropped the rags. With the other hand he released the mop handle. A bunch of the other students had grabbed mops and buckets to help out, but the instructor wasn't having it. He silently waved them off and I guess they heard the earlier tirade because they backed off immediately. After a moment of complete silence, the instructor turned around, looked at the assembled multitudes and said, "Class dismissed."

Turning to his right, he walked to the large bay doors and closed them. The rest of the students began exit. Of course, I lingered in front of instructor's office. I paid good money for this class, you really think I was going to miss this? The rookies did not move one step. For some reason, maybe because I was the only one there who, maybe, didn't want to kill them, all four looked at me. Perhaps they were looking for some advice or sympathy. So, I raised up my arms, turned my hands outward with my thumbs pointed towards me as if to say, "bye and have fun" and I left.

Sometimes it does pay to listen to those who are older and more experienced, bro.

Story 21: The Bad Penny (2016)

Why is it on Monday's that stupid things always seem to happen? On this particular Monday, just short of lunch time, I had a service call to repair a washer dryer combo unit. We call them "stack" units.

The address on the order read that it was located in a mobile home park. There was also a space number. That also means that was going to be a really tight fit once inside. The order said that the dryer was not heating, and it possibly needed two people to assist. The address was located across town and I figured that from where I was at, it would take me about thirty minutes or so depending on traffic and traffic lights, to get there.

By the time I did get there, I noticed a directory on the left side. I stopped the truck to see where I was going. For those that don't know, mobile home parks are usually not laid out in any form of consistency. There was no pattern to follow. Space number nine could be right next to number thirty-two which could be across from sixteen.

The park itself was somewhat rundown and most likely a housing assistance complex. Not that I knew that for a fact but after you've been doing this for a while, you get a sense of things.

I parked the truck in front of the designated mobile home. I grabbed my tools from the back of the truck and headed to the front door. From the outside, the home was old and dirty. I knocked on the door and a few seconds later, I heard footsteps walking through the residence.
A man in his thirties opened the door. He looked me up and down with a stupid look on his face.

"What do you want," he said?

"I'm here to repair your dryer. Someone here called for service," I said back.

The man said he would be back in a moment. I could hear him talking to someone on a cell phone. He was talking in an Eastern-European language that I did not understand. The door opened again, and he said that his brother was the one who had called for service and that I had the wrong address. Oh, joy.

The man gave me the correct address and I wrote it down. I wished him a good day and left. I entered the truck and looked up the new address. It was about two miles from where I started from. I was going to travel back to where I was and now lunch time was about to start. Terrific!

I drove away from the mobile complex, heading to the new address. On the way, I stopped at a drive-through fast food place and ordered lunch. There was no way I was going to have time to stop for lunch. Welcome to my day. As I was eating the last, disfigured French Fry, I overheard, over the radio, that something had happened on the freeway and traffic was being diverted to surface streets. So, instead of it taking me fifteen minutes to travel two miles, I was now looking at a half-hour easy.

By the time I had arrived at my stop at the apartment complex, I finally caught a break. There was a parking spot right next to the apartment. It takes so little to make us techs happy; a straight-forward task, pleasant customers and a decent parking space.

After parking, I knocked on the door and a young lady answered the door. I introduced myself and informed her that I was there to service the dryer. She just looked at me with a confused face, then she did her best to converse with me in broken English. Most of the words she was trying to say, I barely understood. Although, somehow, after her repeating it many times and even some good old-fashioned pantomime, I was able to figure out that her brother had taken the combo unit to yet another address. Miss. Sarajevo was nice enough to write the new address down on a piece of paper and for those of you keeping score, this was address number three for the same job. I thanked her for her time and walked back to the truck.

Once inside the truck, I used my cell phone and called the brother. A few rings later, someone with a male voice answered.

"Yeah, what do you want," he barked out through the speaker?!

"I'm the repair guy. I just left your sister's apartment and she gave me your phone number. So, where's the dryer" I asked?

Judging by the noises I heard in the background, this guy was on the freeway. Lots of honking and some muffled obscenities. Then the brother started yelling at me.

"You want to know where the dryer is?! I'll tell you where it is! I was transporting it in the back of my truck and somehow the straps broke and the it fell off the side of my truck. It damaged the cab and the right-side bed wall, on the outside…"

What? The rant got even weirder as he continued.

"Now, the washer-dryer is in pieces all over the freeway and you're going to come out here and put it back together, then put it back on my truck. I'm going to sue your company for the damage to my truck and you are going to fix it too!"

He was the reason why the freeway was shut down! This guy was out of his freaking mind. I said back,

"Really! I need to know where you get the idea that you can sue for the damages when it was your screw-up that caused this problem and because of your stupidity, you just shut down a major freeway. Good job!"

I continued,

"I am going to cancel your order. I've spent way too much time chasing down your washer-dryer and I'm not willing to wait on the freeway that you just clogged up and do anything for you. Buddy, you're on your own. Enjoy this moment, because it's all you, you moron."

Now, about two weeks later, I received a call to go fix a washer-dryer in a city way out in the county. The little city is a great place to visit and I like going there to do service calls. Mostly, because, the routing office can't locate tech's. Too many mountains. It's nice to be off the leash every once in a while.

As I pulled up to the house, something just did not feel right. I looked a little closer at the address and there was nothing I could recognize. Although, the phone number on the work order looked somewhat familiar, so I fished around in the trash bag I kept under the dash and pulled out the paper that the young lady from the first part of the story gave me.

I walked up to the front door and knocked. A man opened the door. He was standing there in a white tee shirt that dragged to his knees and short pants. He greeted me and asked me to enter the house. It was filthy. I think the paint on the walls where from the 1950's and probably lead based. The rest of the living room needed a good bath or an insurance fire. We walked from the front door and exited into the garage.

Inside the garage was old beat up Ford Ranchero that had been neglected for years. Spread out in front of me were the pieces of a washer-dryer. The side panels were standing off to the side. The dryer's lower drum was crushed beyond repair. The electrical panels were scrapped up and I think there was a tire track on it.

I put my tools down and started to walk around. I wanted to find the model and serial number for this unit. I just looked at the guy and ask him what happened. He was evasive as to why or what happened to the washer-dryer. I asked him, "Who took this apart," again, he said he didn't know.

I found the panel with the model and serial number on it. It matched the same number on my order. Well that's a lucky break. I looked at the guy and asked him if he could open the garage door, so I could get a little more light in the room? He walked over and pressed the button. As the light entered the garage, I could see more of the damage. I stepped more to the front and closer to my toolbox and asked him for the last time. "What happened here?"

Still sticking to his ignorance, he said, "I don't know."

I was now standing toward the front door and he was standing towards the back. I looked at him and said that I have a way of finding out the truth. Just ask my kids. Under my interrogations, they've confessed to things I never even asked them about.

His eyes opened up widely and glared at me, so I pulled out my cell phone and dialed the same number that I used two weeks ago. The cell-phone in the guy's pocket started to ring.
I looked at him and said, "Aren't you going to answer that?"

Busted! I caught him lying straight to my face.

"You were the guy who dropped the washer-dryer off the side of your truck on the freeway, weren't you?"

The guy's face just dropped in shock. As if I didn't have enough evidence already, I pointed towards the Ranchero and the damaged side quarter panel. He knew that I caught him and suddenly he lost all ability to speak English and started yelling at me in a language that sounded like it was from an 1980's action movie.

"Dude, I don't know what you're saying, but I'm going to bill you for $200 dollars for this call."

I picked up my tools and walked away from the damaged washer-dryer for, what I thought, was the last time. But get this.

A few weeks later I had a scheduled service call on a dryer. The order said that the dryer was not heating. That's ok, all the orders say that. I needed to check it out and see what going on.

The residence was located at the north end of the county. Nowhere near where the previous call had been. This house was neat and well taken care of. The yard needed to be cut and a few things needed attending but overall, a clean place.

I knocked on the door and a nice lady answered. She advised me that the dryer was in the back and asked me to enter through the garage door. I turned around and complied.

The door opened and to my honest delight, the garage was clean. No oil stains, clutter or spider-webs. Again, it takes so little to make us techs happy.

We walked through the garage and exited to the backyard. We turned to the right and under a patio cover were several large boxes and a few smaller boxes with parts of a washer-dryer. The two drums were sitting on a picnic table with assorted parts spread out.

I asked her what I was looking at and she said that it was the washer-dryer. Turns out she had bought it on craigslist for only $200 and all it needed was to be put back together. I had a sick feeling in the pit of my stomach.

"Ma'am, can you describe the person you bought this from," I asked?

"I got it from a man a few towns over. I didn't get a great look at him, to be honest. He seemed to be Slavic. Can you believe he only wanted $200? What a bargain."

I slowly walked around the boxes, looking for the panel with the model number and serial number on it. In one of the last boxes I found it. Yup, it was the same unit. This thing just kept coming back into my life like a bad penny. Even if I could re-assemble this thing, it was never going to work.

I started to sigh a little and sat down at one of the tables. I asked the lady to sit down so I could explain the story. When I was finished, she was a little mad that she was taken for $200 for a piece of junk, the exact amount I had charged him for the service call. I wished her good luck and told her to go buy a new unit.

At least, I was pretty sure that I'd never see this thing again and I haven't…at least up until now.

Story 22: Starving For Food or "The Sting" (2000)

In the past few years, my schedule has been pretty packed for a variety of reasons ranging from the company laying off other techs, more generous warranty terms and frankly, things not being as well made as they used to be. As a result of this, often times I do not have time to take thirty minutes for lunch like I'm supposed to. I guess that's why they invented fast food. During one time when I frequented one of those establishments, something interesting happened and I got to fulfill one of my smaller life dreams of being a detective.

It was one of those days when I actually had time to sit down and take a thirty-minute lunch break. Of course, I wasn't that hungry. I think they call that "irony." But, I did have a book that I wanted to finally finish. I'd been reading it for some time, but something always got in the way of me getting to the end. Not today. On that day I had time to take a sit-down lunch break like a regular human-being. This hadn't happened in weeks. I planned to make the most of it but what's that saying, you make plans and God laughs?

So, I had just finished off my morning by replacing a condenser. It was around eleven thirty and I knew there was a new fast food place around the corner. Being new, this bode well because there was a better than even chance that it was somewhat clean, not that it really mattered because all I wanted was a drink and a quiet place to read. That's my version of a vacation.

I parked my truck in the quarter full restaurant parking lot, right next to a Volkswagen Bug. I exited the truck and walked inside to see that a customer was yelling at, what appeared to be, the restaurant manager. I only heard the tail end of it, but the gist seemed to be that there were items missing from the customer's order. The customer was understandably irate, but the manager's reaction surprised me. Basically, I got the feeling that she was being overly apologetic and resigned like yes, it shouldn't have happened, and they'll make it right but it's just something that she's been having to deal with. Maybe she had a problem with her employees stealing. Of course, I was just speculating.

Finally, it was my turn and the apple cheeked teenager manning the cash register asked for my order.

"I'll just have a large drink today," I said.

Before handing me the cup she explained that for only ten cents more, I could have the "Thirst Crusher" which offered an additional sixteen ounces of sugar water, I mean soda. Hey, I know a bargain when I see it and after I was done, I could always use the cup as an above ground pool.

After being handed the bucket, I mean cup, I walked over to the soda dispensing machine and pored my drink. As I was finishing up, I watched the restaurant manager hand a food tray with a few hamburgers on it to a customer. The customer took the tray, thanked the manager and walked off.

I made my way to a booth in the back which I hoped would be quiet. I placed my gallon of liquid on the table and sat down facing the seating area and began to read my book. It was a Tom Clancy novel. I had started it about a month ago and was really enjoying it, but life's myriad of distractions kept getting in the way. Clancy's novels have a lot of characters, military hardware, foreign names and locations. You do have to concentrate somewhat to read it. After the fifty interruptions by my youngest and rereading the same sentence five times, I figured my best shot at finishing this sucker laid outside the home. Now, time to see what happened to that submarine.

As I was digging in, I looked up and noticed a person parking a bicycle in the parking lot. I could only see the back of the guy, but he looked raggedy. His shoes were mismatched and torn as were his jeans but not in a fashionable way. He didn't even lock up his bike. He just parked it. Maybe, because it was older, he figured no one would steal it.

The guy entered the restaurant and I got a better look at him. He was in his late forties and was unshaven and looked like he hadn't slept in days. He looked like he was hooked on meth. Immediately, upon walking through the doors, he adjusted his overcoat, which was down to his knees. After that, he fixed up or patted down his hair using his hands, not a comb. We all want to look as presentable as we can, and this guy was no exception. He sat down in a four-person booth towards the back.

I continued reading my book and actually got through four pages, the most I had been able to in a week. Just as it was getting good, I looked up and saw that the man had stood up. On the other side of the restaurant, a young mother and her three kids walked over to a booth and began to position her kids into the seats. She took the piece of plastic with a number on it, so the server knows where to deliver the food and placed it in the middle of the table. Then she walked over to the restrooms. Maybe because I was reading a novel about espionage, I was naturally suspicious, but I thought it best to watch the man to see what, if anything, he was up to. My instincts proved to be right on.

The man turned to his right and watched the lady go through and enter the bathroom. An employee walked around from behind the kitchen, placed the food tray on the table, took the piece of plastic and walked off. The tray had three kid's meals and a pile of fries with a large burger. The kids were confused and were waiting for their mother to come back and divvy it up.

The man walked over to the kids table and started talking to them. Nothing he said was objectionable, but he shouldn't have been doing it. He pulled some toys out from the bags of food and handed them to the kids. The kids focus was now on the toys and not their lunch. The man took advantage of this and grabbed the large burger and put it in his jacket. Classic misdirection. The homeless magician then walked out of the restaurant and rode off on his bike.

The mom came back from the bathroom area and sat down at the table. I could only see her reactions from the back. She reached into all three of the bags, removed the food and placed it in front of the kids, one at a time. As she finished with the kid's food she began looking around on the table looking for her large burger. Guess what, she couldn't find it.

At that moment, an employee was walking around with a tray of food. The mom raised her hand and motioned to have her come over, which the employee did. From where I was sitting, I could not hear the conversation, but it was probably about the missing burger. The employee walked off into the kitchen and soon after the manager came over to the table. They talked for a minute and the manager walked off.

Several minutes later, an employee exited the kitchen area with a large burger on a tray to replace the one that had gone missing. The mother said, "thank you" and went upon the business of eating her lunch. I was more sad than angry because that man had to be awfully hungry to have to resort to stealing a mother of three's food.

I continued reading my book and got through a few more pages and before I knew it, the man was back again. This time he walked to the rear of the restaurant and entered the bathroom. A few minutes later, he came out and sat down three tables from me.

A customer walked around the corner and placed his order number and glass on a table. The man was clocking him and when the customer left, the man immediately pounced and sat down at the table and when the food was delivered, he took it and moved to another location where he dug in.

When the customer returned from the lavatory, he sat down and waited for his order. Because, the plastic with the number wasn't taken away by the wait staff, the customer just sat there awhile waiting for food that was never going to come. I've got to give the man a little bit of credit here because it wouldn't have occurred to me to deliberately seek out the tables where the employees failed to do their jobs and remove the marker. It definitely bought the man some time.

By now, I couldn't concentrate on my book anymore. Why read about covert-ops when one was happening right in front of me? Finally, the customer went to the counter with the plastic and asked how much longer it was going to be? When the worker said that the food had been delivered a few minutes ago, the customer said that it hadn't. After a few minutes of back and forth, the manager appeared carrying a tray of food, handed it to the customer along with her apologies and went back to the kitchen.

The man finished up his second burger and left the table as any normal customer would, threw out his trash and left. I did notice that this time he didn't take his bike. At this point I had to do something. Not that it wasn't hilarious, but the guy had two large burgers and showed no signs of slowing down. It wasn't about the man being hungry, he was just stealing. If it continued, the manager could lose her job, so I corralled one of the employees and asked if the manager would come see me at my table. He nodded his head "yes," indicating that he would ask her.

A minute or two later, the manager sat down at my table. She looked extremely harried.

"Can I help you," she asked?

"No," I replied, "but I think I can help you."

This definitely caught her interest, so I continued.

"I haven't been here long but in the short time that I have, I noticed that a lot of food has gone missing. Has this been a long-term problem?"

"Yes," she sighed. "I've had corporate breathing down my neck about the losses. Do you know what's been happening?"

"I might and if you want to know too, here's what I suggest. Go back to your office and put on different clothes. Anything that doesn't identify you as someone who works here. Then go to the front counter, like you were a normal customer, and place an order. Make sure none of your employees talks to you as if you were anything but. Then sit down at a table in the back with one of those order markers and after a few minutes, before the food comes, leave."

She nodded in agreement. I like to think that she so readily agreed to my plan because I was so convincing but honestly, she was so desperate that if I suggested she dressed like a chicken and clucked for fifteen minutes, she would've given that a shot too. Nevertheless, she exited my table to prepare for our little sting.

A little while later, she came out wearing a sports jacket and her let hair down to her shoulders. She definitely changed her appearance significantly. Not that it mattered, but she was quite attractive. She placed her order, sat down at a table and left. By now the man had re-entered the restaurant and the customers he had previously stolen from, were finishing up their meals.

A server put the manager's food down at her table. I looked in the direction of where the manager was and moved my head in the direction of the man as if to say, keep an eye on him. She slightly nodded at me. A few minutes went by, but the man didn't take her food.

After five minutes had elapsed and the man hadn't taken our bait, things were looking pretty bad for me. Was he onto us or just quitting while he was ahead? Turns out neither.

In the parking lot was a car full of high school kids and when it parked, they all tumbled out and made a bee-line into the restaurant. There had to be at least twelve of them. As kids go, they were pretty noisy. The man at the table made a note of all of this. By now, I think I knew what was going on. The man hadn't quit while he was ahead, he was working on bigger prey. Why make off with a salad when there were twelve hungry teenagers who aren't the most observant people on the planet?

I turned to the manager and told her that no matter how busy, or hectic things get, just keep an eye on the borderline homeless man. She indicated that she would. By now, most of the kids were finishing up their orders. Yes, they were loud and didn't have the best manners but who does at that age? They took their markers and looked for a place to sit. Since it was now about twelve thirty, the place was filling up and the teenagers were forced to go to the outside tables. Of course, this made it a lot easier for the man to make off like the bandit he was. Hell, he was already outside.

A couple of employees began to walk out from the kitchen, each carrying multiple trays of food and delivered the food outside to the appropriate tables, then walked off. Most of the kids hadn't sat down yet. They were at the soda machine, restroom, etc.

The man got up from the table he was sitting at, turned to his left and then right. He then went outside. I told the manager again to watch him. What she saw was the man getting on his bike and riding past all the outside tables while scooping up food from each one of them! By the time he had finished his pass, I counted that he made off with six burgers, a couple of scoops of fries and a drink. The manager was stunned but not as stunned as I was about to be.

Like a bat out of hell, she ran out of the place and flung a burger at the guy's bike. Amazingly, it caught in his back wheel which slowed him down just enough for her to pounce. She must've grown up with brothers because she could definitely handle herself. She ran up to him, snatched him off his bike and threw on the ground. By the time he knew what was going on, it was too late. This 5'2" petite lady was beating the crap out of him. Trust me when I say, that what she said below was the clean version because the f-bombs were flying out of her mouth like crazy.

"You think you're going to steal from me, you piece of crap?! You think I'm going to lose my job over this?! You've been robbing me for over three months! If you wanted help, you should've asked!.."

Each sentence she got out was punctuated with a punch to the guy's mid-section. I'm surprised that he didn't barf up what he had stolen.

The teenagers thought that this was the funniest thing they had ever seen and instantly started recording the beat down on their cell-phones. It might even still be on youtube. Unfortunately for me, I had to get back to work but no offense to Mr. Tom Clancy, this was more entertaining than any novel. I got up, threw out my cup and exited.

On my way out, I passed the manager who was still pounding on the guy. I would've thought that for sure, she had no idea that I was leaving except that between punches she turned to me and said, "Thanks so much for your help. Come back anytime. Your next meal's on me." Then she smacked him again.

As I made my way to my truck, a police car pulled up with the siren and everything. The officers got out of their cruiser and were a little slow to react. Probably because they were shocked by her tenacity. After a moment or two, they pulled her off him and arrested the two of them and loaded them into the back seat. Man, I would've loved to have been along for that ride.

Since the show was over, I got in my truck and as I drove off I couldn't help but think that if I ever was in the position to hire a manager, she would be right at the top of my list because not only did she have a pleasant demeanor, had excellent customer service skills and was willing to listen to others, she also possessed a wicked left hook.

Story 23: Prank Wars, Executive Edition (The 90's)

Here's a question, how do you welcome your new boss?

Well, I suppose, if you're normal workers, you'd maybe introduce yourself, offer to show the new boss around. Maybe even get a bunch of your co-workers together and take them out for drinks. You know, really make them feel welcome. I think you know by now that techs aren't "normal workers."

A little history first. Our original manager, Ray, had been with us for about three or four years which, for us, was a long time. It seemed even longer because Ray was not a good manager. He was a stickler about things that really didn't matter and always felt like he had to keep a certain distance from us. Come on, it's not like we were in the Pentagon. This was a place that fixed appliances. Worst of all, Ray liked to talk about himself in the third person. A lot of, "this is what Ray wants" or "Ray's going to come down hard on you, if you don't tow the line." The only other person in my life who did this consistently was my old gym teacher and I wasn't too fond of him either. Maybe, in his honor, I should've said, "Rob wasn't too fond of him either."

Our department head, Larry, called to inform us that he was going to be there first thing in the morning with Ray's replacement. After babbling on for a while about who knows what, he requested that we all be on our best behavior. Whoever picked up the phone agreed, knowing full well that that would only last for a day. Who we were kidding? Maybe until lunch. An early lunch.

The next morning, around nine a.m., Larry arrived. By this point, many of the outside techs had already left to make their appointments. That day, I wasn't out yet. I was at my bench working. By the time Larry and my new boss had come around to my corner of the shop, several minutes had passed. I was engrossed in whatever I was doing but I did manage to hear

"Rob, I'd like to introduce you to our new manager. This is Nancy."

Now, this got my attention. We had us a lady manager. I cleared my throat and looked up. Nancy, was an attractive woman who I'd peg to be in her late twenties. She put out her hand, real professional like.

"Hello, Rob," she said as we shook. "Great to meet you. I look forward to working with you. Larry told me a lot about you."

"Nice to meet you as well," I said. "Larry left out a few things about you."

She laughed a little awkwardly, but I took it as a good sign. They walked off to the rear office area and I finished whatever it was that I was working on.

The next few weeks proved that I was wrong about her laughing being a good sign. Quite simply, Nancy had no idea what she was doing or how the appliance repair business really worked. If I had to boil it down to one issue it would be that she didn't realize that she was working with human beings and not stats on a piece of paper. We had meetings. Lots and lots of meetings. Meetings that weren't really about anything except making simple things complicated.

Clearly, she had just gotten her M.B.A. and wanted to try out all her business school theories without realizing that things don't always work that way in the real world. Worse, when this was pointed out to her, Nancy reacted defensively. Remember, most of us had been with the company for many years and had to break in many managers. After work one day, a bunch of us got together to discuss the situation. We agreed that Nancy wasn't a bad person but had to loosen up and ditch her stuck-up all business attitude. We needed to make her feel welcome. Now, how would we accomplish this? Again, normal workers would probably take the rookie out for drinks and dinner. We were not "normal workers." We would do to her what we did to all rookies.

Nancy's day off was Thursday. The next Thursday after work, a few of us went out for beers and came up with a plan. We couldn't help but notice that Nancy was a creature of habit. Every day at 9:00 a.m. like clock-work, she would enter through the front doors carrying her coffee in her right hand and her briefcase in her left without ever looking up. From there, she'd head in a straight line to her office, close the door, sit down in her chair while placing her coffee on the desk and her briefcase on the floor, next to the door. We could work with this and here's what we came up with:

In the back of the shop were pallets of laundry detergent. We stacked the detergent boxes in a maze configuration, making sure that there were no straight lines from the front door to her office. Next, we pulled the hinge pins out of her office door. While we were getting the detergent off the pallets, Schmitty found a lawn mower battery and an old boom box. I came up with the bright idea of mounting the boom box under the desk and the battery in one of the desk drawers. We wired the battery to a switch and mounted the switch under the top drawer. So, when Nancy would push the drawer to close it, the boom box would turn on with the volume cranked up all the way. This was just for starters.

We also managed to put vinegar in her coffee pot. Yes, it was stupid and juvenile, but it would wake her up better than any decaff mocha vente b.s. ever could. There was also a medium sized plant in her office. We removed the dish underneath and placed several antacid tablets on it before putting it back. This would be amusing because right after putting her briefcase down, and pouring a herself a cup of coffee, Nancy liked to water her plant. Lastly, we replaced the paperwork on her desk with phonies that contained a bunch of problems that, if not impossible to solve, would take hours.

Now, what good is a practical joke if almost no one sees it? To tackle this problem, we mounted two video cameras in the shop. One was on top of the office and the other camera we put in a box and placed it in the rear work area. Each camera needed to be triggered manually to start recording.

Friday morning couldn't come soon enough but come, it did. The stage was set perfectly. Everyone in the shop knew what was going on. Well, everyone except for Nancy. All the techs made sure to make their calls before nine and waited outside her office door.

The big digital clock on the wall turned from eight fifty-nine to nine and in came our rookie manager, right on schedule. I'll say this for Nancy, you could count on her. She sipped her coffee as the techs greeted her. She barely nodded. As Nancy passed my work bench. I turned on the cameras. Next thing I heard was her walking into one of the stacks of laundry detergent. Sometimes it does pay to look where you're going. She didn't say anything as she made her way to her office.

By now, virtually all the techs were back inside the shop to witness what was about to happen. I, on the other hand, didn't have to move at all. From my workbench, I had a perfect view of the action. Our rookie manager continued to head to her office.

At least ten of us were gathered to watch Nancy navigate the maze we had constructed to get to her office. The over / under bet was five minutes. I picked the over and cleaned up. Finally, she reached her office door. If she knew something was up, she didn't say.

She reached into her pocket and pulled out her keys. She inserted the key into the lock, turned it, pushed it and watched as the door slowly fell backwards onto the floor of the office. In order to maximize the effect, we made sure to move anything that the door might hit out of the way. The door missed the desk by millimeters. It fell perfectly with a beautiful thud.

Nancy turned and looked around. I looked down and the other techs scurried away. I don't know if she saw us. Next, she did something out of sequence. How dare she! Nancy put her briefcase on the floor and started watering the plant before placing her coffee down. The water went through the soil and right to the antacids. The antacids started to foam out from the bottom of the plant. It looked like something out of a monster movie from the fifties. Maybe she chalked it up to the heat. I don't know.

Next, she placed the coffee on the office desk and sat down. She stopped and noticed that one of her drawers was open, so she leaned forward to close it. By doing this, the switch was activated, and the boom box went off.

Now, "More Than A Feeling" by Boston is a fine song but less so at 9:05 in the morning blaring out from speakers you can't locate. Nancy was so startled that she leapt from her chair and landed on the floor. On her way down, she spilled coffee all over the phony work orders. By now, she was panicked, having no idea what to do. I know this because the cameras recorded all of it. Yes, we were all quietly laughing.

At this point we entered Phase 2. Phase 2 consisted of us leaving the shop and going outside. Simplicity at its finest. The reason we did this were twofold: we were laughing our butts off and it would freak her out if she left her office and no one was there. Thank God for the cameras.

From the outside we could still hear the song. Man, that Brad Delp can really sing loud. Nancy was trying feverishly to locate the source and shut it down but was having no luck. By now there were easily fifty techs, office support persons and inside techs out in the parking lot. We waited for a few minutes. Finally, the music stopped. Hey, it could've been worse. We could've made her listen to Styx.

In my pocket, I had my work cell-phone which were pretty new at the time. I dialed the office number and let it ring several times. Finally, Nancy answered the phone. Her voice was shaken as she spoke.

"Hello?" she said, more asking than telling.

"It's Rob. Hey, can you do me a favor and meet me outside in the parking lot right now?"

"Why?"

"Just come." I hung up, knowing she would.

A few minutes passed and then Nancy came out. She looked so beleaguered that I almost felt badly for her. She saw all of us gathered outside and put it together. Then we all broke into a chant of "One of us! One of us! One of us!" and clapped for her.

A big grin came across her face and she knew that she'd been hazed. She even started to cry a little but out of relief, not sadness. That night we made sweet, sweet love. Kidding! She did take us all out to lunch though.

At that lunch she apologized for being somewhat rigid and promised to be more open to hearing what we had to say and not to implement major changes without giving us some advance warning. We learned that some of the changes she was shoving down our throats weren't hers but were coming from corporate and that she was under a lot of pressure, which we didn't realize. But mainly, we got Nancy to loosen up some and realize that we were on the same team.

Nancy was as good as her word because from that day on, she did everything she said she'd do at our lunch as did we and she ended up becoming one of the best managers we ever had the privilege to work with.

As for the recordings, we played them at the Christmas party. I also sent them to Larry, our department head and asked him to play it during their staff meeting. Hey, I said I'd do better, I didn't say I was perfect.

Story 24: The System (The '90's)

I was in a house the other day where something was not just right. It took me some time to put my finger on it because on the surface, this household was perfect. It was built in 1965 and still had the original furniture, wall coverings and cabinetry. Nothing was out of place. It was like something out of a catalogue.

My reason, that day, for being there was to fix a dishwasher that was leaking. The customer, an older woman named Jane, told me that water was leaking in the front by the door. The problem was easy to diagnose and easier to fix: a loose connection to the inlet water valve. The water inlet valve is located right next to the lower kick plate. Under the sink was the water valve that I needed to turn off to begin the repair. I explained this to Jane and went to work. I kneeled down on the floor, opened the two doors under the sink and saw the first breadcrumb on the path to insanity.

Now, under most sinks, you can expect to find cleaning products, bug spray, rags. One time I even found my youngest's retainer. Believe me, we had a talk that night. But the point is that underneath the kitchen sink is usually pretty messy. Not this place. In fact, it was the very model of organization. You see, each cleaning product had a handmade number written on it.

I had to clear out the cleaning products from under the sink, so I could get to and turn off the water valve. As I was making a path for myself, I noticed a black outline drawn around each item as well as a hand-written code number on the bottom. Leaning inward, I turned off the water valve.

I was right about the problem being a loose connection to the valve. I turned it off, tightened it and did a quick check to see that the dishwasher wasn't leaking anymore. It wasn't. The whole thing took, maybe, seven minutes. Then I started placing the cleaning products back under the sink cabinet. Jane spoke up

"Please stop what you're doing," she said with a slight hint of irritation in her voice.

"Do you want me to just leave these things here on your floor," I asked?

"Of course not. What I want is for things to be put back in their proper place. You see, I have a system and it works very well. Let me show you...watch!"

Ohh-kay. She was paying for my time, so I stood up and stepped back. Jane preceded to put her system into practice, placing the assorted cleaning supplies in their exact right place as dictated by their labels.

As she was doing this, I started looking around the kitchen. Nothing was out of place. Everything was in its' proper place from the towels to the cabinets, to the boxes of cereal. All the magnets on the fridge were at the exact same eye level and spaced out equally. It was like something out of "The Stepford Wives." The whole place just felt very sterile. Freaky.

The kitchen cabinets were original from the 1960's as were seemingly everything else in there. If she wasn't older, I would've sworn that she was born in this house because everything else was original. Jane could not have been prouder of herself.

"You see, Robert, I have a system and the very last thing I needed is to have it disturbed. Do you understand?"

"Uh-huh," I said.

Jane opened one of the cabinets, revealing some old dishes. I mean really old dishes. They may have even been made of lead. She began to explain "The System" without me even asking.

"Here," she said. "Let me show you."

Jane opened one of the doors and pulled out a drinking glass. She turned it upside down, so I could see the bottom and the code that was handwritten on it.

"Do you see this," she asked?

It was two feet away from my face. Of course, I freakin' saw it.

"Now, I'd like you to look at the cabinet floor."

I did. There was a code written on it that matched that of the glass. The lecture continued.

"The numbers should always match up. That's how you know where everything goes."

Jane mistook my silence for interest. Not the first time that's happened. What Jane needed was the name of a good therapist and fast because, unless she stopped doing this, she was going to be the crazy lady that every neighborhood has but instead of yelling, "Get off of my lawn!" it would be more like, "Get off of my lawn unless your sneakers have the same code number as the indentations!"

Of course, she realized none of this and was just happy that she had a captive audience that she thought wanted to learn about "The System." She continued explaining that everything in the house and I mean everything, was labeled and had its spot. The code was simple. Each room had a number, each cabinet or closet had a letter and each shelf or cloth hanging pole had a number. The glass I looked at read, four-U-three. Which meant, the fourth room in the house, the upper cabinet, third from the back. What could be simpler?

Here's where the insanity reached unprecedented levels. Her clothes had a label because if you put the socks in the wrong place in the drawer, it would be anarchy. Her towels had labels. The paper towels were marked. If she had kids, on the back of their necks would be a label.

She wanted to show me everything, like I had nothing better to do. So, we toddled down to the guest room. I half expected to see a skeleton of her mother ala "Psycho," but what I found instead, was nearly as disturbing: lots of framed photos of cats. On their collars was the number, letter, number that denoted "The System." What stuck out was that the letter was the same for each cat. I just had to ask

"Excuse me, Jane, but why do all the cats have the same letter on their collar?"

"Well, the letter is the first letter of their name---"

"Yes, but why is it the same letter," I asked without really wanting to know the answer.

"Because, I decided it was more efficient to give them all the same name, Buster. That way I'll never forget."

She picked up one of the pictures and gestured to his collar.

"The number seventeen means that he's Buster seventeen."

I found this so unsettling that I again scanned the room for skeletons. If I found one, undoubtedly, it would have a "C" marked somewhere for "corpse." Undaunted, she continued with her "System."

"Robert, in the house, I have three inventory sheets: one in the kitchen, one in the hall to keep track of the two front bedrooms and bathroom and the last one is for the back two bedrooms and guest bathroom. I know what you're thinking…"

No, she really didn't.

"How often do I inventory the list? Twice a week so that I could keep track of what I need to buy at the store. That way I never buy what I don't need…"

Okay, maybe that idea had some merit, but a little moderation wouldn't hurt either. She droned on

"I first came up with this system years ago back when I worked at Woolworth's in inventory."

"So, you took it from them." I said trying to be polite. Big mistake.

"I certainly did not. They had no idea what they were doing. Inventory everywhere. Over ordering. Under ordering. That's why they went out of business!"

Yeah, Jane was wound a little tight.

She wanted me to walk with her through the house to see her system at work. I really needed to go. She was driving me nuts with her system. I think she was more lonely than anything else. As she continued prattling on, I tried to make a little joke.

"Hey, maybe I should have a number too since I'm in the house."

"Why would you say that? I don't understand," she said back.

"Just a little levity, ma'am."

"Please don't joke about the system. It saved my life."

Wow. It saved her life? More like prevented her from having one.

"Ma'am, I meant no offense."

She sort of nodded and I took that as my cue to leave.

"Ma'am, the dishwasher is working fine and not leaking. If you could sign this work order, I'll be on my way and thank you for showing me your system.

"It was my pleasure," she replied.

The sad thing is that it really was. We said goodbye to each other and she followed me outside and stopped on the front porch, watching me walk to the truck. I drove off and she waved. I waved back.

I drove the truck down the street and parked around the corner to take it all in and the irony was that out of all the things she wrote on her inventory list, she forgot to write down the one thing she needed the most: a life.

Story 25: Fourteen Stitches (1998)

I was asked to go out to a house to fix the garage door opener. The order read, "The motor ran without the door." It didn't seem to be a big problem. Nothing I hadn't seen before. Best guess is that a motor drive gear stripped out. On my truck, I always carried three of them.

The estimated time for me to arrive was around three o'clock, so I called the customer to confirm if he was home. After I introduced myself as the repairman that was coming out, he had one request and that was to honk the horn three times when I arrived. At the time, I didn't know why but I've been asked to do stranger things before, so I agreed.

The drive over took a while, not that I minded because it was a blazing hot day and any time spend in the air-conditioned comfort of my truck, beat the alternative. About an hour later, I arrived at the domicile. The front yard was completely run down with lots of brown spots. Maybe it would've been more accurate to describe them as "browner spots" since all the grass appeared to be dead. Just some deader than others. Same for the house plants because they were also all brown. Someone had not watered in a long time. If the customer's landscaping goal was for a UPS truck feel, then mission accomplished. I parked and honked the horn with three long blasts.

Several minutes later, the customer walked out of the front door and waved to me while I was still in the truck. Exiting the truck cab, I walked behind and picked up my tool box. The customer met me where the driveway met the sidewalk.

"Thanks for coming out on such a hot day. I'm Bob," he said.

"No problem. I'm Rob."

"Hey, Bob and Rob," he said, gesturing at the two of us like we had some instant connection or something.

"Yup," I said back.

"Let me show you what's not working," he said while walking me toward the garage.

Turns out I was right about the problem being the motor gear. Bob stayed in the garage while I was doing the repair and we had a good conversation and joked about almost everything. Mostly guy stuff like football, the Rams, cars and action movies. After discussing the acting prowess of one Mr. Sylvester Stallone I asked what was the deal with him wanting me to honk the horn three times?

"Oh that. I needed time to put Ferragamo away."

"Ferragamo?" I said.

"That's my dog. I named him after the quarterback."

"I guess you really are a Rams fan. Thanks for making sure he's locked up." I said. "Trust me when I say that dogs and repairmen just don't get along. Turns out all those cartoons were right."

"And mailmen too," he added and we both laughed.

I finished up the repair and Bob walked me back to my truck which was a little unusual, but he wanted to see if I was interested in going to the Rams game with him next Sunday. I wasn't sure because while I liked the guy fine, I felt like there was some kind of line that was being crossed.

Before I could give him my answer, a small scream came from the house and the front screen door blew open with a force that broke the handle. The dog was loose. It wasn't just any dog; this thing was huge and vicious and easily over two hundred pounds. If I had to guess, I'd say it was a St. Bernard / Mastiff mix. Needless to say, Bob stopped talking about tailgating. He was shocked and had no idea what to do. Both owner and canine were poorly trained but for some reason, the dog stopped about ten feet outside the screen door. It was like he was toying with us.

"Stay, Ferragamo. Stay."

Ferragamo started barking and growling. Not good signs. His ears went up. An even worse sign. Then he looked right at me and Bob.

Bob was standing on the sidewalk and I was on the parkway near my truck. It was at that moment when Ferragamo started running full speed right at me. Bob stepped back a few steps waiting. For what, I'm not sure because the dog continued his charge. Time seemed to stop. I can still remember each step, bark and slobber as the dog advanced towards me. It was fight or flight time and I was rapidly running out of flight. I was hoping or more accurately, praying that this Ferragamo was less accurate than his namesake. He leapt and soon was airborne at waist level.

Thinking quickly, I picked up my solid steel, twenty-five-pound toolbox and right as Ferragamo lunged at me, I hit him with the box right under his chin. The sound of the toolbox and the dog's throat cracking was not pleasant. Kind of like that of a beer can being crushed.

After the moment of impact, the two-hundred-twenty-pound beast made seeming out of pure muscle slammed right into my van leaving an eight-inch dent. After smashing into my vehicle, he ricocheted into the street like some kind of demented, rabid pinball.

Ferragamo was sacked for a loss and landed behind the rear of the truck. Bob looked at me, still in shock. Apparently, the dog was trained to do this but had trouble with his "stop" commands. Meanwhile, Ferragamo was scrambling on the ground. I guess the impact of the toolbox was harder that I thought.

"I had been meaning to do that for years," Bob said.

Do what? Bludgeon your dog so that it would stop attacking people? Seems to me that that's the kind of thing he should've gotten around to sooner. It's not like I had a lot of time to think about that in the moment. The adrenaline in my system was starting to set in.

That's when I made a big mistake. The biggest. Nine plus years of martial arts training and I had just committed the cardinal sin of turning my back on an opponent. I turned to my left and stepped to the back door of the truck. I opened the first door and then the second door. as I place the toolbox onto the truck floor, the dog bit me on my right buttocks a.k.a. my right butt cheek. Ferragamo had me good.

He pulled me back a few steps. Thank God, my wallet was in that side of my pants and was full of coins because it absorbed most of the crushing force from the canine's mouth, three hundred and twenty-eight pounds of pressure all on my right ass cheek. Ferragamo ripped off the pocket leaving me with a torn pair of pants and a bloody right buttock. After the longest few seconds of my life, the damned dog finally let go of my pants with my wallet in his mouth. The whole thing felt like it was in slow motion.

Bob fell backwards and was sitting on his dead lawn having witnessed the entire attack. By the way, the dog was still loose. What now? Was he going to go for the other cheek to even things out? Nope. He pranced toward Bob grinning like he did something good. He relinquished my wallet at Bob's feet like it was some kind of trophy. That's when I looked back to see how bad my bleeding was. It was a bloody mess.

Cut to the local emergency room where the attending physician said I was damn lucky. If it wasn't for my wallet, filled with change, I would have more crippling problems, like never being able to sit down or use the toilet like a normal person ever again. I was out of work for ten days and couldn't sleep on my back for a month. To give you an idea of how much I hate to miss work, I once went in with three broken ribs from a sparring mishap. So, yeah, it takes quite a bit to get me to call in sick but an upside-down horseshow scar that required fourteen stitches to close will do that to you.

To this day, every time I sit sideways in a chair, I think of Ferragamo. And sometimes I even think of the quarterback and how he blew Super Bowl XIV with that interception in the fourth quarter. Both incidents were painful in their own way. One physical, the other financial. I lost a hundred bucks on that game and that was 1980 money. So yeah, in their own ways both Ferragamo and his name sake were gigantic pains in my ass.

Story 26: Beam Me The Hell Out Of Here (2002)

I knocked on the door of a non-descript home out in the 'burbs. Non-descript except for the fact that "NCC – 1701" was painted on his mailbox. NCC-1701 is the registry number for the starship Enterprise from Star Trek. How did I know this? I'm a casual fan but I had nothing on this guy.

After the second knock, a man dressed in a full Starfleet uniform answered the door. He smiled and seemed harmless.

"Hi, I'm Rob. I'm here to fix the furnace," I said.

He extended his hand and said, "I'm Captain Lewis. Since I'm off duty, feel free to call me "Tim." Would you like permission to come aboard?"

It took me a few moments to understand what he was getting at. Then, it hit me. His version of saying, "please, come in" was for me to ask permission. What the hell, I played along.

"Permission to come onboard, Captain?"

"Permission granted," he said as he motioned me inside. I went in. From the front doorway, we entered the living room. It was an exact replica of the bridge from the original trek. Everything from the viewscreen, the captain's chair and Uhuru's station were exactly like they were in the show. I was stunned and said so.

"This is incredible. I went to the Star Trek exhibit at the Las Vegas Hilton and this bridge is better than theirs."

"Thanks, and it should be," said the good captain. "I painstakingly created this from the original show blueprints. Some of the buttons and switches are from the original show too."

As was walked in the hallway to the kitchen, I couldn't help but notice that it too was covered with memorabilia from the original show. Lots of pictures of Captain Kirk, Mr. Spock, Scotty, Dr. McCoy, etc. I stopped to look at them. On closer inspection, some were pictures, some were paintings, and some were autographed. On the shelves were action figures, still in, what I'm assuming were, their original packaging. They were probably worth something substantial.

From there, Captain Lewis took me to the kitchen or "galley." To enter, we had to pass through doors that were just like the kind on the Enterprise, even making that famous swoosh sound when they opened. The kitchen or "galley" had undergone quite the transformation as well. All the original kitchen cabinets were taken out to look like the mess. The plates were all commemorative from the various shows. I couldn't help but compliment him on his obsession.

"Wow, this looks exactly like the real thing," I said.

"Well, almost. In Star Fleet, there's no stoves or refrigerators because food is synthesized out of thin air. For about a year, I got rid of them, but it just wasn't practical," he said somewhat somberly. I felt like I had to say something to comfort him.

"Hey, you tried your best, just like Captain Kirk would."

"Thank you," he said, immediately snapping out of the temporary funk he was in.

As we walked down the hall of his home, I noticed that each room was dedicated to a different Star Trek show or film. For instance, the first bedroom on my right was all about "Star Trek: Generations," as evidenced by the giant portrait of smiling captains Kirk and Picard over his bed. Of course, there were action figures and other toys scattered about. The door to his closet was open and full of Starfleet uniforms. All, as he proudly pointed out, from the original patterns.

The bedroom to my left was all about "Deep Space Nine." The centerpiece was a perfect replica of the space station from that show that hung from the ceiling. Captain Lewis told me that it was one out of only 10,000 ever made. There was a TV that was made to look a viewscreen from one of the bridges. When the TV wasn't on, there was a screensaver that looked like we were orbiting a green planet, what I later found out was Koloth IV. Much better than Koloth's I, II and III. By now, we had come to the reason why I was there, to fix the warp drive, I mean furnace.

The furnace was located in a utility closet in the main hallway and I got to work. Starfleet wasn't paying me to goldbrick, right? Captain Lewis exited and went to the kitchen / mess hall and poured himself a drink. Not to judge or anything but Romulan ale before five p.m.?

The problem with the furnace was an easy one to diagnose. The thermostat was not functioning. No return power command was coming back to the power unit of the furnace. The wires had been cut someplace. Could it have been Klingons? Bastards.

"Captain Lewis," I cried out.

He came back in and reminded me that I could call him Tim. Somehow, it just didn't feel right with him in full uniform. I asked if he had a ladder I could use? The Captain said that according to the manifest, one was stored in Launch Bay One or, as you and I would refer to it, "the garage." Yes, Timmy was taking his obsession a little too far, but, again, he was harmless.

A few minutes later, Captain Lewis returned with a six-foot standard ladder in hand. I thanked him and got to work. The crawl space to the attic was at the end of the hall, which was only a few feet away. The ladder wasn't heavy

144

and as I walked down the hall, I was treated to more memorabilia including still more photos and a shadowbox containing a piece of the original Enterprise model that was maybe half an inch, complete with a certificate of authenticity. All right, that was kind of cool. Pretty soon, I had reached my destination, the door that opened to the attic.

It was, fortunately, big enough for me to enter without a problem, so I crawled up into it. Right above the furnace were the wires to the thermostat. They had been damaged not by Klingons but by a creature much more vile, rats. Just think about it, a rat on a Star Fleet starship. The Captain was going to flip out. Then again, maybe he wouldn't. When you think about it, rats are kind of like tribbles.

I repaired the wires and the warp drive cranked right up again. I climbed down from the attic and closed the door. I thought it best to check the furnace out a little better since the bill was going to be quite high. Captain Tim heard that the furnace was working. I know this because I saw him in the kitchen saying this into his communicator / cell-phone. Who was he talking to? Starfleet command? The most obvious guess, would have been his mother but it wasn't. He was talking to one of his "crew members." He couldn't have been happier.

"Tell the rest of the crew that the furnace is fixed, and we can proceed with the meeting on stardate 1313.5…That means Wednesday night at eight," he said disgustedly as he flipped his communicator closed. Good crew members are so hard to find these days.

With that piece of business out of the way, Captain Tim asked me if I was finished with the ladder and I told him that I was. He took it and returned it to Launch Bay One. After he left, I finished writing out the repair bill. It took him awhile to come back. I just hope he wasn't overtaken by Cardasians. Maybe the shuttle bay doors got stuck and Scotty needed his help to fix them. Finally, he did come back, and I presented him with the bill. He asked me if I preferred to be paid in U.S. currency or Latium? My company wasn't crazy about accepting personal checks so there was no way they were going for Latium. I told the captain this and he paid me in cash. Then he asked me if I'd like to see the rest of the ship. I said, "aye, captain."

He took me to different rooms. The other two bedrooms were dedicated to "Star Trek: Voyager" and "Star Trek: The Next Generation." Each decked out with the proper memorabilia for each show. The "Voyager" room was a little creepy because had a mannequin with Captain Kathryn Janeway's head on it. On her face was a come-hither look. I guess it can get lonely in space.

The bedroom dedicated to "Star Trek: The Next Generation" was the most intense. As you entered, you were greeted by a life-sized statue of Lieutenant Worf with his phaser out. Don't worry, that wasn't a euphemism. Once inside you saw several other statues of crew members wearing costumes made from the original patterns used on the show. I know this because Captain Tim told me.

As we walked throughout the house, it was obvious that he was so proud of his hobby and his house and he told me how it took him several years to collect all the pictures, collectibles and full costumes hanging in the rooms that I saw. Tim said that as a child, he was from a broken home and frequently came home from school to an empty house. <u>Star Trek</u> became his friend. It was always there for him. <u>Star Trek</u> never promised to be there for his little league then fail to show up. <u>Star Trek</u> provided good moral lessons like don't judge people or aliens by how they look, treat people fairly, do no harm, etc. The more I listened the more I thought about how this science-fiction program was a better parent than most. Did Tim take it all more than a little too far? Maybe, but he wasn't hurting anyone.

Captain Tim took me outside to his backyard. The first thing I noticed was that it looked like a giant crop circle. Turns out that it was a replica of the arena Kirk was forced to battle Spock on the planet Vulcan from the episode "Amok Time." Leaning against the house were two Lirpa's or Vulcan fighting sticks. Tim picked one up and asked if I wanted to engage in a little Koon-Ut-Kal-If-Fee or physical challenge. I begged off saying that I just had lunch and my doctor told me to wait at least one hour before engaging in any Koon-Ut-Kal-If-Fee related activities. Tim understood saying that he was battling high cholesterol.

We went back inside to the bridge or, as he put it, "his pride and joy." Tim asked me if I'd liked to sit in the captain's chair? You bet I would. As I did, I felt just like Captain James Tiberius Kirk. I gotta say, it felt pretty darn good. Everything was exactly like it was from the show including the lights and sound-effects. It took Tim five years to build it and it was impressive.

"Would you like me to take a picture of you sitting in the chair," he asked?

"Are Kirk and Spock best friends," my way of saying "hell, yeah."

I handed Tim my phone and he snapped me in the captain's chair. And, unlike in Vegas, I didn't have to pay fifty dollars for the privilege.

Tim handed me my phone back and I thanked him. He told me that every Wednesday night, he and a bunch of friends came over and made up their own adventures on the bridge. He said that I was more than welcome. It was a nice gesture from a lonely man and I politely declined saying that the wife wouldn't approve. Tim turned to me and said

"Women just don't understand Trek. That's why I never got married."

Yeah, that's the reason, I thought. That and your entire wardrobe has Starfleet insignias on it. So, while the experience was fun, I figured that this was a good time to beam the hell out of there. Live long and prosper, Captain Tim.

Story 27: Traffic Control (1990's)

This is one of those only in Southern California stories and not just because it involves traffic. It was mid-morning around 10:30 or so and I was on my way to drop off a part that another tech had called me about earlier. I was only a few minutes away from the drop-off point.

The freeway was right next to a shopping mall. You could see the parking lot from the road. Traffic seemed to be normal for this area but as I was exiting I could see that the off-ramp was pretty crowded. There were a few cars stopped at the stoplight waiting for the signal to turn green. The cross traffic was backed up too. Something was happening around the corner off to the right.

The light had turned green two times before I started my entry into the cross traffic. I entered into the number two lane or as refer to it as "the slow lane". In the number one lane, a few cars up, there was a full-size van rocking and shaking to what seemed to be loud music. I couldn't tell for sure because I wasn't close enough, but something was pounding to a beat. The people inside the van were jumping around and obviously having a good time. The van's side door opened for a few seconds and closed. The car alongside the van started honking its horn. Why?

The traffic moved forward a little and the van was still rocking and shaking, and the music was now louder. By now, I could definitely tell it was music. The traffic light in front of us had malfunctioned because traffic was just crawling along one car at a time. Pretty much a typical midtown traffic jam with cars stretching from all sides, left and right. Then the van's side door opened again.

Just by chance, it was my turn to come alongside the rocking van. What the hell was going on in there? Yeah, my curiosity was peeked.

The traffic still was inching along moving along about one car per green light. Both the rocking van and myself moved forward at the same time. The music, from the van, was at it loudest. It wasn't rock music. I couldn't put my finger on what kind of song it was exactly, and I still had no idea why the van was rocking back and forth. Finally, we were alongside each other. I had on my dark sunglasses, looking like a respectable driver hopefully. Honestly, I was trying to look cool.

By now, I really wanted to see what was going on inside that vehicle. My wish was about to come true. My head was tilted slightly to the left, so I could get a good look. It's not like I knew how long I'd have to take it in, whatever it was.

Suddenly, the van's door opened, and I could see inside. The driver was leaning back to his right, looking right at me. In the rear of the van, there were two people. Through the rear side window, I saw long hair. We had a girl in the back and she was completely naked!

She moved quickly to the van's open door and looked directly at me. She could've been plain looking and that would've been fine with me. After all, you can't be picky when it comes to surface street nudity. But she a very good-looking girl with an incredible pair of boobs. As if that wasn't enough, she started shaking them left and right, maybe looking for a reaction from me.

I could see her plain as day. She was having a great time showing herself off and I was having a great time watching her do it. The traffic signal signaled our way again, so we could move up one spot. All the time, she was still shaking her boobs to the music for at least two minutes. I started to wonder if it was just random nudity or if she was drunk. Maybe it was a college prank or something like a promotion for a strip club. Turns out, they were advertising for a local production of "Oh, Calcutta," a mostly nude play from the seventies. Hey, I've never worked in advertising, but something tells me that their sales technique was a lot more effective than a ten percent off coupon. Plus, that's why the music was strange to me; they were forty-year-old showtunes.

What the two thespians didn't know or see was that there was a police officer at the intersection off to my right. I can only assume that it was the loud music and the van's door being open that caught his attention. He was looking right at us. I really hoped he liked plays.

Seconds passed, and I could see in the young girls face that she could not understand why I wasn't reacting. Not that I knew what the charge would be. Is reacting to public nudity a crime? Probably not but why chance it?

The young Meryl Streep started reaching for the van's door, so she could close it or bring down the curtain, so to speak. I needed to do something. I rolled down my partly open window completely, grabbed my sunglasses with my left hand and rolled them down onto my nose. I tilted my head downward, paused and raised my right hand. I extended my thumb and my index finger and rocked my hand like I did not see anything special. Boy, was that a lie.

She stopped moving and her face dropped. Her mouth was open as I waggled my hand. I think she was more embarrassed that I did not react as the others had. The light turned green and it was now our turn to go. I turned to the right and the loud van with the door still open went straight through the intersection with the police car following. I wonder what they were going to say to the police? Sorry, officer, but the Santa Ana winds were so strong they blew my clothes off? Hell, it wasn't that much less wacky than the truth.

So, I went on to give the part to the other tech but with a great big grin on my face. Those crazy kids really made my day. Long live the theater and/or alcohol.

Story 28: New Year's Day Ketchup Bottle (1985)

From time to time, we repairman have to work on holidays. At the beginning of each year we are given a schedule and are told to pick two weekends. I normally pick New Year's Day and Labor Day. Why? Because these days are typically quiet. Customers think we're closed and for me, it's eight hours of overtime money for staying home. Easy money, except for this one New Year's Day.

January 1st, sometime around nine a.m. the phone rang. The caller ID said that it was the head dispatcher calling. My daughter answered the phone and I was standing next to her. Right after she said "Hello" she handed me the receiver. It was my boss. He had received a request for service that could not and would not wait. I walked around the kitchen table to grab a piece of paper to write on.

Hey, it could've been worse. At least it was only one call. According to the address given to me, the customer was more than two hours away and I was ordered to go. I hung up the phone with disbelief. I had a service call today. New Year's Day. For the first time in fifteen years.

I immediately called the customer at his home. The housekeeper answered the phone. I introduced myself and the company I worked for and told her where I was and how long it would take for me to get to her. The housekeeper didn't speak much English. I asked her if she still wanted me to come out? She said, "Si. Hurry."

Now, I don't know about you, but normally, I dress comfortably on my day off in what I refer to as my "bum clothes" and this day was no different. So, I threw on a pair of pants and a clean shirt, kissed the wife goodbye and drove my car to the office, where I switched over to the company service van. From there it was about two hour's transit to the job site.

Looking at this service call from my point of view or as I like to think of it, as dollars. Holiday pay or standby pay is the best. And if we actually are called out to do a call, our pay jumps to double time and a half. Good money to say the least and I started getting paid from the second I put down the phone to the time I got back to my house.

It took a little bit of time to get to this customers house but because it was a holiday, there wasn't much traffic. Again, not that it would've bothered me. The house was perfect, all white and well cleaned. The lawns were mowed, and the trees perfectly trimmed. If I had to guess, the gardener was probably there yesterday. There were three very expensive cars in the driveway. This customer had money. Nice house, nice cars, and a housekeeper. What else? I was about to find out.

I parked on the street, walked up the driveway to the front door and rang the doorbell which was a pleasant chime and I waited. A faint hard-heel walking sound reverberated from the other side of the door. It opened, revealing the housekeeper. She was standing there in a typical maid's uniform. It was black and white with the white skirt draping down to her knees and white ruffle covering her ample cleavage. She was hot. It's good to be rich or so I've heard.

I introduced myself as the repairman and that I was here to fix the refrigerator. She welcomed me into the house and escorted me to the kitchen, through a few corners and a couple of rooms. There were no photos or any kind of personal mementos that showed humans lived there. Frankly, the place looked like a modern dungeon. Finally, we got to the kitchen. It was huge. Easily eight hundred square feet. My first three apartments could've fit in that space.

The housekeeper told me that the homeowner was unable to close the refrigerator door last night and that's why I was there. I looked at the housekeeper and commented, "I guess this is why there's strapping tape on the door!" She answered, "Si."

I placed my toolbox on the rug, close to the sink, so I wouldn't scratch the floor. The housekeeper turned around and walked over to a small file box, like the kind you store recipes in only instead of pulling out an index card for tuna casserole, she came out with an American Express Black Card. You know how many people have these babies? Neither do I but I know it's not many. The maid handed the card to me and I copied the relevant numbers on my work order, so I could start. The exact amount would be filled in after I had finished.

The maid walked off to another room. I noticed a combination of sounds echoing from somewhere in the house. It sounded like someone was yelling at a sporting event playing on a television screen, but it was muffled. I didn't care. My job was to fix this refrigerator.

It was a his and her model, one side's the freezer, the other's the refrigerator and it easily measured somewhere around six feet across. I removed the tape from the refrigerator and the door opened slowly by its self, squeaking as it moved.

The yelling continued from the other room. Alternating between cheers and boos. Also heard was a man's voice and several phones ringing.

The refrigerator door was now fully open. The smell of bad food hit me like a ton of bricks. Clearly, guys lived here because it was obvious that nobody had cleaned in there for a long time. I looked inside the refrigerator and saw a package of soggy, pulsating green cheese in a plastic bag lodged outside one of the lower bins with a squished imprint on it. This thing was a biologist's dream. I knelt down and removed the spoiled food from the drawer. While I was down there, I checked to see if there was anything else. Nothing was noticeable inside the refrigerator compartments. I stood back up and looked around the entire unit. Why wouldn't the door close?

Well, I found it. Was it some highly technical problem that required a full-on diagnostic check? Not exactly. On the lower shelf of the door was a large ketchup bottle. One of the kinds you'd buy at a warehouse store that had a gallon of the stuff in it. That's a lot of ketchup. The bottle was not standing up straight and not laying down completely. It was wedged on a thirty-degree angle. Basically, the ketchup bottle head had struck the rotten food bag when it was hanging outside the food bin when the door would close. We had an obstructed door. What was my high-tech fix? It was something that required years of experience. I moved the bottle to an upright position and wouldn't you know it, the door closed unimpeded. Thank God for all my training. Feeling guilty, for no good reason and being a professional, I thought it best to add a little hinge oil to the washer.

Mystery solved. In the background, I could barely hear the housekeeper with her heels, walking closer to the kitchen. The man yelling over the television was still present and loud. I turned around to my left to grab my work-order from the counter top and started to write out the bill. Now, since I do not normally write holiday work orders, I had to grab a calculator to figure this one out.

The bill eventually read as follows: arrival fee, $75.00 times two. Time/labor charge: 1 hour, parts used: 0. Total billing: $350.00. That was one pricey ketchup bottle.

I finished writing out the bill with the credit card number on the work copy. I needed to call in his credit card for the approval code but, I had left my phone in the truck. I noticed the customer's phone on the counter and asked the housekeeper if I could use it. She handed it to me and I proceeded to call the credit card company. The credit card went through with no problem.

The work order was done. A three-hundred-and-fifty-dollar repair bill to move a ketchup bottle and oil a door hinge on New Year's Day. Wow! I hope it was some fancy gourmet ketchup. The last step was to get the owners autograph on the order.

I placed the work order and credit card in the housekeeper's hands. She turned and walked around the corner. A few minutes went by and then I could hear her walking toward me with those shoes again. The housekeeper approached me and said, "Come, with me," while waving her hand.

We walked for a little bit down two hallways and through a well-appointed living room or seating area. Then we turned down a long hallway and headed toward a large metal door. The door looked as if it was from a bank vault.

The door had some pretty thick iron bars both left and right which were anchored into the walls and ceiling. What was behind the metal door? Did I fix a fridge for Pablo Escobar? As we came within a few feet of the door, the housekeeper stopped. A speaker doorbell combination was on the wall. She reached out and rang the bell.

A man's voice spoke out, "Maria, ok, wait a minute." The metal door finally opened, and I was curious, to say the least. There were two huge men standing on the inside entry. They may have once been professional football players or extras from "The Sopranos." One of the guys asked for the work order and walked off around the corner. The other man just stood there with his dark sunglasses on and his arms folded in front of him. What didn't fit here? The first man came back to the entryway and beckoned me to enter.

I started to walk into the short hall. I was stopped by the second man, the guy with the sunglasses indoors. He said that he needed to pat me down for weapons. I looked right into his eyes, the eyes I could not see because of his shades and said with the deepest voice I had in me, "Sorry man, nobody touches me."

As dark as those glasses were and combined with the darkness as the room, I could not see anything, and I don't think he could see me at all. In the background, around the corner, the man yelled out, "Dude, come on in, they're harmless." Great, I thought, was he referring to the two linebackers or maybe dogs that are around someplace?

I walked forward ten feet or so. Around the corner and to the right, I entered a very large room. There were no lights or windows. Although, as I turned around the corner, I was amazed and shocked too.

The room was completely filled with television monitors. Easily thirty, stacked one on top of another. Six wide and five high, all positioned in a horse-shoe arrangement. Behind the monitors, I saw lights flashing. They were cable boxes and all the hook ups to them on the floor. Inside the horseshoe was a large reclining chair, a desk and a lady typing at a computer terminal off to his right. The man raised his right arm and waved for me to enter.

I started walking toward the man from behind, escorted by one of the human sides of beef. The lady at the computer terminal kept focusing on her screen and continued typing. The man in the chair start screaming. Something happened on the television monitors.

"How did he miss that kick?! It was a chip shot!"

Apparently, some kicker blew an easy field goal. Honestly, I didn't know how he was able to concentrate on any single game since there were so many of them and the volume on all of them were cranked freakishly high. It was deafening. The man was talking on his head set.

"Uh-huh, two dimes on Michigan State." He turned to the lady and repeated it. She typed in the information without missing a beat.

The man was a bookie and obviously a successful one. Because it was New Year's Day, all the Bowl games were on. It was one of the biggest days in his "profession." The phone continued to ring, and he kept taking bets.

"…No, right now we got at it even money…Fine, a nickel on Notre Dame. You got it."

He repeated it to the lady, but he didn't really have to. By this point she knew what he wanted, before he knew he wanted it.

I didn't even know if he was realized that I was even there, but I guess he did because he turned to me and I handed him the work and he signed it.

"Is it fixed?" he asked.

I nodded my head up and down just like the lady did without even realizing it. He did not even look at the charges. He handed it back to me, smiled and returned his attention to the monitors, not that I blamed him. There was a lot of money involved here.

The phones continued to ring, and he picked up one and began to talk. I turned around and started walking to the doorway with the winner of the Luca Brasi look-a-like contest still at my side. I almost made it out when the man called out, "Hey, repair guy, come back here a sec." I turned back around and walked back to him not knowing what he wanted.

The man turned to me, with his best mean look and said," You don't see nothing here, right?!"

Slowly, he raised his hand and reached into his shirt pocket and grabbed something and with the other hand he slid his jacket to one side exposing a side arm. Whatever he had in his shirt pocket was too small to be another weapon.

The man pulled out a tightly rolled paper. I couldn't see exactly what it was, but it was tightly clinched in his hand. The man reached forward and placed the contents of paper into my shirt pocket. I felt like I was in a De Niro movie.

"Remember, you saw nothing here!" he repeated. I nodded my head again and turned around. This time the hired muscle wasn't at my side. He and his twin were at the door, waiting for me to leave the room. I walked out, and the housekeeper was there to meet me.

She turned and started walking to the front door. I followed her and so did one of the goons. When we got to the front door, she opened it for me. I walked through it and turned around to say goodbye to her. Goon #1 continued to walk with me to my truck. He followed me to the rear of the truck, silent the whole time. Either he was trying to intimidate, or the big lug was sweet on me and was working up the courage to ask me out but was too shy.

I entered the truck and started the engine. The tough guy looked right at me through the open window and said, "Remember, you saw nothing here." I paused, not knowing how to respond. He spoke again, lowering his voice this time. "We know where you work! "

This guy just threatened me. So, what to do? I guess the smart move would've been just to nod affirmatively and drive off. Instead, I looked right at him and lowered my voice. Two can play that game.

I said, "Dude, I know where you live, and I know what's going on inside."

Stupid move on my part for two reasons: why was I threatening a guy who was packing heat and why did I try to be intimidating using the word "dude?" Dumb Corleone wasn't finished.

"You have any idea what I can do to you, little man," he said?

'You know what I can do to you," I said back. "You're a big, slow, stupid target and I have nine years of martial arts training."

Then I drove off, day-dreaming as to how I could have handled the situation differently. Turns out I handled it fine. Remember the rolled-up paper the man had put in my pocket? I pulled it out and it was $1,200!

So, to sum this up, I spent five hours traveling and working on the job, which adds to double time plus. I received standby pay for the day and a tip of $1200 dollars all because of a tilted bottle of ketchup. This was a good day. Oh, and I didn't tell my boss or the wife.

Happy New Year!

Story 29: I Can Do Anything You Can Do (90's)

This story didn't take place at work, but I like it and it's always nice to win an argument, especially with your wife.

During a Saturday morning, my wife and I had an argument. I don't remember what it was about but at some point, she thought I was accusing her of being a helpless female. I do remember that that wasn't my intention. I was just trying to say to her that there are many avenues to handle a problem and that the simplest is usually the best.

Now, before the disagreement, she said she was going out for a mid-day lunch with some of her friends and that she was taking one of our daughters along with her. She said she needed some girl time, gossip time, whatever you wanted to call it. Since she was a little short on cash, she asked me if she could have some money. I gave it to her considering it money well spent.

You see, when my wife said, "a girl's afternoon," I heard "Great, a free Saturday." I wasn't dumb enough to say this so instead, "Have fun, honey," came out of my mouth. My wife and daughter threw on some clean clothes and left the house in the family car.

I knew her first stop was the next town over to pick up one of her girlfriends before lunch. An hour or so later, the phone rang. It was my wife.

"Hi, honey. What's up?" I answered.

"Rob, we ran over a nail and got a flat. Can you come and change it?"

I started explaining to her that there was no good reason why she couldn't do it herself and then proceeded to tell her exactly how you change a tire. I also want to add that she was on a quiet residential road and completely safe. But as I was telling her how to perform this simple procedure, echoes of our earlier argument replayed in my head. Specifically, how woman can do anything men can do. I decided that she was right and explained that changing a tire was not complicated and that I was positive she could handle it, wished her luck and hung up.

Unsurprisingly, my wife was not exactly thrilled by this turn of events, but she also knew that because of the earlier disagreement, she couldn't back down. As the Japanese say, she would be losing face. But now she wasn't going to make her lunch date and she was likely to be dirty from the attempt. She also forgot that earlier in the call, she had given me her exact location. I knew I was probably going to get an earful about all this later, but I figured that even I'm entitled to some fun once in a while.

The second I hung up, I jumped into my truck and drove out to area where she broke down. Since I knew the area well, I was able to park a couple of hundred feet away at a vantage point where I knew she wouldn't see me. I got out, walked a little closer to a strange house and hid in some bushes.

What I observed was a man finishing changing her tire. So much for feminism. The guy lived in the house my wife was parked in front of and I thought it was kind of him to help a total stranger on his day off. We don't see enough of that anymore. My wife, being the honorable person, she is, insisted on giving the man some money for his good deed. I couldn't help but notice it was the same money I had given her for lunch.

My wife and daughter got back into the car and drove off. They were safe. I got back into my truck and drove home. When I got there, I noticed that my shoes were full of mud which were a dead giveaway that I was near where the flat happened. So, I placed them in the garage figuring I'd get around to cleaning them later.

That night, the whole family was enjoying dinner. My wife, not normally a big eater, was chowing down like there was no tomorrow. Missing lunch will do that to you. I decided to introduce a little conversation into the meal.

"Honey, I'm so proud of you. You handled changing that tire all by yourself with no help from me or any man. A lot of people would've gone for help, but you didn't. I'm impressed," I said with a big, fake smile.

You should've seen how my wife and daughter were beaming. I do have a question though.

"You know, honey, whenever I work on the car, I always have a lot of trouble getting the grease off my hands and yours are so clean. What soap did you use to clean your them? Tire dirt doesn't come off so easy."

Their smiles sagged just a little bit, but I must say that I was very impressed by the b.s. that was about to come tumbling out.

"Well, Rob, I took the tire down to Pep Boys and they repaired and reinstalled it. I used whatever soap they had in their restroom. It worked great." She proudly displayed her pristine hands as her and my daughter's smile perked right back up.

I knew that I couldn't let her off that easily and that I had to come up with something.

"Last week I took the car to the same place to have the brakes done and I used the same soap to clean up. It didn't work very well. What did you really use?"

Her smile dropped again. She hadn't expected this because whether she wanted to admit it or not, she was now in a chess match. You see, she was caught in a lie and really didn't want to admit that she was unable to physically change the tire. She knew she was caught and we both knew it. However, the secret to a long, happy marriage isn't always being right. Sometimes it pays to be gracious.

"You know what, it doesn't matter. You took control of the situation. You're not helpless, you just handled the problem in a different way. Some stranger came out of the house where you broke down and helped you replace the tire. You properly gave him a tip for helping and then you went to the tire store, so they could finish the job. The important thing is you handled the problem. Great job Honey."

It's a rare occasion when your wife and daughter have the exact same thought at the exact same time. This time it was how the hell did I know everything that happened? All of it. Was I some sort of witch?

Like any good magician, you've got to go while there's still wonderment on the audience's faces, so I placed my dishes in the kitchen sink and left the room. My wife and daughter stayed at the table for some time after reflecting on what just happened. All they had to do was go to the garage, find my muddy shoes and I was busted. For whatever reason, they didn't. The subject didn't come up again and the rest of the night was real quiet too. Yes, I had won that round and while they were thinking it over, I gave those shoes a thorough scrubbing.

After, what I'm guessing, was a long, sleepless night, the next day, my daughter came up to me and asked how could I possibly know everything that happened, exactly how it happened?

I said, "Honey, you think too loud," and walked off. To this day, she thinks I'm part witch.

Story 30: Spirits (1985)

Here is story that I tell at least three times a week. There is no fact or physical proof to substantiate my claim. One thing that I can say is that when I give my word to anything, I always keep it.

The name on the service order is what caught my eye. It was not a normal name or even something that can't be pronounced. It was "Mr. Red Hawk." You have to admit; this customer's name probably had some historical value to it.

I pulled up in my truck and from the outside, the house was small with, maybe, two or three bedrooms at the most. The yard was well taken care of and it seemed like a nice place. I knocked on the front door which had a dream catcher on it and waited a minute or so. The inside door opened slowly, and a voice spoke to me. The man's voice was not of a normal tone. It's hard to describe but the best I can do was that it had the tenor of James Earl Jones or Samuel L. Jackson but with the smoothness of President Reagan. Authoritative but comforting.

When the screen door was fully opened, standing in front of me was an older gentleman who introduced himself as Mr. Red Hawk. Clearly, he was a Native American. He invited me inside and I couldn't help but notice all the beautiful Native American art on the walls and all over. There were hand woven baskets, photos of cave paintings and blankets on the couch and easy chair. I'm no interior decorator but the place looked very nice. Clearly, the man was proud of his heritage and I respected that.

We walked into the rear bedroom where the air conditioner was located. Mr. Red Hawk had a warranty on the air conditioner so there was going to be no charge. He described the problem he was having with the a.c. then left the room. I unplugged the air conditioner and removed the control panel. The main start relay had malfunctioned. I had one on the truck. So, I walked out of the bedroom to go get it.

When I returned, I saw that Mr. Red Hawk was sitting in the living room reading a book about the "old west."

As I walked back into the bedroom, Mr. Red Hawk followed, and we started to talk. He was a Chumash Indian. Now to those of us in Southern California, when we hear "Chumash" we immediately think of their casino and all you can eat shrimp buffet. But the truth is that the Chumash people have lived in this region for over 13,000 years. They've endured many hardships, yet they persevered and remained true to themselves.

Mr. Red Hawk told me that he has seen a lot of things in his lifetime. I was polite and started asking him questions about what he had seen. Somewhere in the conversation, he told me that the book he was reading had gotten the facts wrong.

According to him, the book glorified the authors point of view and was not the whole story. I asked him how he knew this, and he told me that his father and grandfather were actually at the events described in the book and that the author was way off base. I finished the repair on the air conditioner, which only took fifteen minutes or so and that's when things got really interesting.

"Rob," he said in that commanding yet warm tone of his, "would it be all right if I told you a story that my father passed on to me?"

How could I say no? Mr. Red Hawk's voice just kept you listening and clearly the man had wisdom.

Here is what he said; everything around us has been created from the Earth or, as Mr. Red Hawk referred to it, "The Mother Earth." The Mother Earth is in its third or fourth renewal, I forgot which and has a spirit. Everything that has been created from her will has a spirit of its own. This includes plants, trees, all that is green and grows. Also included are things that we manufacture like forks, knives, tables, windows, motorcycles, cars because they are made up of materials from the Earth.

Some of these spirits are asleep, some of the spirits are awake and are listening and a few are not good spirits. These spirits are known for causing trouble whenever possible. The spirits normally cannot move locations unless the shell they are in is broken. I'm still not sure what he meant by "a shell." Normally, I would've interrupted to find out, but his voice was so warmly, mesmerizing that it just would've felt wrong to do so.

Mr. Red Hawk told me to make sure to praise or thank my tools and my truck on a daily basis. He told me that the tools will not break like others would and that my truck will last longer than the other technician's. This to me was a little far out there, thanking my tools for having a good day. Think about it. Me talking to my tools and the truck?

Mr. Red Hawk went on to say that he had a test for me. Almost the same test his father placed onto him. The test was to find out where the bad spirits were. Bad spirits only react to bad thoughts and good spirits react to good thoughts. Naturally, I was curious.

Continuing, Mr. Red Hawk asked me to mark four intersections on my map book. This was before G.P.S. I should pick intersections that I travel on a lot. Of the four intersections, I was to mark two with a bad face and the other two with a good face. These markings were of my choice. Completely arbitrary. The two intersections that were marked as bad, I was to think or say bad things as I traveled through. And as I drove through the good intersections, I was to say or think nice things and say a "thank you" as I passed by. The test was to see if the traffic light would turn red earlier than normal. If they did, it was because of bad spirits and if the good traffic signals would stay green longer than usual as I drove though, it was because of the good thoughts.

As my beeper went off, I noticed that Mr. Red Hawk's story took around an hour but if you had asked me, I would've guessed five minutes had passed. With that voice of his, you couldn't help but listen and be enthralled.

Bottom line, I decided to try it for a year. When you think about it, what did I have to lose? And as time went on, those traffic lights that I thanked mostly stayed green a little longer and the lights that I said bad things about almost always turned red. Look, I have no scientific proof to verify or substantiate my claims, but I swear, Mr. Red Hawk's story was true.

I told this story to my children and when we would approach a traffic signal I would ask the kids to ask the traffic signal to "please stay green." More often than not, it did.

So, Mr. Red Hawk's story had been passed down to him by his father to me from him, to my kids from me and now from me to you. I also followed his advice with my tools and truck and guess what; my tools are now twenty-five years old and they're still going strong. The truck I've recently turned in for replacement had around one hundred and fifty thousand miles on the original motor. The boss wanted to know why the normal mileage on the fleet trucks was around one hundred thousand miles before replacement? I told him I thanked my truck every day. He thought I was kidding.

A year later, I went back to Mr. Red Hawk's home and told him of my findings. He remembered that day! With a proud look, he spoke, in Obispeno, what I later learned was a Chumash dialect and blessed me with good spirits. He even invited me and my entire family to a harvest ceremony where we would be blessed and become honorary members of the tribe. I left the house elated and speechless. Unfortunately, the harvest ceremony was an annual event and we had just missed it. We'd have to wait almost a year for the next one. At least we'd have something to look forward to.

A few months had gone by when I was reading the local newspaper and saw that Mr. Red Hawk had passed away. I decided to pay my respects to a man who, although, I had not spent much time with, had a profound, everlasting effect on me. The funeral was packed that Saturday.

Obviously, Mr. Red Hawk touched many people in his day. I have few regrets in my life but one of them is missing out on the harvest ceremony. Because he passed that story onto me, out of respect for him and what he meant to me and that I gave him my word that I would pass it onto others, I'm now passing it onto you. I hope you pass it onto others. So, whatever you may be doing, just thank the spirits for helping out and do your own test. What do you have to lose?

Story 31: Spoiled Rotten Kid – The '90's

Someone once said that our kids are a reflection of ourselves. This is a story about a four-year-old girl that ran her mother's life, ran the house, and screamed at a pitch that could break a window.

The job was located at a tract house that was maybe two years old. The front yard was nicely groomed. Well, all the yards in the neighborhood were that way. If I was a betting man, I'd wager that a homeowners' association gardening crew took care of the yards. So, yes, it looked like a nice house.

The job itself was a short one: basically, replace a part that another repairman ordered but never had the chance to install. It should've taken around twenty minutes, tops. The lady of the house, a tense but attractive woman in her late twenties, answered the door.

"Hi, I'm Karen. Nice to meet you. Please come in," she said.

"Hi, I'm Rob."

She extended her hand, I shook it and followed her inside. Everything seemed pretty pleasant to this point. I was two or maybe three steps inside the house when I heard a scream so shocking it could only come from a small child. It sounded like she was seriously hurt. I turned my head toward Karen with a concerned but questioning facial expression. Should someone be calling 911? Karen's body language let me know that that wouldn't be necessary. She said that her daughter did this all the time and it wasn't a big deal.

As we entered the kitchen, I saw the noisy kid. She was a blond, little girl standing no bigger than three feet tall with pigtails. Now that I think about it, she looked a little like the girl in "The Bad Seed" and that brat from "Little House On the Prairie." Unknown to me at that point, but which became completely apparent after a short time, was that the kid ran the house. Firmly. Karen explained what was wrong with the appliance and handed me the part.

The little girl was sitting in front of the television watching a cartoon or something. I got to work and after maybe fifteen seconds, the little girl let out another blood curdling scream. Her head tilted back, her eyes were shut, a second breath was inhaled, and off she whaled again. Karen raced to the room where her progeny was seated to see what was wrong. Actually, "racing" is underselling what happened. I really thought Karen was going to hurt herself getting there so frantically. From the other room I overheard,

"What's wrong, Elizabeth?"

"I don't like this show! I want a different show!" the brat wailed.

"Okay, okay, mommy will change the channel."

"Now! Change it now!"

Can you believe this crap? All this fuss because a four-year-old didn't like the cartoon she was watching? If I talked to either one of my parents like this, I wouldn't be around today to write this book.

After some more extensive channel surfing, little Elizabeth was, for a brief shining moment, quiet. As if nothing out of the ordinary had happened, Karen walked back and continued explaining what was wrong with the appliance. Sadly, the peace didn't last long because I heard this from another room.

"Mom! Mom! Mom! Mom! Mom!..." she screamed loud enough to shatter glass.

With each "mom," the noise was getting closer. Lucky me. Just then, Elizabeth darted out of the room and lunged for her mother's leg, but she missed. Of course, this lead to more screaming. Not one to be easily discouraged, Elizabeth tried again and ran toward the backside of her mother's leg.

Obviously, Elizabeth did not want me to talk to her mother and would shout to get her way. If Karen's attention was focused on anything but her precious off-spring, said precious off-spring would throw a fit that would make most men weep.

Suddenly, Elizabeth ran down the hall and into another room. The screaming continued non-stop. However, this time a different noise was added to the mix: banging. It was a smashing sound that happened every five seconds. You had to give it to her, the brat had rhythm. Karen excused herself again and ran down the hall to see what was going on.

After a few moments, I heard Karen yell. Being somewhat sentimental I couldn't help but wonder if that was what Elizabeth would sound like in twenty years. Hey, kids do emulate their parents' actions and their emotions and funny enough, I don't know which one was more spoiled: the woman or the little girl but something was clearly wrong.

It didn't take me long to ascertain why Karen had joined in with her daughter. Little Lizzie was striking what looked to be a very expensive dining room table with a hard, long object to musical accompaniment.

"Living la vida loca," she wailed followed by another whack by what I think was a metal stick and by that point I really didn't care. I just wanted to do the job and get the hell out of there. The concert continued.

"But she'll take away your pain..." Whack. The furniture continued to be assaulted.

"Like a bullet in your brain..." Whack.

A bullet in the brain sounded great at that moment. I guess I should've been grateful because "Living La Vida Loca"'s a short song. She could've sung "Freebird."

Getting back to the repair, normally it takes around ten minutes or so. I say "normally," because on jobs like this, for the most part, there usually isn't a mother and daughter shrieking like complete lunatics. What a pair!

Needless to say, that after ten minutes of this my nerves and patience were being tested. I was about ready to lash out in a non-professional manner. Who could possibly blame me but yes, I am a professional, so I didn't.

Then it got weird again. Maybe I should say weirder. Somewhere in the house I could hear loud footsteps followed by other loud footsteps. Pause. Loud footsteps followed by faster loud footsteps. Footsteps followed by frantic footsteps. The mother was chasing the daughter all over the upstairs. I called out, "Hello-Hello." Karen didn't respond so I tried again only louder this time: "Hello-Hello". This time she responded but was someplace else.

As Karen entered from the other room, the little girl was still screaming and running right behind her. Karen stopped directly in front of me across from a large kitchen island. The island had an overhang on the backside where she was standing. There were two bar stools that were perfectly placed in a way that there was a space between the overhanging edge and the first chair.

Now, I'm not a saint or an especially religious person but I can honestly say that I feel wishing anyone harm is wrong and not the way I like to think. However, exceptions to that rule can be made.

Still screaming in the other room, Elizabeth ran on a straight line toward her mother. I tried my best to keep my composure because as I was speaking about the particulars of the repair, when, wham, the little girl ran right into the overhang of the bar, hitting her forehead right above the right eye.

The sound itself couldn't really be explained but then again that wasn't what stood out in the moment. Rather, it was the complete, utter beautiful silence that followed. Karen dropped down to hug her little girl and both of them remained quiet. Not a word. No crying, nothing. You could have heard a pin drop it was so quiet. Try and think of the most beautiful sound you ever heard like your favorite song, or your child saying, "da da" for the first time and double it because it was that good. Yes, I was laughing inside because justice was served.

A few minutes passed, nothing was said. Elizabeth was breathing but not crying. She was just a little stunned. I thought it best to leave while the getting was good making sure to be as quiet as humanly possible.

A few minutes later I was back in my truck with the engine running getting ready to depart when Karen came out of the house and ran towards the truck. I asked if there was anything wrong with the appliance? No. She wanted to ask me a question. About the repair? Of course not. That would be normal human behavior. Rather, she wanted to know if I would come back to visit her and to help her with her daughter. Apparently, she enjoyed the repair visit very much and wanted me to know that my professional manner was nothing she had ever experience before. My response to her question was that I was a repairman and not a therapist. She looked disappointed, then I looked at her.

"Karen, let me ask you a question; who is the mother?"

There was a long pause. You would've thought I asked her to do Calculus in her head. Finally, after at least ten seconds, she responded.

"I am?"

I resisted every urge I had to say, "Is that an answer or a question?" It just would've confused her.

"That's right, you are." I said. "Now, who's the child?"

More Calculus. If I had to clock the silence, I'd put it around eight seconds. Hey, at least she was improving.

"She is," said Karen.

"Correct, and the fact that it took you so long to answer those simple questions illustrates that honestly, you don't know that! That's a big problem."

She nodded knowingly as if I had just distilled the secrets of the universe to her.

"What can I do?" she asked.

"First thing, get Elizabeth to a doctor and have that cut checked out and after that, both of you need to get some serious professional help. If you don't, it's only going to get worse."

She praised me for being so wise and caring. As I drove off I could see her still standing on the lawn wondering what to do. For all I know, she's still there giving off that blank stare like the lights were on, but nobody was home.

Nut case!

Story 32: Iced Plant Food (1989)

Having a garden can be a peaceful hobby and I've indulged in it from time to time. I've read in a few magazines that placing ice cubes on top of planted pots and even in a garden is a good thing. Think about it, ice melts, thus watering the plants gradually. It's nature's timer and the gardener doesn't have to do anything. So, yeah, it makes sense to do this, but one knucklehead took this a few steps too far.

The day was average. The service requested on the refrigerator had nothing worth mentioning nor did the greeting from the customer at the front door. I thought to myself that this was going to be a boring but easy repair. Boy, was I mistaken.

I placed my toolbox on the floor and my paperwork on the customer's countertop. The customer looked at me with a wistful look. I did not know what to make of it.

"So, Mr. Williams--," I started to say.

"Call me Mike."

"Okay, Mike, can you tell me what seems to be the problem?"

"Well, lately, the ice has smelled funny."

My first thought was that the water filter needed to be replaced or it could've just been old ice. Any time ice is in the freezer for a long time it tends to emit odors due to the hard water we all have to deal with and/or because it's absorbed odor from the surrounding foods. Food gases are easily transferred to water and ice.

Mike walked to a cabinet and grabbed a drinking glass. Apparently, it was demonstration time. He went to the freezer door and placed the glass under the ice dispenser lever and ice started to flow into it. When it was full he handed me the glass and asked me to smell it. I did.

The odor that came from the ice was not normal ice smell. It was not even an old food smell. It smelled like garden fertilizer. I took a second sniff because I wanted to make sure I was absolutely correct. I walked over to the kitchen sink and tilted the glass, so the ice would pour into my hand and looked at it. To my astonishment, the ice was blue-green in color. I looked at Mike and asked him what had happened? He didn't let me down.

"Let me explain. I read an article in a magazine about using ice to water plants and how efficient it is."

"Yeah," I said.

"So, I took it to the next level."

"And how exactly did you do that," I replied, skeptically.

"I bought a bottle of liquid plant food and poured a small amount of it into the icemaker and let it freeze every time the icemaker cycled. I invented ice fertilizer. I'm thinking of calling it Ice-A-Lizer or Fert-A-Icer. What do you think?"

I thought he was nuts but from the look on his face, he could not have been prouder of himself. It took a lot of restraint for me not to refer to him as "Mr. Wizard" from then on. He looked at me for some kind of affirmation. What I wanted to say was, "Why the hell would you do that!?" What I did say was,

"So, you've been using this ice on a regular basis?"

"Yes, I have my one drink a night," said Mr. Wizard, "and to be honest, I can't really taste the fertilizer at all. It's all about getting the proportions just right."

I nodded like he was onto something. Time to play doctor.

"Tell me, Mike, have you experienced any dizziness, fainting, shortness of breath?"

Mike nodded his head "no" with the same sh*t eating grin he had on since the demonstration.

"How about aches, joint pains, blurred vision, bloody noses?"

"Nope," said Mike.

"What about memory loss?"

"Not that I can recall. Why?"

"Just curious," I said, not revealing that I had just gone down the checklist of symptoms for fertilizer poisoning. This bozo had just copped to one and had non-verbally showed signs of others. I decided that I didn't want to know about the rest of his diet.

"Rob, are you a gardener," asked Mike.

"I have a small one at home," I said.

"Great because I've got a couple of bags of Ice-A-Lizer in the garage freezer. Help yourself."

Not wanting to be rude, I said, "No thanks, I'm good."

Enough better living through chemicals. Time to get to the actual reason for my visit.

"What would you like me to do with the refrigerator," I asked.

"The icemaker's working too slow. Can you swap it out for a new one under my warranty?"

This was, by far, the most logical thing he had said since my arrival. The fact was that Mike didn't break anything and I couldn't establish any problem, besides the fertilizer and there was no way I could talk him out of it. I swapped out the icemakers and left.

I've heard of having a green thumb, but Mike was well on his way to having green entrails.

Story 33: Cuckoo (Early '90's)

A little while back I had to make a repair on a home water softener unit. According to the complaint, there was a "funny smell and taste" to the water. Best guess, corrosion on or around the float. This can happen with older units. Man, was I wrong.

I arrived at the house in the early afternoon. It was a nice house. Clean and recently painted an off-yellow. The lawn was well taken care of and there were flowers in several pots near the front door. It's the kind of house your older, never married aunt would live in.

I parked the truck right in front, exited and opened one of the back doors to get my toolbox. I walked right straight across the lawn to the front door and knocked. I noticed that the door had a sticky soap solution on it and a foul odor. Almost indescribable but I'll try. It was a rotten egg Sulphur like smell. If you've ever driven through Amarillo, you have some idea of what I'm talking about. Suffice it to say, it wasn't very pleasant.

The lady of the house opened the door. She was in her early sixties, wore glasses and was wearing a blue house dress. She looked like the kind of person who had just baked a pie. She introduced herself.

"Hello, I'm Maryanne. Thank you for coming."

"I'm Rob and you're very welcome. Is the water softener unit in the garage," I asked?

"Yes, it is. Won't you follow me?"

I did. Maryanne lead me to the north side of the house where the garage was located. As we got closer, I heard the unmistakable sounds of birds chirping. It was soothing. Having a bird chirping while I worked wasn't the worst thing in the world. Now I'll finally know how Snow White felt. Goody.

Maryanne opened the garage door and the chirping turned into a cacophony. This two-car garage was completely full of birds. At least fifty of them. Each one of them had their own cage and the entire garage floor was covered with bird seed. It smelled terrible. Much worse than the outside. Think of the worst pet store odor and multiply it by at least three. It hit me like a ton of bricks. Maryanne was fine with it. I guess she built up an immunity. So much for feeling like Snow White.

After I got over my initial shock, Maryanne walked me over to the water softener unit. I was greeted by several squawks because I felt like I had just entered a Hitchcock movie.

"So, what exactly is the problem," I asked while trying desperately to hold down the two chili dogs with onions I had for lunch. It was my cheat day. Don't judge me.

"Well," she began. "A few months ago, I began to notice that the water started to taste funny and there was an unusual odor that emanated from it."

"Was it coming just from the sink or from all water throughout the home?"

"The stench is coming from everywhere, I'm afraid. From the shower, bath, washing machine and even the dishwasher," she answered.

Obviously, the problem is in the water and not the sink because it was all throughout her house.

"If you'll excuse me, I have to go back inside and finish up my baking for the church bazaar. I'm making my famous lemon squares. They've won the church bake-off the past four years. I'll leave you to it," said Maryanne.

"Okay, as soon as I locate the problem, I'll let you know."

She exited leaving me alone smack dab in the middle of her version of the Enchanted Tiki Room, but unlike in Disneyland, these birds weren't animatronic. They were real, and they were real uncomfortable with my presence. Hey, Polly, I wasn't too thrilled about it either. Also, unlike Disneyland, this place was filthy. There was a white, uneven film on all the windows, which I later deduced was molt. I should've been issued one of those radiation suits before entering. Please stay down, chili dogs.

Not wanting to spend one minute longer than I had to, I got right to work on the unit. I pulled off the lid and looked at the float. I observed nothing at first glance. I removed the complete cover and placed it on the rag I had set down on the floor. Don't forget, there was birdseed and bird crap all over.

As I stood up, I noticed that a yellow feather had just floated by my head. Great. I looked at the display on the water softener unit and saw that the next service cycle was to begin late that night. The service cycle happens about once a week and in theory, it resets the machine to ensure that it's working properly.

The way it works is that water flows through a valve in the top of the tank, down through the resin beads to the lower collector. As the raw water flows through the resin beads, the hardness is removed through the ion exchange process, which is where the undesired contaminants (various metals like aluminum, arsenic, copper, etc.) are removed from water by exchanging them with a less objectionable substance.

The water then passes through the slots in the collector, up the riser tube, through the valve to the main tank where it's filtered for use in the home. Yes, I guess I could've just said that it makes hard water into soft water but sometimes I like showing off.

One of the options on the display was if I wanted to start a force cycle. I did and pushed the appropriate button. Hopefully, this would give me a better idea of what the problem was. The cycle is actually comprised of several cycles. During the second one, a grinding noise came from the main housing. I stopped the unit, hoping not to cause more problems.

I needed to get inside to see what was going on, so I got out a wrench from my toolbox and removed the top housing. Inside it were two off white objects that looked like noodles. I removed them and placed them on a table right next to the unit. I reinstalled the housing and continued the cycle. Maryanne walked back into the garage. Her entrance seemed to sooth the birds at least a little bit.

"Have you found out what's the problem yet," she asked?

"Not yet but I did find these in the lower housing," I said as I pointed to the "noodles."

She walked over and looked at them quizzically. If she knew what they were, she didn't feel like telling me.

"Ma'am, would you mind bringing me a glass of tap water? I need to test it."

"Of course," she said as she left to get it.

The test cycle was finished and out of the corner of my eye, I noticed inside the drain tube was a yellow object. I removed it and dug out another yellow feather from inside it.

However it got in there, it managed to go through the complete cycle. The answer came to me at once because of deductive reasoning and the fact that there was an empty bird cage not three feet away from my head, but I had to know for sure. I looked down inside the main tank and began to dig in the salt which was pretty low. I noticed no more yellow feathers. Maybe I was wrong. Maryanne, re-entered the garage holding the glass of water that I had asked for.

"Any closer to finding out what the problem is," she asked?

"Not yet, ma'am, but I think I'm pretty close."

"Wonderful."

I placed the glass of water close to my nose and immediately wish I hadn't. It was awful. It stunk. The best approximation I can give you is think road kill and chloride. It was not a good combination.

I grabbed a flashlight from inside my toolbox and pointed it towards the main tank. Unfortunately, I was right. One of her birds had entered the main tank and when the unit turned on, it drowned. The salt inside the tank increased the decay of the bird as it cycled every night. Put it this way, there wouldn't be an open casket funeral.

Maryanne just stood there waiting for an answer that I didn't want to give. Throughout my career, I had served many roles from consultant, repairman, occasional therapist and now I found myself forced to play pet grief counselor. I really didn't want to do this, but I had no choice, so I cleared my throat and said

"I think I found what's been causing all the trouble, Maryanne."

I beckoned her to come closer, which she did. I cleared my throat again.

"Maryanne, have any of your birds gone missing about a month ago?"

"Yes, Pee Wee" she said wearily.

"I think I found him."

I looked at her and she looked at me. A few seconds went by. I turned my head back to the tank and shined the flashlight inside the house water system so that she could see her beloved pet one last time.

"Pee Wee," she practically shrieked! "Why? He was so young. He had so much more he wanted to accomplish. Why?!"

I wasn't sure what Pee Wee wanted to accomplish. Maybe write a novel or solve this whole Middle East problem? Finally learn to wind surf? I tried to be comforting but honestly, I don't know how effective I was.

"Ma'am, obviously, I didn't have the pleasure of knowing Pee Wee but maybe we can take comfort in the fact that he was a curious bird. It was that curiosity that lead him to fly into your water softener unit and now he's in bird heaven where there's lots of statues for him to crap on and bells to ring."

Before you make fun of me, it's not exactly like I had a lot of practice delivering on-the-spot eulogies for birds. Plus, I didn't tell her how for the past month she had been eating, drinking and washing with Pee Wee. Somehow, I didn't think this would've helped the situation. Maryanne, sniffed and tried to calm herself down. I like to think it's what Pee Wee would've wanted.

"Thank you. That was very kind," she said. I nodded. Before you read what I said next, I swear I was just trying to be helpful.

"Ma'am, if you'd like, I'd be glad to put Pee Wee in a bag and toss him in a dumpster on my way back..."

Maryanne started bawling all over again. I took that as "no, thank you." Okay, I admit that I'm not the world's most sensitive person. At least she had the other forty-nine some odd birds to keep her company and possibly fly into the water tank. Maryanne eventually composed herself and left while I completed the repair. I didn't even bother to get her to sign the invoice.

The strange thing was that for the rest of my time there, the birds were completely quiet. I don't know if it was out of grief or it was just naptime.

I like to think that it was the former and that they were all remembering Pee Wee in their own special way, but it was probably naptime…or feeding time.

Story 34: Stephen King's Hall (Early '90's)

I call this story Stephen King's Hall for a simple reason: the hall I went down was like something right out of one of his novels.

The houses my company services vary greatly in age. Some homes are so new that you could still smell the paint and others can go back over eighty years. This particular service call came from the latter. It was a very old house.

The work order was dispatched to me via phone call and it concerned a furnace that wasn't working. I wrote the information down and started to head out.

The house was located just off a lake. Not a big lake, but just big enough to fish on or enjoy a nice day. It took me a while to find the house because it was somewhat secluded. Whomever built it originally, placed the house perfectly. It was a large Tudor home, bordering on mansion status. This place was big but not obscenely so like you see in today's McMansions. As I parked the truck I could see that the views from the house were incredible.

I knocked on the door and a man answered. He was older, tall and very thin. There was something almost prim about him.

"Hello, I'm Rob. I'm here to fix your furnace."

"Yes," he answered. "We've been expecting you. My name is Claude. I'd invite you inside, but it would serve no purpose."

He was right, but it seemed like an odd way to put it. Claude exited the house.

"Won't you follow me," he asked?

I did, to the side of the house. Waiting for us was an extension ladder. Claude picked it up and extended it to its full height which met the top of the roof. The roof's highest peak stood around twenty feet. At the peak was a little door. Claude informed me that I needed to climb all the way up the ladder, open the door and crawl inside. Once inside, I would see a sled type device. I was to place my toolbox on the center of the sled and my knees left and right on the board. Not to worry, he added. There was a light switch just inside the door. I would be able to turn it on, then see where I needed to go.

This was not something I was looking forward to. I'm mildly claustrophobic and who knows what I'd find once inside? Did I mention that this happened right around Halloween? So, yeah, my mind did go to a slightly spooky place. I even briefly considered not going but decided that it would be really unprofessional not to, not to mention all the crap I'd have to take from the rest of the techs for wussing out. Ah, the joys of being a man. So, up I went. At least Claude was kind enough to hold the ladder for me.

I climbed all the way up until I was some twenty feet above the ground although that didn't bother me too much. Once up on the ceiling, I saw the door. It opened outward which was rather inconvenient. I climbed inside and found the light switch which I took as a good sign.

An even better sign was that the switch worked and just as Claude said, the sled was the first thing I saw. The second thing was the hall. It was long, and it was narrow. There was a string of lights mounted on the beams, spaced about every ten feet. I could see five of them but no furnace. The place looked like a mine shaft.

"How far down is the furnace?!" I yelled.

Claude's response was muffled but I could make it out. He said, "I don't know exactly. I've never been up there. Just turn to your right at the end of the hall."

Wonderful, I'm going to be in a confined space and I don't really know where I was going. Maybe wussing out wouldn't have been the worst thing in the world to do in hindsight but it was too late for that now.

I placed my tools on the sled that was just inside the door, took a deep breath and climbed into the attic. The door opening was pretty small, but I managed to squeeze through. Claude was right on the money about one thing, though, putting my toolbox in the middle of the sled and my legs to the sides did make it easier to steer because the weight was well balanced. I knelt down on the sled with my tools between my legs and I paddled down the hall like I was paddling out on a surfboard.

One light bulb at a time passed and the roof was very low. Tight places and me tended not to get along too well. I found this out the first time I needed an M.R.I. for my back. I felt like I was in a coffin. Still, my little sled trip continued. Every time I passed a light bulb, I had to bend over even more. I was so close to them that I could feel the heat each time I passed one. The hall seemed like it would go on forever. All I could see was the two-by-fours beams inside of the roof and another light bulb. It really was getting slightly creepy. What was around the corner? An evil clown? A feral dog? Your mind will do that to you when you're in a dimly lit, confined space. By now, my arms were tiring. It took a lot of energy to maneuver the sled because it wanted to sway from side to side. The lactic acid was really making my arms burn. Finally, I reached the end of the hall. I turned the sled to the right and saw seven more light bulbs hanging from the rafters. That meant I had to go another seventy feet at least.

As I got closer to the seventh light, I was able to make out the furnace. I just needed to get there. Easier said than done because when I looked back and saw how far I had gone, then looked forward to see how far I needed to go, I saw that I was only at the halfway point. Time to suck it up and make it to the furnace.

About twenty minutes later, which included two rest stops, I finally made it. There was the Holy Grail, the furnace. By now, not only were my arms hurting, so were my shoulders and back. Plus, I could feel the burn marks on my neck from the lightbulbs and the pungent aroma of burning hair. Not good.

Finally, I caught a break because in the furnace area, a small room opened up that had a lot more room to move. I left the sled in the hall opening and tried to lift my tools. I couldn't. I was that exhausted. I decided to slide them off and placed them just off to my right.

The furnace did not work. It was completely dead. It was a horizontal furnace which meant that the air traveled from left to right. Air would flow through the heat exchanger and come out heated on the other side, into the house. The thermostat unit also wasn't working at all.

One of the testing procedures we use is to start from basics. And the most basic of all is checking to see if the power was on. At this point, Claude was calling out to me from inside the house.

"Young man, have you located the problem?"

"Not yet but the wall outlet doesn't have any power!" I replied.

"I'll check the meter to see if it's working!"

I waited for a few minutes. Then the lights went out. Claude turned off the wrong switch. It was pitch black inside the room and I felt like I was in a coffin again. My eyes hadn't adjusted, and I was stuck there. I didn't even have a flashlight because I had left it in the truck.

Claude was back inside the house and began yelling to me, but I couldn't make out what he was saying. Not that I needed to because I knew what I was going to say

"You turned off the wrong switch! I can't see anything, but the furnace is working now!" I screamed back.

Claude retorted with "Great! The furnace is working!" Then he started talking to his wife while I was still stuck there in the dark. I'll be honest, I was starting to get a little worried.

"Hello! Hello! Could you turn the lights back on, please?!"

Nothing. As I sat there, I could see a little light peeking through some of the air vents on the roof. My eyes were adapting to the dark. I waited and waited. Still no response from old Claude. I yelled out even louder this time asking, no, begging him to turn on the lights. This time I waited even longer. I began to hyperventilate a little and knew that if I didn't do something to calm myself and soon, I would be in the middle of a full-on panic attack. Pretty much the last thing I needed. For some reason, my mind flashed to the Lamaze classes the wife made me take when she was pregnant with our first child. In that class, they taught us to breath in through the nose and out through the mouth in a rhythmic pattern. I did, and it worked. Thanks Lamaze; two words I never thought I'd say.

Once calmed down, I realized that my patience was pretty much at an end and that if I didn't get myself out of there, it was quite possible that no one else would. I placed my tools on the sled and this time I laid down with my stomach on the board. This way I could use my legs and my arms to travel, thus, relieving some of the burden from my arms. I started to move back down the hall, traveling very slowly but at a constant speed. Don't forget, it was still nearly pitch black. The turn came, and I maneuvered it very well. The small door had closed and just enough light came through the cracks.

At long last, I had finally made it to the end without once being attacked by monsters or dead former house occupants. I pushed the door open and light flooded in. I could see again! Turning around in that small hall was a challenge but I was able to swing it. Once out on the roof, I climbed down the ladder slowly. After the adrenalin rush of not being trapped wore off, I noticed that my arms were killing me, even worse than before. I made sure that I locked the door securely.

Once I was on the ground, the relief that I was no longer trapped, gave way to the anger of being put in that position in the first place. I liken it to thinking your car was stolen and being relieved to find out that it was towed. After a few minutes, trust me, you get really angry. There was no reason for my car to be towed, just as there was no reason to keep me trapped in the dark. I walked back to my truck, put my tools away and started to write out the work order.

I had calmed down to the point where I could be barely civil. I walked up to the front door knocked hard. Claude answered the door. He looked at me and his face just dropped. After a few seconds, he lowered his head and said, "I forgot about you, didn't I?"

"Yes, you did," I answered. I told him that I locked the door upstairs and left the ladder leaning against the house. I was pissed off and when I get pissed off in a professional situation I get curt and say as few words as possible. Claude invited me inside and we walked to the kitchen where we both sat at a small table.

I started writing out the repair bill. I could barely do it because my arms and shoulder still ached. Claude apologized, sort of.

"Young man, when you first got up there, my wife asked about our weekend plans and I forgot about you."

"Uh-huh," was all I managed to get out. How do you forget about someone in your attic? He was just talking to me! I wrote out the bill much higher, trust me, much higher that it should have been. Claude was unaware of this and paid by check without batting an eye at the number. By now, he could feel that I was pissed off at him. I placed the check in my pocket and tore off a copy of the work order and placed it on the small table. I left without saying good-bye.

On my way out, I started to wonder if there were any bodies in the attic of the repairmen who had gone before me and if there were, how grateful I was not to have seen them. I went home that night, more in need of a stiff drink than ever before in my life. I poured it, sat down on the couch and turned on the TV. What was on? You guessed it, a Stephen King movie. That drink didn't stand a chance.

Story 35: Freezer Full Of Ice (1982)

If I had to boil this story down to one sentence, it would be this: the rich aren't like you and me.

The request for service form said that the ice maker was making too much ice. This request is not normal. If you have a problem with your ice maker, nine and a half times out of ten it's that the machine has stopped making or dispensing ice. The first thing I thought it could be was that maybe the water valve from the house was not working correctly. Who knows? I'd find out when I got there.

In this case, "there" turned out to be a pretty ritzy neighborhood. This was also unusual. In my experience, when rich people have a problem with an appliance, they don't have it fixed, they throw it away.

The street the house was located on was immaculate. You couldn't find litter, an unkempt lawn or even a non-luxury car parked on the street if your life depended on it. I pulled up into the quarter-mile long drive-way and yes, my truck looked out of place next to the Jaguar and Bentley. Oh well, last, I checked, Bentley doesn't make trucks. Anyway, the front yard was landscaped beautifully with a fountain up front and the hedges were perfectly trimmed. No kid's toys on this piece of grass. So, yeah, these people were pretty well off and it showed. I exited the truck, grabbed my toolbox, walked to the front door and knocked. There was no response for a minute or two.

Finally, the front door opened and standing in front of me was a uniformed butler who stood there like a statue. A small pause lapped before a verbal response was forthcoming.

"May I help you?" said Jeeves, his voice practically dripping with disdain.

"I'm Rob. I'm here to fix the ice maker," I answered.

"Yes, we've been expecting you. The help must enter through the side entrance in the back," he said and pointed to my right.

Great. Now I'm "the help." I was actually now taking crap from someone who picked up other people's underwear for a living. Before walking to said entrance, I bowed. What can I say, I couldn't help myself, Jeeves's eye roll was classic. Someone needed his ass kicked and I was in a cranky mood.

Turning to my right I walked along the front of the house and around to the back side of one of the garages which had a BMW parked inside. I stepped along the pool area and around the swim-up bar. I must admit, I do love a good swim-up bar. The back door was just within a few feet from the pool bar. Slowly, the rear door opened revealing the maid. At least she didn't give me attitude.

"Please come with me, sir," she said.

"Sir?" Hey, I'm moving up in the world. First, I was "help," now I'm "sir." Is this a great country or what? My joy was short-lived because standing in the kitchen was Jeeves. The first thought I had was, why couldn't he had just take me here himself? Would the sight of me using the main entrance really have lowered the property values that much?

After I got over this bizarre logic, I took in the kitchen. It was huge! Maybe around five hundred square feet give or take a few. Located in the kitchen was a trash can with a plastic bag inside with a six-foot dome on top. It looked like a big snow-cone. There was a large grouping of rolled up towels in a semi-circle in front of the freezer which appeared to form a kind of barricade and a big, iron shovel leaning on the side of the cabinet, which was a little weird since I didn't see a coal stove anywhere.

Now to the reason why I was there: the freezer. It measured thirty-two inches in width and the refrigerator was thirty-two inches as well making the total unit measure sixty-four inches wide. The cubic feet just on one side is the largest ever made for this type of refrigerator / freezer. Before anyone gets out their rulers, trust me when I say that this thing was gigantic.

The butler looked at me like you would at a piece of gum stuck to your shoe. He paused before deigning to speak to someone of my low class.

"Would you be so kind as to stand over to the side, behind the wall of towels?"

"Why, yes, Jeeves, I'd be honored to do so," I sarcastically said to myself before walking over to the designated area. The maid strode behind the kitchen island for protection. Jeeves stood just to the left of the freezer door and said

"Please be vigilant and protect yourself."

Was a polar bear about to come bursting out? Was it safe to look directly at the freezer? Should I join the maid behind the island? Needless to say, my curiosity was piqued.

With his left hand, Jeeves grabbed the freezer door and started to open it. As it opened slowly, a cracking sound came from the inside of the freezer. Right after that, a wall of ice came tumbling out, crashing down on to the floor and into the side of the kitchen island that was facing it. How I didn't scream out "Avalanche!" I'll never know because that's what it looked like.

After the spewing was over, there was easily more than thirty cubic feet of ice that had landed on the floor. Honestly, this was like something right out of the movies. It could not have been better or funnier but then again, some people just do not share my sense of humor. Jeeves sure didn't.

Right after the ice-a-lanche, the maid began the clean-up and rescue mission. She scooped the ice around the door first, so I could see what was wrong. After looking at it for maybe two seconds, I immediately diagnosed the problem: there was no auto-stopping arm.

An auto-stopping arm looks a little like half a hanger and goes in front of an ice maker. Basically, it stops the machine from over producing because the ice literally has no place to go which shuts down the mechanism. I assumed that it had fallen or broken off. What's that about why you should never assume? Something about making an "ass" out of "u" and "me?"

Jeeves spotted the replacement part that I was holding in my right hand and said, "I see you have one of those."

"Yes, it's what I need to get the ice maker working properly so that you won't be snowed in every time you open the freezer door. Just out of curiosity, do you know what happened to the old one? Did it fall off?" I asked.

That's right, this commoner asked him a question. Jeeves took a moment to work up to his maximum snooty potential and said

"No, that's not what happened at all. The owner of the house decided that the "auto-stopping arm," as you call it, was not a necessary part of the appliance and not ascetically pleasing, so he forced it off."

What? Not ascetically pleasing? What the hell did that have to do with anything? I don't like the way my brake pedal looks but I'm not going to rip it out of my car. Why? Because, for some reason, I think it's important to be able to step even though the pedal is too wide. This was nuts. I looked right at Jeeves and said,

"And an avalanche every time you open the door is? If there's no stop arm, the icemaker will not stop making ice and it will fill up the freezer until the weight of the ice forces the door open. Then you'll have an indoor unnatural disaster."

Jeeves's one eyebrow rose slightly higher than the other. clearly, he knew this has happened more than a few times. As he exited, and was clearly out of earshot, the maid burst out laughing which, of course, made me burst out too.

I started the repair and then me and the maid started doing our Jeeves impressions. Honestly, hers was better but then again, she had a lot more experience.

Rich people, they're really not like you and me or do they live on a different planet entirely?

Story 36: Engineers Drive Me Nuts! (2011)

"When there is a high degree of intelligence, there is also an abundance of stupidity." This is a quote I heard from a movie I saw a bunch of years ago. Based on an encounter I had a few years ago, I'd rewrite the above statement thusly, "it takes someone really smart to do something this incredibly stupid."

A little while back, I was called out to perform a service call on a refrigerator's ice dispenser. As I pulled up to the house, I noticed that the front yard was a total mess. The lawn was unkempt, there were toys scattered all over and there was even a lawn gnome flat on his back. Maybe he had been drinking. On the front porch was a man wearing a suit with a cell-phone in one hand and a handful of white papers tightly clutched in the other. It looked like the man was ready to leave for work and he was waiting for me to arrive. He was also somewhat agitated.

I parked my truck out in front and exited and walked towards the back door, but the man saw me and motioned for me to come to him. I walked up, and he opened the front door and motioned for me to enter, all while still on the phone.

"…You tell that guy that I have fifteen years' experience and I know what I'm doing. I'll see you when I get there!" he barked into the phone. We entered the domicile and I closed the door behind me.

The house itself was fine, I guess. Pretty average, tastefully decorated with lots of photos of him, his wife and kids. Honestly, nothing really stood out. It almost looked like one of those model homes they show you when you promise to give up an hour of your time in exchange for a set of steak knives. By the way, I still have those knives and they work great so, to my wife, were we really wasting our time that day?

As we walked into the kitchen, the man's phone rang again. He just looked at it and shook his head without answering it. Although it was only nine a.m., it was clear that this guy wasn't having a good day and it wasn't about to get any better.

"By the way, I'm Rob," I said by way of introduction.

He put out his hand, still clearly annoyed by whatever happened earlier.

"Neil, nice to meet you."

I placed my toolbox on the floor and asked him why I was there? He pointed to the refrigerator. There was a giant black spot on the freezer. Neil stood next to the sink with his arms folded. My first thought was, what the hell happened? Then I asked him, "Okay, so what happened?" I cleaned it up. He looked at me incredulously like I was trying to pull something. He responded by telling me his profession.

"I'm an engineer," he said, proudly.

"Really, which train," I said back?

"Not that kind of engineer," he huffed. "I have two engineering degrees. One in mechanical engineering and one in electronical engineering."

Gee, defensive much? Also, there's no such thing as "electronical engineering." He meant "electrical engineering." More importantly, what did that have to do with the giant black spot on the freezer door?

Since he decided to lay out his credentials, I thought it only fair to lay out mine.

"That's great," I said. "I have three degrees including one in <u>electrical</u> engineering."

Before the genius could respond, I walked over to the refrigerator and stared at the door. The giant black spot was in a half oval right above the dispensing housing or where the ice comes out. Clearly, there was a fire. The black spot was comprised of burnt wiring and plastic. Something happened. But what?

I opened my toolbox and found what I needed to open the housing assembly. One tool opened the electrical harness on the top of the freezer door. The screw holding the covering had never been removed. It was screwed tight to the hinge.

I unplugged the harness. This eliminated the electrical power to the freezer door so that I wouldn't get shocked. As I knelt down in front of the freezer door, Neil came up behind me and stood just to the right of me and began to explain what happened.

He admitted to taking off the housing and re-wiring the selector switch with a few added electrical components. Why? I had no idea. I pulled off the panel. Underneath it was melted wires and melted plastic. Yup, there was a fire and what it left behind smelled terrible.

"What did you do here," I asked of the man with two degrees in engineering?

"I'll be right back," he said as he exited the kitchen. Maybe there was another appliance somewhere that needed destroying. I started to check out the panel a little closer. I still had no idea why he did what he did. Luckily, the genius re-entered the kitchen carrying a rolled-up schematic in his hand, which he promptly unfurled on the counter, using the salt and pepper shakers to anchor the edges. He began to explain his theory. I'd explain it to you, but it made zero sense. Neil sat down. I swear, he was practically glowing at the genius of his creation.

I'll give him this, it does take a genius to get everything wrong. You'd think that through sheer dumb luck, something would've been right but nope. For starters, his assessment of the dispensing mechanism was completely wrong. About halfway through his "explanation," I just couldn't take it anymore.

"I have no idea why you did this, but alternating current can only travel in phase," I said.

This stopped him in traffic. I had just disrupted Einstein's thought patterns and crushed his prize workings. The best he could come up with was, "I know that. Don't you think I know that?"

He didn't know that. He really, really didn't know that. I wonder if it was too late for him to get a refund from whatever university granted him his degree. At this point, I turned to the refrigerator and pulled off the lower kick panel. Inside the panel, the manufacturer had placed a wiring schematic for that unit. This particular refrigerator schematic had color coded wiring traces. This makes it easy to locate problems. I walked back to the table and sat down. I placed the refrigerator schematic next to his schematic. He was insulted. I didn't care.

I looked at his wiring attempts. Neil said nothing. I don't know if he was open to suggestion or just pissed off with me for questioning him. The man had routed power incorrectly which made the unit catch on fire. Time to admit failure.

I removed a pen from my shirt pocket and began to explain what he did wrong. I removed redundant circuitry and switches. Just the look on his face while I was explaining the problems was priceless. Okay, so maybe I was a little condescending, but this idiot deserved it.

I could see that Neil was getting a little upset. Forgive me, but I just didn't want to see him burn his house down. True, he was a complete bonehead but why should his wife and children have to suffer? I stood up and walked over to my toolbox and pulled out a multimeter that I use to check voltages. I turned it on and checked to see if voltage was still coming from the connection I unplugged earlier.

The voltage was still good. By some miracle, he had not shorted or damaged the refrigerator's wiring. What's that old saying, "god protects babies and fools?" I'd like to throw "electronic engineers" into the mix.

I removed the dispenser panel and placed it on the table and took out a pair of wire cutters. I explained to Neil that he had soldered the parts on the wrong terminal. He was not taking my comments too well. Clearly, he felt like his pride was being stepped on.

He stood up and the chair fell backwards. Neil looked like he was holding his breath. His face was turning red. He was going to blow. I also stood up. We faced each other. Then he started venting,

"This is my project… I spent weeks on this… I don't need your help…You're just a repairman. I'm an engineer, damnit!…"

This easily was the fifth time he named his profession to me. Then it got weird.

"I have a mitt," he said.

I looked at him incredulously, so he repeated himself.

"I have a mitt, damnit!"

"Hey, I'm here to fix your refrigerator, not play catch. Besides, I was a pretty good catcher, so if we did play catch, I'd probably take your head off."

Neil paused, got even redder and then explained himself.

"Not "mitt." M.I.T.! I have a degree from M.I.T.!"

Oh, so that's what he meant. The Massachusetts Institute of Technology. A fine school to be sure, but everyone makes mistakes. Finally, it was my turn to speak.

"Sir, that's all well and good. And if you were trying to almost destroy your refrigerator and burn down your house, then your project was a complete success. One more thing. I'm not a repairman. Not that there's anything wrong with that profession. I'm a repair technician and I also have taken the same classes in electronics you did. Although, it looks like I wasn't asleep that semester."

Neil was dumbfounded. He just stood there. I closed up my toolbox and secured the locks, picked it up and started to leave. As I turned the corner between the kitchen wall and the living room wall, I stopped in my tracks and did not turn around. I probably should've kept my mouth shut but I just couldn't help myself. I said,

"I certainly hope you're not designing anything right now. At least anything that requires electricity. If you do, please think of your poor family. I'm sure they didn't do anything to deserve this."

Was it unprofessional of me to get that last dig in? Maybe. Was his, seemingly, complete incompetence in his chosen profession a danger to him and those around him? Oh, yeah. Perhaps, if he finally realized how uninformed he was, maybe he'd quit and save some lives. Somehow, I doubt it. Neil's phone rang, and I left.

There's an old saying that I thought was particularly apt for this situation and it went something like this, "engineers can design the world, but it takes technicians to make it work."

184

So, for any and all the engineers who may be reading this, try and remember that. Just because we technicians may have not attended the same fancy schools you did, doesn't mean that we don't know what we're talking about and if you give us crap, there's an excellent chance we'll leave your house and you'll be stuck with a charred refrigerator.

Man, engineers drive me nuts.

Story 37: Temper, Temper (2015)

Here's a little story that just happened the other day. Yes, I needed a couple of days to finally calm down from the childish antics of this one, particular lady.

It was a Tuesday and it was normal except for the high winds blowing. As I entered the office. It was a bad omen. Some days you can just tell that something is up. There was a negative feeling all around. Maybe it was because of the Santa Ana winds.

In terms of volume, it looked like I was going to be traveling throughout the entire county. I had two service calls by the beach and several inland. Of course, none of them were together. But it was the one service call in the outskirts that this story is about.

The municipality that I was heading for was mostly distressed, both economically and socially. I'd say that at least eighty percent of the houses were rundown. The roads were grossly unmaintained, meaning uneven pavement and potholes. This town had been on my route for over thirty years and, sadly, nothing had changed.

As I drove down the main drag, something new actually happened. Off on my right side was an old building that has been empty for years but was now a fast food joint. Not to name names but I did question the business acumen of the executive who came up with the idea of opening a Mexican fast-food joint in a predominantly Mexican neighborhood next to several local Mexican restaurants. I guess I just wasn't cut out for the corporate life. But, at least it was progress. Slow progress.

The address I was headed towards was located in the lower suburbs of a housing track. That meant low income households and multiple families in a single dwelling. I'm not making moral judgements here. I'm just stating facts. As I re-read the address on the work order, I recognized the street. It was worse than I had originally thought. I was headed towards an extremely crime ridden area in a crime ridden community.

It took sometime for me to arrive at the house because the roads leading to the it were even more beaten down and weather worn than the last time I had the unfortunate pleasure of visiting. Yes, it not my favorite place to travel.

According to my GPS, the address was coming up. I was going to make a right turn on the next street when, over the phone, another repair tech informed me that putting sunglasses on would be a good idea. It would help me fit in. I put them on. No, things were not looking good.

I drove pretty slowly. Mostly because I really didn't want to get to my destination and also because, I didn't want to do anything that would make me stand out or alert the locals of my presence, if I could avoid it. The houses along the street had no lawns, no trees but a lot of broken down cars and clothes hung out to dry on makeshift clothes lines. A few of the houses have broken chain link fencing or block walls. This was the wrong place for me to be in, daylight or not.

The address was coming up on my left. Something was truly wrong about this place. For starters, there was a new Camaro parked out front and the blocking wall surrounding the property looked to be of newer construction.

As I drove by, the driveway was freshly poured and painted. The property also had a green lawn which, really made it stick out. What was going on inside?

The road ended at a dirt field. I needed to turn the truck around and park. It was best to be facing out if I had to leave in a hurry. Outside, three men were sitting in chairs on the porch, staring at me as I executed a perfect three-point turn. One of the guys even said, "Gringo can drive." Damn right, I can.

After finishing the maneuver, I glanced to my left and one of the men crushed a beer can in his hand. I wonder if he was trying to intimidate me. Yeah, like a chair ridden, overweight man crushing an aluminum can was going to scare me. Worst case scenario, I could run and that guy could only run as far to get another six-pack.

When this little exhibition of machismo was finally over, I looked at the house. It had a
beautiful Spanish exterior with a wagon wheel and black rod iron gates. The roof was comprised of red Spanish tile.

By now I had parked in front of the house. I could see a light on in one room and nothing else. The front windows were tinted, and possibly bullet proof, with blinds hanging on the inside. Somebody valued their privacy because nobody could see inside this house. If that wasn't enough, the main door was made of heavy metal and imposing. Almost like a prison gate in an old movie.

I made sure to lock the truck, front cab, rear doors and I even put on the club. I figured that if the truck got stolen, I could honestly say that I had taken every reasonable precaution. Time to get it over with. I exited the driver's side door and looked around. Then I walked to the rear of the truck and opened the doors, grabbed my toolbox, clipboard and cell-phone. It was time to enter the property.

One thing that stood out was the ten metal pipes dug into the ground behind the cinderblock wall. I wondered why until I looked around. The house was at an intersection. Most likely a car ran the stop sign and crashed into the house damaging who knows what. That would account for the new construction. Before I let my mind wander too much, I quickly remembered the area I was in.

The front walkway was made of stamped concrete and moved to the left, hooking up with the stamped concrete driveway and to the right, leading to a storage door. Trust me, that kind of work is not cheap.

The lawn was green and freshly mowed. I could even see wheel marks from the mower so, yes, this house was out of place for this neighborhood. Just try to imagine a mansion in a majorly depressed community. Have you ever heard that rule of real estate that you don't want to be the nicest home on the block? Whoever owned this house hadn't.

I rang the doorbell and "Jingle Bells" played. A little odd for June but fine. As I was standing there, something just didn't seem right. Maybe because I was standing on a hand printed concrete scroll.

From inside, I heard a few voices commenting that someone was at the door, which was newly installed and made from solid, composite wood, complete with iron bars. Hopefully, whoever answered it would be normal and not the crazy person I was mentally preparing for.

Finally, the door began to open. A Latina lady, about five-foot-six, stood in front of me. She had shoulder length, dark hair. Her greeting was cordial but no more.

"Hello, please come in. I'm Camila."

"I'm Rob."

We shook hands and walked through the foyer. Adjacent to it, was the living room which contained a fireplace, four arm chairs and a couch. The walls were covered with old black and white pictures of family members who, by now, must have passed on. Everything seemed to have been purchased in the last four to six months. Maybe they got an insurance settlement from when the car plowed into their front area.

Camila and I continued to the kitchen which had an arch opening, wide enough for two people to easily walk through. Just like the living room, the kitchen also appeared to have been redone with new cabinets and brown granite countertops. There were also two dishwashers. Why two dishwashers? In case one broke down? Who knew? Camilia, and she wasn't volunteering. To my right, was the reason why I was there; the refrigerator.

This refrigerator was the Cadillac of fridges. It was sleek, shiny, chromed and had three doors. Name a bell and whistle and this beauty had it. Camilia turned to the left and stopped at the end of the kitchen. I placed my tool box on the floor and my paperwork on top of the tools. As I was standing up I noticed that she was watching me in detail. It got to be a little uncomfortable, so I asked, "Is there something I should know before I get started here?"

She said nothing and continued to stare until she didn't. Camilia started speaking or, more accurately, whining for about two minutes but didn't really say anything. Still, in its own way it was impressive because you can't breathe when you speak, and I can't hold my breath for two minutes. Whatever it was that she was saying, it was obvious that she had practiced it a bunch of times.

I can honestly say that as a seasoned technician, I can normally figure out what kind of person that I'm dealing with somewhere around the fourth sentence. But, because I was so focused on her verbal dexterity which, again, was a two-minute run-on sentence, she threw me off my game.

I just stood there looking like I cared, thinking that somewhere in this verbal diarrhea, there must be some information I could use. Finally, I figured out that was she was trying to tell me that there was a black smudge on one of the pull-out drawers and the housekeeper couldn't get it clean. Why she couldn't just tell me that is beyond me. I reasonably said,

"Ma'am could you please show me the mark in question?"

Camilia walked over to the refrigerator and opened both of the doors. She raised her right hand and finger waved to me to come take a look, so I did. On the left side of the lower pantry pull-out drawer was a dull oval thumb print. The horror. Now, if you aren't familiar with this kind of refrigerator, suffice it to say that you need two hands, grasping firmly on each side to pull out. You didn't need to be Sherlock Holmes to deduce that someone tried to pull out the lower drawer and had trouble doing so.

"This is what I'm talking about," Camilia said while pointing to the offending mark. "This is why you're here."

"Okay, let me in to take a closer look," I said.

At first glance, I couldn't see anything, so I needed to take an even closer look. In my toolbox, I keep a magnifying glass. I had it stored in the sidewall and this was the first time I've had to use it since I bought it five-years-ago.

I reached for the magnifying glass and started looking at the mark. I can confirm that there was a mark with scratches alongside it. I also found four finger prints up underneath the side sliding rail. Camilia hadn't spotted them and I wasn't dumb enough to point them out to her.

At this point I thought it might be nice to show her how to unlock the drawer but my spider sense went off. Camilia was now standing directly behind me at the other end of the kitchen with her arms crossed over her head. It was a weird pose to say the least. I asked her, "What would you like me to do?"

She didn't say anything for a while. We had us a stand-off like a scene from the O.K. Corral. Who was going to make the first move? I thought it best to play innocent. I knew she was up to something and making the first move would prove I was right.

"Ma'am, how did this mark get here," I asked?

She said nothing, just shifting her body weight with her arms folded while glaring at me. I tried again.

"Do you have any knowledge of how this happened?"

Camilia shifted her weight from one leg to the other and lowered her arms to her body. I think she was trying to intimidate me. I tried a third time.

"Ma'am, do you know what happened?"

Now she stood up straight, closed her fists and lowered her arms with fists to her side. She thrust out her chest and had the meanest look I've ever seen on a lady outside of a woman's prison on bologna sandwich day. Honestly, her expression really was that mean. It was a combination of Mary McDonnell in "Dances With Wolves" and Veruca "I Want It Now, Daddy!" Salt from "Willy Wonka."

About this time, I needed to do something.

"Ma'am, I have a spray cleaner in my truck that works great on greasy oil residue on stove tops. I think it'll work in this instance. I'll be right back." I left the abode and when I came back, she had not moved an inch. It was like she was a DVR and I had paused her.

I sprayed the cleaner on a paper towel and began to wipe the thumb print. Not too surprisingly, the spot came off easily. I stood up and turned to Camilia and said,

"Ma'am, the spot is gone now."

I don't think she was expecting this to happen. She, clearly, still wanted something. Camilia walked over to the refrigerator, bent over slightly and stared for a few seconds at the now cleaned thumb print. Her tone changed because in a much lower register she said,

"I still see it. I want it replaced and I want you guys to pay for it!"

She turned and walked back to her spot at the other end of the kitchen and reverted to her "Stands with Fist" position with facial expressions changing about every thirty seconds.

"Ma'am, I not clear why you want me to replace the drawer. The spot is gone and there is no structural damage whatsoever, so I can't justify any replacement," I said.

Just then, her husband, a huge guy who easily weighed two-hundred and fifty pounds, walked through the living room and said under his breath, "Don't make her mad," before exiting.

Why would I care if she got angry? I'm not the one who had to live with her. He took those vows, not me. Still, if a guy who was as jacked as he was,

was afraid of her, I probably should be too but afraid or not, I wasn't going to replace any part because of a thumb print. It was ridiculous.

Then I figured it out. This must be how she got people to do things around her house. Maybe she used this act on the construction people too.

After about five minutes of her angry posing, reality seemed to seep in. She knew I wasn't going to give in to her. Camilia started to walk closer to me while stomping her feet at every opportunity. Whip out your cell-phones because the show was about to start.

"I paid good money for this appliance and service warranty. It's damaged. I want it replaced!"

I didn't move an inch as she continued throwing her temper tantrum. It was cute to watch. Off in the background, the husband walked behind me again. He shook his head, muttered "good luck" and left. The tantrum continued.

"I want a new refrigerator of equal or greater value."

Time to screw with her so, I interrupted her demented monologue by saying,

"Ma'am, I hear you loud and clear. If you want a new unit, we can get you one here, no problem. Probably by tomorrow."

A smile crept against her lips as she said, "Good." In her mind, the bullying had worked again. Then I said,

"Of course, you're going to have to pay for it. Same color as the previous unit, I presume?"

I didn't think it was possible but she was even madder than before.

"No! I want the refrigerator replaced and you are going to pay for it! This thing is a lemon and I want it out here! If you don't, I'm telling all my friends about what a rip-off your company is!"

I seriously doubt she had any friends. Camilia was really working herself up by now. She was holding her breath and stomping her feet something fierce. Her face was turning a beautiful shade of red to match the roof tiles. This must be a great achievement for her because as a light-skinned Latina, she turned as red as an Irishman. Don't you love it when people surprise you?

Time for some logic.

"Ma'am," I said in my best Mr. Rogers approximation, "I need to know why you want me to replace the refrigerator?"

With her eyes staring straight at me and smoke seemingly coming out of her ears, she responded, "Because I said so!"

As much as I was enjoying seeing a woman about to give herself a stroke, I did have other calls to make so, I jumped in.

"Ma'am, let me get this completely straight. There was a black spot on the drawer.
Someone tried cleaning the spot and rubbed some of the shine off. I cleaned the spot so that the naked eye can't see it and the refrigerator works fine with none of its functions impaired in the slightest."

By the way, she still hadn't told me how that spot had gotten there and I had asked her three times.

As, if on cue, the husband passed through again and said, "We are all screwed now" before walking off. Maybe he was, but not me. I continued.

"Lastly, there is no fact, whatsoever, that justifies replacement of your refrigerator other than you saying you said so."

Camilia began to growl at me like Mr. Worf from Star Trek: The Next Generation. I instantly became Captain Picard.

"Let me make this perfectly clear, I'm not going to replace it. Sorry! Also, you may want to calm down a little. You are going to have a coronary or stroke or both if you keep up like this over a smudge that is now gone," I said.

Camilia lowered her sights, now focusing on the contents of my spay can.

"I want one of those, whatever it is".

It was time to exit, before she really had a coronary in front of me. Trust me, the paperwork on that would be a nightmare. I bent over and picked up my toolbox and the bottle of spray cleaner. Camilia was still pissed and was stomping her feet. She lunged forward and tried to grab my bottle. I looked at her shockingly and with my deep voice, said "Get your own."

It was a short walk to the front door. She was still alongside the refrigerator, just growling at me and staring me down the best she could. I swear I could feel her eyes searing a hole in the back of my head. I saw her husband standing in the bedroom hall, listening in. I felt it best to get the hell out of there before she called on her beer drinking neighbors for help. I wasn't worried about the husband too much. Clearly, he was a beaten man.

I made it to my truck, without incident and as I started the engine, Camilia stormed out and stood in her front yard. She was obviously trying one last time to get me to change my mind. She was throwing another one of her tantrums with foot stomping, and her fists punching the air with her hair whipping around. It was a thing of perverse beauty.

I just put my sun glasses, cranked "Slow Ride" on the stereo and drove off, laughing the whole time. Camilia really needed to grow up. I later found out that she was a social worker which really cracked me up. I'm guessing her main method of getting through to people was, don't be like me."

Good advice.

Story 38: Man, You Stink! (2009)

Principles are a good thing. Think about it. Without them, it would be anarchy but how do we know when we've taken them too far? For me, it's when things start to smell.

This is one of those stories that I had to write down right after it happened. My service route for this day seemed just like any other day. The service calls scheduled were of no importance and I was off to my last one.

As I pulled onto this customer's street, nothing seemed out of place. The cars were parked on the street as they should be. Kids were playing soccer in one of the front yards. If there weren't palm trees, this neighborhood really could be Anywhere, U.S.A.

The house I was looking for was about mid-way down the street. Not too far of a drive though. It was on the right side of the street. I pulled my truck up in front of the house and proceeded to exit the cab. As I walked around the back of the truck I couldn't help but notice that the front lawn was all brown. All the surrounding yards were the perfect green, but this lawn was dead. On the sides were some small plants and they were not long for this Earth either. This customer, for some reason, had stopped watering.

The most logical reason for this was that he was planning on putting in a new lawn and before he could do it, the current lawn had to be killed off. I won't bore you with the reasons why but trust me when I say, that's the most efficient way to do it. Mystery solved, right? Wrong.

I walked to the front door and knocked just like on every other service call I've ever made. As I stood at the doorway, I couldn't help but notice that there was a strong smell coming from somewhere. The slight breeze that followed was a welcome release, but it also prevented me from finding out where it was coming from.

The front door opened, standing in the doorway was a slender man dressed in a white "Little Feat" tee shirt and short cut-off jeans.

"Hi, I'm Rob. I'm here to fix your dryer," I said.

"Hey, I'm Gary. Thanks for coming out," Gary responded.

He waved me inside and I followed. If I had to do it all over again, I would've taken a deep breath before entering because it was the last good breath of air I'd be taking for a while. As soon as I entered the home, the smell hit me and hit me hard. The pungent odor was coming from inside his home and it seemed like Gary had not taken a shower or bath in a long time either. He stunk! What was going on here?

Gary closed the door behind me and we proceeded to walk through the house. He was leading me around the living room area. The problem with walking behind someone who stinks is that I was forced to smell his backdraft or as cyclists call it, "tail wind." By now, I was trying to find a breath of clean air and my eyes started to water up. It was almost to a point where I was starting to reach for my tee shirt to pull it over my mouth and nose to filter out some of the stink.

We were heading for the laundry room, which was located right behind the kitchen. As we entered the kitchen, the smell was getting worse. I didn't think it was possible but sure enough, it was. Gary had not done the dishes in a long time. I would say at least a few weeks and they were all piled up with rotting food on them. Shockingly, I didn't see any fleas. Thank God for small favors. Off to the side of the room I noticed that the trash can also had not been emptied and were over flowing onto the floor. The smell of food rotting from the trash can combined with the dirty dishes had just started to make me more than a little sick to my stomach.

We walked by the dishes and the rotting trash and entered the laundry room. Inside the laundry room, clothes were piled up in a matter that suggested that at the end of the day, old Gary would take off what he was wearing for the day and just toss them inside because each layer of the laundry tower was a different outfit. Lots of Little Feat tee-shirts. I'm sure that that very underrated band would be proud to know that Gary was a huge fan.

"So, what seems to be the problem with the dryer," I asked?

"Well, it won't run or really do anything…"

As he was rambling on, it was then that my eyes really began to water. I did my best to not gag in front of him, but my best wasn't good enough. I started to cough in a manner that it seemed like I was trying to clear my throat. Actually, what I was doing was trying to find air to breathe. Gary looked concerned.

"Are you choking," he asked?

I looked up and responded with a comment that would pacify him, so he would leave. I told him that when I swallowed, my saliva went down the wrong pipe. He asked me if I wanted a glass of water. The last thing I wanted was to drink from one of his glasses so, I wasn't thrilled when he walked to the pantry. Fortunately, inside one of the cabinets was a case of bottled water. At least it was sealed and probably not unsanitary but from what I had seen so far, I couldn't tell for sure.

I took a sip which helped a little. Gary took this to mean that I was okay and left, which helped a lot. Back to the dryer. I started to get to work but now I had to contend with the mound of clothes.

"Sir, would you mind moving your clothes out of the way, so I can get to the dryer," I asked quite reasonably?

"Just throw them any place," he responded. Great, now it was up to me to move his clothes. I don't like touching anyone's dirty laundry, let alone this guy. Lucky for me, just off to the side was a mop which I used to push the clothes aside.

The problem with the dryer was a heat fuse that had gone out. In order to replace it, I needed to move the dryer forward a foot or two, so I could remove the rear panel. This was a problem because I needed to move the clothes again and this time push them inside the kitchen. God bless that mop.

Gary was in the kitchen and saw the assorted clothes being pushed out. If he had a problem with it, he didn't say anything.

The rear access panel was just far enough out of my reach so that I needed to use my toolbox to stand on just to access the screws. I did this as gracefully as I could. In the meantime, Gary, like most customers, wanted to strike up a conversation. I must admit that I was more than a little curious about what was going on with his lawn and maybe even about the inside of his house. I just hope I wouldn't gag during his explanation.

"I suppose you're wondering about what happened with my lawn," he asked?

"Oh, is the reason why it's dead is because you're putting in a new one," I asked back?

"Ha! They'd freakin' love that, wouldn't they?"

Huh? Who's "they?"

"I don't understand," I said.

"Those sons of bitches at the Department of Water and Power."

Oh, those sons of bitches. I'll admit to a healthy skepticism about government myself, but I had no idea what he was talking about. Luckily, he needed no prompting.

"Did you know that my water bill rate rose fifteen percent last year and twenty percent the year before?!"

I must've missed that memo. The rant continued.

"They think that I have no choice but to take it but, obviously, they're wrong. I will never use another drop of water provided by this godforsaken city as long as I live!"

For reasons, I don't quite understand, I decided to engage him.

"I hear you. I hate when the rates go up like nobody's business, but you need water," I said.

"I don't."

"What about bathing," I asked?

"My buddy belongs to a health club. He sneaks me in once a week and I shower there. That's all you need," Gary said.

Um, no. Based on what I was smelling, he needed to bathe way more than once a week. He needed to be hosed down. Also, because like in most municipalities, your water bill is combined with your electricity and trash bills. Gary wasn't paying for those either. He explained that all the power was provided by a generator and he just dropped his trash off at local dumpsters when no one was looking.

So, to sum up, Gary wasn't just gross. He was protesting, which is his right but what about my right to not become nauseous?

The part I needed for the repair wasn't in my toolbox. I had to go to the truck for it. Gary was facing the kitchen window and still ranting about how the utility companies were out to get him. He wasn't talking to me. He was talking to the window. It sounded like he has practiced his speech many times and was just waiting for some unsuspecting sap to unload it on. Lucky me, I was that sap.

I made the mistake of telling him where I needed to go, and he just glared at me. How dare I interrupt his wonderful speech!

I opened the door and exited the house. Finally, fresh air! I walked a little on the slow side, mostly because I needed to expel the stink from my lungs and wipe my eyes clean. I got to the truck. The part I needed was in a side drawer. Normally it would take me just a few seconds to retrieve it but not this time. I must have taken ten minutes before I re-entered the house. Can you blame me? Would you be in any hurry to get back in there?

I knew that eventually I had to go back, so walked into the kitchen. Gary wasn't there. He was in the laundry room looking at the back of the dryer. I let him know I was there and he stepped back from the dryer to let me back into the room. Gary went back into the kitchen and I went back to work.

The replacing of the part went really easily. I stepped backward and turned the dryer's timer knob to a setting, so I could test the operation. It started to run. I couldn't have been more happy. In my mind, I was going to be out of there soon. Of course, I was wrong because immediately there was a loud bang. The noise came from the blower vent.

On the floor, behind the dryer, were papers and assorted junk and underwear. Just what I wanted to step onto. As I stepped onto the junk pile, I heard a crunching sound as I stepped down. I noticed that a few of the papers were covered with mold.

I removed the blower vent housing. At first, I did not notice what the problem was. I looked further into the housing and found the problem. It was the remains of a rat skeleton entwined with the blower vent. Without being too graphic, the remains of the rat had, somehow, managed to wrap itself around the blower which restricted the air-flow out of the dryer. Based on the composition of the skeleton, it had been there awhile.

I needed to clear the blower wheel. Fortunately, I kept a pair of gloves in my tool box. You really think I'm going to touch the remains of that animal without protection? Not a chance. As I reached into the blower wheel, an unpleasant thought popped into my head, what else could be in there? I reached into the blower housing with my left hand and pulled out the remains. Yes, it was disgusting but, in that house,, they fit right in. Now I had to retest the dryer because I needed to know if the blower was clear.

Reaching over to the consul, I re-started the dryer. It seemed to be running okay with good volume. I placed my hand in front of the blower vent. Air was coming out of the vent. I reached back over the consul and stopped the dryer and reattached the vent ducting to the blower vent. I started the dryer and it started bogging down again. Now what?!

Something was blocking the air from the outside. As I climbed back over the dryer, something happened. The air started flowing again. Whatever was blocking the vent just flew out and was ejected to the outside. Maybe it was more rat remains. All I cared about was that I would be getting the hell out of there soon. The papers behind the dryer were not a concern of mine and I did not want to pick them up. They just blended in with the rest of the decor. I'd call it "early slum."

I moved the dryer back to its original spot. The papers crunched as I pushed. I started the dryer just to make sure it worked before I left. I started to cough again. The bottle of water Gary gave to me was on my toolbox. I needed to clear my throat bad.

Gary came into the laundry room and wanted to know what I had found. I showed him the half-decomposed rat skeleton I pulled out of the blower. He looked down at it and didn't say a word. Slowly, he turned around and walked out of the kitchen and went somewhere in the house.

It took me a few minutes to locate my tools in the mess and place them in my toolbox. Normally, I take a few minutes to clean up any mess I may have made doing the repair but, somehow, in this house, I didn't think it would 've made much of a difference. It may have even screwed with the decorating scheme.

Gary came back into the kitchen and I met him at the kitchen table. The work order said that the dryer was under a factory warranty. How was I going to justify that the dryer stopped working due to a decomposing rat? I thought it best to not write anything about what I found.

I wrote the order out to say that the part failed out on its own. Basically, I did him a huge favor. I figured that this guy had enough problems.

Gary could not see what I was writing. For some reason he started to get upset. I had no idea why. Maybe he thought I wrote something bad about him. Gary began to raise his voice, getting more angry as he spoke, just short of yelling at me. I gave Gary my best cold, hard stare. He shut up.

I said as reasonably as possible, "Sir, I don't know why you're so angry. I just wrote on the order that a part failed on your dryer and I did not say anything about the rodent. This would void your warranty repair on the spot.

Gary stepped back and paused. Maybe the smell was getting to him too! He raised his hands upwards and said, "I didn't know what you were writing. I thought you were going to charge me!"

I needed to clear my throat again so, I reached down to get the water bottle and I took a sip. Honestly, it takes a lot to piss me off and he just did it. Verbally attacking me while I wrote out the order was not a good thing. I really don't care what this guy does to protest anything. But, with the amount of experience I have, I have found that if I respond to this guy's comments it would do nothing more than fuel his anger. Plus, I've always felt that actions speak louder than words.

I held out the work order and wrote out in large letters. "WARRANTY VOIDED – INFESTATION."

I tore out a copy of the order and placed it on the table upside down. I wished Gary good luck on his various protest as I started to walk out of his house. He asked me why I was leaving? I guess he just wanted to talk to someone.

I started up the truck and started to pull away. As I was about three or four houses away, I looked in the side mirror and noticed that Gary had ran into the street with the copy of the work order in one hand, waving it in the air.

I drove back to the shop to clear my paperwork. As I was doing so, the boss walked up to me. He wanted to know what had happened at this repair stop. Halfway through his question, he stopped and leaned over to me and smelled my shirt. The expression on his face almost said it all.

"You stink! What did you get into today," he asked? I told him about my last stop and the funky odors that resided there, the dead rat, the protest, etc. I handed him the work order and then excused myself to burn my clothes.

Patrick Henry, one of our founding fathers once said, in regard to fighting tyranny and oppression, "Give me liberty or give me death." To that I'd

199

like to add at the end, "and for the sake of everyone around me, give me deodorant!"

Story 39: Hot Rod Granny (The '90's)

Wouldn't you like to take out your frustrations out on that stupid driver who just cut you off? What about on the guy going two miles an hour for no apparent reason? Or the idiot who refuses to use their blinkers like we're just supposed to psychically know when they're going to turn? Yes, there are many idiots on the road and sometimes in Southern California, it seems like we have more than our fair share. So, yes, there have been many occasions when I was on the cusp of road rage. This one time encapsulates what we'd all like to do in this situation.

A little while back, I was in my work truck traveling along one of the major highways. This particular freeway had four lanes and a wide shoulder. I was traveling in the third lane, going about sixty-five miles an hour. That was the posted speed limit for that highway and you can imagine that most people took that as, at best, a suggestion. Nobody travels the speed limit. If you're not traveling at least seventy plus, stay in the slow lane.

Again, I was in the third lane just minding my own business. Way in front of me was a late model, blue Chevy Impala in the far right. The Impala was going about sixty and as I started to pull alongside it, I noticed a pink bumper sticker that read, "Grandma's Rule." Inside the vehicle was grandma driving and talking on her cell phone. She had the phone in her right hand but pressed up to her left ear. Her arm was crossed in front of her and her left hand was on the wheel. Granny was a contortionist.

My exit was coming up and I needed to slow down. As I tapped on the brakes, grandma made a lane change and cut me off. I immediately went from tapping to slamming on the brakes and swerved to the right barely missing her. Grandma crossed from the slow lane straight over to the number two lane. Fortunately, there were no other cars involved. I exited the highway and headed to my stop while thanking the almighty and taking a bunch of deep breaths.

Later that same day, just after lunch, I was driving down a two-lane road with an island in the middle. There was an Impala in front of me driving a little slower. As I gained ground, I noticed the pink bumper sticker again. It was grandma and she was still yakking on the phone. About what, I have no idea. Maybe about her grandkids or how Matlock wears the hell out of that white suit.

This time grandma did something even better. She started signaling to her right. Like a crazy person, I naturally assumed that she was going to exit the road. Needless to say, I was wrong. I don't know why, but I started braking. Call it instinct. Call it experience. Hell, call it self-preservation. Grandma started the right turn into a track of homes and then darted to the left. She was making a U-turn into on-coming traffic, namely me. Grandma crossed in front of me from my right to my left.

I slammed on the brakes. The truck started to skid, and I was heading straight towards her car. No two ways about it, I was about to be hit. Time had stopped. The truck began to turn to the right while skidding.

Fortunately, the angle of the truck was just enough to miss colliding with grandma's car. I eased off the brake pedal and started heading in my new direction. How close were we to smashing into each other? Put it this way, as much as I hate the metric-system, I'm forced to use it here. My truck and her rear bumper were millimeters apart. Way, way too close. Did you think I was out of the woods? Guess again. Yes, I missed ramming grandma, but my new direction landed me on the sidewalk where I promptly smashed into a newly planted tree. Poor tree. Hell, poor me!

With no concern at all, grandma continued her cross traffic turn and yes, she was still talking on the phone. The sound of other car's brake's squealing was everywhere, followed by the sound of crashing metal. I can only guess that grandma did not look as she continued going on her merry way. Yes, kids, grandma caused an accident and not just in my pants. I opened the door of my truck and exited. All told, it was a four-car pile-up. A little while later, the police showed up. I told them what happened and gave them a description of the car. The officer made reference that the car in question has done this before.

Later that evening, sometime around five, I was home and off the clock. My wife and I left the house and went to the supermarket to do a little shopping. I was so not myself that I didn't even put up a token argument. I took the '67 Corvette Shelby, a car that would will cheer any guy up. Honestly, the hour or two I spent doing something else helped calm me down a little. Don't get me wrong, the subject of crazy grandma came up more than once, but I was starting to let it go, at least a little.

As we exited the market, we heard a car crash off in the background, which brought me right back to where I was earlier that day. I looked at the wife and said, "it couldn't be her, could it?" She, quite reasonably, pointed out that the odds of that happening were slim and none. We loaded the bags into the back of the car and started the engine. I pulled out and headed to the mall for round two of our shopping trip.

Now, this particular mall parking lot has three entrances and exits. One, of which, is near a normally heavy traffic exit. It had four lanes leading up to it. This place was designed in the eighties when the philosophy veered towards a high turnover of customers, thus they wanted to make it really easy for you to come and go. Anyway, I noticed that there was a traffic jam in the parking lot. There were three cars in front of me a several coming up from behind. I pulled the car into the line and started to wait. I could not see what was happening, I just knew that we were not moving. Now, here's the thing about the '67 Corvette Shelby, it doesn't use gas. It eats gas, plus, it tends to die in idle so, yeah, we're basically talking about my version of hell.

One of my fellow drivers decided he couldn't take it anymore, so he exited his car and started to yell at the front driver. I turned around to see what was happening and saw nothing. Then I got out to see if it would make any difference. Car horns started to go off. My wife advised me in the same tone she uses when I'm about to get up and sing on New Year's Eve that this isn't a good idea and I shouldn't do it. Of course, like then, I didn't listen.

I slowly closed my car door. A few of the other drivers decided to join me and exited their cars. I started walking and I noticed something. A blue Impala. Yes, it was grandma and she was still talking on the phone. Arms crossed and just sitting there. Her car was running but her engine was knocking. Something was wrong, and it was about to get worse.

I came up behind her. My wife now was yelling at me to come back. I double checked to see if it was her car. No doubt about it, it was the grandma who caused the accident earlier in the day. As I walked past the vehicle just behind grandma's, a man in a different automobile started to exit and as he did, I asked if he would call 911 and report that I have found the car that almost killed me twice today? The look on my face must've told him I wasn't kidding so he dialed.

I walked up behind grandma's car, making sure to stand in the blind spot. I looked into the rear window and noticed that the passenger's door was unlocked. It was like the universe had magically given me the chance to have some fun / revenge. I made sure that grandma didn't notice me as I rounded the passenger side and opened the door. I jumped into the Impala and with a quick motion, I snatched the keys from the ignition. Her arms were still crossed, and she couldn't do a thing to stop me. The car's engine stalled out, just like mine was about to. Grandma could not get away now. Somehow, this snapped grandma out of it and she actually stopped talking. Who the hell was she talking to all this time anyway? I was just getting started.

I exited grandma's car, making sure to slam the door. I had her keys. Unless she had a gun, there wasn't a thing she could do about it. Slowly I walked out and stopped right in front of her car. Then, I started dangling her keys in an attempt to get her to exit the car. It didn't work. She resumed talking as if nothing out of the ordinary was happening.

I started walking to the driver's door. By now, I had an audience comprised of most of the people in the parking lot, waiting to see what I was going to do. Man, was my wife not happy. The look on her face said it all. I was going to pay for this later, but it wasn't later. I needed to finish this. My road rage was just about to take off.

I opened the driver's car door, which was also unlocked. A little piece of advice for all the lunatics out there, if you're going to be a selfish bastard and nearly get people killed, it might be a good idea to lock your doors. After I did this, grandma finally stopped talking. I reached for her phone and ripped it right out of her hand. She didn't put up much of a fight. By now, I figured I'd better say something and soon. To people who were just coming up, I was attacking a sweet, old lady.

"Do you realize that you almost killed me twice today?! The first time when you cut me off on the 23 and you caused me to get into an accident when you made a U-turn into incoming traffic. Because of you, I slammed into a tree! Did you stop? No! Do you realize that, because of you, four other cars sustained major body damage?! Of course not! What did you do? You kept on driving while talking on your g.d. phone the whole g.d. time! Well, no more!"

Say what you want about flip phones but one virtue they have is they're a lot easier to break than your conventional smart phones. I snapped it in half. I took the half with the screen and threw it as far as I could. I used to be a pretty good catcher in my younger days and let's just say that that half a flip-phone had quite a journey, sailing onto the freeway. True, I was going to be guzzling ibuprofen for the next few days for my shoulder, but I didn't care. Right then, I felt great. The part of the phone with the sim card, I placed in my pocket.

Grandma looked up at me and did not move a muscle. She knew. I could see it in her eyes. The people were now standing all around her car. They started clapping and cheering. One of the young ladies in the crowd made a comment about how this was the same car she saw on the news.

A couple of days had passed. I was at home icing my shoulder and filling out paperwork from my accident when I heard a knock on my door. I opened it to find a police officer on the other side. I'd be lying if I said I wasn't a little bit nervous. For all I knew, they were coming to arrest me. Think about it, I had destroyed sweet, old grandma's personal property. Jail would be bad. Not as bad as my wife saying, "I told you so" for the foreseeable future but bad.

Fortunately, I had nothing to worry about. The officer told me that the grandma was part of an insurance scam and had, in just a couple of weeks, caused almost thirty accidents throughout the county. The way it worked was that grandma would be followed by a junker car. Sweet, old grandma would drive carelessly, causing other cars to hit the junker. The junker car would then make a lot of money off the inevitable insurance settlement. Nice, right? The feds and D.A. were going to go after her hard. By the way, I also found out that grandma wasn't a grandma, so they got her on bumper sticker fraud too.

I gave the officer the sim card from granny's phone. Now, they'd be able to find out who she'd been talking to and who was in cahoots with her. The officer thanked me profusely for this treasure trove I had just handed him. He took my statement and said that if they needed me, they'd contact me. He reached out and shook my hand, then left. The pain in my shoulder magically disappeared, at least for an hour or so. If I had to summarize the expression on my wife's face, I'd go with, "I cannot believe you got away with that."

I stared at her and said, "Yes, you're right. What I did was colossally stupid, but it felt so damn good" and I danced away.

Story 40: Garbage House (Early '90's)

According to Wikipedia, garbage is waste material that is discarded by humans, usually due to a perceived lack of utility i.e. stuff that serves zero useful purpose. A "pack rat" or "hoarder" is someone who won't throw anything out. You may think you know pack rats or even been in the home of one, but nothing compares to the house that I was forced to pay a call on.

The repair call came into the dispatcher's office on a Monday afternoon and the service visit was scheduled for that next Friday afternoon. Someone volunteered me to go and repair their oven. To this day, I don't know who volunteered me for that job because if I did find out, someone's got at least a black eye coming to them

Friday afternoon eventually came, and I drove out to the residence. As I pulled up, it seemed to be a regular house with a typical front yard and a nice car in the driveway. It looked like any one of the thousands of homes I've been to during my career. Man, was I wrong.

The weirdness started after I had parked and went to get my toolbox from the truck. I noticed a smell that I didn't recognize, at least not at first. Trust me, it wasn't pleasant. I closed the rear doors of the truck and started walking to the home's front door.

On the front door was a hand-written note with instructions telling to go around to the far side of the garage and enter from the side door. Ok, I've had notes on doors before, so this wasn't a big deal. I just hope there wasn't an angry dog waiting for me.

Despite the note, I knocked on the front door. Why? Experience and habit. Plus, it's just polite to announce yourself to the owners before entering a home. From the back, I heard a man's voice faintly scream out, "Are you the oven repairman?" I stepped back and answered, "Yes, I'm here to repair the oven."

"Didn't you see the note? Go around to the far side of the garage and enter from the side door!"

I placed the note in my back pants pocket and started walking as instructed. On the other side of the house was the garage and next to it, a wooded fence. The fence was comprised of wood slats that were old and extremely weather beaten. The fence stood about six feet. On the right side of the fence was a door with a pull ring protruding from the top. It was obvious that this door has not been used in a long time.

I pulled the ring to unlatch the locking mechanism. The door moved only a few inches. I pushed harder but there was no give. I pushed again, even harder. I looked around the door and noticed that the grass had grown high enough to block it. I went into my old three-point stance from high-school football and slammed the door as hard as I could. It opened just enough so that I could squeeze through. Now, the backyard stood in my path.

The backyard was a complete inverse of the front yard meaning that while the front was neatly manicured and well kept, the back had weeds that stood three to four feet high. It looked like something out of a Vietnam War movie.

There was no walking path to the side garage door. I did my best to maneuver around the foliage, but it was rough going without a machete. Finally, I was able to make it to the garage door. The hinges were rusted, and it looked like it hadn't been opened in years and spider webs hung on top of the door frame. What was on the other side? A portal to another dimension? At this point, nothing would've surprised me.

I turned the knob and tried pushing but it too didn't want to move. I pushed harder, but this time I used both hands and a lot more force. The door still gave very little. Something on the other side was blocking it. I was at an impasse. Do I stop pushing on the door or do I give it a hard shove and risk damaging it? Better yet, do I just forget the whole thing and leave? Damn me and my professionalism, I stayed. I pushed with a lot more effort than I really needed to. Finally, it opened with a crunching sound.

The crunch sound was from objects on the other side. It seemed like nothing broke. What else was behind the door? The door was opened enough so that I could wedge my way inside to the garage. The faint light from the outside allowed me to see piles of trash, some six feet high, some all the way to the ceiling. The door shut because of the breeze. Now I couldn't see a thing. It was completely dark. Great. The small bright side was that I could identify the smell. Have you ever been to a dump? That's what it smelled like.

A man's voice spoke out.

"I'm on the other side of the garage, just walk toward my voice."

"Hello. I can't see where to walk. Can you turn on a light, please?"

I don't know if he heard me or did not understand what I asked, so I asked again,

"Sir, I can't see where to go. Can you turn on a light, please?"

The man responded with, "I heard you the first time, sir. The light does not work."

Terrific. I was now in the garage, standing at the back door with only the streaking light from the sun that came through the door opening. Not exactly a lot of light but just enough to get my footing. Thankfully, I normally carry a flashlight in my toolbox. I placed the box on the nearest pile of junk and pulled it out. Fortunately, it was right on top or else I would've been really screwed.

I turned on the flashlight which was a big improvement. I saw the man standing on the other side. He had a long, scraggly beard and had a huge beer gut. Hard to believe that a guy that lived like this didn't take good care of himself. Separating the two of us, besides thousands of years of evolution, was a large pile of junk.

Now, all I needed was a navigable path to the other side. You wouldn't think walking twenty feet would be that big of a deal, but you try doing it in mounds of junk so high that they exceeded the height of the rafters, so we're talking at least ten feet. They were comprised of old clothes, worn out electrical cords, open and unopened boxes, papers, used food plates, sealed and open bags of trash, etc.

The smell was getting worse from inside. I could only imagine what the house was like. Bad thoughts started going through my head. I'm a little claustrophobic and this situation was bringing it out. Maybe this was a bad deal and I needed to leave.

Then the man called out, "You need to come this way."

Which way, I thought? I bent down and grabbed my toolbox and tried to walk. The crunching sound each time I stepped was really unsettling. I felt like I was walking through the killing fields. Goose bumps and tingles on each step. What was under my shoes?

A few feet in front of me was a stack of boxes, at least I think they were boxes. The man asked me to walk to the stack and turn to my right. I made it to the boxes and I reached out with my free hand and placed it on the stack. It fell backwards, narrowly missing me.

I looked up at the man. We were still relatively far apart from each other and my flashlight was doing its best to light the way as I ventured forward. He asked me to walk forward. I did and as I placed my foot down I heard a crunching sound. It wasn't like the sound of trash under my foot but like bones breaking. What the hell did I just step in? I asked the man what it was.

"Maybe the cat or the dog. I can't be sure. How are they? Can you see them?" he asked.

Now, I was really uncomfortable. What I was stepping on was dead animals. I pointed my flashlight down. All I could see was trash and food plates. But something was underneath it.

"I can't see anything with just my flashlight," I said.

"Well, keep a lookout for them. If you need to steady yourself, feel free to put your hand on that pile to your left," he said back.

I placed my hand about waist high onto the pile and it moved up and down a little from the inside which was a little unnerving.

"Hey, do you know what's inside here? I think I felt something move a little," I said.

"That's my car. It probably needs new shocks," he answered.

Yes, he buried his car with trash and probably not intentionally. You toss enough stuff into a pile and it will envelope anything. I stepped again. This time my foot landed on some rotting food. What did I step in? This is what we call in the repair business "a bad call."

I looked up and said, "I think I just stepped in some rotten food. Is there an easier way into your house?"

I know, I know, a crazy request, right? The man looked a little puzzled. His head started to tilt upwards. What was he thinking and what was he going to do? Hack me up and throw me in one of the piles? Seconds passed but trust me, it seemed like a lot longer

He now turned his attention back to me and stood up straight and spoke with a quiver in his voice like he was offended by my outrageous request.

"Young man, if you don't what to come into my house, then don't! You're grounded for a week. The hell with you, you no good son of a bitch!" he screamed.

There was a lot to unpack here. I was grounded for a week? What the hell did that mean? Was I going to be held prisoner for seven days? Before I had a chance to muddle through any of this, the man began to step backwards through the door. He opened the door just enough, so I could get a quick glimpse into his house. It was more of the same. A lot of trash piled high against the walls. I'm guessing that on his 1040, under occupation he put "hermit" or "nut job." At lease by the look of things, he had mastered his profession and how many of us can say that?

Just then, he exited the garage and slammed the door, this made one of the towers collapse causing a trash-a-lanche. I was now standing in a dark garage, with a terrible smell with the very real possibility of being buried by garbage. What a moronic way to die.

My flashlight was still holding up. Good thing too because the only natural light coming through was from the cracks in the outline of the door. I could not move. My eyes had not adjusted to the dark and I was stuck. What was I to do? I definitely felt a panic attack coming up, so I did my best to calm myself down and then did the only thing that came; make the stupidest call in the history of 911. I grabbed my cell phone from my belt and dialed and yes, it was embarrassing.

"911, what is your emergency," the operator asked?

"My name is Rob. I'm an appliance repairman and I'm locked in a customer's garage," I answered.

"Excuse me," she said back.

"I know, I know. I was out on a call and found myself in a hoarder's garage. I said something that offended him, and he left leaving me here alone. I can't find my way out," I explained.

I heard stifled laughing on the other end.

"I apologize, sir," she said.

"Don't worry about it. If I were you, I'd be laughing too. Just, please send someone, okay?"

She promised she would and I gave her the address and all the other relevant information. I didn't know if it was 911 policy or the lady just took pity on me, but she stayed on the line until the fire department arrived. I'm not too proud to say I was grateful. You try being in total darkness surrounded by God knows what and see how cool you are.

The firemen arrived just as my flashlight went dead. Talk about good timing. I heard a knock.

"Is there anyone in there! This is the fire department!"

"Yes, I'm Rob. I made the call!"

Another voice was heard. It was the man who yelled, "Get out! Get off of my property!"

"Sir, we will, just as soon as we rescue the man trapped in your garage," said one of the firemen.

"He's not trapped! He has a bad attitude and now has to live with the consequences," said the man.

"That's not really relevant, sir," said a fireman.

Great, these two were having an argument over semantics while I was trapped. Lovely. Then, another fireman came around the side gate. He opened the door but was standing outside. Light came into the garage and finally, I could see again. The fireman looked at me and signaled.

"Are you all right," he asked?

"Yes, I'm not hurt but I am stuck," I said back.

A couple of additional fireman came to help, and a police officer came too. When two of the firemen entered the garage, they stopped abruptly. It was the smell. The terrified looks on their faces was something I will never forget. When guys who run into burning buildings are scared, that doesn't do wonders for your confidence. They immediately put their oxygen masks on.

The police officer entered the garage and stopped just behind the two firemen. All three of them looked at each other and paused for a second to look around.

"Crap" someone said.

Yes, exactly. Lots and lots of crap.

I was now facing them, and you should've seen the smirks on their faces. They apologized which made me feel a little better. I told them to go ahead and laugh. Hell, now that I wasn't going to die in there, it was hilarious. They took up my invitation and started to guffaw. Maybe a little too much.

By now, after all that time in the dark garage, my eyes had almost adjusted, but it was still a huge relief when another fireman opened the same door that the man used, and the garage was flooded with light. I started walking through the trash, toolbox in one hand and a dead flashlight in the other, slowly heading to the backdoor. As I was walking, I found what seemed to be a towel. I stopped and wiped my feet on it.

I exited the garage, followed by the firemen and police officer. Once outside, I was greeted by the fire captain who asked me if I was hurt. I told him that I wasn't. I just needed some fresh air and a moment to clean myself up. They cracked up too.

The police officer wanted to know what happened. The three of us walked out to the front yard and I explained. Trust me, I did not leave any details out. I told the police officer that Social Services were needed as well as several very large trash dumpsters with heavy equipment to remove the trash. Then, I turned to the firemen and suggested a more satisfying solution for me and a more practical one for them, a controlled fire! Honestly, I wouldn't shed a tear if the owner was in the house when that happened. That guy was nuts!

Story 41 - The Front Door Cat (1981)

My service van was pulling up to the front of a house with a nice brick flower bed to the right of the front door. The planter was pretty big, about three feet wide and twenty feet long. What was a little weird was that there were no flowers, just dirt but it's not my job to critique a customer's landscaping preferences. I was there to fix the stove. My phone rang. Mind you, this is when you could actually take calls while driving. It was my kids, specifically my eldest daughter and our youngest who just lost a tooth and had an adorable lisp.

"Hi, daddy!"

"Hi, kids," I said.

The eldest put the youngest on which was a little unusual.

"Daddy!" she said.

'Yes, sweetheart?" I answered.

"Can we get a puppy or a kitty cat! Pleassth!"

Aha! That's why the youngest was on the line, to plead for a pet. My eldest was no dummy. Who can say no to a seven-year-old with a lisp?

"We'll take care of him and feeth him and walk him and love him…" My eldest took the phone back.

"You and mom won't have to do anything," she promised.

Adorable lisp or not, I knew darn well that despite what could be their best intentions, the wife and I would be the ones taking care of said animal. So, I did what all parents do when they want to postpone a decision and yet still give some hope. I opened my mouth and said:

"We'll see." and hung up.

At the least, it bought me some time. I hung up, cleared my head and refocused on the task at hand. A moment or two went by, then I knocked on the door and waited for the customer to answer. While waiting, I noticed that there was a fat cat sitting in the planter, not really doing anything.

Now, when animals are concerned, respect is given or earned there is nowhere in between. The cat was around three or four years old. I slowly guided my finger toward the feline's nose. He greeted me and let me pet him. Nice cat, or so I thought until, out of nowhere, he took a swing at my hand and clawed me good. A fair amount of blood was drawn. I now had a two to three-inch gash on my hand that I still have to this day.

I can't be sure, but I swear the cat was laughing as he ran off. Fortunately, I had a clean rag in my toolbox. As I was cleaning the blood off my hand the customer opened the door. The customer, an average looking woman I'd peg to be in her thirties, looked at me and said, "I see you've met Timmy". I answered in return, "Yes, I have," as I entered the house.

She explained that her stove needed service. That it wouldn't come on and wasn't heating. Without even needing to see it, I knew the igniter was out. As an experienced technician, the work order told me everything I needed to know. What I had to find out was which igniter needed replacing.

After a few minutes, I located the defective igniter. Conveniently, I had the part on my truck.

"Ma'am, I located the source of the problem. I'm going to my truck to get a new igniter. I'll be right back."

"Great," she said from another room. "Take your time. It's so beautiful outside."

She was right about the day, but I wouldn't because after her I had three more jobs and maybe I should have this brand-new hand wound looked at. Anyway, I went to my truck, found the part, still in its metal box, put the box in my other hand, turned around and started walking back to the house.

As I was walking up the driveway, who was at the front door? My old friend, Timmy. I don't know if he wanted a shot at the other hand or if he wanted to draw blood from an entirely different body part but one thing I knew for sure, this time it would be different.

By this point, my wound had stopped bleeding. The pain was there, throbbing, but it wasn't anything I couldn't handle. As I walked closer, the cat was looking at me and I could tell that he was just waiting for me to pet him again. So, I did.

Remember how I said this time would be different? As Timmy closed his eyes and lowered his head feeling my hand stroke his fur backwards, I took a few steps back in anticipation. Just as I predicted, he lunged at me. Only this time, at the last possible second, I placed the parts box in front of me so instead of chomping on my flesh, the cat kissed a nice chunk of good old American steel. Without a doubt, it was the worst kiss of Timmy's life. How to describe the sound? Well, it was kind of like a thud with just a hint of "meow." Can't say I felt badly about it either. As Timmy saw stars and did his best to clear his head and regain his bearings, I swear I heard the classic cartoon "boooing" sound. I re-entered the house.

Once inside, I removed the busted igniter and was in process of putting in the new one. I glanced up and saw that Timmy had somehow entered the house and was in the walkway between the living room and the kitchen, just sitting there doing nothing. The lady was amazed.

"You must really be a cat person because Timmy never comes around people," she said.

"I guess I just have a way with animals, ma'am." I replied.

I'd be lying if I said I wasn't laughing on the inside, but you know, in a weird way, I respected Timmy. Cats are funny creatures. They do what they want, when and where it pleases them. When a cat wants to be noticed, he will be.

As I was talking to the customer in the kitchen, Timmy came over and started rubbing back and forth on my leg looking, somehow, for a pet rub. Was this cat's way to get back at me or did he change his mind and want to be friends?

"Wow, he's never done that before either," she said.

"Lucky me," I think.

Honestly, I did not trust the cat. Maybe he was going to bite my leg or something. The customer was so shocked that I tamed the feline and how nice he was capable of being. But I could tell that Timmy was up to something. Best thing for me to do was to leave and not give the cat another opportunity to attack.

As the customer and I walked toward the door and I handed her the receipt, the cat followed us. When I exited the house, so did Timmy. The customer wanted to know what was my secret? Was I some kind of cat whisperer? I just told her that when Timmy first stared at me, I returned his gaze and would not be the first one to turn away.

"It's all about dominance," I said.

What the heck, it sounded good. Anyway, the customer walked to the end of the planter, thanked me and said goodbye but good old Timmy stopped at the end of the driveway. Maybe running smackdab into the part box did him some good or maybe not.

One thing I did know, if me and the wife caved and got the kids a pet, it was definitely going to be a dog and named anything but Timmy.

Story 42: Ooops, I Fell (The '80's)

One of the maxims of this job is you can't always tell what's going on, on the inside of a house just by looking at the outside.

I pulled up to what seemed like a normal abode but turned into anything but. The first sign that something might be a little off was the high wall surrounding the house. This customer clearly wanted her privacy. I parked the truck, walked to the back and grabbed my toolbox. I walked up to the front door and rang the bell. A few seconds went by and a female voice answered.

"Coming. Just a sec."

I could hear footsteps walking towards the door. The anticipation was building and what opened the door, didn't disappoint. The customer, I believed to be a woman, cracked open the door. I say "believed" because this person was covered by a blanket over her head and hanging down to her knees. All that was showing were her lower legs. Perhaps, the whitest legs I've ever seen.

"Come in, please hurry," she said, more than a little agitated.

"I'm Rob," I replied as I entered the home.

After I went inside as quickly as possible she said, "I cannot have any light. Any! It's poison."

Oh-kay. Something was clearly off but then again, if she had a medical problem, it was none of my business. I really hoping that during this repair that I did not have to listen to any of her health issues. You'd be surprised by how many customers want to use a tech as their shrink. One lady spent over an hour going over her commitment issues. If I was smart, I would've sent her a bill for $200 for therapy.

Anyway, as we entered the main door, I was stopped right in my tracks. Not by the décor or animals or other people inside but because I couldn't see a thing. The house was almost completely dark. Practically no light at all. Just little shining lights plugged into wall sockets. In the doorway was a standing coat rack. Clearly, Martha, the customer, was deadly serious about this whole light is poison thing. She pulled off the blanket and hung it up. I guess the blanket was just for outdoors.

Why Martha kept her house so dark was none of my business, except it was because I was virtually blind. I'm not exaggerating when I say I couldn't see more than a few inches ahead and that was thanks to my watch.

"Follow me," said Martha.

I wanted to say "How? It's pitch black. Do you have a miner's helmet I could borrow?" I guess this wasn't the first time this had happened to Martha because after a few awkward moments, she grabbed my hand and said to follow her. Normally, I don't like people touching me without my permission but honestly, I welcomed the help.

By the time we got to the kitchen, my eyes were somewhat adapting to the dark house. Martha explained what the problem was with her appliance. It was under a manufacturer's warranty so, there would be not charge for the repair.

I did my best groping around in the dark to find out what parts were broken but it was difficult. After almost slicing my finger because I couldn't see, I decided to take action. Did I turn on a high-powered flashlight, did I start a fire or light a sparkler? Nope. Instead, I had the nerve to install a 25-watt bulb in her refrigerator because the previous bulb had burned out. To those of you who may not be familiar with the whole watt / lumens in terms of brightness definition, suffice it to say, a 25-watt bulb doesn't exactly produce blinding light. The fact is, it was still pretty dim. Not that you'd know it by Martha's reaction.

"Turn that off! It's too bright! Are you trying to kill me?!" she practically screamed.

Honestly, at that point, I wasn't. I was just trying to see. I'm funny that way. Then, I made my fatal mistake.

"Martha, I realize you like to keep it dark but I'm having a lot of trouble seeing. Would you mind turning on the kitchen light, so I can see a little better?"

I swear you could hear the insanity building up in the silence but what I imagined paled in comparison to the real thing.

"I knew this was going to happen! You were sent here to send lethal microwaves into my house to give me brain damage!..."

She was nuts. Her rant got even crazier.

"You don't think I know what you're up to? It's all rigged. They know who's going to win the election before a single ballot is counted. It's all done by the same people who steal money from internet sites to fund human trafficking..."

It got weirder and weirder. I was shocked that little green men and Bigfoot never entered her monologue. I guess there was only so much room in her head, even for crazy. Then came the topper.

"It's all your fault I can't have sexual relations with my ex-husband! The microwaves make it impossible for me to breed, don't you see?"

I didn't but if it was true, then the ten men who supposedly ruled the world in a cave located somewhere in the Alps got one thing right; this woman should definitely not breed. If I ever had a doubt that I possessed self-discipline, this call proved that I do because I was biting my tongue so hard, I'm shocked it wasn't bleeding.

"…It's the entire reason why the moon landing was faked. If you don't think it was fake, then how come there weren't any stars in the pictures?" she continued.

I just couldn't hold it in anymore and busted out laughing. This did not go over well.

"Let's see how hard you're laughing when you're in chains in Denver being forced to mine the Artigone they need to power their ships. Enjoy life as a slave, you fool…"

Okay, I admit that that doesn't sound like much fun. I had to get the hell out of there before she started talking about the Trilateral Commission and broke out the tin foil hats. The problem was I still couldn't see where I was going after I left her kitchen. I was lost in a proverbial carnival fun house. What was it they sang in "Hotel California?" "You can check out anytime you like, but you can never leave?" This chick checked out a long time ago.

Since I had no visual markers to determine where I was, I used her voice. The farther away it sounded, the more progress I figured I was making and better I felt. After banging my knees and elbows into what I'm assuming were walls, I was eventually able to grope my way out of the house and get back to my truck.

I'll say this for Martha, every time I microwave a burrito, I think of her and space aliens. Thank God for Taco Bell.

Story 43: The Burrito Drop Test (Early '90's)

There's an old saying that if you want to know where to eat, ask a truck driver. I'd like to add service tech to that list.

In every profession, there are daily rituals. Sometimes, you don't even realize them as rituals. For techs, it seems like at the start of every morning, a bunch of us are sitting around a table asking each other how many repair stops we have on tap for that day, how far we have to travel to make those stops and most importantly, where are we going to eat lunch?

During one of those conversations, one day, I found myself talking to Rosa. Rosa had been on the job for about a year and had earned all of our respect by being a hard worker, taking our hazing in the spirit in which it was intended and actually knowing what she was doing. Plus, it couldn't have been easy being the only woman in a gang full of Neanderthals like us and we admired her for fitting in and for not complaining or taking any unwarranted crap. So, yes, I liked Rosa and thought of her like a kid sister. As luck would have it, that afternoon would find us working in the same city and she suggested that we meet up for lunch. I didn't have any plans and didn't know the area well at all, so I was happy for the company. Rosa wrote the address down on a piece of paper and handed it to me.

Lunch time rolled around, and I followed her directions and found myself at a tiny Mom and Pop style market. This did not look like a restaurant at all. Plus, the surrounding area was sketchy to say the least. I wouldn't exactly say "war zone" but it was "war zone" adjacent. I double, and triple checked the address and sure enough, it was correct. My next thought was that Rosa was playing a practical joke on me which, under normal circumstances would've been fine (Hey, if you dish it out, you've got to be able to take it) but I was really hungry that day.

Just as I was mentally estimating how long it would take me to find a burger joint to grab some food quickly in the allotted time, Rosa came bounding out of the market to greet me.

"Oh, cool, you made it! It can be a little tricky to find for some people," she said cheerily, and she wasn't wrong. Most buildings in this area didn't have numbers. She continued,

"Come on in. Hope you're hungry."

"Don't worry, I am," I replied as we both entered the market.

The inside of the place was not an improvement on the outside. The Formica floor had to be over twenty-five years old and had the stains to prove it and the walls were all faded wood paneling. On the left was the cash register, flanked by the Mexican equivalent of Slim Jims and behind it was a wall of alcohol. Must be a big seller in this neighborhood, I thought to myself. Manning the counter was an old Mexican lady who looked like she was at least a hundred but was probably in her sixties, who was sitting in a torn vinyl chair. This wasn't shaping up to be a good lunch at all. In fact, I was more concerned about contacting Hepatitis. Those thoughts promptly vanished when I was hit by "the smell." Now, in previous pages, every smell I described was disgusting. This smell was the exact opposite. It was the smell of someone cooking with spices who knew what they were doing. Pungent, flavorful and aromatic, it literally made my mouth water. It was coming from the back of the store.

If we were in a cartoon, we would've floated over there but since we weren't, we walked. It didn't take long to reach the back where an old man was cooking up Mexican food. It smelled even better the closer we got. This guy clearly knew what he was doing.

Rosa greeted him in Spanish and he nodded back, not wanting to be distracted from his art. He handed us a well-worn paper menu with stains on it. Turns out that this hole in the wall market in the middle of nowhere was really an authentic Mexican old-style kitchen complete with a table and chairs near the rear counter.

The old man, let's call him Javier, spoke in Spanish to Rosa and took her order. Then he turned to me and asked me the same question, yes, in Spanish. Now, I had four years of high-school Spanish which meant that I had absolutely no idea what this gentleman was saying. Not being a complete idiot, I assumed he was asking me for my order. I answered in English that I would like the "Drop Burrito." I had no idea what I ordered. What was a Drop Burrito? But I figured, when in Montebello...

Javier nodded to me and got right to work on our orders. It smelled amazing. To kill some time, we walked around the market, specifically over to the far wall where there was a row of refrigerators with soft drinks, water, beer and whatever else people purchased in stores like this. I swear I saw a jar of pig's feet. We picked up a couple of Mexican Cokes when Javier called out to me.

"Senor, Senor...," he called out.

Even I understood this and walked back to the counter. He wanted to know how hot I wanted my burrito. Rosa acted as translator and communicated that I wanted my burrito mild with spice. Truthfully, normally, I would've asked for spicy, but I didn't know what "spicy" meant here. I mean it wasn't like we were at a Taco Bell. This was the real thing and the last thing I needed was for my mouth to be set on fire. Javier turned around and started making my lunch. Taco Bell and Del Taco were both put to shame here. Behind the counter were at least three full burner stoves with all kinds of stuff cooking. Javier placed two homemade large tortillas on a plate and scooped large amounts of beef, beans and assorted fixings onto it. He put down the plate on one of the wood tables in the cooking area and wrapped, then rewrapped the burrito in foil.

All of a sudden, he raised his hands, cradling my burrito over his head. He then released it to fall on the counter, making a loud thud. What was this about? Is that the secret to making great Mexican food gravity? Just then, the old lady screamed, "Mas, mucho mas!" It was clear that she was talking to Javier and that she ruled the roost. I guess this was their version of quality control because he immediately went back to work. Frankly, I was shocked that she could hear a burrito drop from that far away. Clearly, she knew what a "Drop Dead Burrito" was supposed to sound like and I wasn't going to argue. What I later found out was that with a "Drop Dead Burrito," if it moves after dropping it, then it ain't done.

Javier sliced open my burrito with surgical precision and added more beef and fixings to it. It was big before, now it was huge or, more appropriately here, gigante. It was now time to close so Javier rewrapped the burrito, only this time in another tortilla, so now there two. Again, he raised both of his arms over his head and dropped my lunch. When it landed on the counter this time, there was a louder thud and some of the bottles shook. I guess the extra weight had something to do with it. It didn't move. This time the old lady said nothing. She just nodded in approval.

Javier placed my food in a shopping bag and handed it to me. I took it and immediately noticed that it was a lot heavier than it looked, at least five pounds. This was one dense burrito. I thanked him for his efforts. Rosa took her lunch and she and Javier conversed in Espanol, much too fast for me. I was completely lost. I cracked open my Mexican Coke and took a sip. It was a lot sweeter than American soda and really hit the spot. Then I walked over to the front counter and paid for both of the lunches. The old lady thanked me politely for coming, mixing Spanish with English.

We exited the market and sat in the chairs outside and went about the business of eating our lunches. It was great. Probably the best Mexican food I have ever had. The juices dripped down my face and onto my clothes. Some was trapped on my moustache. I didn't wash if for days because it smelled so good. We did our best but, in the end,, we couldn't finish all the food. I was set for the whole day. My afternoon would go slowly as I fought going into a food coma.

A month later, it was my wedding anniversary. I told the wife that I'd take care of everything and told her to dress up. She looked fantastic. I made sure to tell her this right before I asked her to put on the blindfold I had in my right hand. She looked at me suspiciously, but I said, "trust me." She put it on.

Try and picture it. I'm driving with a suit on and in the passenger seat is my wife wearing an elegant dress, wearing a blindfold. Because it was Southern California, naturally, no one thought anything of it. Finally, after about an hour, we arrived at our destination. I helped my wife out of the car and positioned her perfectly. Then I said, "Happy Anniversary, honey. Take off the blindfold."

She did and by the look on her face, if she could've divorced me on the spot, she would've. Again, I said. "trust me." We went inside and were greeted by the old lady. She remembered me from earlier before and if she thought it was odd that two dressed up gringos were in her establishment; her facial expression didn't let on.

Because I am a romantic, I took the liberty of ordering for the both of us. We ordered four "Drop Dead Burritos," then we sat down at the table and watched the show. Javier was a little more animated this time. He was showing off, who doesn't in front of a beautiful lady? The food flew in the air like Tom Cruise in "Cocktail."

When it came time for the show-stopper, the dropping of the burritos on the counter, my wife could not believe what she was watching. This time a bottle of hot sauce fell over on the counter as the third Burrito impacted. It must have been real heavy, and it didn't move. When Javier was finished, I asked my wife to carry the bag to the front counter while I paid. I wanted her to have the experience of carrying twenty to twenty-five pounds of burritos. None of her friends could lay claim to having done that. She had to use both hands. Then it was time to dine al fresco. We went outside to my usual table.

I pulled out a chair, for my wife and she sat down. Then I went to my car, popped open the trunk and took out a bottle of champagne from the ice chest I had put in there when she was getting ready earlier. I took the bottle back to the table and opened it. I was a little nervous about doing that because in that neighborhood, the pop from the bottle could've been misconstrued as a gun-shot. Thankfully, it wasn't, and we started eating.

From her first bite, any anger my wife felt towards me instantly disappeared. She agreed that it was the best Mexican food we've ever had. It was a great dinner and if memory serves, neither one of us ate anything else for the next thirty-six hours. So, not only was it delicious, it was economical too. Throughout the meal, the old Mexican lady came out every so often to check on us. She was perfect. Attentive without getting in the way. I've been to four-star restaurants where the service wasn't as good. So, there we were, two people wearing the wrong clothes, in the wrong place and of the wrong ethnicity but we were having a great time. Looking back maybe it wasn't our best anniversary celebration and it definitely wasn't the most expensive, but it certainly was our most memorable.

To this day, I probably go there about once a month. The old Mexican lady and Javier died about five years ago and their kids took over, but something was missing. Don't get me wrong, it was still good but not the same. Javier took some of his secrets with him to his grave but, even with him gone, it's still the best Mexican food I've ever eaten and for that I say, muchos gracias, Rosa.

Story 44: Obsessive-Compulsive (The 90's)

Up until today, I thought that "obsessive-compulsive" wasn't a real thing. That it was made up by day-time talk show hosts in order to get a new batch of weirdos to appear on their shows. I mean, is there anybody who really has to flick a light-switch on fifty times before entering a room or wash their hands twenty times a day? Or, whenever they enter a room, it has to be with their right foot or the world's going to blow-up or something? Well, after this late afternoon service call I found out that Maury, Oprah and Springer may not be completely full of it. At least not on that.

The Boss came up to me that morning and asked me to go out to a special repair call later that day. He informed me that a few other repairmen had already been there, and I was just to verify a problem with the appliance. Based on previous experience, it sounded like it was going to be a pain in the ass, but I felt like I couldn't really say "no." I had a small route that day and he was my boss. So, off I went.

The house was located in a wealthy housing tract. The houses were huge and multi storied. As I drove up, I noticed that the cars weren't parked in garages but in carriage houses. Basically, a building separate from the main house. They're designed to look like mini-homes or cottages but are three-sided so that automobiles could pull right in. I say "automobiles" because these structures were much too fancy for simple "cars."

The front yards were perfectly groomed as expected but the streets and no cars on them. Maybe they were all inside their fancy carriage houses or it was street cleaning day. Who knew? But, as I drove through the housing tract and all I could think about was how this sure looked like a television advertisement for the good life.

The mansion I was looking for was located just up ahead. I pulled the truck up in front and parked on the street. Being the only vehicle on the entire street, I'm sure I stood out. Put it this way, if the F.B.I. ever wanted to do surveillance and pulled up in a flower van, they would get made in about thirty seconds. After I parked, I grabbed my gear, exited the truck and walked up to the address on my work order. There was a brand-new Jaguar parked on the circular driveway. The walkway was made from hand laid carved stone. It looked very nicely done too. I headed to the front door.

I knocked on the door and waited for a few minutes. The lady of the house answered the door. She looked very prim and proper. Not that surprising considering where I was but what did stand out was that after opening the door, she stepped back at least twenty feet. In her hands were a brand-new rag and a bottle of liquid disinfectant.

"Hello, I'm Rob. I'm here to work on your garbage disposal."

I put out my hand, but she didn't reciprocate. I decided not to take it personally.

"Diana Whitney, please stay at the door for a moment."

"Sure," I said back to the woman who calling "Diane" or "Di" would not have gone over well at all. Trust me.

She closed the door. I figured she wanted to straighten up or put the pure-bred German-Shepard into his air-conditioned cage or something. A few minutes later the front door re-opened and I noticed that Ms. Whitney, who was now standing by the staircase, had placed a sealed folded see-through plastic bag on the inside of the front door. A brand-new broom was leaning against the railing.

"Would you mind putting these on," she said gesturing to the bag?

As far as I could tell, inside the package were a surgical gown complete with shirt, pants, a mask, booties and gloves. I didn't see the harm in doing so, so I agreed. Maybe someone in the home was ill and couldn't be exposed to germs from the outside or she was concerned that I might catch something. What a nice lady, right? Wrong.

I finished putting on the surgical clothes and Diana walked towards me. She stopped ten feet or so away from me and pointed in the direction of a hallway. We started walking down the first hall and hung a left turn to the second hall and into the servant's area. As I was walking, I couldn't help but notice that she was dusting the floor behind me. Every step I took was followed by her swinging the broom back and forth with ninja-like skill. Clearly, she had done this many times before. Who knows, if this rich lady thing didn't work out, she'd have an excellent shot at making the curling team for the next Winter Olympics. Finally, we arrived at our destination, the servant's quarters which was equal in size to a small home. The kitchen alone was about five-hundred square feet and had a mini-bar and was very tastefully decorated. I wish I had a kitchen like this. I wonder if Diana was taking applications. Diana didn't enter the room. She stepped into a closet that was just behind me and with her left hand, pointed where I need to go and start my work, which was underneath the sink.

Walking around the mini bar, I placed my toolbox on the rug just behind the opening. What got me thinking was that I needed to crawl into a small area. Who knew what I was going to find? I stopped and looked at the work order to maybe glean any kind of insight about what the problem might be. It told me nothing. I opened two cabinet doors and climbed inside. It was at that moment that I realized I was having trouble moving. The surgical clothes were restricting my movement. I guess that's the reason why you don't see too many surgeons underneath sinks.

Diana had now walked into the entry way of the main door and was watching me. With those medical clothes covering my person, I needed to be able to move a little more freely. I crawled back out of the cabinet and looked up to see if I could see her. I could.

"Ma'am, would you mind telling me what exactly I'm looking for," I asked.

By the expression on her face, you would've thought that I had just farted in church.

"If you can't see it then you don't have to be here," she said incredibly rudely.

Firstly, I wanted to hit her with my pipe wrench, secondly, what's "it?" I stood up with a concerned look on my face.

"I want it out of here, right this instant," she barked. "Do you understand?"

Honestly, I didn't.

"Ma'am, I'd probably be glad to, if I knew what "IT" was. What am I looking for?"

Silence followed by a long pause. We were having us a stand-off. She won because I kind of wanted to find out what was under there. I walked just in front of the counter wall and just in front of her, leaving about ten feet distance between us, which I thought she'd appreciate. Diana stepped back.

"Ma'am, I have to remove some of these clothes. They're too restrictive and I can't do my job while wearing them," I said as calmly as I could. Her eyes opened with a fright. Something was happening inside there.

As I started to remove the hair cap and gloves, Diane started rocking back and forth on her heels. The she started stomping her feet and waving both of her hands in panic. The cherry on the crazy sundae was her starting to scream hysterically.

"No, you'll contaminate everything, you idiot! Don't you understand?! Put them back on now this instant!"

You know, on second thought, maybe working for Mrs. Diane Whitney wasn't the dream gig I originally thought it was. I just stood there next to the counter with the two gloves and a hair net in my hand. Diane dropped the dust mop and rag and ran off somewhere in the house. I could hear her hysterically screaming as she ran off and yes, it was more than a little unnerving to say the least.

I stood there for a few minutes not really knowing what to do. This wasn't covered in the training. I called out, "Hello! Hello!" No answer was forthcoming. I had no idea where she went. The dust mop and cleaning rag she had in her hands were now on the ground. So, what to do?

I should've poured myself a good, stiff drink from the mini-bar but instead, I turned around and walked back to the bar area and took a second look inside the cabinet. I still couldn't see what she had wanted me to find.

Everything about Diana bothered me from her prissy attitude to her treating me like "the help." I'm not the help and yes, I do work for a living. Dirt is something that just happens. Maybe I should've had some sympathy for her because, clearly, she was suffering from some kind of mental illness and I suppose I would have if she was the least bit kind, which she wasn't.

There really was no reason for me to be there so I reached for the work order, picked up my toolbox and started to walk to the hall. I placed the gloves and hair cap on the floor just in front of the dust mop. Before I turned to the second hall, I stopped and placed the toolbox back on the floor. I knew that if I took off the surgical gown and dropped the items all over the house it would've really bothered her. So, what did I do?

I took off the top and threw it on the floor. Then, I stepped back and kicked my toolbox along the floor. The bottom of the toolbox was filthy, and it left a beautiful grimy streak all over the floor wax. Next, I took of the pants and threw them in the opposite direction, all the while still sliding the toolbox toward the front door.

I walked to the front door and stripped off the rest of the gown. I left the face mask on the front door knob and noticed a pair of slippers nearby. I took the slippers and used them to prop open the door so that it wouldn't close. I knew that would freak her out big time, the thought of all the germs from the outside just flooding in. I was almost sorry that I was going to miss her reaction. I left the house with a big smile having never loved germs more than I did in that moment.

Story 45: Anybody Thirsty? (Late '90's)

It was my first year with the company and it was a perfect Southern California spring day with the temperatures hovering around seventy-eight degrees. Honestly, the day was so beautiful I didn't want to work at all. I wanted to be at the beach, or fishing or just driving my own car with the sun-roof open, blasting Tom Petty. But, Tom Petty doesn't pay my bills, this job did so work, it was.

At least the service call I was on, was a nice drive out in the country or as close to it as we get out here. As I got closer to my destination, the last mile or so was even on a dirt road. At the end of it was a picturesque farmhouse, complete with a porch and rocking chairs, that looked like they had been there a few hundred years. The trees around the house must have scaled around seventy to eighty feet. It was like something out of a painting.

I parked the truck and noticed a big man, wearing bib overalls, sitting in a chair and leaning back against the main support beam. It was almost a shame that he wasn't witling. On his head was a dirty trucker's hat that had seen better days. I couldn't be sure, but I think it read, "Semi-Retired Boob Instructor." Sure, it seemed silly but who was I to make fun of a man's chosen profession?

With a big, country smile and a slight, guttural, Southern accent, he greeted me with a big, "Howdy there, young man."

I briefly considered saying "howdy" back but it just didn't feel right coming out of mouth so, I had to settle for

"Hello sir, I'm Rob. I'm here to fix your chest freezer."

The man bounded up from his seat and walked towards me with his right hand extended to shake.

"Don't call me "sir." Call me "Randy. All my friends do."

"Okay, Randy."

With that out of the way, I grabbed my tools from the back of the truck and Randy escorted me inside the farmhouse. The inside could best be described as what hipsters would call "shabby chic" meaning faded colors with cracks in the paint so that you could see the wood underneath. But, unlike the hipsters, I highly doubt that Randy paid over a grand for a weather-beaten coffee table. No, this table looked that way because it was old as was most of the furniture. But the place certainly was homey and comfortable.

We went into the kitchen where the freezer was located. Man, this place looked like something out of the 1950's. There was lots of chrome and old tile. The refrigerator looked to be at least twenty years old and it hummed like it too. Then, the reason why I was there; the chest freezer.

"So, Randy, what seems to be the problem," I asked?

"Well, the dang thing ain't freezing," he said back and yes, he really did say "dang."

"I can see where that would be a problem with a freezer. Let me take a look-see," I responded. I felt myself becoming more countrified by the moment.

I did a quick inspection of the condenser coils to see if they were dirty. They weren't. Then I checked the evaporator fan motor. Bingo. It had simply burned out and a replacement was needed. This was Randy's lucky day because, in my truck, I had a used but perfectly good replacement part that would cost about half of what a new motor would cost and should run for years to come. I called the big guy in.

"Hey Randy, your motor burned out," I said, holding up the part and showed him the proof.

"Dang, I was really hoping it was the coils. I did a little reading up on it and it doesn't cost that much to fix, right?"

"Right, usually you can just clean them, and they'll work fine," I said.

"But a motor. Shoot. That can run into real money. I need this freezer to work to make my living..."

Normally, I don't like to cut people off, but Randy was really worried, and he didn't need to be. I told him the good news about how it was only going to cost him about half of what he thought. Country Randy could not have been happier. I swear, the man danced a jig. It looked like something out of "The Country Bear's Jamboree." I exited the farmhouse to get the part from the truck.

I re-entered the farmhouse and started swapping out the motors. During the repair, Randy and me had a good conversation about a wide variety of subjects. Mostly about sports, action movies, cars, fishing. Your basic guy stuff. After talking about the Rams secondary, Randy asked me a very straight forward but strange question.

"Is the back of your truck open?"

"Yes," I said back. "Why?"

"Oh, no reason," he said with a twinkle in his eyes. No doubt, Randy was up to something but what?

Randy exited the kitchen saying there was something he needed to take care of. Something told me it wasn't international banking. I had about twenty minutes worth of work to complete, including testing the new motor, before I was done.

Honestly, I had some not great thoughts about Randy in his absence. Why did he want to know if the back of my truck was open? Was he going to steal equipment or somehow damage it? Yeah, that would've been fun to explain to my boss who I didn't get along with in the first place.

Just as I about to completely spiral out, Randy came back. Believe it or not, this relaxed me. Why? Because whatever was done was done. I was finishing up testing the motor when Randy sat down. It worked fine, and I told him so. He was one happy country dude.

I finished up the repair, cleaned up and started the paperwork. He paid me in cash, as working people are prone to do and our conversation continued punctuated with plenty of laughs on his part. Randy was in a good mood and I just hoped it wasn't at my expense

He walked me back to my truck, stopping just short of it, making me a little uneasy which, I did my best to hide. Here's what I saw: my truck was sagging big time in the rear and leading up to it were tire tracks from a hand truck.

I approached the truck and opened the back to stow my toolbox. What I saw immediately filled me with relief and thanks. What I saw was redneck heaven, for my truck was now full of Coors beer.

Perhaps, I'm not doing it justice. When I say "full" I meant "full." The truck was packed from floor to ceiling with liquid gold. How he was able to load all this beer into my truck in such a short period of time was beyond me. All I could think say was "wow" and "thank you." I've never meant anything more.

Now, for the record, company policy clearly dictated that service techs and forbidden to accept any tips or gratuities so, I was in a bit of a moral bind here. The last thing I wanted to do was insult Randy. What he did was completely from the heart and I really felt like if I asked him to take it back, it would've been like throwing it in his face. I decided to keep the beer and deal with the repercussions later.

Randy reached out for my hand and, once again, shook it heartily.

"No, Rob. Thank you. You saved me a bundle on the freezer motor and I'm much obliged."

It felt really good to have helped this guy and the beer didn't hurt either. We said our goodbyes and I drove off, praying that I wouldn't hit any major potholes because with all this extra weight, I might've busted an axle. I started the engine and drove back to the main road. Once I spotted a pay phone, I pulled over to call the boss, Al, over at H.Q.

I told him I was a few minutes away from the shop and asked him to meet me in the rear of the service unit. I told him that I had a problem and I had to show him what happened. He was suspicious but agreed.

Twenty minutes, or so, I pulled into the lot and the boss wasn't there to greet me. I entered the back-access door into the shop and the boss was standing there. Al did not look happy.

"What's the problem," he asked?

"You know, it's better if I could just show you," I said back.

"You weren't in an accident, were you? You're still on probation, you know," he shot back.

That really ticked me off. Not to brag but I had been a model employee. Never late, never complained and here was this guy assuming the worst of me. Would it have killed him to give me the benefit of the doubt? I had certainly earned it. Anyway, we exited the office to the truck. He noticed that the rear was sagging. Stevie Wonder would've noticed it, that's how obvious it was.

"There was no accident," I said.

"Really," he said sarcastically.

I don't know what possessed me, but I stopped and asked him point-blank why he mistrusted me and why would he assume that I was lying? I received no answer. Maybe he thought that since he was the boss that he didn't have to answer.

As we walked closer to the back of the truck, I spied Al looking at the sides to find any accident damage or anything he could use to justify his b.s. comments.

I opened the back of the truck, revealing the beer. He was momentarily speechless, the second miraculous occurrence of the day. Walking up behind us was Stan. Stan was Al's boss and he and I got along just fine. Both of them were drooling at the sight of my cargo. I looked at them both and asked

"Anyone thirsty?"

I swear, Stan's face dropped to the floor with excitement.

"Now Stan, I have to get a hand truck to transfer my treasure from the truck to my car. It will probably take at least seven minutes before I get back. If any of the beer should, shall we say, go missing, I'd have no way of knowing."

It wasn't exactly subtle, but I wasn't trying to be. Al, the lesser boss looked at me to see if I would extend the same courtesy to him. Yeah, right. After the way he had treated me? I simply walked away to get a hand truck to unload the brew.

That weekend most of the people I worked with came over to the house for a big fish fry complete with plenty of Golden, Colorado's finest to help wash it down.

Guess who wasn't invited.

Story 46: Offensive Tackle vs Door (Early '90's)

One of the things I like to do is listen. Listen to what people have to say and somewhere good memorable information will come out. In this case, the information I gleaned from listening, may have saved me from great bodily harm.

It was a normal day with normal repair stops and normal traffic. Yeah, it was just another day at the office, completely average in every respect. The work order said that the customer's freezer wasn't cooling well enough which, was a little unusual. Usually they stop working completely. Best guess was that there was a leak somewhere in the unit. Of course, I wouldn't know for sure until I got there.

It was about 10:30 when I headed out to the customer's house. I used my phone to confirm that they were home, but the machine picked up. The message I left was short and to the point, "This is Rob from the appliance company and I'm scheduled to be at your home in about thirty-five minutes to repair your freezer. Bye." Hopefully, someone would be there when I arrived.

The address was in a nice neighborhood. I knew the area fairly well because it was on my regular route. The house wasn't hard to find. The address was clearly posted on the house, which I really appreciated. In front was a Ford SUV and from the lack of license plates, whoever owned it had recently purchased it. I parked the truck across the street, grabbed my tools in one hand and my clipboard with paperwork with the other and walked up to the house.

It was a very nice-looking house. Approximately, ten to fifteen years old. The driveway was made of sculpted hand pressed concrete and colored brown to match the exterior. I placed my toolbox on the porch and just as I was about to knock, the door began to open. The woman, attractive and her mid-thirties, must've seen me walk up. She was wearing blue-jeans, a t-shirt and pink slippers. She introduced herself.

"Hi, I'm Abby. Thanks for coming out."

"No problem. I'm Rob. Nice to meet you."

We shook hands as we walked inside. Abby showed me down a short hallway which was lined with pictures of her family, her kids but what really stood out where the photos of a man in a full football uniform. We turned right around a corner to enter the kitchen where there were even more photos of someone playing football. There were pictures of him playing in high-school, college and the pros. I slowed down because I had to look. What can I tell you, I'm a huge fan. I even played in high-school.

Once inside the kitchen, I noticed that there was a large piece of foil covering the freezer door. Holding it up were souvenir magnets. Lots of them. I placed my toolbox on the floor and Abby calmly said that her husband would be right out to talk to me, then she left. While I was waiting for her hubby to arrive, I checked if the model number and serial number were correct on the order. I wanted to make sure that I was working on the right product. I was and right then, a shadow covered me and my clipboard. It was the husband.

This guy was gigantic. Standing about six foot four and weighing about two hundred and sixty pounds, all of it muscle. His neck could've easily measured twenty inches. He was wearing a Dallas Cowboys t-shirt and was, obviously, the man in the photos. Another thing I noticed was that his forearms were covered with "Sponge Bob, Square Pants" band-aids. Kind of an interesting juxtaposition if I do say so myself.

"Hey, I'm Billy," he said.

"I'm Rob, good to meet you."

He extended his hand and I shook it. Man, did he have a strong, powerful grip which, I told him. Billy said I did too. I don't know if he meant it or just wanted to make me feel good. For the sake of my ego, I chose to believe the former and not the latter.

"So," I said. "I guess that's you in the pictures?"

"Yes, it is. They're from my entire career."

I asked what position he played, and he proudly told me "Offensive Tackle. It's my job to protect the quarterback at all times."

"Yeah, I said. You don't want to let those pretty boys get hurt, do you," I said.

He laughed, and I asked him what team he was playing for now? Billy told me and went on about the proud history of that franchise and how that team was better run than previous ones he'd played on. As a football fan, I was loving it big time.

We talked some more about football and how it had saved Billy's life. He grew up in a tough area with no direction until he discovered America's favorite game. He said it gave him discipline and a sense of community, not to mention plenty of money. As much as I was enjoying talking to him about the N.F.L., I had to steer the conversation back to the reason why I was in his home.

"So, what's going on with the freezer," I asked?

"Funny story," he began. "A couple of weeks ago, I was watching the Redskins play the Giants. If the Giants won, we'd be in the play-offs so, I had a lot riding on it."

I nodded, not entirely sure where this was going.

"Right," I said. "I watched it. Weren't the Redskins leading with something like two minutes left when Manning hit Beckham in the End Zone?"

Billy wasn't too pleased with that outcome and said so.

"Yup, the 'Skins lost, and we didn't get in. Cost me a goddamn fortune in play-off money."

He was getting a little agitated so, again, I tried to coral him into the present.

"Yeah, that's a tough break, missing out like that. I'm just not sure what that has to do with your freezer not working?"

Billy's eyes began to dart from left to right but, after a few moments, he calmed himself down enough to continue.

"Right, sorry. Anyway, on that last play, Josh Norman—"

Josh Norman was the cornerback for the Washington Redskins. The cornerback is the guy who covers or plays defense against the wide-receivers. Billy had known and played with Josh Norman previously, I forget on which team, and they were friendly. Apparently, Billy gave Josh some intel on how to cover Beckham which, Josh ignored. Billy was not in a forgiving mood because money and prestige were on the line. Billy continued

"…Beckham faked to the left and Josh fell for it! I told him a thousand times that Odell loves to do that. It's a little stutter-step he makes, don't fall for it! Guess what, Mr. I Know Everything About Playing Corner And, You Know Nothing falls for it, hook, line and sinker! The worst part is I could see it happening before it happened by the way they lined up at scrimmage."

Uh-huh.

"I went to the 'fridge to grab a Coke. Went to the freezer, to get some ice and I heard Al Michaels say, "Touchdown, Giants!" After that, I don't remember what happened."

I was more than a little perplexed but if Billy knew anything else, he wasn't going to tell me.

"Okay, thanks for telling me. Let me have a look at her."

Billy grunted something and exited the kitchen to watch TV on the big-screen in the living room. As he did, I grabbed the door handle on the freezer door and opened it. Inside was a large quantity of frost and ice on the freezer floor. It looked like a snow storm was going on inside. I then opened the refrigerator door to gain access to the main controls, mostly looking for the defrost timer. I found it and started a manual defrost operation.

With the freezer door completely open I stood there watching the defrost heater slowly turning on not realizing that the problem was over my shoulder and watching professional wrestling in the next room. The heater came on and frost was returning to a natural water state.

My first thought was that the door didn't close completely. Judging by the amount of frost in the freezer, it had been opened for at least twenty-four hours. Under normal circumstances, this would've been a pretty good guess. As I was about to find out, these weren't normal circumstances.

What I had failed to notice was a rather large hole in the freezer door. I closed said door and removed all the magnets and the foil, exposing a hole approximately eight inches in diameter that went completely through. There was a kitchen towel stuffed to prevent cold air from escaping. Let's just say that it didn't work. You didn't have to be Sherlock Holmes to figure out that someone had punched their hand through the door and that someone was cheering on Ric Flair in the other room. Because of the hole, warm, humid air from the outside was combing with the cold air on the inside. That's how you get frost and, in this case, lots of it.

Having solved this relatively simple mystery, I went about writing up an estimate. Then a scary thought hit me, there was no warranty in the history of mankind that would cover this type of damage. How would Billy react when I told him this? I decided to not find out. I mean, if he could punch a hole in a freezer door, what kind of damage do you think he could do to me? I did have a family and was fond of my internal organs.

Billy came back in and asked if I figured it out? I told him yes and that I'd need to go back to the shop to get the parts necessary to complete the repair. I asked him if he'd be home that night, so I could call him with the details. He said that he would, and I shook his hand again and exited the home.

Later that afternoon, I went into the office to look up the parts for Billy's freezer. As I was doing so, my boss came up to me and asked what I was doing, pointing out that I could have easily made a phone call from the customer's home for this information. I told him that I was quite familiar with the process and that there was a very good reason why I was doing it this way, namely that I didn't want to get punched or worse.

He wasn't sure what I was getting at, so I recounted earlier events. After I was finished, he had a stunned look on his face and said, "Who would punch and break the freezer door? Nobody would do that!"

I further explained the circumstances like losing out on play-off money, Josh Norman not listening to him. How Billy was getting agitated just remembering it, etc. Wanting to make my point even further, we walked into the boss's office and looked up Billy on the internet. Not only did my boss see how huge this guy was, he also saw that Billy had some arrests on his record for violence and "assorted mayhem."

My boss had finally agreed that I had done the right thing. Safety first, right? The boss did have one request though: he wanted to listen in when I called Billy. Fine by me. We dialed him up and Billy answered after a few rings.

"Hello," Billy said.

"Hello, this is Rob. I was in your home earlier today about your freezer," I said back.

"Hey, what's up?"

"Nothing much," I replied. I decided to get a little brave since I wasn't right in front of him. "If you don't mind me asking, those cuts on your forearm, where they entrance or exit wounds from when you punched a hole through the freezer door," I asked?

There were a few moments of awkward silence. Had I angered him? If I had, at least I'd have some time before he tracked me down. Finally, he said, "Okay, you got me. I busted through the door after Beckham burned Norman's ass. I admit it."

Okay, so far, so good. I took a deep breath and in my best professional voice I said, "The cost to fix the door, including all parts and labor comes out to $410."

There was a grunt on the other end of the phone.

"Yeah," he said.

Now the tough part. I swallowed hard and said, "Of course, since you inflicted the damage, it is not covered by the warranty."

More silence. After about twenty seconds I heard, "Hhhmmm. I really think that that's too much money to repair the door. I'll find something to cover up the hole or go and buy another refrigerator. Thank you for your time." Click. He hung up.

The boss and I just sat there and looked at each other for a while. Both of us admitted that we had never been in a situation like this before.

My boss said, "Man, that guy was scary calm. Those are the kind of guys you have to look out for."

I agreed and said, "True, but you know who I really feel sorry for?"

"Who's that," inquired my boss?

"The salesperson that has to tell Billy that a comparable unit will run him about two grand."

We both laughed in relief knowing that whomever that poor son of a bitch would be, it would not be us.

Story 47: Seasonal House (2005)

Can you think of two more different holidays than Christmas and Halloween? With the possible exception of Passover and the 4th of July, I can't. Here's a story about a house that celebrated the birth of our lord and savior and a day devoted to all things macabre. Hey, it's a crazy world but someone's got to service its appliances.

My second stop that day involved repairing a wall unit air-conditioner. What was unusual was that this call was in the middle of November and it was cold outside. Who wanted cold air when it was cold outside? To me, that's the same logic as going to a tanning salon when it's ninety degrees out.

Like I was saying, it was a cold day. The truck windows were closed, and the heater was cranking out toasty warm air. As I pulled up to the house, I noticed that the mail box was decorated like a giant candy cane with a hand painted snowman on the side. It was cute. Someone sure likes Christmas and hey, there's nothing wrong with that.

I exited my truck and walked to the rear. As I turned around to the back end of my truck, a flash of a light from the house caught my eye. It came from a pine tree decorated like a real, live Christmas tree. In fact, that's exactly what it was. I later found out that the tree was the couple on the inside's Christmas tree from five years ago. They loved it so much that after that year's holiday had passed, instead of throwing it out, they planted it in their front yard. By now, it had grown to about twelve feet at its highest point. It's always a good idea to re-plant, when you can, and it looked pretty great.

I took a moment to check out the house from the street. The car, in the driveway, was painted red, white and green. The planters were white and had sparkly glitter and icicles dangling from them. The plants they contained, Poinsettias, Azaleas, and Garden Sage were red, in keeping with the Christmas theme. The house itself was painted green with red trim except for the garage.

The garage, which was detached from the house, was painted white and black with what looked like a short knee-high fencing off to the side. The fencing surrounded what looked like a graveyard that you would find in the movie. "Nightmare before Christmas." Something didn't completely seem right here.

As I walked up to the house, the walkway was decorated with small Christmas tree ornaments and artificial snow. It caught my eye because I thought I might slip and fall.

I stopped at the front door which was covered with a wreath and more Christmas decorations. I looked around for the doorbell. Shockingly, it wasn't a conventional doorbell. It was Santa's face. I pushed Santa's nose and waited. Hope this didn't put me on "the naughty list." A doorbell version of "Silent Night" played. Why was I not surprised?

A minute or so went by. Then the door finally opened. On the other side was a lady dressed, from head to toe like Mrs. Santa Claus in a red velvet dress with white fur lining the edges. Her permed hair looked like it came from the 60's. Her black gloss shoes had gold buckles on the front and closed in in the rear with two-inch heels. If it wasn't for the rip on one of her stockings, she would be perfect.

I needed to do a reality check. Whose door did I just knock on? The North Pole or a track home?

Mrs. S smiled and greeted me with a dish of cookies.

"Hello, young man. Would you care for a cookie," she asked?

I stood there in shock, it really took me off guard.

"Now, don't be shy. They're just out of the oven and, if I do say so myself, quite delicious."

I recovered, thanked her, took one, bit into it and she was right. They were delicious.

I entered the house. Mrs. Claus and I both started to walk into the foyer area. Off to the right was the formal living room. It was completely inundated with Christmas decorations. Tables, wall units, the floor and cabinets were all full of Christmas stuff. There was even a small train running through all the displays. As the door closed behind me, a lighting system took over and a light show of snow falling appeared on two of the walls. It looked so real. All I needed was a coat and a set of skis.

We passed through a few more rooms that were also covered with Christmas decorations. There was even a couch in one of them that was flanked by matching Christmas trees that looked just like night stands. Santa and his sleigh hung from the wall and wrapped around the television. Just imagine a hobby blown way out of proportion and you'll have some idea of what I'm talking about. Too much time on her hands, I guess.

Mrs. Claus and I turned to the left and walked over to a large door. She stopped and knocked.

"My husband will take you to the air conditioner," Mrs. Claus said to me.

I thanked her again for the cookies when the door opened. I instantly turned into a five-year-old. Was I about to meet Santa? Turns out, I wasn't.

Standing in front of me was the mayor from the movie, "The Nightmare Before Christmas" complete with top hat, spider bow-tie and a ribbon that said "Mayor" on it. He too looked great. Disney really should contact these two and have them walk around their theme parks.

He greeted me warmly and beckoned me inside. I entered, and you can guess that it was completely outfitted for Halloween from grave yards, to dead trees, ghostly figures traveling across the walls, pumpkins which talked as you walked by, caskets opening and closing with a voice screaming, everything that you can imagine. The room also had an extra kitchen dinette area for food preparation. The only conventional item in the room was the air conditioner that was mounted in the window, off to one side.

We walked over to the unit. I placed my tools and paperwork on the floor next to a dummy stuffed with hay that resembled a dead body lying underneath the table. The Mayor advised me that the air conditioner was as dead as this room. I took his words as fact.

The Mayor walked over to his arm chair and turned on the television. On the screen appeared a classic black and white movie, "The Creature from the Black Lagoon. What a night and day house. Christmas to Nightmare. You could not be someplace more opposite than here.
I turned my attention back to the air conditioner. It was dead.

It took me a few minutes to move some of the Mayor's stuff from in front of the unit, so I could get a closer look. The entire wall, top to bottom was covered with Halloween stuff.

The control panel was not lighting up. I needed to move the toy dead hand from the panel to get a better look. The problem was a simple one to diagnose; no power. The power cord traveled off to the right and behind a grave yard headstone. I moved it and found a very not scary power strip.

On every power strip is a reset button. It was tripped. No power, period. I can confirm that all six plugs were in use and I guess that the amperage draw from the air conditioner was a little too much for the breaker bar.

I double checked that the main plug was plugged into the wall and it was. I reached down and turned on the power strip. Now all six plugs were active. One of the plugs powered a motion sensitive figure of Jack Skellington. Wonderful! More theme stuff. The other four plugs went off to a wall shelving unit. A lot of collectables lit up. Why didn't this guy notice what the problem was?

The air conditioner's light lit up. On the panel was a simple on/off switch. I turned the power on and cycled the "air only" function. I wanted to make sure that it ran before I exceeded the current level and tripped the power strip.

Around this time, the Mayor leaned forward and in an over the top, straight out of the movie way, praised me for saving his collection. Like the real mayor, he was somewhat clueless because I really hadn't done anything. On a side table, next to his chair were several cans of Bud Light and days of old dirty clothes. I turned on the compressor sequence and cold air started to flow out of the vents. The Mayor's day was just gotten a little better. I felt like I had done my good deed as an honorary citizen of Halloweentown.

I picked up my tools and paperwork and began to wonder, what do I charge him flipping a switch on a breaker? I thought it best to just charge him the house call and leave it at that.

The Mayor was happy for what I did and in return, he gave me a DVD set of classic black and white horror movies. Very cool.

It was all going well when, for some stupid reason, the Mayor looked at me and wanted to know why I made no comment about the house and all the deco. He was baiting me into a compliment. Basically, he wanted me to justify his Halloween obsession. I wanted no part of his delusion so, I just looked at the Mayor and responded,

"I've been in a lot of houses in all my years and if this is your hobby, go for it. If that's your wife's hobby, have fun!"

Not taking the hint, the Mayor asked, "Do you want to know why my house is divided into two different holidays?"

Not particularly. I needed to stop this subject dead cold.

"Mr. Mayor, how you live your life and whatever hobby's you and your wife have is your business and it's not for me to judge," I said in return.

The guy wouldn't let up. For a third time, his mayorship baited me to get me to ask him about the whole Christmas vs Halloween decorating theme, only he was starting to get more aggressive about it. I had to stand my ground and push back but do it respectively. What part of, I don't care do he not get?

"Mr. Mayor, do you really want me to answer your question? You may not like the answer you hear," I said.

He didn't say a word. It was now time to leave the house. I picked up my tools and the paperwork and started walking to the door. I opened it and Mrs. Claus was sitting on the couch knitting.

"Is everything working now," Mrs. Claus asked?

The Mayor responded, "It is back working again!"

Mrs. Claus put down her knitting, picked up the plate of cookies and grasped Mr. Mayor's hand. Both of them escorted me to the front door. As I opened it, the image of the two of them together really hit me; Christmas holding hands with Halloween, kind of like a deranged Ozzie and Harriet. Unlike peanut butter and chocolate, these two just did not belong together.

Story 48: Prank Wars 3 (2000)

As you may have read earlier, we techs like to play practical jokes on each other and sometimes even on our bosses. The reasons for this are several: it's a great way to blow off steam. Believe it or not, being a service tech can be a very stressful job. The customers sometimes demand the impossible and when you explain why their request / demand isn't feasible, they don't want to hear it. They can be obnoxious and verbally abusive, but we have to take it, within reason, of course. Also, with corporate profit margins getting smaller for reasons I won't bore you with, we're forced to work even harder. As recently as ten years ago, I was expected to make six to eight service calls a day. Currently, it's not that unusual to have to make anywhere from ten to twelve. Plus, practical jokes are a lot of fun to plan and pull off and we get to show off our creative side.

A little while back we had a supervisor named Ted. Ted was one of the good ones. Partially, because he started out as a service tech so not only did he understand what we were going through, he never forgot where he came from. He was genial, funny and down to earth. He was also out of his freakin' mind. Why do I say that? Because he was the only boss we ever had who played practical jokes on us.

They ranged from the classics like the whoopie cushions placed strategically during the morning meetings. The more annoying like being told you left a tool behind on a call to Ojai and after driving all the way to Ojai realizing that you left behind no such tool. Perhaps, the one he was most remembered for was welding the back bumper of one of the trucks to a parking sign. The poor S.O.B. who got that truck that day just keep gunning it and couldn't understand why the dang vehicle wasn't going anywhere despite the smoke and smell of burning rubber coming off the tires. Finally, he put it in reverse, lead footed the accelerator and plowed right into the side of our office, taking the parking sign down with him. In fairness, I should point out that that truck was due to be retired later that week. Ted just moved up the process. And after every prank, rib or practical joke, he'd always say, "harmless practical jokes are good for the morale of the unit." Of course, I saw this as a challenge. I knew it. The whole office knew it and most importantly, Ted knew it.

Ted was looking over his shoulder for the next few weeks because he knew one or more of us would invariable strike back. What he didn't know was that we had all gathered and promised to leave the poor guy alone. Why? Because we were such nice guys? What book have you been reading? No, we knew that Ted's anticipation / paranoia would drive him batty and it did. Finally, after about a month, when Ted bragged that no one had gotten anything over on him and he "won," we pointed out that constantly looking over your shoulder, checking underneath your car and never allowing your phone receiver to touch your head isn't exactly a huge victory. Yes, we explained, by not playing a joke on him we had played the best joke of all. Can you believe he bought that load of crap? I can't and best of all, it allowed him to lower his defenses.

Cut to about three weeks previous. I was out on a rare commercial job fixing the cooling system at J & M Manufacturing in Simi Valley. I had finished up when the floor manager asked me if I wanted a tour. Normally, I would've said "no, thank you" but it was so hot out that day that spending twenty minutes in a nice, thanks to me, air-conditioned factory didn't sound too bad at all. Truthfully, the tour was kind of boring. At least until we got to the loading dock. What made this one was so fascinating was the several gargantuan see-through garbage bags in the corner. They seemed so out of place, I just had to ask.

"So, what's over there in the bags?"

Ernie, the manager, replied, "Oh about 15,000 ping-pong balls."

"Sounds like someone's planning a helluva tournament."

"Only if it's at the city dump," he said back.

I was intrigued.

"You mean these aren't for an order? You're throwing them out? Why?"

"Because there was a screw-up in the last stage of manufacturing. They're weighted incorrectly so we can't sell them," he explained.

"Is there any law that says that you have to throw them away?"

Now, he was intrigued.

"No, we just can't have them here. Why? Do you want them?"

"I might at that."

"What are you going to do with them," Ernie asked quite reasonably?

"Oh, I'll think of something."

"If you can pick them up in the next thirty-six hours, they're yours. If you can't, I can't have them around here, so they'll be going to el dumpo."

I promised Big Ern that the ping-pong balls would be picked up within his deadline. Right after giving him my word, I hightailed it to my truck and told all the techs to meet me at our usual place for lunch, a burger stand that was far enough from the office and seedy enough that most upper management types stayed away.

Everyone showed up. I explained about the ping-pong balls and a rough idea of what I had planned for them. How into it were they? Well, let's just say that everyone showed up after work at J & M Manufacturing off the clock. One guy even borrowed a pick-up truck from his neighbor to help haul the balls away. Eventually, we were able to get all of them into our vehicles which did take some time. Now, what to do with them? Luckily, I had an idea.

For the most part, our office floor plan is pretty wide open. There's work benches, assorted cubicles and some offices. The offices are essentially cubicles with four higher walls that didn't quite reach the ceiling, which was perfect. The plan was to almost drown Ted in a sea of ping-pong balls. Step one was figuring out how to get all the balls to drop down in a relatively small space. The inspiration came from a packing store. I don't know if you've even been to one or observed their process but basically, they have a big funnel above them that contains packing peanuts, those white, infinity shaped foam bits. Whenever a worker needs some peanuts for a package, he pulls on a string and the peanuts fall down from above. This could work.

With the help of some good buddies, I was able to fabricate a funnel but instead of the opening being six inches, this one was about eight feet or the width of Ted's office. The whole drop motion was connected to a string. A string I would be holding. After several successful test runs, we decided on a time to strike. The coming Friday seemed ideal. If Ted got a kick out of it, we could all go out and get drunk after we knocked off. If he reacted badly, unlikely but possible, there was always the chance that by the time Monday rolled around, he would've calmed down some.

A bunch of us got to the office at the crack of dawn because this would take some time to set up. It's not like any of us had any experience installing a temporary funnel over our boss's offices and loading in 15,000 ping-pong balls. For the most part, it went pretty smoothly except for a false alarm when we thought Ted was coming in early, but it turned out to be Viola, a member of the cleaning crew who left something behind. She walked in, saw us idiots loading the ping-pong balls, shook her head and left. I like to think that the fact that she didn't even question what we were doing marked her as one of us. Unfortunately, there just wasn't enough time for a test run but we were pretty confident it would work. We made sure that the boxes and funnel were the same color as the ceiling, so they blended in fine. The string, the item that would release the balls was taped right alongside the door frame. No one would notice it, unless you were looking for it. Even then it would be a challenge because we were using fishing line filament which is really thin. Hey, if you're going to drop 15,000 ping-pong balls on your boss's head, you might as well do it right! Finally, we were ready.

Noon rolled around, and Ted was on the phone in his office with the door opened. I decided to stand outside his little window, doing nothing but with a grin on my face. When he acknowledged my presence, I'd walk off. I did this three more times. Just enough to unnerve him and drive Ted just a little crazy. Next, I appeared in his doorway without entering.

"Can I help you with something," he said sarcastically?

"Nope, I'm good," I said as I walked off.

I did this two more times and I really think he was on the verge of a nervous break-down which is exactly where I wanted him to be. For the third time, I made sure that everyone in the office was looking in. I removed the string from the door frame and made sure Ted saw it. Why? to build up anticipation and besides, he wasn't going anywhere.

"Don't you have some work to do, Rob, or are you just going to stare at me," he barked out?

"Can't a man just look in on his boss with admiration," I asked with all the faked sincerity I could muster up.

"Not if that guy's you," he volleyed back.

"Well, that just hurts my feelings."

I held up the string to eye level.

"What's that?"

"It's a string, boss. Don't they teach you upper-management types anything," I said with a bare minimum of snark.

"I'm not an idiot. I know it's a string. Why are you holding it?"

Good question. This was my answer.

"To do this."

With that, I pulled on the string and 15,000 ping-pong balls descended from the heavens! Okay, so not the heavens but from the funnel that me and my team had painstakingly created. What a great sound they made! The first waves hit the floor and bounced up but in no time at all, the floor was covered so they'd hit each other, making a rumbling noise. Before you knew it, thirty seconds had passed, and the balls continued to rain down. Ted, to his credit, didn't even try and move. In his mind, I think it would've been like taking a crayon and making an "x" on a Picasso. It's just wrong to ruin a masterpiece and that's what this was.

After another minute or so, the impossible happened. We were almost out of ping-pong balls. Of course, Ted was literally up to his neck in them and I actually know what the word "literally" means and used it correctly. Finally, the last one hit him perfectly in the middle of his head. That's the kind of thing that makes you believe in God. With perfect timing, Ted looked at me and the entire office staff and asked, "Now why would you do that?"

I shrugged and said, "Harmless practical jokes are good for the morale of the unit." Then I walked off to make my morning calls to the applause of the entire staff. And even though his arms were buried under the avalanche, I like to think Ted was clapping too.

Story 49: Horse In the House (The '90's)

Have you ever felt like you were in the middle of nowhere? You weren't, trust me. The place I'm about to tell you about makes the middle of nowhere look like Times Square.

It was a Thursday, around mid-day. My dispatcher routed me the service call and gave me a little extra time to reach my destination because it truly was in, what the Australians call, Woop Woop or the boonies.

As I turned the repair truck onto the street, there were no houses visible. All I saw was miles of rolling hills, all covered with lemon trees, oranges trees and grapefruit trees. As I slowly drove along the street, I had trouble getting my bearings. Besides not seeing many houses, the ones I did see didn't have any addresses on them. The only consistent thing on this road were telephone poles. Where was this customers house?

The road seemed endless but after about twenty minutes, I came to the end of it, still no better informed about where I was or where I was going. It takes a lot for me to admit this, but, yes, I was lost. I began to turn the truck around, making a three-point turn. I finally straightened out the truck to go back down the long road. As soon as I placed my foot on the gas pedal, I noticed that there were three high voltage wires heading to the groves. There was also a planted palm tree in a large aged wooden container on the side of the road. Could this be a signal that civilization was near?

Next to the palm tree were several other planted trees. What caught my eye was that they were really out of place compared to the citrus trees all around. I stopped the truck and turned off the engine, yes, right in the middle of the road. Not to state the obvious but under normal circumstances, you don't do this. I, however, wasn't worried. There was nobody around for miles. I started to walk to the two potted trees. They were at least twenty feet apart with overgrown plants and trees surrounding them. The palms were being outgunned by a Weeping Willow tree, the branches almost touching the edge of the aged wooded pot.

On the other side, we had planted cactus in large plastic containers. A couple of those plastic pots had cracked their sides and the roots had grown out of the container and into the ground. Around that time, a gust of wind blew through the area. Thank God it did because it revealed a sign that arched above the plants. It read, "Locally Grown Nursery." Wow, this was a plant nursery.

To the left, above the cacti, and attached to the large sign was a smaller sign with an arrow instructing any customers on how to enter the property. It looked like something out of "Jurassic World" where the plants grew over the famous sign, only with present day foliage.
The smaller sign was seriously weather worn. I could barely make out an arrow that pointed to the left.

Ok, what to do? Do I drop the repair call or investigate a little more? My curiosity took over. So, walked under the large sign. I started looking around for something, anything that identified that humans lived here. I entered through the foliage without a machete and traveled about fifteen feet towards the entrance. There was still asphalt under my feet, which I took as a good sign but the further I walked, the less secure the ground seemed to be.

On my last step, I noticed that there were potted trees lining both sides of the road and were growing out of control as far as the light would take them. Just like jungle foliage. Noticeably, they had not been taken care of in years. The road leading in front of me was made of small granite stones. This gave me hope because small granite stones are a good base for large trucks. It takes a tremendous amount of weight, we're talking thousands and thousands of pounds, to make them buckle. I learned this from watching the National Geographic Channel.

I turned around, ducking my head as the wind blew the plant growth all around. My truck was in sight, although, as I stood up, I heard a horse whiney. Honestly, it sounded more like a donkey than a horse.

I got back inside my truck, started the engine up and turned on the radio. What was playing? "Don't Look Back" by Boston. Was this an omen or merely the local classic rock station playing the same ten songs?

I turned the truck towards the large sign and was worried if it would fit under the sign or get scratched up the cacti on both sides? I drove slowly, about five mph. I crossed myself before going under the sign and made it cleanly through. Now, I was driving down the gravel road.

I must have traveled about four hundred feet when the road turned slightly to the left. As I turned the truck's steering wheel, I could see a large semi's load container with the back door facing me and the front heading toward the foliage. On the side of the container, toward the front, I could only see two red letters. These two letters said "ER."

My driver's side window was open. I wanted to listen for something as I slowly drove down the granite road. As I continued the left turn, I noticed four more semi-trailers in front of me, all parked in the same way, the back door opening to the driveway. The ground plants had overgrown these trailers too. I wasn't exactly sure what all these semi's were doing in the middle of nowhere. Perhaps, they were there for storage of gardening supplies. To the side of the last trailer were several concrete storage containers with ground cover materials which, the plants had left untouched.

Off to the left, were three business type travel trailers. These three trailers were gathered in a u-shape configuration. The front trailer had a wooden and metal walking ramp leading to a large door and on the door, was a rotting wooden sign saying, "were open." Their spelling, not mine. Incorrect spelling or not, nothing had been open here in years.

There was a parking area in front of the ramp, overgrown with plants and roots. I thought it best to park the truck there. At least at some point in time, this is where people parked their cars. I turned off the engine and exited, but just before I got out, I thought it best to honk the horn three times to announce my arrival. That way, if someone was looking to kill an outsider, at least I had made it a little easier for them. I got out of the truck and left the driver's window open and the truck unlocked. Maybe it wasn't the smartest thing to do but I figured that there was nobody else around. Wrong!

I grabbed my toolbox from the back and still had not heard a sound from anyone in the house, so, I made sure to slam the door. Hopefully, the only thing I'd wake up would be humans and not poisonous snakes. I walked through the dead ground cover, heading to the walkway. There was the back of a horse corral. I saw enough to know that somebody lived around here.

I found the walkway, which was made of more rotting wood and framed by some kind of rusted metal. I placed my feet to the sides of each plank because there was a better than even chance that if I put my feet in the center, the weakest part of any plank, I'd bust through and be in danger of braking my ankle or getting tetanus. I thought I was up to date on my vaccinations, but I wasn't positive. Keep in mind that, after all this, I still hadn't officially started the service call.

As I reached the top of the walkway, I placed my toolbox on the platform, stood up and knocked four times, loudly. Then, I waited. Nothing was happening, no sounds or movement. As experience has taught me, trailers do not have a solid foundation. They are built up on stilts. As a person or animal walks around, you can hear their footsteps echo and the tone changes the closer they get to more solid beams in the floor. I knocked again. This time I heard something. CRAP! Someone was home and was approaching the door. The sound was getting louder. Then I heard a loud crashing thud from inside. This alarmed me somewhat. Did this person fall, trip over something or what? I called out, "are you okay?"

More seconds passed, and I still heard nothing. I started to head down the ramp when, suddenly, I heard a sliding motion like a chair leg traveling on a floor. Then another sound, it was a quick short hand bang. Finally, the door started to open.

Standing in front of me was disheveled guy in his fifties wearing a button-up shirt and blue jeans that probably hadn't been washed in years. His hair hung down on both sides of his heads and he could not look greasier. On his head was a baseball caked with dirt and grime so caked on, you couldn't tell what the insignia was. He might have even been suffering from mal-nutrition. One more thing, he was flat on the ground. I helped him up and introduced myself.

"Hello, I'm Rob, the refrigerator repairman."

He barked out, "what do you want!?"

"I'm Rob. I'm here to fix your refrigerator."

Silence then, "I called you yesterday and I waited all damn life day for you? What took you so damn long?"

"Traffic," I said. Believe it or not, this seemed to satisfy him.

This man, let's call him "Dusty," was drunk as hell. His eyes were bloodshot and yellow. They may have even been bleeding at some point. Basically, standing in front of me was Neanderthal man. His beard had flakes of dead skin on is and there were open sores on the right side of his face and the smell coming his body was more than a body odor, it was more like growing fungus. No one had ever told Dusty about the upside of moisturizing.

We stared at each other for a few seconds, then he spoke again. "Are you going to come in or what?" Keep in mind that he never asked me to enter in the first place. Truthfully, I was kind of hoping he'd tell me to leave but no such luck.

I picked up my toolbox and began to enter the trailer. The smell hit me hard. You could've poured gasoline all over, lit a match and it would've done nothing to extinguish the foul odor that was, seemingly, everywhere. Dusty turned to his left and we began to walk into an office area. There were papers all over the desks and the floors. Of course, it was a total mess. I sarcastically said, "So, this must be the nerve center of the entire operation, huh?" He just looked at me.

We continued to walk a few feet through a half partition wall to what might be called a hallway. It was obvious that this was what Dusty had tripped over because there was a hunk of his shirt on the partition and I noticed that there was blood trickling down his left arm. Not a beautiful sight, to be sure.

As we walked down the hallway, there were two rooms adjacent to each other. The doors were open. Each room was cluttered with empty cardboard holding containers ranging from about 18' to 30' in size. I would say there was anywhere from two to three-hundred empty containers in each room. Whatever they were used for, there was a lot of them.

The hall was coming to an end. I couldn't see where we were going. As Dusty walked down the hall he was using the left wall to support himself. The blood from his arm continued to trickle onto the floor. We stopped at the end. Where were we going? Did I have my affairs in order? Had I told my family that I loved them lately? Probably. Dusty reached into his pocket and pulled out a set of keys. I was surprised that it only took him a few seconds to find the right one. He opened the door that lead to another hallway.

We were now in trailer two. This trailer's hall way was about forty-five feet long. There were four door openings leading to four additional rooms. Two of the doors were closed and two were open. In the two open rooms, I could see sun light rays shining through the outside growth and into the room. I could see the air particles floating in the hallway. But what was in those particles? The Ebola virus?

Dusty and I continued our jaunt down the hall. We passed an open door on the right and inside the room were cases upon cases of Budweiser beer. The room was stacked wall to wall and right up to the ceiling. Although, I didn't have the opportunity to count them, I'd wager that there about one thousand cases with twenty-four cans of beer in each one. Someone was thirsty.

Dusty continued to walk and bleed down the hallway. The second room we passed was also crammed with beer. Two rooms, both full of beer. Call me crazy but I'm guessing that the two closed doors also contained plenty of suds as well. To take a rough count, that would be more than four thousand cases of the stuff. Around here, it was never too early for Octoberfest. Then it hit me, the "ER" on the side of the trailer was from "Budweiser!" These were old Budweiser trucks that this guy had decided to live in. For an alcoholic, it was almost ingenious.

I followed Dusty down another hallway. This time it was a short walk, about twelve feet.
This hall opened up to a third trailer. To the left was the kitchen and to the right was the living room and dining area. In the living room were open pizza boxes mixed with various take-out food containers. Some of it looked like Mexican food.

My work order said that the "refrigerator was leaking inside." Dusty pointed me in the right direction and exited to the living room, through a sliding glass door. What was he doing? I don't know. Maybe bleeding and drinking.

I placed my toolbox on the floor directly in front of the refrigerator and started to read the work order. The kitchen was a total mess other than a small corner next to the refrigerator. That's where I decided to spend most of my time. The place was gross. No beer here though. I guess they already had enough…for several lifetimes.

Upon checking the work order, I noticed that the model number on the order didn't match the refrigerator. Dusty had made a mistake. Hard to believe that someone as meticulous as him would screw-up but screw-up, he did. It ended up working out fine for me as this fridge was easier to fix than the one I was supposed to.

I walked to the sliding glass door that divided the kitchen and living room to find and confirm things with Dusty. On the couch, laid a woman in her twenties, wearing short panties and t-shirt. Her hair was a mess and she stank of vomit. Next to the princess in waiting were several cans of beer and a full case next to the couch. Dusty was face down on the ground about twenty feet from the trailer steps and in a position where somehow, he knocked into the horse's stall gate. The gate was open, and a horse just stood there waiting.

I now was getting a little concerned, is Dusty all right? I yelled out, "Dusty, are you okay?!"

He moved his legs a little, so I guess he wasn't dead. I was this close to calling 911. Not that if Dusty was in real trouble, that they could've gotten here in time. I thought it best to leave things alone and head back to the kitchen. I needed to do the job and get the hell out of there and back to the planet Earth. By now, the girl on the couch was stirring. My earlier yelling had woken her up. Time to start the day! It was about 12:30.

As I opened the refrigerator door, surprisingly, there were more cans of beer. Boy, was I shocked. I would've been shocked if I found diet soda. Inside the freezer I found food, actual, real food like bags of nuts and ice-cream. There's your protein and dairy with the beer filling in the wheat group.

I cleared the food from the freezer compartment and found an almond stuck in the drain tube. This is what was blocking the water from exiting. I needed to check the drain, so I reached down into my toolbox and grabbed a bottle type container. I walked to the faucet. As I turned it on, Dusty had re-entered the trailer and was in the process of sitting down at the dining table.

Dusty looked at me with his eyes half open and slowly lowered his head onto the table top. Time for a power nap, I guess. I filled up the water bottle and returned to the refrigerator drain. As I was pouring the water into the drain, Dusty stood up and walked over to a kitchen cabinet. He opened the door and grabbed a can of food. I couldn't make out exactly what it was, but it was probably a safe bet that it wasn't vegetables. He placed the metal can in the microwave and turned it on.

I just had to stop what I was doing and watch this. Every idiot knows you don't put metal into the microwave. Dusty hadn't received that memo. After a few seconds, the can began to spark, and a small light was coming from the inside. We had us a small fire. Dusty just stood in front and waited. He was unfazed and was simply waiting for his food to be done. Alcohol might kill Dusty, stress wouldn't.

The microwave made a sound indicating that it was done. Dusty reached over to a small slide out drawer and fumbled around a while, I guess he was looking for a spoon. He sort of succeeded because he pulled out a large spoon, like the kind you used to stir a small pot but small enough to get inside the can. Dusty grabbed a dishrag and removed the can from the microwave. Thank goodness, it wasn't on fire because I don't think it would've stopped him.

Dusty ambled over to the kitchen table and started to eat one small scoop at a time. Keep in mind that this food was just out of the microwave and was on fire just a short time ago. The heat didn't stop Dusty for a second. He just kept shoveling it in. Hey, no brain, no pain, right? Then things got interesting.

Why did I say that? Well, because, just then I heard a clopping clip clop sound right behind me. Then another about five seconds later. As the clopping sounds continued they changed tone. Then a new smell had wafted into the room.

I closed the refrigerator doors and turned around. Standing in front of me was a horse. A well fed, white in color but dirty gray due to the dirt, horse. Somehow it had walked up the steps by the backdoor and entered the living room. The horse let out a loud whiney, again sounding more like a donkey. I was thinking, as the horse stood right in front of me, should I take him back outside or do nothing?

Maybe I'm nuts but I thought it best to escort the horse outside. It would be the right thing to do. I walked forward to the horse and grabbed his bridle. Right then, the horse, began to pee all over the living room floor. Have you heard the expression, "peed like a race horse?" Well, it doesn't apply to just race horses. This was a gusher. I'm just glad I didn't have prostate problems because I would've been really jealous of what this equine could do. By the time he was finished, I'm surprised we didn't need waders. The horse then walked over to Dusty at the dining table.

To give you a better idea of the geography involved, I now had a two-thousand-pound horse's rear end inches away from my face. I couldn't move. It was a little scary. I mean, if Mr. Ed decided to get nasty, it's not exactly like anyone was going to rush to my aid. Finally, the horse did move. He took a step...right on my tool box, knocking the contents all over. None of this disturbed Dusty's meal. He went right on eating. In his state, I don't even know if he was aware of what was going on.

The horse sidled up to Dusty's right side and made several attempts to nudge him. Dusty reacted by giving the horse some of the food from the can. Actually, more than "some" because soon, the can was empty. The spoon clanking on the bottom of the can gave it away. The horse was still hungry.

Dusty made a bad attempt to stand up and fell again. This time his left arm, which was bleeding, bled on the table top and it stuck as he tried to stand. Dusty was completely unfazed. Falling was second to nature to him by now.

While Dusty was on the ground, the horse backed up a few steps and was pushing me into the refrigerator. You know, on my first day training to be a service tech, this was not a scenario they talked us through. I was not having fun. Dusty finally was able to get up and he pushed the horse and grabbed the bridle harness. He walked the horse around the dining area and out the back door.

For some reason, I think Dusty had done this before. The horse somehow knew exactly what to do. Dusty came back inside and staggered over to a wall cabinet. He opened the door and began to sway his head up and down. I was just waiting for him to fall backwards and fall again. How was this guy still alive?

Dusty stopped, just stopped. I wasn't sure what was going to happen next. Was he having a stroke, passing gas or both? He was that talented. With his two arms, Dusty grabbed two new cans and opened them with a left-handed can opener and put them into the microwave. Yup, they sparked but old Dusty had it under control.

The sparks turned into a small fire. Dusty bent over. I couldn't tell if he was breathing or not as I was still standing by the refrigerator. My paperwork was on the other side of the kitchen. I turned my attention from watching Dusty and his stupidity to finding my tools the horse knocked all over the kitchen floor. A few seconds into this chore, the microwave buzzer rang. Dusty magically awoke, found the dish rag and reached for the cans. This time, Dusty turned the cans in such a way that I could make out what was inside. It was dog food which explained why the horse liked it so much.

In the middle of eating the first can, Dusty stopped suddenly. He turned his head and looked at me. He just stared at me for about thirty seconds. Dusty somehow conjugated a full sentence and asked me, "Are you all done and how much do I need to pay you?"

Right after he stopped speaking, Dusty stood up the best he could and removed his hat. Inside the hat were hundred-dollar bills. He began removing a good handful of them and placed them on the table right next to his food, then put his hat back on. Great, money crawling with lice. Again, Dusty stopped moving.

My tools were now all cleaned up and back in my toolbox. At some point, I'd probably have to run them through the dishwasher. I didn't know what was on Dusty's floor and didn't really want to. Dusty was still in a hunched over position with his head hanging over the two cans and his hair covering part of them.

I needed to fill out a repair charge for my services and I really didn't know what amount to fill in. I was completely overwhelmed. I started thinking about horror movies where the bad guy does something unexpected as the innocent victim approaches. Would Dusty lunge at me with a rusty knife? An idea came to me. Find some type of peace offering or something to block any forward movement he might try.

Inside the refrigerator were several six packs of Budweiser. Yeah, they were big enough to block anything that Dusty might try. So, with a six pack in my left hand and my right arm free, I walked over to Dusty at the table. I slowly took as many hundred-dollar bills as was necessarily to pay the bill and placed the six pack right next to his dog food.

Just about this time, I heard the same clopping foot-steps from the rear. The horse was trying to enter the house again. I guess it was time for the second course. The horse used his nose and opened the door just like a dog would do and entered. Well it was time to leave before something else happed. I placed the money on my clipboard and walked over where my tool box was sitting. As I bent over to grab the handle, the horse was in the house and heading right for me. I shouldn't have been worried. I didn't have any food on me. By now, the young girl on the couch woke up again.

She staggered for a few steps, straight through the urine from earlier and headed in my direction. I wasn't me she was interested in, it was the beer. I greeted her with a "Afternoon, princess." She just grunted something.

I exited out the sliding glass door and headed straight to my truck. As I turned the corner of the trailer I heard the sound of beer cans being crushed and squirting. Then the unmistakable sounds of something solid dropping out of an animal. Now I really needed to get out of there but before I did, I had to sneak a peek. After doing so, I wish I hadn't. I'm not exaggerating when I say there was a six-foot pile of crap next to and on top of the assorted broken pots and beer cans. As I started the truck, I could smell Dusty on my clothes.

I didn't want to make a big deal about leaving, not that Dusty was the sentimental type or anything. As I made a hasty exit, my truck kicked up a bunch of gravel. One of the unkempt trees managed to leave a nice scratch on top of my truck so, that was a nice little bonus.

I was about ten miles from the closest small town and I needed to clean up a little before heading to a bank to exchange the dirty money for something less disgusting. I did the best I could with napkins and wet-naps but based on the reaction I got from the teller and the other people in the bank, I really hadn't succeeded. I didn't know if the stink was coming from me or the money, not that it made any difference. Stink was stink. At least they let me cut to the front of the line.

After completing my transaction, I hopped back into my truck and drove home. As I was driving, I was doing my best to think of a reason to call the authorities on Dusty, the horse and the young lady on the couch, but I couldn't.

Yes, they were living in squalor, but the girl was of legal age, the animal wasn't being neglected and Dusty was an adult. As gross as the set-up was, they weren't doing anything illegal, as far as I could tell but, if you ask me, I think the horse had made the best out of the situation.

Story 50: The Green Fog (Late '80's)

It's been said that inside of every man, lives a little boy. This day was one where we just had to let him out.

Back in the mid-eighties to mid-nineties, we techs had to wear something called "beepers." You remember them, right? Those annoying little devices you clipped to your belt that preceded cellphones? The company called them beepers, we referred to them as leashes. So, one day, I was on the road when that godforsaken device went off. I hated that beep, beep, beep noise. The code on it told me to call the office asap. Since I was driving, that meant one thing, I had to go and find a pay phone.

Even back then, a working, non-disgusting pay phone was tough to find. After a bunch of false starts, including one where the handset was on the receiver, but the cord was cut. After a bunch of missteps, eventually, I found a working phone next to a Burger King.

I called in to the dispatcher who wanted me and another tech, Chris, to go over to a customer's house and help the customer with a freezer. It seemed simple at the time so back on the road I went.

The house was located at the end of a street, in a high money track. I wouldn't go so far as to call them McMansions, but they were close. They were nice but a little too large for the amount of land they occupied. As I pulled up, I noticed that a large trash dumpster was located in the street. The dumpster was the kind that could comfortably fit in the back of a semi. It was situated between the customer's house and their neighbors.

As I exited my truck, I spotted Chris walking towards me from the other direction. I had worked with Chris a few times before and liked him. He took the job but not himself seriously and he liked to have fun. A fact that would come in handy a little later. After greeting each other and seeing if either one of us had any additional information, which we didn't, we walked up to the customer's door having no idea what we were getting into.

The customer of the house walked out to meet us and introduced herself as Karen. She explained that her freezer had a problem so the three of us walked to her garage. She used a clicker to open the door and in we went.

Karen pointed out the appliance. It was a large chest freezer. According to the order, it was about twenty-five years old. We asked what was wrong with it and she answered by saying, the fact that it's here. We weren't there to fix it. We were there to throw it into the giant trash bin out front. I have no idea why the boss wanted to do this at all, let along asap. We were repairmen, not garbagemen. Odds were that she was related to someone high up in the company. At least she was nice about it.

"I've been in Paris for over eight months and I think that the freezer has been off for at least that long. Whatever is in it, I want out of here, please," she said.

We nodded. Of course, both or our curiosities were piqued. What was inside? I wanted to know. Scratch that, I needed to know.

Now for a quick aside. Do you remember the first "Alien" movie, especially that scene towards the beginning where John Hurt goes down to the planet and pokes around in the cavern where all the alien eggs are and how they were all covered with a white thick, dry ice fog? Try and keep that scene in your mind.

Back to the task at hand. Karen pointed out two hand dollies and a pile of rags we could use. She finished up what she had to say and walked back inside the house. Little did we know that she had just played us for suckers.

Chris and me looked at each other and decided upon a plan: he'd unlock the dumpster doors and I'd grab the hand dollies. It looked like I had gotten the better job because Chris was having trouble opening the doors whereas I had no problem getting the dollies down from the wall. At this point, the parable about how curiosity killed the cat sprang into my mind. Fortunately, or unfortunately, depending on how you looked at the situation, I decided to ignore it. Why? Because I was dying to know what food or meat in particular, looked like after going months without refrigeration. Simply put, I needed to open the freezer lid.

As I approached, the freezer, I began to feel like Indiana Jones. I took a breath and used the rags to open the lid. Big mistake on my part because as I opened it, a dark green misty fog came out of the freezer. Now that it had fresh oxygen for the first time in months, it escaped and began to swirl and even leak out onto the floor. What a beautiful sight and quite possibly a bio-hazard. The smell was nothing I had ever smelled before. It literally knocked me over. Think of being punched in the face by the most disgusting odor you can dream up. Then, multiply it by five. You're still not close. I actually was knocked down but before I hit the garage floor, I managed to shut the lid. The green fog didn't even really dissipate. It just kind of laid there above the garage floor. My nose burned and my eyes teared.

Chris saw all this and after laughing his ass off, asked if I was all right? I didn't know how to answer his question. I had just seen the gates of hell inside an old freezer. After a moment or two, the odor hit Chris hard.

"What the hell is that smell," he asked?

I didn't answer because I really didn't know. We both waited for the dark green fog to dissolve while we stood by the freezer. After a few moments of dead silence, we decided to try and get on with the job. I placed a hand dolly under one side and Chris did the same with the other side. As we lifted it up, we heard whatever was inside slosh from side to side. I didn't want to lift the freezer too high because all I need was the contents to come splashing out onto the floor or even worse, onto us. Luckily, we spotted a roll of duct-tape on the workbench. I grabbed it and we went about taping the lid shut. It didn't work. The green mist still managed to leak out from the cracks.

After that, we preceded to drag the freezer down the driveway and into the dumpster. The doors were open and we, eventually, managed to get the freezer inside the dumpster. As we were closing the trash bin doors, we heard a rumbling noise coming from inside the freezer. Maybe when we moved the dang thing, it's contents shifted around. The noise stopped for a few seconds and then started again only this time louder and the freezer moved a little. We needed to close the dumpster doors now! Obviously, we had woken up the alien monster!

We started walking up the driveway to return the dollies and rags to the garage. Just as Chris and me entered the garage the freezer lid exploded! Food guts were all over the trash bin!

Needless to say, we were shocked. As we turned around we noticed that the dark, green fog had returned and was flowing over the sides of the trash bin which were seven feet high. The dark green fog was taking its sweet time to dissipate. In fairness, it had been trapped for a long time.

Karen came running out from the house and said, "Oh my God, I heard the explosion. Are you okay?"

"We're fine," I said. "At least I think we are."

"What was that and what is that green fog," she asked?

Both good questions that we did not have the answer to. Now onto more practical matters. She wanted to know if we were going to clean up the mess. I guess it was our responsibility.

Karen handed us a garden hose and pointed to a broom and shovel and left, leaving us with the dirty work. We started to clean up. As I walked around to the trash can doors I noticed the liquid food stuff was leaking out. I climbed up the side of the dumpster and what I found was astonishing.

When the freezer exploded, it had fallen over on its side. On the floor, next to it, laid a boneless butterball turkey. It was wrapped in a yellow wrapper and a tight nylon fish net bag just like you see in the supermarket. What I was able to deduce was that the bacteria inside the turkey expanded when it mixed with oxygen and because of the expansion, it was now pushing hard against the wrapper through the nylon fish netting. It looked like one of those Alien eggs. Truly a beautiful sight and it was ready to pop.

Here is where we decided to have some fun. Inside my truck, I had a box of 16d nails that were three and one-half inches long. Just long enough to throw and pop the wrapper. I asked Chris to climb up and check this out. He did and readily agreed with me.

We quickly finished the clean-up and now it was time to explode that turkey. It sort of looked like bubble wrap but inside each bubble was noxious gas. We couldn't wait.

First, we started tossing the nails into the trash bin. Each nail had an arc of fifteen feet, then fell, hopefully, into the turkey. We tossed several nails, each of them making a metal impact noise when we missed. We had some minor success but the big one eluded us. Clearly, one at a time wasn't getting the job done. Time to up our game.

We each took a handful of nails, counted to three and tossed them into the dumpster. <u>Kablooey</u>! Turkey guts exploded causing the dumpster walls to vibrate and buckle. Turkey or, whatever biologists would classify this thing as now, guts flew out everywhere. It was great! Yes, it added to the horrific smell, but we didn't care because we weren't two techs in their forties. We were two idiot twelve-year-olds and we loved it.

That night, I went home and asked my wife for a nice, big hug. For some reason, maybe because it was because I stunk to high heaven, she refused. I pointed out that she was constantly asking me to be more affectionate. This argument didn't persuade her. I guess I'll never understand women.

Before being allowed in the house, my son had to hose me down in the backyard. The water was freezing cold, but I had the biggest grin plastered on my face the whole time. We had blown up an alien!

Story 51: The Nooner (2013)

Every morning like clockwork, I call my customers to let them know when I'll be arriving. This particular customer, who needed their air-conditioner looked at, was scheduled for mid-day and I advised them that I'd be there between 11:00 and 1:00. And unlike your local cable company, we actually get there when we say we will.

I parked the truck in front of the house and looked closer at the work order to see what the problem was. Apparently, water was leaking on the floor. Exiting from the truck, I walked around to the back and picked up my toolbox. As I closed the truck's rear door, I heard a faint lady's voice that was screaming. It was a pulsating faint scream. Because the house was on a busy street, I couldn't locate where it was coming from. Hopefully, no one was being murdered. I'm guessing that would require a ton of paperwork.

I started walking up to the front door and heard moaning. I knocked several times with no response but plenty of groaning. I thought somebody had left the Playboy Channel on. Finally, the lady's voice stopped but there were no commercials. I knocked again and from upstairs, a man's voice yelled out, "I'll be right down!"

The wait was longer than usual. It sounded like people were getting dressed in a hurry. Suddenly, the door opened. The lady of the house, she was cute and, in her thirties,was standing inside the archway and wearing a long tee-shirt like you'd would wear to bed.

"Hi, I'm Rob. I'm here to fix your air-conditioner."

"Hi, I'm Joan. Come on in."

I entered the home and I noticed that to the right was a room that was used as an office. Off to the left and down the hall was the mister, standing somewhat bent over at the waist and wearing a faded blue housecoat. Why was he bent over? It was not obvious to me at that time. Maybe he had a medical problem not that it was any of my business. I called over to him,

"Hi, I'm here to fix you're A/C I'll try and get out of your hair as quickly as possible."

"Thanks, man," he said back.

Myself and Joan continued to walk around the house and headed into a room that was just off from the living room. It was completely empty. The only thing in there that wasn't from the original construction was an air-conditioner which was mounted in one of the windows. Joan explained that it did not work at all. Nothing was working. No fan or display was present on the unit. As she finished explaining what the problem was, she closed her legs suddenly. It was like she snapped to attention. At the time, it didn't make any sense.

Joan walked out of the room and I started to work on the air-conditioner. Moments later, I heard the toilet flush. Some time had passed, and I continued working. In the background, I overheard the conversation that the couple were having.

"You just couldn't wait until he left, Brad," she asked but not really.

"Oh, come on, it's fun almost getting caught," said Brad.

"What do you mean "almost?" We were caught. I had to walk out on the repairman when it dawned on me that I wasn't wearing any underwear!" she whisper-screamed.

That would explain why she stood up, ramrod straight. They continued their dialogue, starting with Brad.

"I'm still ready for you. I hope he gets out of here fast."

"Relax," said Joan. "You took your blue pill an hour ago. You should be good for at least four more."

Obviously, it was her voice screaming, or should I say "moaning" from outside the house. It was Playboy Channel quality moaning. The two of them were having a nooner and I interrupted them. Hey, not that I'd ever watch a dirty movie, but don't they usually start out with a repairman making a service call? Now, I really needed to finish the job and get out of there. The last thing I'd ever want is to stop someone from getting laid. Not cool.

Fortunately, for them, the repair was simple. No power was coming from that wall socket. First thing I needed to do was test the wall socket. I walked out of the room and headed towards the front door. I needed to get my extension cord from my truck and test the air-conditioner, using another outlet.

As I approached the front door, I saw that Brad and Joan were in the office. I tried hard not to look, but I glanced slightly. He was in a chair and she was in his lap kissing him. The wonders of modern pharmacology.

I walked out of the house and headed to my truck. The extension cord was just inside the back door. After obtaining the cord, I paused for a moment. Obviously, I needed to re-enter the house and finish the job, but do I go in asap or let a little bit of time pass? I decided that it wouldn't be fair to my other customers or the company if I didn't finish this job or any job as fast as I could while still doing the repair right. Not that it was going to be easy going back in or not potentially embarrassing.

I re-entered the house, making sure to open the front door slowly to make some noise and started walking back to where the air-conditioner was. Brad was still in the chair with his back to me and Joan was missing. I walked to where I needed to be and plugged the air-conditioner into the cord and the cord into a wall outlet in the living room. Miraculously, the air-conditioner started to work.

Clearly, the problem wasn't the a.c. but the lack of power in the room. We repairmen have a highly technical saying for situations like this, "no power, no workie." I turned around and saw that Joan was standing behind me.

"Yeah, so the problem isn't your air conditioner," I explained. "It's that you're not getting any power from your outlet. I plugged the unit into a different outlet and it worked just fine. I'd suggest calling in an electrician to fix the outlet problem."

My work here was done, and Brad's was just about to start up again. Joan thanked me and walked me to the front door and asked if I could recommend any electricians, so I named a few. Guys I had worked with before who were good and weren't crooks.

Joan opened the front door and I noticed that I was facing the office where Brad was now sitting. Right before exiting, I called out

"I'm done, and you may continue. By my count you have at least three hours before the blue pill wears off. Godspeed."

Brad was a little embarrassed but nodded to me anyway. Joan's face dropped just as Brad stood up. Not to be graphic or anything, but he was clearly ready to go. I walked back to my truck just in time to realize that I really had to go to the bathroom. Do I go back in and ask to use the facilities, or do I find a fast food restaurant with a restroom? I decided to not go back in. I didn't want to delay their fun anymore.

My first nooner and I wasn't even one of the participants!

Story 52: Game Over (Early 2000's)

It was an average day, nothing out of the ordinary was going on. One service call after another, each seemed the same. I had one more repair call to do just before lunch time. My thoughts were of where to go and what type of food I was going to eat. Maybe I'd even try that Korean BBQ food truck like I'd been threatening to do for months now. But, business first.

I pulled out my trusty Thomas Guide and began to look up the street address. The directory gave me a page number, column and row. The street was located in a very old part of town and the house address was right down the street from an elementary school. My first thought was that I was going to travel by the school just as the kids were being let out for lunch. I really wanted to avoid this for reasons that should be obvious, so I put the truck into "drive" and took off.

It took me about thirty minutes to get there traveling on the freeway and a few surface streets. According to the Thomas Guide, the address I was looking for was going to be on the left and a few houses down from the school.

I made a right turn and as I completed it, right in front of the truck were countless cars waiting to pick-up their children as they exited the school. All these cars that were trying to make a left turn had to wait because the local Middle School and High School were also letting out. Yup, we had three schools letting out at the exact same time. It was right around that moment when I really wished that home schooling was much more popular. How bad was this traffic mess? Well, we techs called this area the "Royal Street Parking Lot."

Lucky for me, I caught a break because the house I was looking for was on the right, so I didn't need to battle the left hand cross traffic and in a big truck, that's a blessing. Maybe things were starting to go my way.

As I pulled up to the house, I noticed that the front yard was run down. The plants showed little life. The tree on the right had not been pruned in years and the newest thing on their yard was a bag of trash that an animal had torn open. Because the street was packed, I had to park in the driveway, or what was left of it.

The house was old, most likely built in the 1920's. The roof was made from old clay dirty shingles and the walls were constructed from masonry concrete and not from stucco. This is old school material. I'm sure that at one point, this place was chock full of asbestos. Hopefully, it wasn't any longer.

I got out of the truck, grabbed my tool box and made my way to the front door. Easier said than done because the steps were clogged with bags of trash. Whoever lived there could care less about outward appearances, much less safety.

As I navigated my way up the steps, I had to use my foot to push the owner's belongings off to the side just to find the step itself. Once I had made my way through this maze of crap, I noticed that there was no doorbell to ring. I don't think doorbell were around when the house was built. The front door was made of thick hard wood, probably oak. I knocked. The sound was deeper than the sound you get from knocking on a modern pressed wood front door.

While I was waiting, from the inside I could hear a few young adults playing a video game. From where I was standing, I could not tell which game they were playing but from the sound of multiple gun bursts, it was a first person shooting game. I later found out it was "Goldeneye," a very popular game in the late nineties based on the film of the same name. Actually, the game was much better than the film but I'm no critic.

After I knocked again, the door opened revealing a young, Latino boy who I'd peg to be around sixteen.

"Yo" he said by way of introduction.

"Yo. I'm Rob. I'm here to fix the refrigerator," I said back.

In fairness, I don't think it was so much him being rude as him being interested in the game. Still, I wanted to smack him but, of course, I didn't. "Yo?" What the hell is that? Anyway, this future member of Toastmasters General asked me to wait by the door while he got his uncle. I hoped this was progress.

A short minute went by when a man in his forties stood in the foyer. I introduced myself again and this time I was invited to enter the home. He said his name was Jose.

We entered the living room and the first thing that stood out was the 60" flat screen mounted on the wall and the half dozen or so "gamer chairs" all pointed in its direction. The rest of the room looked like it should be condemned. On the wall opposite the big screen were wooden panels that were in the process of falling. There were a bunch of plastic house plants that needed a serious cleaning. I felt like I was in a dentist's office in Manilla.

In front of the TV were two tables which held the Nintendo or whatever gaming system they were using. I say "they" because there were three guys, four, if you include "Yo" who all should've been in school which was only a couple of hundred yards away but going by their attitudes and demeanor, they probably hadn't been for a long time. To put it simply, they looked shady.

All were trying to grow moustaches with varying degrees of success and all were wearing plaid button-down shirts. If they weren't in a gang, it wasn't from lack of trying. All eyes were glued on the game which they had been playing for a while.

To get to the refrigerator, I had to commit the cardinal sin of walking in front of the television. This did not go over too well because I was preventing some secret agent from getting killed. I think it's fair to say that in that brief moment, I got a pretty thorough tutorial of Spanish curse words. I'm also pretty sure my mother was brought into it and not in a complimentary way.

The kitchen was just off to the left. Now, in these older homes, most of the kitchens are small with the stove, refrigerator, table, sink and laundry equipment all in the same area. It's really tight and hard to work in.

I placed my tool box down on the floor and my work order on the table. The cabinets in the kitchen were very old and the several doors were about to fall off. The paint on the wall and the windowsill were cracking in spots. The paint appeared to be from the 1960's and might have been lead based. Hey, who wants to live forever anyway, right?

Jose started to explain what the problem was with his appliance: it was making a squealing noise as it ran. I knew what the problem was, and I had the part on my truck. This was going to be an easy service call. The Korean BBQ truck was sounding better and better. Maybe I'd even beat the long lines.

Just as Jose finished his explanation, an older lady entered the kitchen from the back half of the kitchen. She must be in her eighties and did not maneuver too well as she passed the both of us.

"That's Abuela," said Jose. I nodded "hello" but if she noticed me, she did a good job of hiding it.

By the way, "Abuela" is Spanish for grandmother. She looked a little gray and out of it and didn't say a word to either one of us as she continued on her way out of the kitchen. She passed in front of the TV. I was curious to see what the g.b.i.t.'s or "gang bangers in training" would say. At least she'd be able to understand them.

Fortunately, they said nothing. Maybe I was wrong about the kids. Maybe I was too harsh on them because they respected their elders. It was the second wrong assumption I made since I entered the home. Seven more and I'd get a free sub.

I started to tear down the appliance because I needed to visually check the motor. There was a lot of noise and distractions in the other room as the boys played the game and I couldn't remember the part number I needed.

As I was almost to the motor, Abuela walked back into the kitchen from the same entrance as before. This time, the old lady stopped and looked at me then spoke. I was not sure what language she was speaking, but I picked up that a few words that were slurred and somewhat garbled.

The old lady sat down in one of the chairs that was located next to the table. She put her left hand on top of the table with her palm down. She was shaking a little and looking around in a somewhat confused fashion.

I found the motor housing and the part number on the side. I reached into my pocket for my note pad and wrote the number down. I then stood up and started to exit the kitchen. As I was leaving, I looked at the old lady. Her eyes were wide open, and she was shaking a little.

Honestly, I didn't think too much of it as I needed to walk in front of the video game twerps again. This time, nothing was said. I was almost grateful that there were just dirty looks. As I exited the house, I was thinking about the old lady and her medical symptoms as I walked back to the truck and entered through the rear doors and crawled inside.

The motor I needed was on the shelf. I grabbed it and after stalling for three minutes, I decided it was time to re-enter the house. Something came over me before I left my truck. My little voice in my head told me that I needed to grab my cell-phone before I went back in. This was before cell-phones were commonplace.

I walked back into the hacienda and the boys were playing the video game very intensely. As I turned and entered the kitchen, Abuela was still sitting on the chair next to the table. For the five total minutes it took me to get the part, she had not moved an inch.

I started to install the motor in the fridge and as I reached into my tool box for a larger screw driver, I heard a throat clearing noise. I thought the old lady was just clearing her throat. I was wrong.

Abuela's head had tilted backwards, and she was gasping for air. Her right arm was shaking, and her hand dangled as the movement processed. The old lady's posture began to bow backwards in the chair and somehow her left arm had not moved. It was right then when I harkened back to my college days.

Before you all think that there's something seriously wrong with me, the reason why I was thinking of college was that for an elective, I had taken First-Aid. True, the reason why was because of a beautiful girl was also taking it but at least I had paid attention and because I had, I knew there was something out of the ordinary happening here.

I put down my tools and walked over to her. I looked at her face for a second or two. Then I knelt down in front of the chair and tried to start a conversation. I didn't get a response, so I placed my hand on her left hand and it was cold to the touch. Then I, with effort grabbed, her right hand which was shaking and weak but steady. I continued to try and talk to the lady but with no response.

Mind you, while this was going on, the boys continued to play their game. I called out a few times for Jose but got no response. Finally, one of the boys, it may have even been "Yo," said, "Uncle Jose went to the store, holmes."

Just wonderful, I thought, I stood up and looked more closely into the old lady's face. I placed my hand on her forehead, looking for a fever. But there was none. In fact, her whole body was cold to the touch, despite it being in the mid-eighties.

I, then, used both of my hands and put her head upright to clear her air way. All of a sudden, she opened her eyes and her mouth opened up fully and then her eyes rolled backwards into her head.

<u>Oh my God, she's having a stroke</u>! I needed to do something quickly knowing, that the boys would not help.

I grabbed a towel from the counter and twisted it to a point so that I could use it as a makeshift neck brace to stabilize her neck. This was crucial because if the head wasn't stabilized, major arteries in the neck can be severely damaged because of the sometimes violent head spasms. After I was fairly sure that Abuela couldn't move her neck, I called out to the boys and asked for help.

"Guys, grandma Is having a stroke, I called out" nothing happened. Unbelievable! This woman could die and all they cared about was killing someone in a stupid video game. I peeked my head around the corner and found a pillow that no one was using. I quickly walked over to get the pillow and placed it under her arms while the game continued. Now that she was in a position where she couldn't hurt herself by falling, I called 911.

A lady answered the phone and I told her what was going on and all the symptoms the old lady was having, also what I did to assist her. The 911 operator told me that I did everything that I needed to do, and I was to wait for the fire department to show up. She promised that it wouldn't be long.

While I waited for their arrival, I continued to talk to the operator to keep her informed as best I could. Thank God, I hadn't taken that ceramics class instead.

It only took a few minutes for the fire engine and paramedics to pull up to the house. They must have been close by to get there so fast. Whatever the reason was, I was grateful. I ran out to the front yard to greet the firemen and tell them all about the situation.

The Captain spoke calmly but with authority to his men and they got to work obtaining whatever they needed from the truck. The Captain and I walked into the house and right in front of the big-screen TV where the game was still being played. The boys had no reaction to our presents except for one dirty look.

The Captain and I got to Abuela. He looked at what I did to help her with the towel and pillow and complemented me to my makeshift first aid treatment. He even referred to me as "MacGyver with a tool box." Pretty high praise if I do say so myself.

The rest of the firemen entered the house, all in full fire gear and they walked in front of the boys. Since the kitchen was very small, two of the fireman had to stop right in front of the TV. This really pissed off the boys. One of them even had the balls to scream out "move your fat ass!" I bet he wouldn't say this to a policeman. How do I know this? Because, moments later, three policemen entered the house, and no one said a word. Gee, I wonder why?

After the police entered, they were followed by two paramedics. By now, the little house was becoming quite crowded, so I wasn't at all offended when the fire captain asked me to move out of the kitchen. I did, and the paramedics went to work. As they did, me and the Captain walked into the living room and were joined by one of the police officers. They needed some information from me about what had happened.

The boys were now standing up and leaning up against the wall panels that were falling down. The Captain excused himself mid-sentence and turned to his crew and said, "Clear a path for the paramedics."

Here is where the fun started. All four of the fireman grinned and began lifting two of the chairs and threw them across the room to clear a path. The fact that the chairs and later the tables were chucked right at the boys, I'm sure was purely a coincidence. Funny, how none of them said a word this time. I'm sure it was because they were thinking about that poor woman in the kitchen.

It got even better because one of the fireman picked up the videogame console, and with a jerking motion, disconnected all the cables and power cord while the game was still on. Somehow, I resisted the urge to yell out, "Payback's a bitch!" Even without saying it, I felt so good in that moment. Time seemed to stand still as the boys watched their scores disappear forever.

While this was going on and the hole was "cleared," the paramedics continued treating Abuela. They could not have been more competent or professional. One of the medics was on his Bluetooth talking to the hospital. It was like something out of that old TV show, "Emergency," only, instead of Roy and John, we had Dave and Brad. I'm sure DeSoto and Gage would have been proud. Overall, I'd say that this whole process took about 30 minutes from arrival to carrying the old lady out on a stretcher and into the waiting ambulance.

The room was about to be cleared out and thank God I was almost done too. As I cleared up my tools, one of the boys walked into the kitchen and rudely asked me if I was done and berated me for all the "trouble" I had caused. I was stunned. I guess I should have let the old lady die so as to not disturb their stupid game.

I looked into the brat's face and asked if he noticed what had just happened? He said yes, but he was more interested in the video game that the realization that old lady may not come back. The compassion he showed was overwhelming.

"You're really an idiot," I said to his face.

The boy stepped forward and got in my face, he said that I would not live to see tomorrow and blew me a kiss as he raised his right hand to his side, simulating that he had a weapon there. This is what the law would call a "terroristic threat."

Clearly, I was dealing with the height of his stupidity. Instead of responding, I picked up my tool box and exited the kitchen. As I turned, I looked at the boy's clothes more closely. The reason I did this was not because if I ever caught my son dressing like this, I'd disown him, but because if he was packing a weapon, it would've made a bulge on his waist that would be visible. I saw nothing bulging out. I turned to my right and headed to the front door.

Still standing in the room was the captain and two of the police officers. I noticed that one of the officers had three stripes, meaning he was a sergeant and likely the one in charge. I walked up and kindly informed him of the conversation I had with the piece of crap in the other room. The sergeant assured me that he'd take care of it. Then I exited the house. For the first time in my career, I left a job not caring if an appliance worked or not.

As I was headed out, I saw the sergeant speak into the radio on his shoulder. What exactly did he call out for, I couldn't say. But I can assume that he asked for back-up. Police tend to take death threats seriously. They're funny that way. I placed my tools in the back of my truck when three police cars arrived at the house, sirens going. It looked like the boys were finally going to be taught about respect. What a day. Finally, I took off.

Now, about four days later, I was in the neighborhood and I thought I might go by and see what had happened to the old lady. I pulled up to the house, exited my truck and walked carefully to the front door. The man who took off that day, Jose, answered the door. He was shocked, to say the least, to see me. Because the gamers had gone missing, he wasn't able to piece together the events of the other day, so he asked me, and I told him about the cops, firemen and EMTs. I asked about the old lady. Jose told me that Abuela had, indeed, suffered a stroke but was on the mend and would make a full recovery.

After we had finished exchanging information, I turned around and headed for my truck but not before Jose had a question. He wanted to know what happened to the four boys who were there. Mind you, this was four days later! I'm guessing this wasn't a close family.

I told him that since it was a good assumption that they were rounded up by the police, maybe he should try calling the county lock-up if he wanted them back. Jose shrugged. Something told me that he wasn't going to get right on that.

I can only hope that those kids found prison as stimulating as that video game they were playing. Think about it, video games sell themselves on the fact that they are so realistic but tell me, what you think is more realistic: playing a fighting game or actually having the crap kicked out of you?

Something told me that they'd have a long time to figure that one out.

Story 53: How High Can You Jump? (2009)

Seriously, how high can you jump when necessary? Basketball players can jump to incredible heights. Same for Major League Baseball Players, National Football League players, not to mention certain track and field athletes. They can reach heights that we, as mere mortals, can only dream of. Some animals, like frogs and even fleas can leap insane distances. But my question still stands, if you felt like your life depended on it, how high could you jump?

On this one particular afternoon, I pulled up to a house that was having trouble with its water line. The front yard was under construction and by that, I mean that the front yard was entirely dug up. The construction workers were installing a sprinkler system and major holes were everywhere. The twelve-year-old in me thought it was kind of cool. There were plywood planks over most of the trenches which allowed people to walk in or out of the house.

I exited the truck and made my way toward the front door. Even though it wasn't entirely necessary, I walked on the planks. Sometimes it's fun to pretend to be a pirate. The construction workers saw me do this and knew exactly why I was doing it. That's the thing about men, deep down and in some cases, not that deep down, we're all basically twelve-years-old. After walking the planks, I knocked on the front door and waited for someone to answer. It was a short wait as a middle-aged lady opened the door and greeted me.

"Oh, thank God you're here," she said. "I simply must have this problem taken care or right away."

"That's why I'm here," I said, and she motioned for me to come inside.

The house was older, and it was obvious that major construction work had been recently done. The interior looked absolutely amazing. Whatever construction company that did the work, did an incredible job. The living room, in particular, looked very elegant. There was a lot of gold leaf and the leather sofa was large, quilted and in a style, that I found out later is called "Chesterfield." Honestly, the place had an almost museum-like quality to it. It just wasn't very homey. The lady, whose name was Andrea, showed me to the kitchen.

It was pretty large, and it was shaped like a dogleg meaning it was a little off the beaten path and it bent. It, too, looked great with brand new granite counter tops, beautiful colors and cabinets that tastefully matched the rest of the interior. In the center of it all was an island complete with a sink and gold faucet built right in. Andrea must've spend a fortune to have this done and it showed.

Apparently, the water hose to the refrigerator had come loose. All I needed to do was find the leak and repair it. As I started to pull out the refrigerator, I got a nice little shock which threw me back some. If Andrea was concerned about my well-being, she didn't let on. Needless to say, something was wrong. The first thing that came to mind was that maybe some water had sprayed onto the wall socket and I received a residual shock.

Stepping back from the refrigerator, I reached into my toolbox and pulled out two rags to ground myself, in case of future shocks. I put them in my hands, grabbed onto the side walls and pulled out the refrigerator.

"Ma'am, would you mind getting me some towels? Having this water near electrical appliances isn't safe," I said.

"Of course. I'll be right back," she said before exiting the kitchen.

Surprisingly enough, there was only a small amount of water on the floor. Not really enough to cause an electrical shock situation. In my toolbox were the tools I'd need to remove the rear cover of the refrigerator. I reached into the box, grabbed the tools, walked back to the refrigerator and sat down behind the unit. After removing the rear cover, I noticed that the two wires traveling from the main terminal block on the right side to the compressor relay on the left had been gnawed at in several spots, most likely by a mouse. What caused the shock was that the red wire was touching the main frame of the refrigerator cabinet, not the water.

I unplugged the refrigerator because, and call me crazy here, I did not want to get electrocuted. Andrea re-entered the kitchen with the towels I requested. What I was expecting were old, over bleached towels you used to wash your car. What I got were lush, luxury towels. The kind you'd find in the Four Seasons. Clearly, Andrea didn't hang onto old towels.

"Will these do," she asked?

"And then some. Do you have any old towels? I'm just using them to wipe up the excess refrigerator water," I said. She had no idea what I meant. I tried again.

"These are too nice. It would be a shame to waste them."

"These are the only towels I have."

"Okay, then. Guess they'll have to do," I said. Back to the job at hand.

The wires needed to be replaced and spliced in to the main terminal block. Exiting the house, I walked the plank again back to my truck. I opened the back door and found the wires I needed to finish this job. One wire was red and the other was white. Lucky for me, no odd color wire splicing was needed which would've made the repair a lot more complicated. I re-entered the house and Andrea was standing in front of the island sink. She asked me if I had located the cause of the problem? Somehow, I knew this wasn't going to be fun.

"Ma'am, the wires that lead to the compressor have been eaten by a mouse. By the looks of it, the mouse has made a little home for itself using this fiberglass insulation as its building material—"

She flipped out.

"Excuse me, but there is just no way that a mouse or any rodent could be in my home. It's impossible," she said while standing up ramrod straight. I tried to soften the blow.

"You know, it's really not uncommon for this to happen to houses where construction is being done. The mouse's habitat is being ripped up, so they go inside where it's warm." She wasn't buying it.

"I have paid top dollar to have this work done and there is no way that my home could be infested," she bellowed like one of those fancy ladies in old movies.

"Oh-kay," I said and went back to work.

I rewired the main terminal block to the compressor using the wire I brought, during which I had to listen to her prattle on about how clean her house was. I finished the job and plugged the refrigerator into the wall. It started up right away. Taking great care, I used my voltage meter to recheck to see if I was going to be shocked again if I pushed the refrigerator back into it original spot. No voltage was found.

I stood up and walked around to the front of the refrigerator and pushed it back to its original spot and stepped back. Again, Andrea wouldn't shut up about how clean her house was. I believe the phrase, "you could operate in here" was tossed out more than once. After I just couldn't take it anymore, I turned around and handed her the wire that had been eaten. I had overestimated her because Andrea had no idea what I just gave her.

"Do you see these little spots where the insulation has been stripped away? These are bite marks from a mouse," I said, quite reasonably.

"I'm telling you that it's impossible," she said.

At that point, reasoning with her was damn near impossible. It was like that old joke about the husband who was caught, by his wife, in bed with another woman who said, who are you going to believe; me or your lying eyes?

I explained to her what I had found and what I needed to do to the refrigerator. Basically, some rewiring and a few components had to be swapped out. Nothing too complicated. Andrea had no idea what I was saying. I tried to explain the problem in a different way. I almost drew her a picture. Not that it would've made any difference. All she cared about was that I had insulted her by saying she had mice in her palatial estate.

Suddenly, a small scratching noise came from the lower cabinet of the island. This caught Andrea's attention because for the first time since I had come in, she was silent. We both looked down at my feet. The noise continued. It went on for about a minute. I bent over without moving my feet and looked at the corner of the door.

Three short whiskers appeared out of the molding. They wiggled for a few seconds. We both continued to stare at the molding. Just then, a small mouse's head popped out. Andrea stood up in shock. She was speechless.

After the mouse's head popped out, then came the rest of him. Mickey popped out of the hole like he was being pushed, clearing the molding by two inches, followed by a faint plop sound from when he landed on the floor. He moved his head around looking for something. Food? His mother? Seconds passed. At this point, I was still kneeling down. The mouse started running forward a foot or so, then stopped and restarted. He did this several times. I guess the little guy was scared. He darted ahead and stopped between myself and Andrea. Her shock level had increased to its highest level. She couldn't move. Visions of the movie "MouseHunt," a very underrated movie, if you ask me, danced in my head.

I stood up and turned my focus on the mouse. Silence overtook the kitchen and an eternity of anticipation took over. What was Mickey going to do?

His little head tilted upward. He found Andrea's feet and he took off, traveling straight between her shoes. Then the little guy started doing laps around her feet. It was something I had never seen a rodent do before. If I didn't know better, I'd swear that that mouse was deliberately screwing with her. Good for him. Andrea tried to get away, running around the kitchen, but the dang mouse kept following her. Now, I don't know if this mouse was Andrea's reincarnated dead father like in "MouseHunt," but going by the mouse's actions, it almost seemed like it was personal.

Andrea completely flipped out and honestly, at that point, I didn't blame her because it was getting a little unnerving. Have you ever heard of people being able to perform incredible physical feats when they or someone they loved was in danger? Remember how Bill Bixby threw the car off the side of the road because the jack failed in the opening credits from "The Incredible Hulk" show? True, he was a victim of gamma radiation poisoning, but it was still darn impressive. Or like almost any one of Blake Griffin's dunks? I saw something even more awe inspiring because Andrea jumped from a completely standing still position onto a table that was at least three feet tall, missing by inches the light fixture hanging from the ceiling, sticking the landing perfectly. She didn't even take a cheater step. It was damn remarkable. It's too bad there weren't judges there. Not that she had any idea of what she accomplished. No, all her attention was on the mouse and then to me. Then the screaming started.

Andrea was pretty much hysterical, which I found hysterical. It was just a little mouse. Yeah, they're a nuisance but come on. Her earlier attitude dictated my actions. I reached down and closed my toolbox. I then picked it up and stood directly in front of her.

She continued screamed, only this time, right at me. "Do something!" she pleaded.

I did do something. I wished her a pleasant rest of her day and headed towards the door. She was still kneeling on the island. Once more, she screamed, "Do something!"

I turned to her before exiting and said, "My apologies but your warranty, that you did not pay for, does not cover mice. Have a nice day." I left with an all too self-satisfied smirk on my face as I closed the door behind me.

So, for any professional sports team general manager, who may be reading this and needs their players to jump higher. Forget specialized training and nutritionists and the rest of that crap. Simply enter a rodent into the equation. You don't need to pay me. A couple of center court tickets will do just fine.

Story 54: Christmas Eve Shot (Late '80's)

In the service trade, seniority does have its privileges. I'm not sure the approximate amount of years that I had at the time this story took place. I do know that I was low on the ladder when it happened.

It was December 24th, only one day before Christmas. The routes were full and only a few techs showed up for work. The holidays are usually one of our busiest times of the year. Hey, if you have a bunch of relatives coming over, you'd better make sure your television works or you're going to have to talk to them. So, there were a large amount of calls that needed to be handled. I took off that morning with my heavy route, hoping I could get to them all.

The morning calls went fine. Nothing out of the ordinary and I was able to fix all the appliances. I took lunch around 12:00 o'clock or so. I remember thinking that if the afternoon went as the morning had, maybe, just maybe, I could actually start my Christmas early. Yay!

My penultimate or second to the last call for the afternoon, sorry, I just really like the word "penultimate" and don't get to use it that often, was a television that someone previously had ordered parts for. The ordered part was an old dial tuning tuner or, as you civilians call it, "a knob." This is the kind of thing I could knock out in literally ten seconds so, the problem wasn't the job, it was the location.

Now, mind you, this was before G.P.S. so I had to rely on my Thomas Guide which is a book of maps. I looked up the address and the house was located several miles outside of the city limits. The news didn't get any better when I saw that the road on the map became dashed. That meant that the street had become a dirt road or worse. You ever drive a two-ton truck on a dirt road? Neither had I and I wasn't exactly looking forward to it. Great. I'm gonna be out in the sticks and may have significant trouble getting out. Goodbye, early Christmas.

I headed off to the call and me and the Thomas Guide were right, the road did end and became dirt. There were coyotes running across like they owned it. Where the hell was I sent? Lucky for me, the house was within visual sight and I drove up to it. It was a farm house that had a long front porch with a swinging chair and all painted white and yellow. It looked weathered and ugly. Almost like something out of the old "Andy Griffith Show."

I parked the truck in a conspicuous place so that it and the signage could be clearly seen. If I was going to disappear, I was going to leave something behind to find me. I got out, opened the back and pulled out my toolbox and the television part and walked about forty feet to the stairs just in front of the porch. I knocked. I waited and waited. No answer. By now, several minutes had gone by. I knocked again and this time I waited only a few minutes. Yes, I'm going home early. They're not home! In my mind, I was already drinking eggnog, the good kind and eating Christmas cookies. I started to turn around when, in the background I heard someone walking towards the door, in boots. It was a large thumping sound with each step.

The front door opened slowly, and I couldn't make out who was there. No sounds no nothing. Complete silence.

"Hi, I'm Rob. I'm here to fix your TV. Merry Christmas."

There was no answer. Icy silence. Then I heard a noise that chilled me to my bones. It was the unmistakable sound of a shotgun being cocked. Just then, I saw a two-barreled, Winchester aimed directly at my head. The only thing between the gun's barrel and me was the screen door. For some reason, I didn't think that the torn mesh would offer me too much in the way of protection.

I could not move. I was so scared. My legs seemed frozen to the floor. Finally, the man behind the door spoke.

"What do you want?!"

I gulped. "Sir, I'm here to fix your television."

The shotgun was still aimed squarely at my face.

"I don't know you. Get off my property! Now!" he barked.

Because I had lost the ability to form words, I nodded and did my best to move. Easier said than done. My legs were heavier than lead. I stepped backwards keeping the gun barrel in sight while turning around slowly. Pausing, waiting for the blood to return to my feet and knowing that there was a gun aimed at my back, I eventually was able to walk away. I don't know how I remembered to breathe. Honestly, that was the longest walk I had ever made.

After what seemed like an eternity, I finally made it back to my truck. I opened the doors, one at a time. I had trouble lifting my arms to get it open. I placed my toolbox in the back of the truck and stepped inside the doorway, using the door as a shield. I looked up at the front door trying to see if the man was still there. I couldn't see him, but I wasn't taking any chances. He might still be aiming at me but from a different angle. Like I needed any of this.

Closing the truck doors slowly, I walked to the cab door, entered and started the engine. It was at this moment that I was finally able to slow my heart beat down to normal human levels that I noticed a pungent odor. Was it from the farm or animals? Nope. It was me. I had pissed myself. Something that no grown man wants to experience but completely understandable given the circumstances. With the cab seat wet and my feet and arms slowly regaining control, I managed to drive down his driveway and out into the street. About a mile or so later, I pulled over to the side of the road. I needed some time to collect my thoughts and change into the extra set of clothes I always carried although never for this situation.

Over the next thirty to forty minutes, I grabbed the cleaning solution from the rear of the truck and was cleaning both myself and the truck as best I could. Honestly, the extra time was needed to wait for the cleaning fluid to dry. Just as I was finishing up, the cell phone began to ring. Caller ID indicated that it was the boss. I answered. He yelled.

"Rob, I just got off the phone with your customer, Bill Johnston! He said you left without fixing his set. Why the hell would you do that!? That's very unprofessional! I know it's the holidays and we all want to get home early to be with our families but jeez! You have any idea how bad this makes us look?!"

Mind you, this was going on while I was still putting my pee stained clothes into a sack. He continued:

"I promised Mr. Johnston that you were going back to fix his set right away and I expect you to apologize for your rudeness and unprofessional behavior. And when you get back here, you and I are going to have a talk...'

Un-freakin-belivable. I almost got my head blown off and now he wants me to go back there and apologize? I don't think so. What would that apology even be?

"Hey, Mr. Johnston, it was so rude of me to come to your house, like you requested and not let you kill me. Won't happen again," I thought.

His rant continued on for about five minutes. Eventually, the Boss stopped. Maybe he expected me to say something or maybe he just ran out of breath. In either case, I didn't tell him that I placed the phone on the truck dash so that I could hear him without really hearing him. After he exhausted himself, I picked up the phone from the dash and finally spoke.

"OK Gene, do you feel better?" I asked. I continued by saying, "I'm guessing that the customer left out a major piece of the story."

"What the hell would that be?" he asked without really asking.

"He greeted me with a shotgun pointed at my face and ordered me to leave..." I said.

"What?" he cleverly answered back.

"That's right, Gene. From the second he answered the door, Mr. Johnston had a two-barreled shotgun pointed directly at my face. Not exactly the warmest welcome I've ever received. When I turned around to leave, it was pointed at my back. The only thing missing was him not saying in a Southern drawl, "You're not from around here, are you?" There was a moment of silence coming from the other end.

"Rob, I had no idea," said my immediate supervisor.

"Let me ask you this, after having been told that this customer might've killed me the day before Christmas, do you still expect me to go back there?" I put it mildly.

"No, of course not," he said with a humbled tone. "Forget about it. I'll take care of it," then he hung up.

Two days later, on December 26th at 8:00 am, while I was gathering some supplies to put into my truck, Gene called me into his office. All the other techs watched me walk down the hall like something out of the "Green Mile." I entered his office.

"Close the door, please" he said as we both sat down. This was the first time I ever heard the word "please" come out of his mouth in a non-sarcastic manner. It got better.

"Rob, I want to apologize for my actions two days ago,' he said. "It was wrong of me to go off on you without knowing all the facts. Again, I'm sorry."

Wow, this also never happened before. It was a Christmas miracle! I thought that that was it, but there was more.

"One question, if I may, Rob,"

"Sure," I said back, not sure where this was going.

"Two days ago, you had every right to go off on me after what you had already been through, but you didn't? I want to know, how come?"

I didn't see this coming, but a thoughtful question deserves a thoughtful answer, plus, it takes a big person to admit when they're wrong. I cleared my throat and said

"It would not have served a purpose to yell back. You did not have all the facts. Also, at the time you were yelling at me, I was still in trauma. Sometimes it makes more sense to listen than to speak."

Not a bad little speech, if I do say so myself. Yes, I substituted the word "trauma" for peed myself, but I think I got my point through nonetheless. Gene nodded his head.

From that day on, not only was my relationship with Gene different, Gene was different. He changed from a yell first, yell last then yell some more kind of boss to a nice, thoughtful one who had our backs. Don't get me wrong. By no means was the man perfect. Believe me, there were days when I still wanted to throttle the guy, but those days were much fewer and between. Yes, no doubt about it, respect was built that morning.

Call it corny, but I think the holidays may have even had something to do with it. We all tend to let our guards down that time of year and are more open to doing and being good. We, at least, try to think the best of instead of the worst of people. So, even though, I was almost shot and peed my pants that Christmas Eve day, I still consider it one of the best Christmases I've had. Why? Because instead of a sweater or tie or a homemade birdhouse from one of my art challenged kids, I got a great present that lasted over ten years; an understanding boss. We wished each other a Merry Christmas and I left his office.

About ten years or so later, Gene retired, and we had a big dinner for him. A bunch of people spoke and a lot of them mentioned about what a jerk he had been his first year with the company and how over his first Christmas with us, how he changed. In our speeches, neither me or Gene mentioned our talk that day because we didn't have to. It was between us and that's where it stayed.

Gene retired to Montana and eventually we lost touch, but I'll never forget the guy and if I ever develop prostate problems like incontinence, rest assured, I'll think of him.

Story 55: Grandma (Late '80's)

There was nothing special about the service call I was about to make. I was to go to a customer's residence and clean and service their appliance. I had done this many times before and it was beyond routine. So, it wasn't the task that made this call special, it was the customer.

On my way over I couldn't help but notice that there was no address number. Instead, there was a space number meaning it was a mobile home. Again, nothing terribly unusual about that. I've been to many trailer parks. Sometimes it's a tight fit for my truck but other than that, nothing I hadn't seen before or couldn't handle.

I entered the complex and looked for the directory to get my bearings. I found the sign post which had a crude hand drawn map on it. The space I was looking for was located just around the main office. Slowly, I traveled down the streets looking for the right space. As the numbers on the houses counted one at a time in sequence, I noticed that for the most part, it was a pretty nice complex with clothes lines, kid's bikes, bbq's, etc. Your basic Americana. Norman Rockwell could've painted the place. At the next corner, I turned the truck to the left and saw that the house I was looking for straight ahead.

As I parked the truck, I noticed that the windows for the home had an assortment of teddy bears. Not just a few but, at least twenty or so. Ok, maybe the customer likes stuffed teddy bears. This was not what I was there for. I exited my truck, waked around the back and got my toolbox.

The customer was standing at the back door. When it comes to mobile homes, most do not use the front door. So, entering through the back door isn't unusual. The customer was a lady in her senior years, I would guess in her seventies. Speaking of Norman Rockwell, if he had to paint a grandma, he would've painted this woman. Silver hair, kind smile, bifocals, etc. She smelled like clean linens. The only thing out of the ordinary about her was what she was wearing. She had on a dress that would be worn in a square dance. It was bright yellow with ruffles on the sleeves. The skirt jutted out and probably had hoops underneath. It was hard not to burst out into "Oklahoma!" but somehow, I contained myself.

"Hello, I'm Mrs. Johnson. Won't you come in?" she said sounding like Mrs. Brady and the nicest first grade teacher imaginable.

"Hi, I'm Rob and I'd be glad to," I replied. I swear that with her appearance and mellifluous voice, I wouldn't have been surprised if she asked me to salute the flag.

I entered the domicile through a small hallway where the washer and dryer were located. Mrs. Johnson had to use both of her hands to hold down her dress, so she could walk past. We entered right into the kitchen area and I placed my toolbox on the floor. As I looked up I was amazed as the amount of stuffed teddy bears around the living room. The bears encompassed the entire room. There was a hand knitted sign on the back wall which read, "Teddy Bear." The place was packed with no room to spare. It was obvious that she had either a collecting hobby or an addiction. Maybe it was unprofessional of me to ask but I just had to know.

"Mrs. Johnson, may I ask why you have so many teddy bears?"

"Oh, you noticed them? I guess you couldn't help but notice them. I used to teach school..."

I knew it! She continued.

"...One year I had a small teddy bear on my desk. I don't remember who gave it to me but for some reason, my students thought I really liked them. So, on every Christmas, instead of jellies, note pads, soaps, things you might give your teacher, they gave me teddy bears. You should see how many I used to have. Could've filled another home. I just kept my favorites and gave the rest to the local children's hospital."

"That's very nice of you," I said. "I'm sure you were a wonderful teacher..."

"I did my best, just as I always asked my pupils to do."

"Now, how can I help you? What's wrong with your stove?"

"Not a thing. It's working fine."

"Okay..."

"But, according to my contract, I'm entitled to a cleaning at no charge."

She handed me her contract and sure enough she was right. Honestly, with the way she looked and with the sound of her voice, I would've done it contract or no contract.

"Mrs. Johnson, you're correct and I'll get right on it," I replied.

The kitchen table was right next to the counter. I started to check out what I needed to do to the stove as Mrs. Johnson excused herself and left the room. Her contract specified that I was to only clean the components that related directly to functioning parts. Basically, just the parts that were most likely to get dirty and worn down. This wouldn't take long, not that I was in any particular hurry.

As I started cleaning the parts, Mrs. Johnson returned with a wash bucket, soap, scrubbing tools and a floor mop. She placed the scrubbing supplies right next to the kitchen table and some of the smaller ones on top of the table. She walked right in front of me and stopped.

"Robert?"

No one, except for my grammar school teachers, ever called me "Robert." What a wonderful time warp I found myself in.

"Yes, Mrs. Johnson?"

"Would you mind moving out the stove and washing the floor and wiping the dust off the walls behind it when you're done?"

What a smoothie! Here I was, the whole time, thinking I was talking to Mary Poppins and the whole time she just wanted me to do her housework for her! I've got to be honest, I did not see it coming.

What did I do? Did I tell her that it wasn't my job to do her housekeeping for her? Did I immediately pack up my tools and exit while disconnecting the gas line? Nope. She got me, and I fell for it hook, line and sinker. Saying "no" to her would've been like saying no to your grandma. I don't know about you, but I can't say no to mine. After I finished cleaning the designated area she asked without really asking

"If it's not too much trouble, Robert, and since you're here already, would you mind terribly cleaning the rest of the kitchen?"

My first thought was "Really? Anything else I can do for you while I'm at it like fold your laundry or clean your windows? How about I wait here for hours for the cable guy while you run errands? Better yet, you stay here, and I'll run the errands! It would be my dream come true!"

Funny how much the first thought changed as it went from my head to out my mouth because I stayed there for an extra hour and cleaned what she asked me to clean; the floor and the walls for the rest of the kitchen. One thing I want to make abundantly clear is that I didn't do the dishes. Some lines just aren't crossed. So, I did my good deed for the day and I was feeling pretty good about it too. When I finished and was packing up, she handed me a small package wrapped in tissue paper that smelled mouthwatering.

"I baked these earlier. It's my secret chocolate chip cookie recipe. I hope you enjoy them."

"I'm sure I will. Thank you, Mrs. Johnson."

"No, thank you, Robert."

"My pleasure. Now that I'm done, can I go?" I said reverting to my eight-year-old self.

"I think you meant to say, "May I go?"" Once a teacher, always a teacher.

"May I go?" I responded.

"Yes, you may," she said as she walked me out of the home and down a handicapped ramp, all the while carrying the mop and bucket. I couldn't help but notice a number of members of the greatest generation eyeing me through their windows and hearing the wheels in their heads turn. If Lucille can get the repairman to do her housework for her, maybe I can too. Nope. Time to high tail it out of there. I turned to Mrs. Johnson and said,

"It was nice meeting you, Mrs. Johnson. You take care now."

"You too, Robert and remember to drive safely," she said.

I promised that I would and got back into my truck and back into reality. At least I still had the cookies. They were delicious.

Story 56: A Good Deed Returned (Early '90's)

In my travels doing in-home appliance repairs, I have been asked many times to do favors for people. Some of them included repairing plumbing, moving furniture, fixing lights, crawling under a house to get a kid's toy, etc. And yet, with all the countless good deeds I've done over the years, only two have been returned back to me. This is the story of one of them.

It was a beautiful Sunday morning, around nine o'clock and I needed to pick up a part from a hardware store. It was about thirty miles away but at this time of morning there usually was no traffic. The part I needed wasn't physically large so instead of taking the truck, I thought I'd take the classic car I keep in the garage, a beautiful, red, 1980 Ford Pantera. I only take it out on weekends for a bunch of reasons, one of them being gasoline. Specifically, the cost of it.

My truck's fuel mileage isn't that great but it's a work truck. The Pantera's mileage is even worse. To best describe it, you can't go wrong with "really sucks" since I get, maybe, eight miles to a gallon. Logic be damned, I took the classic car. What can I tell you, it's a guy thing. A fast car, with the windows open and the roar of the engine as you eat up the highway. It's a feeling that can only be described as "cool."

I was traveling northbound on the highway doing the speed limit. Okay, that's a lie. This car could really move and there was just no way I could restrain myself and only drive fifty-five. There's a reason why Sammy Hagar wrote that song, the reason being is that it's true.

Just as I was really enjoying myself, something happened to the car. I blew a tire. Lucky for me it was the rear tire and not the front because traveling at the speed I was going, I could've had a serious accident. I pulled over to a safe spot and got out. I also was fortunate in that there was little to no traffic.

My first thought was, it's only a flat tire, no big deal. I can fix that. I am a tech. I can do almost anything. I walked to the rear of the car and pulled out the spare tire and it was flat. How was I going to get to the store or back home?

I quickly ran down the checklist of options in my head. I could leave the flat tire on the car and slowly travel to the nearest tire store. Problem was that this would damage the rim beyond repair. I could install the spare but risk damaging the tire and rim. Another option, involved walking to the nearest phone.

As I was standing next to the car, not knowing what to do, to my surprise, a car passed me. He was traveling the same direction and as he passed me, I saw the brake lights go on.

The car came to a complete stop right in the middle of the highway. Then the reverse lights came on because he was backing up and headed my way. Man, did I feel relieved. Approximately twenty-feet away from my car, they stopped again. I don't know why someone would do that unless they were trying to help but I'm not the kind of person who likes to count their chickens before they hatched. Some might say that's pessimistic but to me, it's being realistic.

A man and woman exited the car. He greeted me with open smile and a firm handshake. The woman came up to me and gave me a hug. This was a little weird. I did not know these people or, so I thought.

They both stepped back, looked at each other and both at the same time said, "It is him." Boy, was my curiosity peaked. Not wanting to screw this up, I responded by saying "Thank you for stopping." I was still a little in shock.

"What a small world," the man said.

"What are the odds it would be him of all people?" she said back.

"A zillion to one?"

They laughed for a short time as I looked at them more closely and frantically searched my memory. How did they know me? Was it from a sporting event, school, friends of friends? Like the tires not spinning on my car I, for the life of me, could not remember. Finally, I just couldn't take it anymore.

"Guys, this is driving me nuts. Where do I know you both from?"

They laughed again and then explained.

About two years ago, I was doing a repair at their house while a contractor was there. As they remembered it, the contractor wanted to perform a service that I felt was not necessary and really overpriced. I now had a vague memory of this event and think it involved rewiring.

As a result of my opinion, they decided not to hire the contractor. Later on, they found out that he had ran off with another people's money and could not be found. Apparently, I had saved them a bunch of money and a whole lot of hassle.

Ironically, the car they were driving was from the same dealer as mine. The mister, who had later introduced himself as Glen, turned around and headed to his car. The lady, Maura, continued to talk to me, thanking me for being their savior. It felt really nice knowing I had such a big effect on these two without realizing it at the time. A smiling Glen came back rolling his spare tire and handed it to me.

The first thought that went through my mind was why? Thought number two was, would it fit my Pantera's wheel hub? I was all set to find out by myself when Glen insisted on helping me. We took off the old tire and viola, the spare did fit. I could now drive to a tire store and get my car fixed. This whole operation didn't take too long although Maura never stopped talking. She was so happy. Even happier than I was.

After we finished replacing the tire, what they did next really caught me off guard. They told me to keep it. They also asked if it was ok if they could escort me to the tire store to make sure I arrived safely. I was in shock. Honestly!

They were good people doing the right thing all the while talking about all I had done for them. But after the great kindness they had shown me I had to ask myself, who was really the savior here?

Story 57: The Delivery Package Dog or More Fun With Animals (2007)

Every story in this book actually happened to me. This one happened around me. Let me explain.

One Tuesday, I went to a house to repair a dishwasher. The repair was ordinary. The door gasket was leaking which caused water to leak on the kitchen floor. It was an easy fix for me but not for whoever was going to have to fix the damage to the kitchen floor. Oh well, not my problem.

As I was leaving the house I noticed a delivery person in the process of delivering a package to the next-door neighbor. My daughter, the lawyer, says I can't identify the company the man worked for but let's just say he was wearing brown. The delivery person was carrying the hand-held computer that they ask you to sign for your packages in his left hand and the customer's package in the other hand. My daughter, the lawyer, says I can't identify which hand he was using but let's say it wasn't his left. Okay, so the last sentence isn't true. What is true is that I like to give her a hard time and it's my book.

Anyway, I was thanking the customer for her business and not mentioning how crappy the front lawn looked and how the bushes that were under the front window were overgrown with weeds that overwhelmed the grass. I also failed to mention that the house was in dire need of a paint job? Why didn't I mention those things? Because I'm a people person.

So, the delivery person was now standing at the front door of the house next door and I was about eighty feet from him. The delivery person knocked on the screen door and then stepped back. I turned to my left and started to walk back to my truck.

All of a sudden, I heard a dog starting to bark, franticly. It really sounded like a large dog and for a moment, I feared that I was going to be bitten by it as I walked back to my truck. I was almost there when I noticed that the screen door was all torn, most likely by the barking dog. Not a good sign. The unseen Cujo continued to bark.

I almost made it back to my truck when, with a crashing motion, the dog bolted right through the screen door which made the delivery person jump back so that he was standing about twelve feet away from the door. What kind of dog was Cujo? He was a small, fluffy French poodle with a horrendous attitude. For whatever reason, this thing was really pissed off.

My initial thought at that moment was that this guy was going to be in trouble with the ankle biting dog. I put down my toolbox and started walking in his direction. Again, I'm a people person.

The dog, who I decided to call Fifi, had some momentum as he came through the screen door and had some distance to make up before he was able to get to the delivery person. He seemed intent on making it up in a hurry because he ran full speed towards the delivery person.

I was now on my third step when Fifi lunged at the delivery person. Yes, the rat dog was small, but it could bite and with its lousy attitude could cause some damage to the poor sap who was just trying to drop off a cook book or whatever was in the package. I just hoped that I was going to get there on time because, in the moment, it didn't look good.

The delivery person suddenly made a move that took little effort. He just lifted his right leg backwards into a right angle. He stood there on his left leg as Fifi missed him. As Fifi tried to stop, his paws dug into the grass and he began to flip sideways until he landed a few feet behind the delivery person. Nice move, I thought.

The delivery person put his right foot back on the ground and stepped off in such an angle so that he could see the dog in front on him. I was just about to start to run over to him. Honestly, I didn't know what I would do once I reached him but, having been in similar situations, I just wanted to help.

The dog regained his footing and started to attack the delivery person again. Usually the French give up at the first sign of trouble. Maybe this dog had some German in him.

The delivery person carefully reached with his right hand and secured the package from his left arm. He then placed the package on the ground in front of the dog, blocking Fifi from reaching him. Another smart move on his part, I thought. Clearly, this wasn't the delivery person's first rodeo.

The dog stopped at the package. Still barking and growling as he stood there. By the way, where was the owner when all this was going on?

Finally, from inside the house came a faint voice.

"Sorry, I'll be right there," she said.

The dog stopped barking. Maybe the owner's voice calmed him down or distracted him because, just at this moment, the delivery person reached down and grabbed Fifi by the scruff of his neck. The dog just froze up. Taking advantage of this, the delivery person, with one careful and swift motion, side armed the dog over his head and threw it onto the roof. Holy crap!

At this point, I was now in the middle of the yard and stopped walking. This guy no longer needed my help. Honestly, I think the delivery person was in shock about what just happened too. He watched Fifi land on the roof and not once did he mention hang time. To be fair, I think he was really worried about whether the rat dog was going to stay on the roof or if he was going to fall off.

He paused for a few seconds and then reached down and picked up the package he was there to deliver. He was just about to place it on the front door step and get on with his life when the owner finally answered the door. I overheard their conversation. She was an older woman.

"I apologize for taking so long. I was indisposed," she said.

"Not a problem, ma'am. Please sign here," said the delivery person.

She did so, and he handed her the package. Just before going back inside she looked around and said to the delivery person

"Have you seen my dog? He was barking his head off to protect me. Isn't that adorable?"

"Yes, ma'am and no, I haven't seen your dog," said the delivery guy.

Of course, the dog was right above her and for whatever reason, wasn't barking.

"Okay, thank you and sorry for taking so long," she said.

"No worries, ma'am. Enjoy your day."

And with that she went back inside her house and he started to walk away. A few steps after leaving the door, he looked in my direction and saw me for the first time. Mind you, the whole encounter with the dog probably lasted about sixty seconds. We both looked at each other. His face was ghost white. He knew he had done something really wrong and now he knew that I had seen everything.

I did not know what to do. We both just stared at each other for a long few seconds wondering what was going to happen next. I thought it best to say something. With a somewhat loud voice I said,

"That was great! I need to remember that move. Are you all right?"

The Delivery Person exhaled. He did not say a word to me. We both turned in the direction of the dog, namely straight up.

What we saw was the perfect ending and I swear this is true, Fifi walked up the roof and urinated on the chimney. Obviously, Fifi was okay and would live to bite another day.

We both turned back towards each other, now with different view-points and paused for a few more seconds. We just stared at each other then, busted out laughing. Then we both turned and started walking back to our trucks wondering how that annoying little fur ball from hell was going to get down from the roof to torment another service person.

Story 58: Soap Opera Lady (Late '80's)

It was mid-day on a Tuesday as I pulled up to the house. I was called out to repair something on this customer's television. The service order specified that there were lines in the picture. This was before flat-screens. This was the era of televisions weighing over a hundred pounds a.k.a. "the mover's nightmare."

As I normally do, I pulled out my toolbox from the rear of the truck and started walking to the front door. The house itself was a little run down and kid's toys were all over the front yard. Nothing too bad though. A normal but functional house. I knocked on the front door and waited.

A lady's voice came through the door, "I'll be right there!" I don't know what your definition of "I'll be right there" is but I bet it's not a few minutes. Finally, I could see her walking to the door. She was a thin, blond woman in her mid-thirties. She opened the door.

"Sorry to keep you waiting. I'm Grace. Thank you for coming."

"I'm Rob and no worries. I can see by your lawn that you've got young kids. I've got kids too and believe me, I know they can be a handful."

"Yes, they can. Please come inside," she said.

We entered the home. Inside was also cluttered with kid's toys but clean. We walked into the living room and then Grace showed me her television. It was a twenty-five-inch console, circa 1984. It was already on and she pointed out the lines on the top of the screen. The good news with dealing with a model this old was that when I took it apart, it only had a main mother board that I needed to contend with.

The problem with her picture is called vertical fold over. For those of you under fifty, vertical foldover is when the picture is squashed down vertically and there's around five small white lines cross the top of the screen no matter what station is being viewed. You can still watch your show, but it does get quite annoying. Lucky for me and her, I had seen this problem before and knew how to fix it. The part needed is a small circuit which would take a very short time to solder in. In a normal world, this would take, maybe, twenty minutes in and out. This was not a normal world. This was soap opera world.

Grace was watching ABC, specifically "General Hospital." Grace sat down, completely transfixed. It was like I wasn't there. The house could've been on fire and it would've made no difference. I left the room and the house to get the part I needed which was back in the truck.

It was now about twelve-twenty. As I re-entered the house, with part in my hand, I noticed that that Grace had not moved. If she was breathing I didn't notice. She was transfixed and catatonic at the same time. It was almost like she was in a cult which, now that I think about it, she kinda was. A commercial came on and so did Grace.

She stood up and without even missing a beat asked if I could fix the problem? Whoa. What a space cadet. I had explained it all to her not seven minutes ago. She didn't even realize I left her house.

"Grace, like I told you earlier. The problem is a circuit has burned out. I went out to my truck to get the replacement part," I re-explained. She tried to cover.

"Oh right, now I remember," she said, covering. "So, what happens next?"

"What happens is I write down an estimate based on the cost of the part and how long it will take me to install it. If you approve it, I'll get right to work. If you don't, you make your peace with the white, squiggly lines on top of your screen."

She nodded and was about to say something when "General Hospital" came back on. She sat down. Once again, mesmerized.

I finished filling out the estimate, presented it to Grace and asked her if she approved. She did not move. I don't think she heard me at all. The kids were in the back of the house yelling. I think they were fighting. At least they were smart enough to pick their spots. They could quite literally have gotten away with murder as long as it happened when G.H. was on.

I had to wait for another commercial break before I could get a response from Grace. Finally, after several excruciatingly boring minutes, a commercial for some kind of woman's hygiene product came on. My quick twenty-minute service call was going to be a lot longer.

As the tampon commercial played on, I handed the paperwork to Grace and she approved the estimate. She asked me what had occurred to make the part go bad. I said it was excessive use. I'd bet anything that this baby was on twenty-four hours a day. I walked over to the television and turned it around, so I could unscrew the back cabinet. "General Hospital" started up again. I think someone's twin was trying to kill them or someone was having an incestuous relationship. How the hell would I know? I don't watch this crap. What I did know was that I needed to unplug the television. When I did, Grace became unhinged. It was borderline scary.

"No!!!" she screamed out.

I looked up at her. She threw up her hands and screamed out again.

"No! Please turn the television back on now!"

I did what she asked and for the moment, peace was restored. What I had forgotten was that after unplugging the set, I had turned it to channel three. For reasons I won't bore you with, back then, we had to turn it to that channel in order to perform the necessary tests. She continued to freak-out.

"I need to know what happens with Luke and Laura. Turn the channel," she cried out!

As I turned the station back to channel seven, Grace was contented once again. This chick was on the verge of having a heart-attack because of some make-believe people who, in my opinion, weren't very good actors.

I looked at my watch and then at Gracie. I had some bad news to deliver.

"Ma'am, this program has almost thirty minutes to go and if you're going to make me wait for it to be over before I can do my job, you're going to be charged extra for it," I advised her.

Remarkably, this time Grace heard me. She slowly sat down on the floor with her legs crossed and re-focused on the program. She raised her arm in a gesture that I interpreted as "okay, I'll see you in a half-hour. Fine."

Ok, now what do I do until 1:00 o'clock? I left the house and went out to my truck. Good thing I packed my own lunch today. It was going to be a long one and I was going to enjoy it. I make a pretty great brisket sandwich, if I do say so myself. To wash it down, cherry lemonade and for dessert, homemade chocolate chip cookies and Grace was paying for it.

I finished my lunch just shy of 1:00 o'clock and re-entered the house. By now, Luke and Laura should be done with their shenanigans for the day. Grace still hadn't moved an inch from when I last saw her. The kids were still fighting.

The credits were rolling so I deemed it safe to get back to work. I walked over to the television and knelt down next to the cabinet. Grace had snapped out of her trance. First thing she did was look at me from a sitting position on the floor.

"You moved, how did you do that?" she said.

I wanted to tell her that in my spare time, I was an amateur magician. She would've believe me too. Man, did she have a serious problem. She stood up and walked down to the rear of the house. She went into the kid's room hopefully to quiet them down. I started working, removing the cabinet from the television.

I continued working on the television. I needed to solder the part into the chassis. Several minutes had passed. Grace came back into the living room. She stopped at the back on the sofa and watched me soldering.

"Excuse me, sir. How long will this take? I have another program coming on in a few minutes that I would like to watch" she said.

I stopped soldering and looked at her.

"Ma'am, I need some time to do the repair right, so if you don't mind, I'm going to get started again," I responded.

She sat back down on the couch and started fidgeting with her hands. Then she changed positions on the couch a bunch of times. After that, she started playing with her hair. Now, I don't know a lot about addiction but, it appeared to me that Grace was actually going through withdrawal over soap operas. The more time passed, the worse she became. A lesser man would've stretched this thing out for hours, but not only did I not have the heart to do that, I was really worried that she'd hurt herself. By the way, this had to be the dumbest addiction ever.

Finally, I had finished the repair and Grace was practically bouncing off the walls and was scratching herself violently. She turned around and screamed at the kids.

"Knock it off, Preston! Mama's in no mood today!"

This caught me completely off guard and I jumped more than a little. I wanted to yell back at Preston that mama was not screwing around. Of course, her screaming was not the smartest thing for her to do while I had my hand inside the television's chassis, the appliance that made her life worth living.

As I turned around to secure the rear cabinet, Grace's eyes opened up wide. All I need to do was screw the cabinet back on. When I was finished with the last screw, she stood up in, what I thought was, blessed anticipation. Life would finally be worth living again for her. I plugged the set back in and turned it on. She cheered. What a whackado.

The television was working normally now. The lines up top were gone. The picture was crisper, and the colors were more natural. The skin tones of the actors were much more life-like too. As the opening credits to whatever the next soap was starting to appear, Grace sat back down on the couch and froze again.

I cleaned up the small mess I had made and began to fill out the bill. The estimate I presented her with earlier didn't reflect the extra time I spent sitting in the truck eating lunch or waiting for a commercial. How could it have? I didn't know she was crazy when I first entered.

I handed the work order to her and she paused a few seconds before she signed it. While never taking her eyes off the screen she reached for the credit card that was on the coffee table and handed it to me. I got the hell out of there toot sweet.

Later that day, when I was finished with my route, I drove back to the shop. On my desk was a note to call Grace because she had a question. Hopefully, it wasn't about "General Hospital" because, once again, I don't watch that crap. I called her, and her husband answered.

"Hello," he said.

"Hi, this is Rob, the service tech. I'm returning your call," I said.

"Thanks. I wanted to know why my bill was so high. I called around to other repair centers and their price was significantly lower. Are you trying to gauge me?"

I took a deep breath, so I wouldn't lose it.

"Sir, the reason why your bill is significantly than your estimate is because I was not allowed to work while "General Hospital" was on.

"What?"

"Your wife would not let me complete the repair while that program was on. The extra time I spent doing nothing and eating my lunch is reflected on the bill. I wasn't thrilled about it either," I said.

There were a few moments of silence on the other end of the phone. I'm guessing that this wasn't the first time that something like this had happened. Honestly, I thought that I might get yelled at. Not that I was afraid of it, but it was a hassle I didn't need. Finally, he spoke.

"Thank you for your time, sir. The picture on my television looks great. Have a good evening." As he was in the process of hanging up, I distinctly heard him say, "Goddamn it, Grace! Enough with those stupid soap operas!..."

Poor Grace and to think of how much of a difference a VCR, a DVR or "On Demand" would've made in her life. Some people are just not born in their proper time.

Story 59: A Fish Story (Late '80's)

Some days you just get lucky. For me, one of those days was when I had a service call to make in the city of Santa Barbara. The call was scheduled between 1-2 in the early afternoon which was perfect. It was just one of those days where the schedule worked in my favor, as we repairman would say.

My morning schedule wasn't difficult at all. I only had three calls to make. Here's how that would break down: do a repair and take a break. Do another call, take another break. Then take a real break of thirty minutes. After that, the third call, then take the third break. After that, lunch. It just might have been the easiest work morning I've ever had, which was really appreciated because I was battling a bad head cold. Now, it was time to go to Santa Barbara.

For those of you who aren't familiar with the place, Santa Barbara is located on California's central coast, right on the beach. It was settled by the Spanish in the 1700's and you can still see their influence on the architecture which still has plenty of stucco buildings and red tiled roofs. Unlike a lot of beach communities, Santa Barbara is lush with vegetation and there's plenty of interesting stores and places to explore. I know I'm sounding like I'm working for the chamber of commerce but it's really a nice place and I was getting paid to go there.

As an added bonus, the drive north was really enjoyable. I was on the 101 North, a road, in which a major section, passes right alongside the beach. There was no traffic due to the time of day, so I drove with my window down to catch the gentle ocean wind. The weather was pretty much close to perfect. Warm but not too hot with a comfortable breeze and zero humidity.

I arrived in town around one fifteen and had some time to kill so I stopped at a country store to purchase a drink and to take another break. Hey, I'd only had three up to that point.

Inside the store, in addition to sandwiches, sodas and homemade ice-cream, the owner also carried an impressive array of fishing equipment. This was a nice surprise so, not having anything better to do and time to waste, I went shopping. I looked at some Kistler's, Falcon's and Fly Logic's before deciding on a really nice Carbon X angler spinning rod and reel, that was, as luck would have it, on sale. I also picked up some salt water lures and a couple of shank hooks also for a reasonable price. I stowed the newly purchased equipment in the rear of the truck. The only official duty I had left was that one last call that afternoon. Yeah, I'll admit it, I was quite the slug that day.

I arrived at the service call around 2:30 pm. The house was relatively modest. I say "relatively" because this was a wealthy area so even this 900 square-foot home easily could've been worth in the high six figures. The customer needed his freezer fixed. The note on the work order said that the unit had stopped completely. When an order says that it has stopped completely the question is; for how long?

The customer, a guy in his early fifties, who was probably a life-long surfer, judging by his seemingly permanent tan and being semi out of it, greeted me at his front door and said that the freezer was in the garage.

"I'll open the garage door for you, buddy" he said. "By, the way, I'm Mike. Thanks for coming out. I get that this must've been quite a hike for you."

"I'm Rob and you're welcome. It was really no bother," which could not have been more true.

I looked at the freezer and on my first check noticed that the inside light was working but it was not getting cold. Easy call. Something was wrong with the compressor. I pulled out the freezer and looked behind it. I noticed that a mouse or rat had chomped through one of the electrical wires, which was lying on the floor. This was going to be a really easy fix and it wasn't like the day had been difficult to this point.

Repairing the wire was a breeze mostly because I'd seen this many times before. After fixing the wire, I helped Mike remove the freezer's contents, several pounds of rotted fish and put them in the trash. Hey, no one ever said that this job was glamorous.

I left the house and bid Mike adieu around 3:00 o'clock and started the drive back. I needed to be back at the shop around 5:00 o'clock so I could complete my eight-hour day. So, what did I do? Yes, I took another break. Now you know why most but not all repair men are usually late. We tend to take a lot of breaks.

On the way back down the 101, I stopped at the little country store again to get another drink. This time I parked my truck on the beach side of the freeway. After getting back to the truck, I looked at my watch and notice that I still had time to kill.

In the back of my truck was the newly purchased fishing equipment. I needed to try it out and since I was right at the ocean, I rationalized that it would be wrong not to. I mean, if I tested it out at home and it didn't work, I'd have to take a long drive to get back here. Yes, the responsible thing to do was to go fishing right here and right now. Why not? I hooked up the reel to the pole and ran the fishing line through the eyelets, tied on a fishing lure and tossed it into the Pacific. I must have casted it out at least fifteen times.

My lucky day continued because a fish took the bait. I caught a bass! I don't care how many times you do it, it's still a thrill. And it took me no time at all to bring him onto the shore. He didn't have a chance. Hey, my new equipment just caught a fish. Looks like this was going to be my new lucky pole. I threw the bass back into the ocean, cleaned up what I needed to or at least I thought I did and drove back to the shop almost on time.

An hour or so later, I entered the parking lot where the rest of the trucks were and parked right next to my car. More good luck. I placed the equipment in the car without anyone seeing me. I didn't want my boss to notice what I had purchased on company time. Something told me that he might not have been as understanding as I would've liked him to have been.

I walked into the shop area to complete my paperwork, so I could go home. As I was filling out my forms on the rear counter, the boss came around the corner. He stopped to talk to some of the repair guys. Nothing important. just chatting.

"...Any of you guys have a barbecue pit? I'm telling you, it's the way to go," he said. Suddenly, he stopped talking, made a face, looked around then said, "What the hell is that smell? That's fish!"

Crap, I was about to be busted. My heart started to race. I knew that that day was too good to last. It was so perfect, something bad was bound to happen and now it had. If it wasn't for my head full of mucus that I was carrying, I would've notice the stink. What was I going to say to my boss? What I needed to know was come up with something and quick before my face turned beet red but what?

What a minute, the truth could actually work. After all, I was checking out a broken freezer with spoiled seafood in it!

"Stuart," I said, "You sent me to Santa Barbara today to fix a compressor on a busted freezer. Yeah, well, there was a bunch of rotten fish and other spoiled food inside. It must've rubbed off on me without me noticing. Honestly, because of this dang head cold, I didn't notice the stench. Sorry."

Now what? He paused, took another breath which he instantly regretted, shook his head and said, "You need to wash up right now." He bought it!

So, I headed to the men's room, leaving my paperwork on the counter. Stuart told me to make sure not to spread the smell onto the counter then walked off.

What I said had worked and the day had remained lucky. I went to the washroom, gave myself a thorough scrubbing and took a few deep breaths. Then I walked back to the counter to finish my paperwork.

One of the senior repair guys, Fred, walked over to me and faced me and said, "Rob, you are so full of crap. It wasn't the freezer. I know exactly what you did. You bought some new gear at that country store and decided to try it out, right?"

Okay, so I was busted but I just had to know how this guy saw through this line of B.S. that I had so beautifully crafted and that our boss had just bought hook, line and sinker.

Sheepishly I said, "Yeah, I did. How did you know?"

The guy grinned and said, "Because I did the exact same thing last week. We all do whenever we go to Santa Barbara. Although, at least we're smart enough to wash up before coming back." I nodded and hung my head in mock shame. Fred wasn't quite done with me though.

"Since you like to fish, a bunch of us are going out on a charter this Sunday in La Conchita. Why don't you come with," he asked?

"Thanks. I'd love to. Can I bring anything?"

"We got it covered. Just make sure you don't smell when we start the trip. See you at five a.m., Sunday."

Fred grinned and walked off.

So, to summarize, I had a light day, got to drive to Santa Barbara, bought some new fishing gear, caught a fish, almost got busted but due to my quick thinking, didn't. No doubt about it, this pole was lucky. I mean really lucky because the next day, not only did I get in better with some of the senior techs, I pulled three bass out of the Pacific and my head cold was gone too.

Story 60: Prank Wars Part 4: Dude, What's that Smell?! (Late '90's)

Early in my career, I had a manager who loved saying, "Practical jokes are good for morale and I encourage harmless but fun jokes." This about one of those times I took him up on it. If you play with the big dog, expect to be bitten.

One Wednesday morning, the manager in question, Mario, called a meeting for nine-o'clock. Now, I liked Mario and not just for self-preservation. The guy was about 6'5" but he had started out as a tech and he never forgot what that was like. He did like to screw with us though and we felt free to screw right back.

Anyway, I arrived at the host service unit around eight-thirty. Having a little time to kill, I thought it would be a good opportunity to clean my truck out of all the junk that I had accumulated. I parked next to the main trash cans and started to clean it out. It truly is amazing how fast crap can add up. Did I really drink this much soda? No wonder my dentist could afford a new Jacuzzi. Then there's the small mountain of phone books that I kept forgetting to throw in the dumpster. Don't even get me started on the amount of windshield flyers that were wadded up in the back. If any of the people who distribute them are reading this, I know I speak for everyone when I say, we're not interested in making money from home, we're happy with our regular dry cleaner and if I want to refinance my home, I'm not going to use a bank that advertises this way.

As I was discarding the 1995 yellow pages, someone sneaked up from behind me and screamed. "What are you doing?!" Needless to say, he scared the crap out of me. Who in his right mind would do such a childless act? Then I turn around and saw who it was. Of course, it was Mario. He looked at me and said, "Robbie, I got you." He was the only person who called me "Robbie," but from him, I allowed it. I said back to him, "Mario, payback will be a bitch."

Mario was laughing it up big time as he walked off towards the shop area. Okay, so he got me and I almost needed a new pair of underwear. In his mind, he was probably paying me back for some joke I had played on him. Since we did it to each other constantly, sometimes it was tough to remember whose turn it was to get got. But, no doubt about it, it was now Big Mario's turn.

By now, it was eight fifty-five and the meeting was starting in five minutes. I finished the clean-up and parked in the rear lot. Then I walked across the parking lot and entered the building. The main offices are in the front of the building. The first one belonged to Harmony who did scheduling. She and I would constantly send each other Shakespeare quotes and we'd have to guess which play they came from. Trust me, once the obvious ones got used up, it got pretty obscure pretty fast. Anyone can recognize "To be or not to be" from <u>Hamlet</u>. Try placing "And sleep, that sometime shuts up sorrow's eye, steal me awhile from mine own company." It's from <u>A Midsummer Night's Dream</u> and yes, I had to look it up.

Mario's little and I do mean little office was next to hers and mine was next to his. In between the hallway and his office are the call center operators and the main dispatchers. All and all, I'd say around thirty or so personal normally work in the office on any given time. Basically, a lot of people work in a relatively small space. Perfect. But what to do? Hhmm...

As I walked past, I couldn't help but notice that Mario and his buddies were in their offices and showed no signs of leaving. Great, everyone was in roughly the same place. I had me an audience but for what?

Someone once said that the best practical jokes are the ones that are never played. Okay, so I said it, but I think it's a pretty darn good saying and it sounds deep. Time to put my nonexistent acting skills to the test.

I jerked my head like I smelled something that needed further investigating. I took a deep breath and walked further into the office area. Stopping a few feet to my left, I took another deep breath. One of the ladies at a phone bank, Marge, stopped what she was doing and looked right at me. This was a good start as Marge was the phone bank manager and those under her would follow her lead.

I took some more steps, stopping at and end of a table and took another deep breath, only this time I made a funny expression with my face. A few more of the office personal stopped what they were doing. I walked slowly into the main office conference area. This is where everyone could see me and what I was going to do.

I walked up and down the hallways, often serpentining through the various cubicles, each time taking a deep breath, pretending to try and locate the location of this fictional but noxious odor. After a few laps around the office complete with funny faces and more breaths, I pretty much had all the office personnel's attention.

From the corner of my eye, I could see calls being put on hold and workers nudging one another to look at me. Of course, I pretended that I didn't notice any of this. As far as they were concerned, I smelled something terrible and was trying to figure out the source. Some of them even joined me in taking deep breaths. Finally, Marge couldn't stand it anymore.

"What are you doing," she asked?

"You mean you don't smell it," I said back?

Just then, another operator joined in.

"Oh my God, do you smell smoke? Is there a fire?!"

Two thoughts occurred to me in that instant: I hadn't anticipated this and maybe I could've been an actor, but I had to put this to a stop immediately. I wanted to have some fun, not start a panic.

"Nope. It's definitely not smoke. There is no fire. I'd bet my life on it," I said with as much conviction as humanly possible.

"Then what is it," asked Marge?

"I'm not sure. It's like really bad body odor mixed with rotten eggs, sewage, skunk and dirty sweatsocks. Almost like when someone's had oral surgery and hasn't been allowed to brush for days," I said. The key to every good lie is details. Disgusting, nauseating details.

At this point, the power of suggestion had firmly taken hold because one of the operators claimed to smell it too. Then another, followed by some more. Those that weren't, were right on the verge. I needed to do sometime really good because I had stopped the office from working. Turning around again, I stopped. This time facing Mario who had scared the crap out of me earlier.

Now I was center stage, I had the whole office wanting to know what I was smelling and where it was coming from. I raised my head for the last time and took a deep breath. This time I started choking. I covered my mouth with both hands and I made it look like I was going to throw-up.

One of the operators came over to make sure I was all right. She placed her hand on my back and tried to look into my face. It was time for the payoff.

I suddenly and with a concerned look on my face looked straight at Mario and started my speech,

"People of this office, I feel for you. Putting up with this smell every day is just wrong. I've only been in here a few minutes and I can barely take it."

A bunch of others nodded in agreement.

"These are unsanitary working conditions. Maybe you're all used to it but take it from someone who isn't here every day, this isn't right. You shouldn't have to work in this environment."

Just as people were about to call their union reps, I looked at Mario and took a deep breath. Time seemed to stand still as I milked the moment like a dairy farmer. Finally, I spoke.

"Mario! The smell is coming from Mario! Mario, I beg of you, see a specialist immediately. I'm concerned about your health, big guy. But I'm even more concerned about the health of everyone around you. These are not odors that come from a healthy human."

The entire audience immediately caught on and cracked up and then started clapping. The Oscar for best acting in an office prank went to me. Mario pulled his head right next to mine and said, "I'm gonna get you next time, Robbie."

I looked right back at him and said, "I don't think so, Mario."

And he didn't. Yes, over the years, he certainly attempted to but no matter how hard he tried, he could never match the humiliation that I had heaped upon him.

A few years later we learned that Mario had passed. He hadn't worked with us in a while but for those of us who knew and loved him, many a dreary Monday was made a little better by recalling Mario stories. Like I said earlier, he got us, and we got him. The funeral was well attended and while it was fun seeing people I hadn't seen in years, obviously the occasion that drew us together wasn't.

Later on, at the wake, I talked to Mario's widow, Marlene. After paying her my condolences we swapped our own Mario stories. Someone, I forget who, mentioned the Mario smells story and Marlene's eyes lit right up. She told us that he thought it was hilarious and he brought it up all the time.

You know, sometimes we don't realize the effect we have on each other's lives. Let's face it, people pass in and out of ours as we pass through theirs and we never give it a second thought. We're busy. We've got jobs, family, responsibilities. Friendships and relationships can fall by the wayside. We don't mean them too. We may even still really like the people we've left behind, but, like I said earlier, other things get in the way.

That's why what Marlene said meant so much to me. I knew what effect Mario had on my life, but I don't know if I had any effect on his. The fact that he remembered our friendship and back and forth made me feel good. Even better, it made me feel proud.

Story 61: I'll Get You! (Late '80's)

There's only a few things that really upset me to the point where my anger comes pouring out and I can barely contain it. Number one on that list is child abuse. I cannot express how much I deplore this. Thankfully, in all my travels I have only had one instance to speak about but once is still one too many.

The day was a scorcher. Temperatures ranging around the 100's or so. At least there was no humidity to speak of. Thankfully, the A/C in the truck was working well. When the day is that hot, any relief is welcome.

The job I was sent out on was on a busy street right where the residential zoning area ended. Meaning, that while there were private homes near the address, fast food joints and assorted other stores were close by. As a result of this, the street was busy with cars driving fast on both sides. Because there were no visible addresses on the curb or on the mailboxes, the house was really hard to find. I drove by the house several times trying to count up and guess where the right place was. The last thing I needed was someone coming after me with a shot gun or a dog attacking me. Yup, it was that kind of neighborhood. Sketchy and dangerous which made sense because most people wouldn't choose to live blocks away from a convenience store unless you were really into lottery tickets, Slim Jim's and menthols.

There was a small break in the traffic and I had enough time to enter what I thought was the correct address. Standing on both sides of the driveway were two concrete pillars. Both were overgrown with plants and looked terrible. It really needed to be cleaned up. There were several trees around the house and they were overgrown and possibly diseased. It was obvious that no one had taken care of the yard for many years. Frankly, the place was downright depressing. The driveway curved off to the left with the house slightly to the right.

I pulled the truck forward to what I thought was the front door. The door opened, and an old lady came out.

"Hi, I'm Mrs. Williams. I'm so glad to see you!" she said.

Apparently, I had guessed right. I had the correct place. Little did I know that this was the last good thing that was going to happen for a while.

"I'm Rob. Your house isn't easy to find," I replied.

"Sorry about that but we do cherish our privacy around here. Won't you come in?"

I removed my toolbox from the back of the truck and proceeded to walk towards her. We entered the house. What a mess! I don't think anyone has cleaned in here in decades. There were old newspapers, opened cans of food, the smell of kitty litter or what I thought was kitty litter. Lots of fly paper on the walls with a bunch of dead insects on them. How could anyone live like this?

Mrs. Williams seemed to be nice at first. She explained to me what her appliance was not doing and how much grief it had caused her. I always keep a rag in my rear pocket, so I can clean my hands of whatever I need to which came in handy in gross places like this. I placed the rag on the floor and my toolbox on it. My intent was to not drag her dirt onto the bottom on the toolbox. If that seems like overkill to you, the floor had a sticky film that made a smacking sound as you walked so no, I wasn't taking any chances.

Mrs. Williams left the room, so I could work on the refrigerator. The problems with her appliance were extensive. The timer on the front did not move and the motor made a humming noise. Plus, there was a grinding sound coming from the back. There were so many problems that added up, it would cost substantially more to fix them then to simply buy a new one.

As I was going through my checklist, from the other end of the house I heard someone being slapped, followed by a scream. At first, I thought maybe it was coming from the television, but it happened again and this time, there was no mistaking it, someone was being hurt. It worried me. Something was going on and it wasn't good.

A minute or two went by and the same thing happened again. Smack and scream. This time the scream went right through me. As I was finishing up my assessment of her appliance, it happened a third time. Someone was getting beaten. My first thought was that it was Mrs. Williams. Elder abuse happens more often than we'd like to think.

I walked out of the kitchen and slowly headed through the living room. I entered the bedroom hallway and Mrs. Williams met me at the entrance. She started to walk in front of me like she was trying to block my view. From what, I had no idea. I did know that it wasn't Mrs. Williams who was being beaten but who was? As Mrs. Williams walked by me I saw a young lady walking in the hall. She was morbidly obese and had no clothes on.

The young lady looked right at me. She had red hand marks across her face. You didn't have to be in the F.B.I. to realize that the sound was Mrs. Williams slapping the young lady's face. From the time I entered the house, I counted four slaps, but this was four slaps too many! Mrs. Williams and I walked into the kitchen and stopped in front of the refrigerator.

I advised her that her appliance was not worth repairing because it would cost more to fix than to replace it. For some reason, Mrs. Williams wanted it fixed even though it made zero economic sense to do so. Midway through her whining, the young lady entered the room, still naked. She said, "Grandma, I went poo."

Clearly, this young woman was mentally disabled. Mrs. Williams explained that while her granddaughter was physically twenty-four, she was mentally four years old. Turns out that Mrs. Williams's daughter was in a car accident and died. As a result, it was she who was now taking care of her granddaughter. She continued to explain that is how she makes her go to the bathroom. By slapping her on the face when she is on the toilet. The granddaughter turned around and skipped out of the room with her flesh jiggling with every step.

I was beyond stunned. Hell, criminal charges should be brought against her. I'm sure raising someone in her granddaughter's condition could be a frustrating and at times exasperating experience but that does not excuse in the least what Mrs. Williams was doing to a member of her own family.

Slapping someone, especially someone who is mentally handicapped is never right. All people have dignity and should be treated with respect, especially those that cannot defend themselves. I turned around and grabbed toolbox from her dirty floor. I stood up and looked Mrs. Williams directly in the eye and said

"Lady, granddaughter or not, physically striking someone on the face is sick! I'm leaving your disgusting house and I'm not fixing your appliance. Goodbye."

I was so shaken and disturbed by what I had witnessed that I actually have no memory of how I got into the parking lot of a 7-11 but somehow, I pulled in. I found a pay phone (this was before cellphones), called the police department and filed a complaint. I knew I did the right thing and immediately felt better after doing so.

That evening, somewhere around ten o'clock, I was getting ready for bed and turned on the television. The local news was on and the anchorman started reading a story about Mrs. Williams. Unbelievable. There was footage of Mrs. Williams being dragged out of her house and being put into a police cruiser. As she was ducking her head, I could clearly hear her say, "I'm going to get that repairman!" Please. I'd love to see her try.

I'm not sure what happened to the granddaughter. Hopefully, she got the help she needed but I knew I did the right thing because anything is better than being slapped while going to the bathroom. I wouldn't do that to an animal, let alone a member of my own family. What is wrong with some people?

That wasn't the end of it. The story so unnerved me that I just had to unburden myself, so I went to the Catholic Church that me and my family regularly attended, and I talked to Father Michael. My family and I knew Father Michael for years. He was a kind hearted, empathetic man who really cared about people. Best of all, he was a really good listener. Father Mike is pretty much everything you'd ever want in a religious leader.

I told him what happened, and he greatly sympathized and then he quickly sprang into action, getting the church's charities involved. We both kicked in some money as did many members of the congregation and we raised a bunch of money and donated it to organizations that helped people like the granddaughter in this story and others like her. Yes, I could've done more but at least I did something.

We can all do something.

Story 62: Dark House Crybaby Lady (Early '90's)

I received a repair order from the dispatcher and the address was close by, so I thought I would head right over and be done in about half an hour. Little did I know.

As I pulled up to the house, I noticed that all the windows were covered with aluminum foil like Elvis used to do. I assumed the customer was a day sleeper and not an Elvis impersonator. Then I looked at the order, wondering what was wrong with the oven. The inside light was not working which is pretty straightforward and a quick fix.

I parked the truck and I walked up to the door as I have done countless times and knocked. The door opened. Someone was standing inside the archway. A hood was covering her. It was really dark inside. Too dark for my liking.

"Hi, I'm Rob. I'm here to fix your oven," I said by way of introduction.

"I'm Gertrude. Thank you for coming. Won't you come in," she asked?

She removed the hood and looked vaguely familiar. She was an older woman, probably in her late sixties. I couldn't place her or even where I might know her from. Yup, this was going to drive me nuts but not right now because I had a job to do. The first part was navigating in near, total darkness. Once inside, I could only see a couple of feet ahead of me. She closed the door and then the room went completely dark.

Gertrude asked me to follow her as she walked away. My eyes hadn't adjusted to the lack of light and wouldn't in the next few seconds. Fortunately, when Gertrude entered the kitchen, she turned on a very low light. I could still barely see. What I could see was trash. It was at least five feet in height and it smelled but not like spoiled food or normal trash. No, it smelled like really old newspapers. Moldy and musty. You know the smell. It's kind of like when you go into somebody's basement. As for Gertrude, she was, apparently, a hoarder.

I found my way into the kitchen, barely. Gertrude stood there in front of the oven. She reached up and pressed the light switch, demonstrating for me that it didn't work. I placed my toolbox on the floor, next to the oven and opened the door. Inside my toolbox I kept an old flashlight. Of course, it was buried on the bottom. While I was trying to dig it out, Gertrude started in about how her life depended on that oven light bulb working correctly. It was b.s. but moderately entertaining b.s.

I finally located the flashlight and aimed it inside the oven, then turned it on. She screamed, grabbed the flashlight right out of my hand and threw it out of the kitchen! I was so stunned that it took me a few seconds to comprehend what had just happened.

"Why did you do that," I asked? "It's only a flashlight, not a laser."

She took a few steps backwards like she was fleeing from me.

"I'm sorry but the light blinded me. I'm allergic to light.," she said.

That's a new one or at least it was to me. Then she started crying which transitioned into sobbing. Now, what I'm about to say next might seem cold but trust me, this is years of experience talking; whenever a grown adult cries on a repair call, they want something. The question is what?

As this was going on, I turned around and started to walk out of the kitchen to retrieve my flashlight which was still on. Thank God because otherwise, I still might be looking for it. Both of Gertrude's hands were covering her face. I went back into the kitchen and headed to the oven and looked directly at her.

"Ma'am, I need to check your oven to see what the problem is. That's going to require the use of this flashlight," I stated rather than asked.

Her hands moved away from her face and I could see that the crying was a con job because there were no tears. At least, she was finally going to say what she wanted.

"Sir, I'm on a fixed income and I do not have the money to pay you. Would you be so kind as to help an old lady?"

Gertrude had screwed up. By crying so early in the process, I knew what she was up to. She would've stood a better chance had she waited till towards of the end of the visit.

"Ma'am, why don't I see exactly what the problem is and then we'll talk," I offered reasonably.

She said, "all right" and the crying ceased. The next order of business was locating the house breakers, so I could turn the power off. Of course, she had no idea where they were. I walked out the back door and sure enough, to the left were the breakers which were covered in spider webs. No one had been there in years. I almost needed a machete to get rid of them. I lifted the lid up and turned off the power to the kitchen, then headed back so that I could diagnose the problem.

When I got back inside, she was talking on the phone, as calm as could be. The second she noticed me, she hung up and started the fake crying again. I got inside the oven and found the problem: it was a bad door latch switch assembly which I didn't carry on my truck. I would have to order a replacement through the factory if they still made them. The stove was old. I told Gertrude what the problem was and how the switch network had simply just worn out.

I asked Gertrude if I could use her phone to call my office. I needed to get the part number and the price. She started crying all over again. It had less than zero effect on me. At least she let me use the phone, provided it wasn't long distance. I assured her that it wasn't and dialed.

I made the call and promptly was put on hold. My eyes, which had adjusted somewhat to the dark by now, wandered around the room. On the wall, off in the living room were several pictures of Gertrude as a young woman. If I had to guess, they were from the late '50's, early sixties. Upon further inspection, I could make out that these photos were of television and movie sets and Gertrude was alongside people who you had definitely heard of. That's where I knew her from! Gertrude was an actress and had been on a bunch of sit-coms I remembered from when I was a kid. I may have even had a small crush on her at one time. That explained the phony theatrics.

During my trip down memory lane, a clerk came on the line and informed me of the price and model number of the part I needed and that it could arrive in several days. I wrote all the info down and headed back into the kitchen to see the actress.

"OK, ma'am, I now have your estimate for you." I said. "Parts, tax and labor. Your estimate comes to $353.00 dollars and I can have the part ordered and be back here on Friday." She began to cry again, only this time, harder.

"Sir, I don't have the money to pay you. Can you find it your heart to do this any other way? Could you, maybe, come back after work on Friday and I will take care of you in another way," she asked while still crying?

I was stunned but managed to get out, "What did you mean by "taking care of me?"

Gertrude stopped crying and started unbuttoning her shirt. "I'll take good care of you," she repeated as she walked up to me and with her other hand started touching my hair.

Whoa, this wasn't good no matter how you looked at it. First of all, I was and am a happily married man. Second, even if I wasn't and wanted to "date," I would limit it to women in my generation. Yes, at one point, it might've been cool to be able to say you had a fling with the secretary from the Gomer Pyle show but that point was a long time ago. Third, what if it was some kind of a set up?

It's not as farfetched as it sounds. I fix the oven and later get blackmailed or thrown in jail for taking sexual advantage of an elderly woman. That would be a good way to end up in prison. Believe it or not, this actually happened to a guy I once worked with. He didn't go to jail, but only because he got unbelievably lucky. And, by the way, repairman like myself, are not stupid. After being on the job for even a short while, we can see a set up and can read customers quite well.

I told Gertrude to button her shirt back up in such a way that she knew I meant business. I didn't want to buy what she was selling. Of course, she started crying again with both hands on her face. It was pretty apparent why she didn't go further in her chosen profession.

I took advantage of the false hysterics to make my hasty retreat. I turned around with my toolbox in hand and left the kitchen but because it was so dark, I walked and turned the wrong way down the hall. Old Gertrude continued her crybaby act and didn't know that I had screwed up. I opened a door and found myself in her bedroom. I felt like the proverbial fly caught in the web. All I could make out was that it was four poster, canopied bed with lots of dolls and stuffed animals. I had to get the hell out of there and fast. The last thing I needed was her to find me there.

I turned around and walked as fast as I could. Fortunately, bumping into bundles of newspapers tends to not hurt that much. Good thing she didn't hoard sharp objects. Finally, after several wrong doors, I finally found the front one and got out of there while she was still sobbing. I don't even think she noticed I had left.

I made it back to my truck and noticed that my flashlight now wouldn't turn on. I've had that thing for over ten years. Oh well, still a small price to pay for escaping the clutches of the crazy, old, horny actress lady. Sixties TV would never be quite the same for me.

Story 63: Anybody Need Change? (Late '80's)

One of my hobbies is to study historical events and the writings of the past, specifically weird laws. Perhaps, you've seen a collection of them on restaurant placemats like how in California a woman cannot drive while wearing a house coat or that in New Jersey it is illegal to frown at a police officer or that in Alaska, you can't push a live moose out of an airplane? Here's a story involving a weird federal law that almost paid off big time for two different people, one of them being me.

It was a normal morning at the shop. Everyone was in line to punch in at 8:00 am and, as usual, I was one of the last people in line. After I did so, I passed the cashier's office and heard one of the cashiers say that she was running a little short on coins. I still have no idea why that snippet of a conversation stuck in my head, but it did. Then I left the building and climbed into the company truck to start my route.

Just after lunch and with a full stomach, a service call came in that didn't really seem too out of the ordinary. It was about a thirty-minute drive out to the house. As I entered what might be generously called a housing track, with no sidewalks, no curbs, no visible or marked roads, just dirt, I spotted the house I was looking for.

The house had a white picket fence in the front yard with an archway and small gate, so someone could enter the yard. On the gate was glued a pair of dice. Why? The bushes around the front yard were loosely maintained but clean. I parked in front of the house, so the owner could see me clearly. Common courtesy.

The walkway leading up to the house was made of red brick and very old. The house looked like it was built about sixty-years ago. I can only guess that when they laid the brickwork. I knocked of the door, stepped back a step or two and waited.

A lady in her fifties answered the door. She was pleasant and weathered with a cigarette dangling out of her mouth. She was wearing a house coat. Good thing she wasn't in New Jersey and wanted to drive.

"Hi, I'm Rob," I said by way of introduction. "I'm here to fix your washer."

"Hi, I'm Thelma. Please come in," Thelma said back.

We entered the home and walked into the living room and headed to the laundry room. The house was decorated solely with old and new Las Vegas stuff. Pictures of entertainers like Dean Martin, Liberace, Elvis and, of course, Mr. Wayne Newton adorned the walls. There were two yellow lamps on the tables and blue dish plates hanging all around the room all with the names of various casinos engraved upon them.

"So, what seems to be the problem," I asked?

"Well, I don't think the timer is working. The wash cycles are taking hours to finish," she said.

This made for very clean clothes and very high water bills. Basically, the timer needed to be replaced and I told her so.

The good news was that I knew this washing machine and had I've done this repair many times before plus, I had the proper part on my truck. The bad news was, actually, there was no bad news because the estimate came to only $148.46 including labor. Not too bad at all. Thelma signed off on the paperwork and I started the job.

Now, it only takes a few minutes to remove the console from the washer. A few screws and a bunch of wires. Lucky for me, the part number is located on the back of the timer. I wrote the number onto my work order and exited through the house. I told Thelma that I was going to my truck to get the part. She said "fine" and I exited the home and headed to the truck.

I went to the truck and got the part which was on a shelf, more towards the rear. I grabbed it and noticed that the box was a little beaten up. I opened the box, looked inside and saw that the timer was not damaged. With the part in my hand, I started to walk back to the house still wondering how old was this brickwork?

As I entered the doorway, Thelma was still sitting on the couch only she now had a large dirty tan cloth bag between her legs and several stacks of quarters on the coffee table, all stacked in a short row.

I went back to the washroom and began to install the timer. The repair went well. The timer gave me no attitude or troubles going in. When a part gives me trouble, I always recall a service call from an earlier story when a gentleman told me that all objects have "spirits" and to be nice to them. By being nice to them, they are less apt to give you trouble. I figured it couldn't hurt.

During the twenty minutes or so that it took me to install the timer, I could hear from the living room that Thelma continued to count out the coins and placed them on the table, one short rattling clank at a time. This was kind of odd. Why was she counting out the loose coins? I wondered who was going to wrap them all up? Not me. Even weirder, while this was going on, she was listening to Wayne Newton's "Live At The Frontier, Las Vegas." This may have been the first time in recorded history that someone actually owned and played a Wayne Newton album.

Anyway, I finished the job and reconnected the console to the washer. Now it was time to test the timer to see if it worked so, I started the first cycle. Water was starting to enter the drum and I switched the temperature knob from cold to hot to test it. Above the washer, hanging on the wall was a picture of Bugsy Siegel, the man who founded modern Las Vegas. Who was this lady?

Satisfied that the washer was working fine, I cleaned up, gathered my tools and placed the old timer inside the beat up box. I called out to Thelma that I was finished, and she asked me to come to the living room, so I did. Thelma smiled at me and invited me to sit down in the chair. To my great surprise, she had counted out all the money and itemized them on the coffee table: $148.64, all in coins.

The rows of quarters were perfectly lined up. Ten rows and ten columns of quarters which added up to one hundred dollars. A short space separated the other forty-eight dollars and sixty-four cents. The money bag from earlier was still sitting on the floor, next to her left leg and there was still plenty of coins left inside. I look at her and asked her if she wanted to pay with a credit card or check? Thelma smiled and looked down at all the coins equaling the entire bill. You see, I knew what she was up to and it went something like this: she was going to offer to pay me all in coins and I was going to refuse. If I did, I was going to be the one out $148.63. Luckily, I knew the law she was trying to exploit, and it went something like this:

Many years ago, commerce and trade were different compared to today. When a retailer had a product or service that they provided, it was called a "trade" or "trading." In today's commerce, the term still applies but it's called purchasing in some cases and now it is also called "shopping." When you "pay" for something, you're essentially making a trade of equal value or the price. In fact, if you ever listen to the elderly speak of business transactions done long ago, they always refer to it as "trading with them."

So, if a retailer, for any reason declines or refused to take U.S. currency, then the customer gets the item for **free**. If you look at any U.S. one-dollar bill, you'll notice that on it, it says, "this note is legal tender for all debts public and private." It was one of the many ways that the federal government claimed legitimacy when it was first starting out. Now, if the money presented was not U.S. currency like Canadian dollars or Mexican pesos, the retailer can refuse with no penalty.

As I sat in front of Thelma, she just stared at the coins with a stupid grin on her face, hoping that I'd refuse her payment. Didn't mean that I couldn't ask her some questions though like where did she get all those coins? Thelma responded that she just got back from Las Vegas and that she had won them. Really, all coins and no bills? Wasn't it just a little bit possible that she exchanged her bills for coins for the specific purpose of this scam? Well, if she did, she wasn't saying.

Thelma looked at me and asked if I was going to take the coins? I did not have a choice, so I said, "Not only will I take them but you're actually doing my company a great favor. This morning, some of the cashiers were saying how they were crazy low on change. This will save them a trip to the bank. Thank you so much!"

Thelma had to pretend that she was happy about her "good deed" but she wasn't a good actress. No matter, I pulled out the old timer I had replaced from its beaten up box and began placing all the coins inside of it. After collecting all the money from the table, it was full and quite heavy. I needed two hands to hold it. As I walked out and thanked her for her business, Thelma sat back into the couch's pillows and tilted her head in disbelief.

I walked through the front door and she asked me why I took the coins? I just stood there for a few seconds with my tool box in one hand and the coins propped against my hip, I turned my head in her direction and commented that I know that statue too. She just shrugged her shoulders and gave me a look that I took to mean "touche." I respected her for trying and I like to think she respected me for knowing.

Later that day, I returned to the shop. One of the things you have to take care of after completing your route is to turn in the money we collected and the paperwork that went along with it. The cashier was still in her office. I called her over and we had a short talk about the day. I placed the paperwork on the shelf in front of us and with a struggling motion, placed the heavy box of coins on the shelf. Her eyes opened up widely. I told her that it's the money collected on this work order. The cashier looked at the total and thanked me for the coins. I said, "don't thank me. Thank Las Vegas." Then, I walked off.

A few months later, I noticed that the five-gallon water jug that I put my spare change in had finally filled up. This happened about every three years. So, inspired by Thelma, that Friday night, I moved the jug down to my living room and emptied the contents on the floor. The whole family joined in and we had us a counting party. It took us most of the night, but the payoff was worth it because the grand total was in excess of $2,400 dollars! What to do with all that found money? I had an idea.

On Saturdays, it is my families weekly trek to the local grocery store. I think it was the kids mission to drive dad and mom crazy with all the crapola they wanted. On that particular Saturday, I decided that we were going to pay for all our food with coins. Why not? It was money, right? Even more shocking, my wife agreed with me. So, I took the cloth, heavy-duty bag with a draw-string that was in the kitchen and loaded it up three-hundred dollars' worth of change. In my defense, they were mostly quarters.

Naturally, the bag was quite heavy and my oldest daughter, who was about 10 years of age, was more than willing to help out. She moved it about two inches before giving up but hey, it was the thought that counted, right? So, we piled into the car and drove off to the market. We got there, grabbed a cart and proceeded to do our shopping.

Parenting note: when your youngster places a box of food in the cart and asks if they can have it with a multiple "pleases," say "yes" but be sure to remove the box from your cart when you hit the next aisle after they turn their back. Works like a charm and I saved a fortune on dental bills. Believe it or not, not too long ago, there was a cereal actually called "Sugar Smacks." Now, it's called "Honey Smacks" with zero change in ingredients. The genius of advertising!

Now, the manager of the supermarket was someone I played co-ed softball with on Sundays. I knew him for many years and we were friends. Pizza and beer followed every game, so we could hang out and razz each other about our various screw-ups during the game. This was going to be fun. In fact, when I first told my wife about the plan she looked at me and said, "He's going to kill you, you know," meaning Dave, the store manager. I did not care.

The Saturdays escapades were as entertaining as normal. Aisle by aisle with the kids wanting things and dad placing them back on the shelf. Paper towels being thrown like footballs, the girls grabbing cans of food and rolling them on the ground but aimed at the cart. Somehow, the necessities ended up in the cart. It was fun and yes, we are a fun loving crazy family and I could only visualize what the store employees were saying when we came in to shop.

After forty-five minutes or so, the shopping cart was completely full, rising over the top of the basket and some products were stuffed around the baby who was sitting in the seat. It was time to head to the cashier. Cashier aisle number five was open, the poor bastard. Time to pull my stunt.

We all joined in on unloading the contents of the cart onto the conveyor belt. A minute went by and I was able to grab the bag of coins. I then placed the bag on the table and opened and proceeded to count out the quarters in dollar stacks. The little signing table, for the two people a year who still write checks, began to get over crowded with quarters. The cashier stopped a few times and noticed that the quarter were beginning to pile up and now I was stacking them on the main counter top.

As the family was emptying the cart, another customer pulled up behind us. I stopped counting and advised the customer that we may be a while checking out. Today, I was the jerk customer who nobody wants to be behind. It felt kinda good. The customer just stood there and rolled his eyes and who could blame him?

The cart was finally empty. The cashier continued to scan the food through the bar code scanner. One at a time, beep, beep until she was finally done. The total cost of the food came to over the $300 I had brought with me. Damn, maybe the day had finally come when I had outsmarted myself.

It was at the precise moment when the cashier looked at me and asked for my discount card. Phew! I had forgotten that this store gives discounts for members. Silly me! I hadn't outsmarted myself. At least not today.

As the cashier pushed the final button, the total on the display monitor began to count down the total. This took a few seconds and the total amount came to $287.56. All the food I purchased was now in two carts and ready to go.

I guess, out of habit, she asked me for my credit card.

"No thank you. I think I'll pay with these quarters that I have painstakingly taken the time to count out," I said.

She didn't know what to do. Suddenly, she excused herself and had a short conversation with a co-worker. The customer who, for whatever reason decided not to move, was now watching more closely. What was going to happen?

The cashier came back and advised me that she was unwilling to take the money I put in front of her. Our conversation was somewhat short.

"Young lady, that's U.S. money. It is legal tender here. Why won't you take the money?" I asked.

She did not respond, not a word. So, I slowly picked up all the quarters and placed them back into the bag I brought. When I was finished, and the last quarter was in the bag, I turned to her and thanked her for her time. My wife, children and I walked behind both of the shopping carts and exited the building.

As we were putting the food in the car, Dave, the store manager walked out of the store and up to my car. We had a short conversation.

"Rob, what are you trying to pull here," he asked?

"I'm not trying to pull anything. I offered to pay your cashier with legal, U.S. tender and she refused which means that I'm entitled to have the goods for free. I'll be glad to show you a copy of the law that I have in my pocket," I said back.

"Of course, you have it in your back pocket," he said back. I grinned.

He looked at me and said, "If you do that, that girl is going to lose her job. Do you really want that?"

"Of course not," I said as I handed him the bag of quarters. "There's three hundred dollars in here. Do you want it?"

"No, but I'll take it," he said as I handed it to him. He almost gave himself a hernia lugging it back to the store. Dave wasn't, shall we say, in prime shape.

"You can give me the thirteen dollars in change I'm due at the next game," I shouted to Dave who was now halfway across the parking lot.

The hand gesture he gave me may be interpreted by some people as obscene. I prefer to think that Dave was saying, in his own special way, that I was number one.

Man, the crap I pull sometimes...

Story 64: Kids Just Can't Throw These Days (2010)

It was a nice sunny day, one in which I would continue to improve my tan and just cruise through the day. I arrived at the residence for my repair call. As I briefly looked over the order, nothing on it really stood out. Fine, by me. It's not like I was looking for excitement.

The house itself was in an average housing track. I did notice a bike lying down in the front yard, a soccer ball behind a large tree and the garden hose strung out across the yard. At the end of the hose was a sprinkler which was turned on. Yup, this was one boring house.

As I exited the truck, I noticed that the mail box was not closed all the way. A few pieces of mail were sticking out. Mostly oversized postcard coupons. Maybe I'd mention the problem with the mailbox to the home owner.

With my toolbox in one hand and work order in the other, I walked on the dry section of the lawn and up to the concrete walk way heading to the front door. I stopped at the door and just before I knocked, I heard a young boy speaking loudly and aggressively to someone or something inside the house. The only words I could clearly make out were "stupid" and "moron." Swell.

The front door was made of wood and glass. Most likely it was the original door from when the house was built, sometime in the 1960's. I knocked and waited. In the background, a lady's voice rang out, "Coming!"

A few seconds had passed, and I could see the lady of the house walking towards the door and around a partitioned wall. The door opened, revealing a woman in her thirties who looked kind of flustered. Honestly, I don't remember what she said but, with her raised right hand, she waved me inside.

It was a short walk into the house entry. There was no front foyer, just a short hall. I closed the door behind me and the lady started walking to her right through the living room. As I turned the corner, I noticed that there was a young boy about fourteen years in age, sitting at a desk and it looked like he was trying to do something which involved a lot of paperwork. He was so pale that he made Steve Martin look ethnic. I swear, it was like this kid had never been outside or even seen the sun.

As we walked through the living room and straight in front of the young boy, we passed a couch on my right with clothes spread all over the place. The couch pillows were on the floor and food wrappers were spread throughout the room. On the table, in front of the couch, were empty glasses and potato chips. Basically, a mess.

On my left was a large flat screen television with an X-Box control center. The paddles still had cables attached to them, so I knew it was an older unit. Playing on the flat screen, was an old cop show from the 1970's. It might've been "Columbo."

The walls had several pictures of landscapes and old houses. Whoever hung these paintings, back in the 1960's, must have had real bad taste.

As we passed through, on the way to the kitchen, the young boy tried to look over the papers on the table. Also, on the table was a laptop computer, which was also very old due to the fact that its base was very thick, and the screen was large. Personally, I prefer screens to be big, but it doesn't seem to be the trend these days. Nope, everything's small.

The lady, whose name I later found out was Kim, and I entered the kitchen. The ceiling was very high. It looked like some custom work had been done. At the end of the room was the refrigerator. It was a two-door side by side and made of stainless steel and really clean. The ice maker was not working, or, at least, that's what it said on my work order.

Kim explained what the problem was, and I got the sense that she was being honest which, isn't always the case. I placed my tools down and I put my work order on the top of the toolbox. I opened the freezer door and removed the cover housing for the ice maker. Kim walked back to the young boy and both of them started to talk about math equations.

On this particular model refrigerator, the ice maker was mounted on the left side wall. Underneath the ice maker was a large auger bucket. An auger bucket is a bucket with kind of a cork screw in it that churns the ice. I looked inside it and noticed that there were popsicle wrappers in it and an empty box pushed backwards, behind the ice maker.

I stepped back a foot or so. I wanted to see what exactly she had in there for food. Yes, it was none of my business but based on the condition of the living room, can you really blame me for being curious? Not shockingly, it was a disorganized mess. There were unwrapped food containers, spilled food products and fallen veggies all over the place. It had not been cleaned in a long time. Then I looked at the ice maker itself. Wouldn't you know, there was something wrapped around its fingers. I needed to remove the ice maker from the freezer section and get a better look to see what was wrapped inside.

As I turned to locate the desired tool to get it out, I heard the young boy begin to scream at his mother. He said,

"You're wrong! You're just a stupid bitch who knows nothing and your equations are stupid!"

Holy crap. I had to look up and see what was going on. Kim just sat there and took his verbal abuse. Honestly, I don't think she was phased, in the least, by his comments. Clearly, this wasn't a unique occurrence. If I had dared to speak to my parents even remotely in the way that he had just spoken to his mother, you wouldn't be reading this book.

I removed the ice maker and found a plastic wrapper wrapped around the fingers. The wrapper was what was stopping the rotation from harvesting to complete the cycle.

I reached down into my toolbox and found a knife to cut off the plastic from the fingers.
As I finished removing the plastic wrapper, the young boy spoke again. He continued insulting his mother. This time, Kim sat back and covered her mouth with both her hands. No one ever should talk to anyone like that, let alone your own mother. What were they working on that was making him so upset?

I re-installed the ice maker and started a new cycle. As the water began to come into the ice maker, the young boy stood up, turned to his mother, looked down at her and called her a "worthless human." Kim was still sitting on the chair with her hands covering her mouth for a few minutes.

It was pretty obvious that this kid was in need of a serious ass kicking. I called out to Kim and told her that the ice maker was repaired. I think she welcomed the opportunity to leave the warm embrace of her child's presence. She slowly got up, wiped her face off with her hands and started walking over to me. The young boy now turned and stared directly at me.

Kim was in the kitchen, standing next to me and I started to explain what I had found; a plastic wrapper stuck in the ice maker and the box stuck in the back of the freezer and that it was now fixed. The young boy, who was still a little upset, did not approve of me. Why? Because I had just taken him away from his mother.

Mom was a little confused and hurt and the same time. She looked at me and said, "I have no idea how this could have happened." I had a rough idea and he was sitting a few feet away from me. I paused a few seconds and turned to my right and stared right back at the kid.
I didn't say a word and I didn't have to. Mother and child both knew what I was implying and who the guilty party was.

All of a sudden, the young boy reached under the table and grabbed an unopened soda can in his left hand. He raised it over his shoulder and threw it at me! The can moved slowly and traveled in a high arch. It seemed like it would take a week to get to me. This kid had no athletic skills whatsoever.

As the can came closer, I had two options. Catch it in mid-flight or lean back and let it go by. Kim yelled, "Look out!"

So, I let the can whiz by and it struck the freezer door, leaving a half moon smiley face on it. The can fell to the kitchen floor and spun around a few times. The little bastard had just assaulted me. I could've sued them and won, no problem but I'm not that type of guy. Kim
looked at me and asked if I was ok? Then she looked at the freezer door. She asked me how I was going to repair the mark.

Was she serious? I was going to clean that up? I looked at her quizzically and said, "Ma'am, flying soda cans which damage freezer doors are not covered and if you want it repaired, I'm going to charge you for parts and labor."

Junior decided to re-direct his harsh comments toward me. He said,

"You're going to fix it and fix it for free, dumbass…"

Kim was in shock. I think she thought that I was going to take out the fruit of her loins. Believe me, I thought about it but, I decided it best not to answer. It just would've escalated things for poor Kim and I was the lucky one who would soon be leaving this nut house. I replaced the tools I used back into my tool box and closed the lid.

As I was bent over, I noticed that the soda can was in arm's reach, so I picked it up in my right hand. I walked over to the young boy and stopped just left of the table next to the chair his mom was sitting on.

I stood right in front of him. The look on his face was a little troubling. Would he go psycho? It was a real possibility. Plus, it was obvious that he has never been confronted with someone my size and I think he was trying not to show any fear.

I stood there for a few seconds, waiting for him to flinch. I turned my head slowly down to the paperwork spread all over his desk and noticed that he was studying basic algebra. The last equation that his mother wrote down was correct and his answer was missing a major factor. He did not transfer a square to an enclosed equation.

I put my tool box down on mom's chair and pointed to the missing factor in the equation. With a surprised look, he turned to the paperwork and began studying it. It took him about a minute to see what his mistake was. Then he stood up as straight as he could and let off a verbal insult directed right at me.

"You're just a repair guy. What do you know?"

"I know how to do basic algebra. Looks like you're the only one in this room who doesn't," I said back.

I needed to leave, this was getting ugly. Mom was now next to me on my left.
There was no way this little fart was going to insult me and get away with it.

I placed the soda can on the desk, right on top of his papers and next to his computer. I reached with my right can and placed my hand on top. Do you know what happens when a soda can is shook up or thrown at a refrigerator? Junior was about to find out.

I pulled the can's pull top and the spray of the soda began to burst out big time. It drenched all over the paperwork but somehow not on the computer. All his work was ruined. He was so stunned. No one had ever given him crap back before and I was so happy to be the one to do it!

I picked up my toolbox and began my exit from the house. As I grabbed the front door's door handle, the young boy decided not to quit while he was behind and uttered another stupid but threatening comment.

"I've been working on this all day, you ass! I'm going to kill you and drag your body outside to the street and watch people drive over you. Then I'm going to put your guts into an oven and burn you

Oddly, his rant sounded familiar. Then it hit me. Everything he was saying was from TV or the movies. If you're going to threaten me, at least be original. Is that really so much to ask?

I stopped in the doorway of the house. I have had enough of this little turd's comments. I turned to him and said, "Ok, I accept your stupidity. Meet me this Saturday at 9:00 am at the high school's baseball field, on the pitcher's mound. Let's rock!"

My last sentence was from "Married…With Children." Hey, if he could plagiarize, why couldn't I?

Kim just stood there and did not say a word. I shut the door and left.

Soon, it was Saturday morning. I went outside of my house to get the mail. One of my neighbors is a police officer. We started a conversation about that stupid kid. In our conversation, I learned that the officer was having a problem with his dryer and he wanted to know if I would help him out. I said "sure." He was a neighbor and it's not the worst thing in the world to have a cop as a friend. Basically, he'd help me and I'd help him.

The part I needed to fix his dryer was at a parts warehouse and we needed to drive there to purchase it. On the way, we stopped at the high school, parked the car and walked to the baseball field. It was nine. There was no one there.

We waited for about fifteen minutes and talked about the issue at hand. Sadly, my neighbor informed me that he could not let any harm come to the kid, no matter how much he deserved it. I decided that Mr. Algebra wasn't showing up. We left the field.

It was a long walk back to the car. As we opened the doors, the stupid kid actually came flying up and announced that he was here, skidding the tires on the bike to stop. He was almost completely out of breath. It was probably the most exercise he had in years.

"Ok, I'm here," he said.

He had a backpack strapped to his back, maybe he thought that I was going to help him with his math homework. Yeah, right!

Since, I couldn't hurt him, I needed a way to save face. I opened the car door and looked at him, standing just alongside and said, "It's 9:30 and YOU'RE LATE. Go home, you stupid brat! And see this man here?"

I pointed to my neighbor.

"He's a cop. If you ever talk to your mother like you did the day I was in your home, this man will kill you in your sleep and guess who they'll call to investigate the murder? This guy. Got it?"

He gulped, and as a wet spot formed in the front of his pants, I started the car and we drove off. It was a short drive to the parts store and on the way, my neighbor asked me what I would have done if he did arrive on time?

I said, "Nothing."

He laughed and said that he wasn't allowed to kill minors in their sleep anymore, even obnoxious ones. Something told me that the kid probably figured that out, but he wasn't a hundred percent sure about it either.

I had a feeling that Kim was going to have a much easier parenting experience from that point on.

Story 65: It Must Have Been The Roses (2016)

A few weeks ago, I was sent out on a call to help a customer with her new garbage disposal. My dispatcher had no idea what the problem was, just that the store she bought the disposal from was asking for our help.

It was a short drive in terms of mileage but in Southern California, with traffic and assorted other nonsense, we measure trips in terms of time. It took me about forty-five minutes to travel five miles. Too many traffic lights. Too many cars on the road but that's just me complaining.

As I pulled up to the house, I couldn't help but notice that the yard had a large crop of roses of different colors planted along the white fencing next to the sidewalk. It was striking and since a lot of the homes I usually service placed a minimum of importance on yardwork, a pleasant change. I went to the rear of the truck and reached for my tool box. Around this time, a nice breeze kicked up and I inhaled the smell of roses that was coming from the yard.

There was a white, wooden gate that opened inward, but it swung just out of the reach of the beautiful looking roses. The walkway leading up to the front door was made of hand laid brick and the front yard was just mowed. What was missing, if you want to call it that, was any other type of flower or planet. It was roses from front side to back side. It was roses, just roses. The place was lousy with them. Maybe the owner was a florist.

The house itself was nicely painted with a color I later found out was "Simply White" with a nice brown trim. The windows did not have a spec of dirt on them. The house looked like a model home or maybe even something from one of those old Doris Day movies.

It took no time to arrive at the front door. The doorbell switch was off to the right and made of polished brass. A little much for a doorbell, in my opinion. I reached out and pushed it. While I was standing at the door, again, the smell of roses filled the air and now was a lot stronger. Good thing I didn't have allergies. I turned a little to the right and honestly, there was no wind blowing. Where was the smell of roses coming from? I was about to find out.

I stood there for a few minutes, but the smell was so good and relaxing that I really didn't mind. Suddenly, the door opened and a nice lady in her sixties with gray hair greeted me. She looked like the kind of person you'd see on a food label; warm and inviting and she greeted me with politeness.

"Hello there. I'm Mildred. Welcome to our home," she said.

"Thank you," I said. "My name is Rob and I'm here to help you with the garbage disposal you purchased."

"Yes, that would be wonderful. Come on in."

As I entered the home, it was like walking through the gates of Saint Peter's, it was heaven. Everything was immaculate and shiny and smelled great. Why? You've probably guessed by now. Yes, Mildred's home was covered from front to back with roses. Red, white, pink and even green. The sizes ranged from small to large and some were even oversized. I would say there was at least a thousand roses and hundreds of vases holding them, all told.

As I closed the door behind me, I stopped for a few second and looked around.
I really needed to say something, so I did.

"Ma'am, if you don't mind me asking, what's your favorite flower?"

Maybe I was being a bit of a wiseass, but not too bad. Honestly, I don't know if she heard me or not because the next thing she said was, "Please come in to our house and be welcomed."

I had never heard that phrase before, but I had to admit that I liked it. We started walking into the main hallway and then into another room before we entered the kitchen. On the way to the kitchen, of course, more roses. All different, all long stemmed and all perfectly groomed.

In the kitchen, roses and their vases lined the entire room. Anywhere there was an open spot for a flower vase, lo and behold, there was one. They even covered the small dining table in the breakfast nook. The other places made sense but why put roses there? On the floor were roses peddles. Best guess was that someone was pruning the long stem roses and did not clean up after themselves. But that was nitpicking. This home was a welcome respite and I had maintained my good mood since entering. I placed my toolbox on the floor and my paperwork on top of the box. Off to the left of the sink was the garbage disposal, still in the box. Obviously, Mildred had not made an attempt to do any work that was claimed on the paperwork.

Around this time the doorbell rang. From somewhere in the house came a noise. A man in his late sixties, wearing a pair of slacks, dress shirt and cooking apron with gardening tools hanging by his side, answered it, revealing a delivery person. She had three boxes at her side. Each box stood about four feet in height and about two feet around.

The man signed the paperwork from the delivery girl and he moved the boxes inside the house without speaking a word, which was a little odd. He didn't open the boxes right there. Instead, he picked up one box at a time and walked them through the house straight to the backyard patio area. He did this a total of three times. Once for each box.

Mildred came back to the kitchen and told me a little bit about why I was there. Apparently, the garbage disposal under the sink wasn't working so she went out and bought a new one. The salesperson at the hardware store advised her that it's a really easy job to do and that she'd have no problem taking care of the installation. Wrong. Any kind of plumbing job is intimidating, especially for someone who had never attempted anything like it and clearly, Mildred hadn't. I asked her if I could check things out before I started the installation. Maybe I could figure out what was wrong with the old one and fix it. She readily agreed.

I opened my toolbox and my flashlight was right on top. I didn't have to dig for it like I had in my previous stops. Now that I think about it, good things just seemed to happen in that home. The smell made it impossible not to be at least somewhat calm. Around this time, the man started opening the boxes. Inside were, if you can't guess by now, yes, more roses. Why were so many roses being delivered to her home and why so many?

Now that I had my flashlight, I walked over to the garbage disposal and shined the light down the opening. I wanted to see if anything was blocking the blades from turning. I flipped the switch to see what was going to happen. Nothing did. It took a few minutes, but I found a brass colored object caught in the side wall of the unit. That's likely what stopped the motor from turning.

On the bottom of most disposals is a reset switch. It can be a little hard to find if you don't know where to look. Reaching under and fumbling around for a little bit, eventually I found the switch and reset it.

As I was standing up, the man entered the kitchen, carrying a bunch of roses in his arms and walked straight towards me like I wasn't there. I stepped aside to get out of his way and away from the sink area. He began to pick out the roses one at a time, inspecting them in close detail, top to bottom so he could clean them up and de-torn them if necessary.

Mildred entered and apologized for his rudeness and made her best attempt to engage the man in conversation, but it was no use. The man did not recognize her and made no physical gesture to acknowledge her presence. He just continued cleaning each rose, one at a time, in detail. I could tell that this greatly upset Mildred, but I decided to stay out of it. It really wasn't any of my business.

The man was now finished with the pruning of the first box. He grabbed the whole bunch and walked away inside the house someplace. Mildred was shocked, not knowing what to say or do. I tried the power switch and a loud hum came from the garbage disposal. Normally, we hate the sound of the disposal but in this instance, it was a good thing. Now all I needed to do was remove the brass thing from inside and me and the disposal would be good to go.

The man came from the back of the house and walked to the backyard where the other two delivery boxes of roses were. I saw all this from the kitchen window. I needed to move quickly and remove the brass object, preferably before he came back. In my toolbox was a set of pliers. I was able to grab the brass object, but it wanted to fight me.

The man, who had now opened box number two and removed the contents was heading back into the kitchen to clean the new batch. Again, he did not see me and walked straight to the sink. I thought it best to move aside and let him by. Mildred felt like she needed to say something.

"Robert, let me apologize for Milton. He doesn't know he's being rude—"

I tried to stop her because it was clearly making her a little uncomfortable and if I'm being completely honest, it made me uncomfortable too.

"It's okay--," I interjected.

"No, I feel like you should know this," she said as she soldiered on. "My husband is quite ill with Alzheimer's disease. The symptoms started about five years ago when he would lose his train of thought and speech. He'd lose his balance. Walk into things..."

She was starting to tear up but stopped herself. I was impressed. There was so much dignity in how she felt that it was important for her to finish, so she did.

"We've seen so many doctors at the V.A. and outside it. The doctors put him on some medicine, but I honestly don't know if it's working on not. They insist that it's slowing the progress of the disease but who can really tell?"

Not knowing what to say, I said, "I'm sorry."

"Thank you," she said back. "About two years ago, even the doctors noticed that it was getting worse. He was falling even more and couldn't be left alone because he could really hurt himself. You should've met him before all this. This isn't him. He was so strong and thoughtful."

All I could do was nod.

"During one of his episodes, he fell and hit his head and since then this is what he does all day, tend to the roses. My husband speaks to no one else but me, in a language I don't really understand. The only times he stops are twice a day to eat, then back to the roses."

She motioned to the small table and gestured. "This is where we eat. The part of the table that's empty. He's in his own world, doing the same thing seven days a week. We wake up around seven and go to sleep at eight. Stopping only to eat. It's like his mind is stuck in a loop. Over and over again."

She went on to tell me that after all the doctor and hospital and ER visits, the insurance company and doctors thought that this was the best course for him. It kept him occupied and limber. Alzheimer's patients who are confined to bed don't live nearly as long as those who are active. So, this is what they did. They had roses delivered to the house twice a week, paid for by the insurance company, as a kind of therapy. I really hoped that she didn't hear my smartass comment earlier when I asked what her favorite flower was.

Mildred told me that it wasn't like she even existed to him anymore. She told me that her kids come by sometimes to visit and give her a precious hour or two outside the home but it's so overwhelming. The last thing she said to me was, "I miss my husband." Imagine missing someone who's five feet away from you.

Why was she telling me this, I wasn't sure? Best guess is that after having to put on a brave front on for everyone, maybe it was helpful to spill her guts to someone who she'd probably never see again. I felt like I had to try and help and/or say something.

"Ma'am, I'm not a doctor, but obviously, you need some help here. Later today I will make a phone call to see if there is anything that can be done."

Milton walked out of the kitchen for the second time and I had about five minutes to get that brass object out of the blades. Finally, I did. I flipped the switch and it turned on. Turns out, the brass object was a packing staple from one of the big boxes of roses. Somehow it got caught inside the blades.

I told her that she could return the new disposal and get her money back. Call it my good deed for the day. She was so happy.

As I was cleaning up my tools I noticed that Milton was opening the third box. It was time to leave. Mildred and I began to exit the kitchen as her husband came back into the house from the backyard. We were still standing in the hallway together. I was trying not to bump into any of the roses.

Just like the previous two times I had witnessed, Milton placed the roses on the sink then something strange happened. He stopped what he was doing, turned around, looked straight at me, walked three or four steps and stopped. I did not know what to do. Did I do something to upset him? I hoped not.
He looked at me and out came two words. His voice was very guttural and garbled, but he clearly said, "thank you." I nodded and said, "you're welcome."

Mildred stopped and turned around, looking straight at him. She began to cry. "Honey, you spoke." She walked over and hugged her husband, openly weeping.

This was one of those special moments. Only between them. So, I gave them their privacy and started to leave the house. As I began to turn the door knob, she came up from behind me and thanked me for what I did. She referred me as "an angel" and asked if I wanted to take a few roses home with me?

"As you can see," she said. "We have plenty."

"Thank you but that's really not necessary."

"You don't understand. Those are the first words he's spoken in eighteen months. You must be a special person. Thank you," she said.

Now, I was the one who was overwhelmed. At the entrance of the front door was a bunch of white roses in a vase. Mildred removed them and handed them to me as I exited. "Give them to your wife," she said." I thanked her and promised that I would.

Later on, I placed a call to social services on her behalf and was able to get a home aide to visit her house for a couple of hours a few times a week. It wasn't much, but it was something.

By now, all the roses that Mildred gave me are long gone except for one. I have it pressed inside a book to remind me of that day. It's one of my most prized possessions.

Afterword

Thank you for reading through all sixty-five of my stories or however many you've gotten to, if any, before reading this. Maybe you're the kind of person who likes to read the "afterword" first. I don't know why anyone would do that, but you bought it and can read it in any way you choose.

It was a lot of fun writing and reliving these stories and I hope it was enjoyable for you to read them. There have been some changes since I've started this book. The biggest is that me and the wife have moved or "downsized" to a smaller house and yes, it was by choice. Why? Mostly because with all our children moved out (Yay!) we realized that we didn't need all that square footage. The fact that we got a really good price on the old house was incidental. What spurred us into this change and what made us empty nesters in the first place was that last year, a different daughter got married in Las Vegas and the theme was a "1920's gangster wedding" with everyone outfitted in appropriate gangster and moll attire. It was a blast. Yeah, we like to have a good time.

So, what have I been up to since this book went to the publisher besides moving and marrying off my youngest? Well, so far, I've got seven new stories and if experience has taught me anything it's that the world will never run out of weirdos or, as my wife would have me put it, "unique individuals." Bottom line, don't be at all surprised if I write another one of and if I do, I hope you buy it and get a kick out of it. Thanks again from your friendly, neighborhood service technician or, as most people would refer to me, home repairman.